GENDER <u>IN</u> HI!

Series editors:
Pam Sharpe, Lynn Abrams, Cordelia Beattie and Penny Summerfield

The expansion of research into the history of women and gender since the 1970s has changed the face of history. Using the insights of feminist theory and of historians of women, gender historians have explored the configuration in the past of gender identities and relations between the sexes. They have also investigated the history of sexuality and family relations, and analysed ideas and ideals of masculinity and femininity. Yet gender history has not abandoned the original, inspirational project of women's history: to recover and reveal the lived experience of women in the past and the present.

The series Gender in History provides a forum for these developments. Its historical coverage extends from the medieval to the modern periods, and its geographical scope encompasses not only Europe and North America but all corners of the globe. The series aims to investigate the social and cultural constructions of gender in historical sources, as well as the gendering of historical discourse itself. It embraces both detailed case studies of specific regions or periods, and broader treatments of major themes. Gender in History titles are designed to meet the needs of both scholars and students working in this dynamic area of historical research.

Living in sin

MANCHESTER
1824

Manchester University Press

LIVING IN SIN
COHABITING AS HUSBAND AND WIFE
IN NINETEENTH-CENTURY ENGLAND

⊷ Ginger S. Frost ⊷

Manchester University Press
Manchester and New York

distributed exclusively in the USA by Palgrave Macmillan

The right of Ginger S. Frost to be identified as the author of this work has been asserted by her in accordance with the Copyright, Designs and Patents Act 1988.

Published by Manchester University Press
Oxford Road, Manchester M13 9NR, UK
and Room 400, 175 Fifth Avenue, New York, NY 10010, USA
www.manchesteruniversitypress.co.uk

Distributed in the United States exclusively by
Palgrave Macmillan, 175 Fifth Avenue,
New York, NY 10010, USA

Distributed in Canada exclusively by
UBC Press, University of British Columbia, 2029 West Mall,
Vancouver, BC, Canada V6T 1Z2

British Library Cataloguing-in-Publication Data is available

Library of Congress Cataloging-in-Publication Data is available

ISBN 978 0 7190 8569 7 paperback

First published by Manchester University Press in hardback 2008

This paperback edition first published 2011

The publisher has no responsibility for the persistence or accuracy of URLs for any external or third-party internet websites referred to in this book, and does not guarantee that any content on such websites is, or will remain, accurate or appropriate.

Printed by Lightning Source

Contents

Acknowledgements

Having worked on this project for over a decade, I owe more debts than I can possibly repay. I want to thank the anonymous readers for Manchester University Press and the entire staff there. I am also deeply grateful to my wonderful mentors, Marty Wiener, Martha Vicinus, and John Gillis, who never hesitated to give support, advice, and letters when needed. I'm particularly indebted to the two readers of the original 900-page manuscript, Gail Savage and George Robb, who helped plan the necessary cuts and who, for some reason, are still friends with me. I also thank commentators at various meetings where I gave papers, too numerous to specify, and the readers of separate chapters, including Julie Early, Rod Phillips, and Nancy Fix Anderson. My colleagues at Samford University, especially the chair, Dr John Mayfield, offered much support and encouragement. Similarly, I also want to thank the 2002–03 fellows of the National Humanities Center, particularly the Victorianists: Harriet Ritvo, John Kucich, Diane Sadoff, Molly Rothenberg, and Jonathan Riley. Joshua Bearden put together the Bibliography, and for that I am grateful. Finally, for intellectual and practical support while in England, I thank John and Sue Stewart.

I also owe much to the librarians at many institutions, including the British Library; National Archives (Kew); University College, London; Bishopsgate Institutional Reference Library, London Metropolitan Archives; British Library of Political and Economic Science; Institute of Advanced Legal Studies; the Institute of Historical Research; University of Michigan Library; Duke University and Law Libraries; Lambeth Palace Archives; National Research Library, Chicago; Centre for Northwest Regional Studies, Lancaster University; Bodleian Library; the Women's Library, London Metropolitan University; and, especially, the National Humanities Center, Triangle Park, NC. Anyone who has spent a year at the NHC knows how helpful and supportive the staff is, and my year was certainly no exception. I also received crucial monetary support from Judson College, Samford University; the National Endowment for the Humanities; and the Rockefeller Foundation, which funded my sabbatical year at the NHC.

The following works have been previously published and are part of this manuscript, and I thank the publishers for permission to include any copyrighted materials here. These include the following: ' Through the medium of the passions : cohabitation contracts in England, 1750–1850', *Proceedings of the 23rd Annual Consortium on Revolutionary Europe* (1994), 181–9; 'Bigamy and cohabitation in Victorian England', *Journal of Family History* 22 (1997), 286–306; ' He could not hold his passion : domestic violence and cohabitation in England, 1850–1900', *Crime, History & Societies*, 12 (2008), 25–44; and ' Love is always free : Anarchism, free unions, and Utopianism in Edwardian England', *Anarchist Studies*, forthcoming.

Finally, thanks to my support system of friends and family, especially my mother. I could not have gotten through this long process without you.

Introduction

I N JULY 1875, George Henry Lewes, a man of letters and a scientist, accepted an invitation to a garden party which the Queen of Holland attended. During the course of the afternoon, Lewes had a conversation with the monarch. She complimented his writings, then added, 'as to your wife's – all the world admires them.'[1] What is startling about this story was that Lewes's legal wife, Agnes, had never written a book in her life. Instead, the queen referred to Lewes's cohabitee, Marian Evans (George Eliot), with whom he had lived for seventeen years. Nor was the Dutch queen unique in her sympathy. Queen Victoria, a byword for prudery, nevertheless let Eliot know how much she enjoyed her books, and acquired the signatures of both Lewes and Eliot for her collection. Princess Louise, her daughter, attended a party with the couple in 1878 and talked privately with Eliot for some time.[2] Though Eliot was exceptional, her experience – along with many others – indicates that the Victorian attitude to unmarried cohabitation was not one of blanket condemnation. Instead, it was complex and contingent on many factors.

Although the large number of cohabiting couples in England dates only from the 1970s, free unions are at least as old as marriage itself. In the nineteenth century, the choice to cohabit rather than marry crossed classes and regions and revealed conflicting motives and desires between the genders. It also problematised the whole notion of 'marriage' and 'family', and the state's role in these institutions. As Chapter 1 will make clear, the law of marriage in England changed several times over the course of the century, but was based primarily on the Hardwicke Marriage Act of 1753. The state took over the definition of marriage and most of the adjudication of marriage cases at that point, and even more so after the Divorce Act of 1857. Though the law never recognised common-law marriage as a legal status, the English courts nevertheless dealt with such relationships repeatedly. The civil courts decided disputes over bonds and wills, while the criminal side oversaw bigamy trials and instances of violence. The Victorian courts' reaction to these relationships combined official disapproval with pragmatic acceptance. Such complications were almost inevitable, since these relationships had all the roles of spouses but no legal sanction. In the end, the issue boiled down to the definition of marriage – as a status, a sacrament, an institution, and/or a relationship.

The legal difficulties posed by cohabitation are therefore examined in the first two chapters of this study, but most of the book examines the cohabiting couples themselves, including their interaction with each other, their families, and wider society. Though cohabitees were a small minority of couples, their experiences highlight important issues in family history, because those on the margins of society offer a unique perspective on the 'norm'. In particular, these couples threw into disarray the traditional definition of marriage. Most of them insisted that they *were* married in all important respects. They fulfilled spousal duties, shared the same last name, reared children, and had lifelong commitments. In short, they defined marriage as a relationship, an idea, or an act of will. What, then, was the exact difference between cohabitees and spouses? Cohabitation's differences from, as well as its similarities to, marriage is a major theme of this book.

Second, this work stresses the consequences of irregular cohabitation. For example, cohabitees offer new ways to look at the roles of kin, neighbours, and wider society in domestic life. Though their reactions differed by class, not all families rejected cohabitees as 'fallen'. Many otherwise strict moralists made exceptions, as in marriages with a deceased wife's sister. In addition, these couples had several special difficulties which forced them to call on the help of their families and friends, particularly in the working classes. In the majority of cases, the families answered the call. The wider society also had a nuanced approach to marital nonconformity, and this grew as the century went on. In short, the amount of ostracism depended on many factors, including class, gender, generation, and most crucially, the reason for cohabitation.

The consequences also came out in the legal system. The role of the state in defining marriage, but also partly supporting cohabitation, is a third major issue in the book. Criminal and civil assize courts, police courts, and church courts had great difficulty in adjudicating a status that did not, in fact, exist in law. Over time, the actions of thousands of couples, and their public redefinition of marriage, helped to change social and legal norms. By the end of the century, voices from all classes protested the strictness of the divorce law, and a combination of working-class and middle-class actions had lifted the ban on one type of affinal marriage (to a deceased wife's sister) in 1907. Critics revealed inequities in marriage and demanded changes to the laws of divorce and illegitimacy. Though reforms only came after the First World War, the social basis for them was already in place beforehand, showing the importance of pressure 'from below' in revising marriage laws.

In order to explore these three themes, I have located as many examples of cohabiting couples as possible, collecting approximately one thousand. These couples divide into three major groups. The first and largest group were those, like Eliot and Lewes, who lived together because they *could* not marry. Such couples include people who were too closely related by blood or marriage as well as those who already had spouses and could not divorce. Couples in this section wanted to marry and blamed the law, not themselves, for their irregular status. The challenge these couples posed was to the legal definition of marriage, making them especially troubling to the state, but allowing family and neighbours to sympathise with their plights more readily.

The second group were those who *did* not marry, either from indifference, lack of social pressure, or class concerns. This section includes the very poor, those in 'criminal' pursuits, and the parallel world of the demimonde. Some professions required flexible domestic arrangements, but in all occupations of the poorest classes, stable cohabitation offered a rational alternative to legal marriage. Since these couples chose not to marry, they challenged marriage more directly, though they did not often dissent from its expectations, especially in gender roles. The second group in this section were cross-class couples. These pairs were almost always a well-off man with a poorer woman, putting both class and gender differences in stark relief. The relations to the state in all of these instances were, again, complex. The demands that men keep promises and support dependants could sometimes mitigate the disadvantages of poorer women and their children.

The third group were those who *would* not marry, as a conscious protest against the institution. Though this group was the smallest, it had cultural impact out of proportion with its numbers, due to the public nature of its marital dissent. This section, unlike the previous two, is organised chronologically, showing both the continuities and the changes in challenges to marriage. I have called these couples 'radicals', though I am aware that this term is problematic, since it indicates a specific political approach in the nineteenth century, and also because some of the couples wanted only reform of marriage rather than abolition. I use the term simply for convenience; it indicates those who had conscious reasons to disdain marriage and then acted on those beliefs. Readers should remember this definition when perusing these chapters.

Within each of these groups, I highlight class and gender differences. In general, the working class had a more tolerant attitude than the middle class, especially in urban areas. On the other hand, the sexual double standard meant that men faced less ostracism than women in all classes. Men's gender advantage recurred in every type of cohabitation; the male partner was reluctant to marry far more often than the female one. In addition, women fulfilled wifely roles and made long-term commitments more readily, whatever the legal status of the union. Still, the issue was not simple. Precisely because of men's roles as providers and protectors, the courts expected them to keep their words and enforced demands for support from women and children. As a result, men paid a legal price for cohabitation, though the social and economic costs were greater for women.

Though most of the chapters centre on socio-legal history, I also demonstrate the difference between the cultural and social significance of figures such as Mary Wollstonecraft and George Eliot. These public 'fallen' women acted as touchstones for conservatives and reformers alike, but their family experiences were much like other cohabitees. This was also true for many of the 'pioneers' historians have studied, including painters, novelists, and socialists like Eleanor Marx and Edward Aveling. When put against the backdrop of hundreds of similarly circumstanced couples, the way that these pairs both resembled and differed from their peers becomes clear, and the similarities outweighed the differences. Moreover, circumstances, not choice, usually forced these couples into irregular unions.

Whatever the context, most couples, including those who chose not to marry, showed a desire for a ritual and a life-long commitment. As this work will make clear, those who lived in free unions usually wanted a permanent, stable union, not promiscuity. Thus, cohabitees' challenge was to the terms of the union, and to the role of the state, but not to the idea itself. In light of this, marriage's survival into the twenty-first century is not a surprise. Ironically, by dissenting from marriage, these couples helped to redefine it, but also equipped it to survive an age of mass cohabitation and no-fault divorce. This conclusion would have horrified some, and delighted others, of the couples in the following pages.

Definitions and limitations

I have limited this study in a number of ways. Due to limitations of space, I was unable to explore generational tensions between parents and children in any detail, though I hope to return to that subject in my next project.[3] I have also largely eliminated the aristocratic couples. Their social mores were distinct, and they made up only 2 per cent of the English population. A few nobles appear in the sections on the demimonde and cross-class cohabitation, but they are otherwise absent. I have also limited this study to those who resided in England and Wales. Scottish and Irish laws were different, and including those countries would have added many more pages to a book already too long. In addition, I have concentrated on couples who lived for substantial parts of their lives in England, rather than English subjects abroad. Expatriates in Paris and Italy had communities with laxer social mores and offered an escape for those with irregular relationships, but because of those differences, they need a study all their own.

Finally, I have limited myself to heterosexual cohabitees, for several reasons. First, other historians have written on gay history and done it very well; I do not need to replicate that work.[4] Second, such a discussion would add to the length of the book by hundreds of pages. Third, and most important, same-sex couples were in a different legal position than opposite-sex couples. The latter at least had the possibility of marrying. Even if they were already married, they might outlive their spouses and then be able to marry their cohabitees. This was not the case for same-sex couples; the law did not allow civil partnerships for them until 2005. Thus, the dynamic with the state was distinct from opposite-sex cohabitees in a crucial way. Because of all of these reasons, this book will focus on heterosexual cohabitees.

Except for Chapters 8 and 9, these chapters are organised holistically. My time frame is the long nineteenth century, from the 1760s to the First World War, but, because of the limitations of sources, much of my evidence is from the 1830s to 1914. The continuities are greater than the changes in most of these groups, but I have tried to indicate change over time when important. Overall, the period between 1760 and 1840 had more open marital nonconformity, while mid-century had stricter propriety, at least in appearance. After 1880, the *fin-de-siècle* period saw renewed openness about sexuality and criticism of the 'hypocrisy' of mid-century. But all of these changes were tendencies rather than strict rules and differed by class and region. The working class always had a higher percentage of couples outside marriage than other groups, and the laws of marriage tightened in the course of the century, thus pushing more couples out of the marital fold. Rural areas also tended to have fewer such couples than urban areas, where they could be more anonymous.

Naturally, the definition of 'cohabitees' is vexed. In general, I defined a couple as 'cohabiting' if they lived 'as husband and wife' for a month or more. This term was a common contemporary phrase and meant that the couple had sexual relations, but also that they presented themselves as married to society. At least one of the partners, then, believed that the relationship was committed. These unions might not be permanent, but they were exclusive for the time they lasted (at least for the women). Because the sources are often silent on sexual issues, some couples are included who may not have had sexual intercourse, but who lived together and had emotional intimacy. I also included couples if the bulk of their relationship occurred before 1914, even if it continued past the First World War. In addition, some couples, unsurprisingly, do not fit neatly into one category or the other. For example, many of the couples who could not marry legally also dissented from marriage for philosophical reasons. I have, then, included a handful of couples in more than one category.

Sources

Middle-class cohabitees have left numerous records, and some are famous – the writings on Eliot alone run to thousands of pages. The sections on these couples, then, are necessarily partly synthetic. I did not redo work already done well by other historians, though I did consult printed collections of letters, autobiographies, and diaries when available. I have supplemented these accounts by finding a number of more obscure cohabitees, drawn from legal records, diaries, Court of Arches records, Royal Commissions on Marriage in 1848 and 1912, and newspapers. The legal sources include disputes over bonds and wills, bigamy and violence cases, and church court cases such as nullity, incest, and false declaration of marriage. Though only a minority of the latter dealt with cohabitation, they are valuable in giving insight into higher-class couples when other types of evidence are scarce.

Middle-class couples also appear in government documents. The Royal Commission on Marriage in 1848 was primarily concerned with affinal and consanguineous marriages, illegal after 1835; the commissioners took hundreds of pages of evidence, including testimonies of those who had defied the law. The Royal Commission of Marriage and Divorce of 1912 centred on divorce reform – the expansion of grounds, equalisation between the genders, and lessening the cost. This Commission's report contained numerous statements and letters from those who lived in adulterous unions. Those giving evidence wanted to influence the government to change the law, but this does not mean that their testimony was not valid. Many subjects described their own situations, and their problems were echoed in a variety of sources. These more obscure examples show that though the famous couples reaped more publicity, their experiences were not unique. Eliot was culturally more significant than others, but her decision to cohabit, the reaction of her family, and the consequences for her life, were mirrored in the lives of others.

The working-class sources were of a wider variety. Some couples had biographies and diaries, but these were, by definition, unusual. I have used the work of historians such as John Gillis and Barry Reay to make generalisations about the numbers and change over time of working-class cohabitation. To find more specific examples of working-class couples, I amassed collections of both bigamy and violence trials from newspapers in London, Lancaster, and York, as well as neglect and desertion cases and trials involving the Poor Law. I used newspapers, rather than assize or Old Bailey reports, because I wanted to get cases from the police and magistrates' courts as well as the high courts. Once I identified the cases, though, I consulted the relevant court records, especially those in the Home Office files and the Old Bailey Session Papers, so I could get a complete picture of the trials.

Newspapers are also limited in that most of them published regularly only in the last half of the nineteenth century. To cover the first half, I consulted the Foundling Hospital records at the London Metropolitan Archives. I looked through all of the rejected petitions from 1810 to 1856 (the last year then available to historians under the 150-year rule). I consulted only the rejected petitions, since, by the rules of the Hospital, no cohabiting woman could have her child adopted. The Hospital only accepted the infants of women who had 'fallen' with one man, due to a promise of marriage, had only the one child, and whose child was under a year old. The Hospital rejected any woman who lied on her petition or who had lived with her lover. The rejected petitions were also by far the largest group and so would have been the majority of applicants in any year. From these records, I found 177 petitions by women who cohabited with the fathers of their children.[5] These are a small percentage of all petitions, which numbered over one hundred a year by the 1840s. But this was unsurprising, since cohabitees were not welcome, so many women would not have tried. Most of those who did apply admitted their relationships openly, but even if they did not do so, the Foundling Hospital investigated all petitions rigorously, so the investigators usually found them out. Since a cohabiting relationship was a bar to acceptance, any woman admitting to this was probably telling the truth, though she might exaggerate the man's culpability.[6] I have taken into account both the women's stories and the investigations in using this source.

Other records for the working class match those of the middle classes, including the two Royal Commissions of Marriage in 1848 and 1912, which had numerous working-class examples. The Women's Cooperative Guild, made up primarily of the wives of artisans, also surveyed their members in 1911 and recorded several instances of adulterous cohabitation. A fourth type of evidence was that supplied by middle-class observers of the poor. Henry Mayhew published four large volumes of investigations of the London poor in the 1850s, and Charles Booth published seventeen volumes on the London poor at the end of the century. Many other investigators abounded, especially in the late Victorian and Edwardian periods when the middle and upper classes rediscovered poverty. In using these sources, one must take into account that middle-class observers may have exaggerated the vices of the poor. But the historian has little choice but to consult these compilations in order to get some idea of the number of cohabiting couples, and the reluctance of some poor people to talk to a stranger partly balanced out the tendency of middle-class investigators to overstate their depravity. Though Mayhew, in particular, focused on the pathos of his subjects, his broad patterns were probably accurate, especially when other sources confirm his deductions. Finally, I consulted Elizabeth Roberts's oral history collection in Lancaster as an alternative to middle-class views.

This book is a national history, not a close study of one region. I have relied on local studies at many points, but have not conducted such research myself. I have tried to guard against too much London-centred history by using two provincial newspapers, the *Lancaster Guardian* and the *Yorkshire Gazette*, and I have used violence and bigamy cases from across the country as well. Yet the bulk of my evidence comes from urban areas, since cities received most of the attention from social reformers, and London couples dominate in the records of the Foundling Hospital and the Old Bailey reports. Since the number of cohabiting couples in the country was never huge, I have had to take a large-scale approach to garner a representative group, but regional variations certainly existed. Future research will illuminate all the complexities of the marital/nonmarital situation across England. My purpose is to set out broad themes and to allow, as much as possible, the cohabitees to speak for themselves over the next nine chapters.

Notes

1   R. Ashton, *G. H. Lewes: An Unconventional Victorian* (London: Pimlico, 2000), p. 271; W. Baker (ed.), *Letters of George Henry Lewes*, 3 vols (Victoria, BC: English Literary Studies, 1995), II, 211–13, G. H. Lewes to Charles Lee Lewes, 11 July 1875.

2   K. Hughes, *George Eliot: The Last Victorian* (London: Fourth Estate, 1998), pp. 303–4.

3   G. Frost, "'The black lamb of the black sheep': Illegitimacy in the English working class, 1850–1939', *Journal of Social History* 37 (2003), 293–322.

4   H. G. Cocks, *Nameless Offences: Speaking of Male Homosexual Desire in Nineteenth-Century England* (London: I. B. Tauris, 2003); S. Brady, *Masculinity and Male Homosexuality in Britain, 1861–1913* (New York: Palgrave Macmillan, 2005); M. Vicinus, *Intimate Friends: Women Who Loved Women, 1778–1928* (Chicago: Chicago University Press, 2004).

5   The numbers break down as follows: nineteen cases between 1810 and 1819, ten cases in the 1820s, twenty-five cases in the 1830s, sixty cases in the 1840s, and sixty-three cases in the 1850s.

6   B. Weisbrod, 'How to become a good foundling in early Victorian England', *Social History* 10 (1985), 193–209; F. Barret-Ducrocq, *Love in the Time of Victoria: Sexuality, Class, and Gender in Nineteenth-Century London* (London: Verso, 1991), pp. 39–43.

1

Cohabitation, illegitimacy, and the law in England, 1750–1914

THOUGH CONSERVATIVES liked to believe otherwise, the legal definition of marriage changed over time, including and excluding couples as it did so. The key legislation in these transformations was the Hardwicke Marriage Act of 1753, a watershed in family law. Parliament took control over the regulation of marriage, challenging the principle of marriage as an eternal sacrament, since the state now determined who was married and who was not. In addition, this act and subsequent pieces of legislation tightened the laws of marriage and defined marriages more rigorously. As English law divided those married from those unmarried, a growing number of couples found themselves outside its parameters. The legal consequences were considerable, so the provisions of the law were vitally important.

Prior to 1753, the marriage laws of England were chaotic. The validity of marriages was a major source of litigation, because couples could marry secretly in a variety of ways. A man and woman could simply state 'I marry you' in front of witnesses, and the church recognised the union as legal. Couples who said 'I will marry you' and then cohabited were also married. Though the church courts became increasingly unwilling to validate such unions as the eighteenth century wore on, clandestine weddings remained popular. As a result, many couples bound themselves for life without licences or their parents' consent.[1] In the Hardwicke Marriage Act, Parliament abolished the binding power of betrothals and much of the authority of the church courts in England. Many factors influenced Parliament to make the change. First, the confusions of the law led to difficulties, especially when prior contracts threatened long-standing marriages. Second, the upper classes wanted to stop their under-age children from making unwise marriages, a reassertion of patriarchal control. Third, the act gave more freedom to men, since regularising cohabiting unions became much more difficult. Thus, the only legal marriages were those performed on certain days of the week, at specified times, and at registered Anglican churches (exempting Quakers, Jews, and the royal family). The wedding had to be performed after a reading of the banns three weeks in a row or the purchase of an expensive licence. In addition, no marriage was legal unless both parties were over twenty-one or had the consent of their guardians. In other words, all secret marriages of minors, all clandestine marriages, and all oral contract marriages were void.[2]

As Ralph Outhwaite has pointed out, the act was not the 'last word' on marriage reform. Opponents of the bill tried to overturn it several times, and repeals passed the House of Commons in 1765 and 1781, but failed in the Lords. The entire law was repealed in 1822, only to be reinstated in an amended form in 1823. Most especially, Parliament had to address the grievances of Dissenters, whose religious ceremonies were now invalid. Marriage by civil registration, which came into law in 1836, began this process. After 1836, couples could obtain a licence from the local Registrar's office (created in 1835) and marry there. This law broke the monopoly of religious establishments over marriages, since Dissenters and Catholics could marry by registrar and then have their own religious rites as they saw fit.[3] The original act had intended to cut through the confusion of church marriages and define a legal marriage in unambiguous terms. Nevertheless, difficulties remained, in part because of the very specificity of the act. Couples who made mistakes in the parish registers, married at the wrong times, or picked an unregistered chapel might not be legally married at all. At times, a man or woman might assume that a marriage with some minor mistake was not legal and so remarry, thereby making a possibly bigamous marriage. Furthermore, both Ireland and Scotland had different marriage laws, which meant a couple might be married in one country, but living in 'concubinage' in another. In short, the law meant to clarify the definition of marriage instead offered a host of new problems.

Further complicating matters was the fact that common-law marriage did not exist as a legal category in England. Indeed, commentators rarely tried to describe 'concubinage', though they spent scores of pages explaining marriage, since anyone who did not marry legally automatically fell into the former category. Those who did attempt a description often had to reference marriage; cohabitation was not something positive in its own right, but a 'non-marriage'. James Cookson, writing in 1782, described 'concubinage' as 'the cohabitation of a man and woman in the way of marriage, without its ceremonies and solemnity, – the marriage of nature; but below that of positive Institution.'[4] Cohabitation, then, was a lesser relationship and never compared favourably with marriage. But what, specifically, was missing?

Obviously, cohabitees lacked the sanction of the church and the state. All the same, they had often been through a ceremony of some sort and were parents. After the passage of Civil Marriage in 1836, some married couples also evaded the religious ceremony; though they had legal sanction, they were not all that distinct from couples who lived together. Thus, in a number of circumstances, cohabitees mirrored those legally wed. In fact, the attitude of many people to cohabitation was connected to their opinion of a 'true' marriage. If the person saw marriage as an institution and a sacrament, he or she was more likely to condemn concubinage. But if a commentator stressed the relationship as the basis of marriage, he or she tended to be more sympathetic to those who lived 'in sin'. In the end, however, the key point for the law was the lack of legal standing, even more than the lack of church sanction. Without a legal marriage, a family lost many benefits, particularly women and children.

Despite this, some couples still lived together irregularly and relied on reputation and long cohabitation to give their unions public sanction; without property considerations, the ambiguous state of the union rarely mattered. And even when the courts did get involved, judges might declare the marriage valid, since one of the axioms of English law was that such reputation could be taken as proof of marriage.[5] All the same, those who cohabited were vulnerable. If one partner determined to leave the relationship, he or she could use the law to end the union. In fact, Hardwicke's critics foresaw this possibility. Robert Nugent pointed out that 'to declare a marriage void, if not celebrated with all the punctilios prescribed by this Bill, is really to divorce the husband and wife'. His prediction was accurate, sometimes with serious consequences.[6]

On the plus side, no legal penalty to cohabitation existed. With the decline of the church courts, punishments for fornication withered away. Though some local leaders disliked the new licence, they could do little about it. In 1842, a magistrate wrote to *Justice of the Peace* to complain about a couple who lived 'in a n avowed state of concubinage'. He asked if the local clergyman could force them 'either to separate, or to marry?' The editors replied that 'such parties are usually left to the punishment which society inflicts upon them ... if they move in any decent sphere of life.'[7] In other words, if the couple did not care about public reputation, they could live together as long as they pleased.

Nevertheless, such freedom came at a price, particularly for women. Women who cohabited with men now had no legal claim to the status of wife. Critics of the bill had pointed out the hardships it would entail for women; Charles Townshend, for example, predicted that it would be 'the ruin of a multitude of young women'. As late as 1838, the editors of *Justice of the Peace* asserted that 'the choice was to be made between the inconveniences of clandestine marriages and the destruction of one of the bulwarks of morality, and the legislature adopted the former'. Furthermore, children born to these unions were illegitimate, and this was no small consideration, since the English bastardy law was the harshest in Europe. Illegitimate children were literally parentless at law (filius nullius), and even the subsequent marriage of their parents did not legitimise them.[8]

The position of illegitimate children became even more precarious after the New Poor Law of 1834. This law's Bastardy Clause placed the responsibility of maintaining illegitimates onto their mothers. Women could no longer name the putative fathers of their children and receive support from them. Although some changes occurred in this law in 1844 (and more substantially in 1872), women remained at a disadvantage in collecting support; in addition, the amount of maintenance was small and ended when the child reached thirteen.[9] And even if women avoided the legal and financial penalties, they were far more likely than men to face social snubs. In short, the Hardwicke Act, combined with the New Poor Law, made marriage both more difficult and more necessary for women.

Accidental cohabitation?

Despite the changes in 1753, the church and secular courts still had to define legal marriage in the nineteenth century. This should have been straightforward, due to the specificity of the Hardwicke Act, but it was not. Many Britons disagreed with the new marriage law and tried to get around it. More exalted examples of this phenomenon were the children of George III, who tried to escape from the strictures of the Royal Marriages Act of 1772 (which specified that the monarch's children could not marry legally without the sovereign's consent). The Prince of Wales married Maria Fitzherbert in 1785 by bringing a clergyman out of the Fleet prison and bribing him; though the marriage was illegal, Fitzherbert had the position of a pseudo-wife.[10] Similarly, George III's sixth son, the Duke of Sussex, married Lady Augusta Murray in 1793. Murray was the daughter of an earl, but the king still had the marriage voided. Their son, Sir Augustus D'Este, petitioned frequently to be legitimated, to no avail.[11]

Less elite examples of attempts to get around the marriage laws also abound. In *Reddall v. Leddiard* (1820), the bridegroom, who was twenty, swore out an affidavit that he was of age, and the bride and her two guardians acquiesced in the lie, all so that he could marry without his parents' consent. Sir John Nichol, one of the judges, complained, 'they trifle with the sanctity of an oath in a manner to undermine the very foundation of society.'[12] But judges would remain disappointed in the population's regard for marital oaths. In 1830, the Consistory Court in London heard the case *Wiltshire v. Prince*, a typical case. Henry John Wiltshire married Elizabeth Prince on 5 February 1828 after the reading of the banns. Henry was a minor who changed his name – from Henry John to John – in order to conceal his marriage to the family cook. When his parents found out, they sued to have the marriage annulled. The court invalidated the marriage; this couple had clearly acted fraudulently to get around the statute.[13]

In other words, in this and similar cases, couples defied the law, but the courts enforced it strictly. The fact that couples refused to accept the new legal definition was worrisome, however. Furthermore, other sources showed that people married illegally in a number of ways, and, unless parents intervened, the government was reluctant to prosecute. In 1866, a parson wrote to the Home Secretary, trying to get him to prosecute two cases in which apprentices had gone to local Registrar's offices and 'obtained clandestine marriages through fraud & perjury.' The Registrar General refused to help, so the parson turned to the Home Office, who, likewise, declined to get involved, despite the clergyman's insistence that something must be done to stop 'so serious and encreasing [sic] an Evil.'[14] The only time the authorities prosecuted was when one of the couple had defrauded the other or committed bigamy, both more serious offences.

Even more disturbing than this flouting of the law was a second complication. At times, the courts made decisions that ignored the original intent of the parties. In these cases, couples found themselves to be accidental cohabitees. In 1830, the common law courts invalidated the marriage of Joseph and Mary Betts. The two had married in 1817 by banns. The groom used the name Joseph Betts, but the clergyman called the bride Mary White, though her name was Hodgkinson. Since the parents did not object to the match, and both were of age, the clergyman had simply made a mistake. Despite this, the court voided the marriage. The very strictness of the Act, then, led to uncertainties. The issues were especially complicated for illegitimates. Because they had no legal parents, their Chancery Court guardian had to approve any underage marriages. In *Days v. Jarvis* in 1814, the husband did not have permission from the Court of Chancery, and so a marriage that had been celebrated twice in 1805 was nevertheless set aside.[15]

Yet a third problem arose when unscrupulous spouses tried to use irregularities to rid themselves of their mates. John Cope sued to nullify his marriage to Sarah Burt in 1809 because she had declared herself a widow and lived under the name of Melville when they married in 1793 (she had never previously married). Though the outcome of this case is unclear, Burt's false declarations put her marriage at risk.[16] *Wakefield v. MacKay*, a Court of Arches case in 1808, was more complicated. Isabella MacKay married

Daniel Wakefield in 1805 under the name of Jackson. When Daniel became disenchanted with her, he sued to have the marriage nullified. MacKay countered that Jackson was her legal name, since she was illegitimate, yet the courts found for Wakefield.[17] As MacKay's case indicates, illegitimate children had special difficulties. In 1796, Harriet Lydiard, a minor, had her mother's permission, as well as that of the guardian her father had appointed for her, when she married. However, she did not have the permission of a guardian from Chancery. Her husband used this loophole to invalidate the marriage in 1799.[18]

To avoid such problems, church courts in particular tried to discover the intent of parties when marrying. Judges invalidated long marriages only if they could find evidence of fraud. In 1821, a wife could not escape her sixteen-year marriage, since the court did not believe her husband intended to defraud her when he changed his name on the banns. Similarly, Maria Dormer could not extricate herself from her marriage to William Henry Williams in 1838, since Dr Lushington believed only one of the parties had 'guilty knowledge'.[19] But these cases contradicted some of those in civil courts, adding to the confusion.

These difficulties led Parliament to revise the Hardwicke Act, first in 1822, with an act which was practically a repeal of it, and then with an amended version in 1823 that substantially reinstated it. In the 1823 act, Parliament acknowledged that some breaches in the regulations were inadvertent. Thus, they left it to the courts to determine the intent of the parties. Though this did not help the Bettses in 1830, it did lessen the number of marriages voided on technicalities. In 1872, for instance, the court used the 1823 law to uphold a marriage. This case concerned the 1841 marriage of William Frederick Gompertz and Georgiana Adelaide Harvey. The banns were published in the names Frederick Gompertz and Adelaide Harvey, when the couple were nineteen and eighteen. Frederick insisted that he shortened the names 'for brevity's sake only.' They lived together for twenty-four years until Adelaide's death when a dispute over her will led to the court case. The Chancery Court found in favour of Gompertz, because there was no fraudulent intent.[20] Nevertheless, the general public remained confused, and many couples must have feared making even slight errors in their marriage ceremonies.

Blood, empire, and nationality

Another seemingly unambiguous issue was that of marriage within the prohibited degrees. Any marriage with those too closely related by blood or affinity was void. English laws followed, for the most part, the decrees from Leviticus 18, which barred marriage with kin of first and second degrees: 'parents, siblings, aunts and uncles, children and grandchildren, and half-siblings; plus their spouses and equivalents by marriage.'[21] But even here, the issue became muddled. Before Lord Lyndhurst's Act of 1835, such marriages were voidable, but not automatically void, at law. In other words, if someone challenged the marriage during the lifetime of the parties, the marriage was invalid. If not, then the marriage, though illegal, was not invalid and the children were legitimate. A typical case was *Watson and Watson v. Faremouth and Others*, heard in 1811. Samuel Watson was Catherine Kingwell's brother-in-law, but they married and had children. When Watson's mother died, his relatives sued to have his marriage voided so that they could inherit the entire estate. Since Watson and Kingwell were still alive, the Court of Arches duly found against the marriage, declaiming 'this was an incestuous cohabitation that ought to be put an end to'.[22]

Despite this danger, many couples married illegally, particularly if they were confused over the status of illegitimate siblings. In *Ware v. Ware*, Ann Ware married a pair of half-brothers; her second mate was Thomas Ware, who was illegitimate. When she sued to have her second marriage nullified, Thomas defended himself by insisting that illegitimate siblings were not included in the laws of consanguinity. The court nullified the marriage, since Ware's assumption was incorrect.[23] This would seem to have settled the point, yet almost 150 years later, couples still claimed confusion on the issue. In 1901, William Perry was charged before the Exeter Assize Courts with lying about his relationship with his niece, Alice Jackman, whom he married in December 1900. Perry's defence was that 'the mother of the girl the prisoner married was an illegitimate daughter'. Because of his apparent ignorance, the jury acquitted him, though his marriage was still invalid.[24]

To add to the difficulties, only registered chapels could perform valid marriages, and people did not always know which ones were legal. Furthermore, as the population boomed, the Anglican church could not keep up with the explosion. Parliament had to pass bills expanding the number of legal sites for marriage in 1781, 1804, 1825, and 1830.[25] As the empire grew, the problem became global. In 1867, J. D. Powles, the chair of a mining company in Brazil, petitioned the Home Secretary to register the local Anglican church to perform marriages. The nearest place to marry was in Rio de Janeiro, too far for poor miners. Most of them, then, cohabited; in fact, two doctors working in the area had not married legally either. The undersecretary wrote to assure Powles that the bill was being prepared; these kinds of bills must have been necessary wherever the British Empire spread.[26]

Adding another layer to the confusion, English law was different from Scotland and Ireland, as well as most of continental Europe, and the courts had to determine which foreign marriages to recognise. In 1777, Edmund Middleton, aged eighteen, married twenty-eight-year-old Martha Janverin in Flanders without the permission of his mother, his guardian. When they returned to England, they kept the marriage a secret. In 1780, Middleton refused to support Janverin, and she sued for maintenance. In this instance, the judges declared the marriage void because they concluded that the marriage was invalid both in Flanders and in England, but they saw the principle as wider than this. Sir W. Wynne concluded, 'It is true that a marriage had abroad is not within that act. But it does not follow from thence that it is good by the law of England.'[27] English subjects had to follow English marriage law, and under the latter, Middleton was too young to contract a marriage without his parent's consent.

English judges equally had to deal with cases coming out of Scotland, as Scottish law on both marriage and divorce varied from English law. The English law of divorce was quite strict. Divorce virtually did not exist before 1857, and even after the Matrimonial Causes Act of that year, it was limited. The Divorce Court met only in London and the process was expensive. Furthermore, the grounds for divorce were few and biased in favour of men. Men could divorce for a single act of adultery, while women had to prove adultery and some other offence, such as cruelty, desertion, or bigamy. In addition, divorces required an innocent party; if both mates were guilty of actionable behaviour, the court almost always refused relief. As a result, most legal marriages were lifelong unions.[28]

The Scots had a looser marital regime. For one thing, they still recognised irregular marriages. For another, Scottish law allowed divorce on the grounds of desertion of four years and, for women, simple adultery. As a result, English couples eloped to Gretna Green to marry secretly, since it was just over the English–Scottish border and couples could wed there without parental consent from age sixteen. English couples also tried to get Scots divorces when their English marriages failed. Scots courts accepted jurisdiction at times, but English courts did not uphold their decrees. Samuel Beazley married a Miss Richardson in 1810 in England, but they separated in 1813. Mrs Beazley went to Edinburgh in 1823 and divorced Samuel on the grounds of adultery. On the strength of that divorce, Samuel married Emily Conway in Edinburgh. In 1831, Emily, too, found Samuel's society uncongenial and sued to have the marriage annulled on the grounds of bigamy. The question, then, was if an English marriage could be ended in a non-English court. The English court found that because Samuel and his first wife were both English subjects, they could not divorce in Scotland.[29] In short, the first Mrs Beazley used the difference between the

Scots and English laws to escape her marriage, and this allowed the second Mrs Beazley to escape hers as well.

The differences between Scotland and England sometimes worked the other way. In *Fenton v. Livingstone* (1859), the issue was reversed. In 1808, Thurstanus Livingstone married his deceased wife's sister in England; both husband and wife were English and their son was born there. Since no case was brought to void the marriage before the death of Mrs Livingstone in 1832, the marriage was legal in England. However, Livingstone had property in Scotland, and when his son tried to succeed to the land in 1859, he could not, as the Scottish courts considered him illegitimate. In Scottish law, marriages with a deceased wife's sister were automatically void.[30] Thus, though some couples managed to use these escape clauses, the majority did not. If the English courts would not accept Scots divorces, English couples had little incentive to attempt it, and the number of such attempted divorces reduced to a trickle by 1820.[31]

These high court cases show that many issues unsettled marriages, but the uncertainty of marriage law is even clearer when reading the correspondence of magistrates across England. The main journal of these men was *Justice of the Peace*, and in each issue the editors included a section answering questions from JPs. Magistrates were primarily concerned with finding support for those chargeable to the parish. If a woman was not married to her mate, he was not responsible for maintaining her or her children, at least after 1834. Thus, magistrates constantly sought guidance in defining a legal marriage. Their questions showed how many people ignored the law, as well as the limited knowledge of many JPs.

Sometimes magistrates asked about basic provisions of the Marriage Act, showing a worrisome degree of ignorance; for instance, one JP (in 1839) did not even know that a marriage of a minor without parental consent was void. Most, though, were about the many grey areas of the law. One correspondent wrote in 1868 about a marriage in a Mormon chapel; the editors duly informed him that it would only be valid if the chapel were registered for marriages.[32] Magistrates also had trouble determining the validity of inter-faith marriages, particularly those between Protestants and Catholics, as well as those made outside England.[33] Considering the number of court cases about such issues, the difficulties of local JPs in keeping to the rules was not surprising.

Many of the puzzling cases had to do with a wide array of consanguineal and affinal unions. In 1852, an 'Old Subscriber' wrote in, asking for help with a man who had married his niece. The man lied in order to get the licence, and the subscriber wondered if the parish could prosecute for perjury. The editors recommended bringing a charge of 'obtaining the marriage license by means of the false oath', since a jury would be less likely to convict for perjury.[34] Other readers questioned marriages between uncles and nieces, nephews and aunts-in-law, daughters-in-law and fathers-in-law, half-siblings, and others. In each case, the marriages were in the prohibited degrees and void. Clearly, the marriage laws were not well known or enforced among the common people, and this caused difficulties for women and children and headaches for local magistrates.

Cohabitation contracts

All the same, the picture was not entirely bleak for female cohabitees, since some couples who lived together made contracts with each other. These usually involved one of two things: a bond made to support a female cohabitee after the man's death, or a will that left some support to the children of the union. Interestingly, the common law courts were not unsympathetic to cohabitees. Chris Barton, who surveyed cohabitation contracts over a long period, found that female cohabitees prevailed in about half of the cases. Without actually condoning immorality, the courts found ways to support former mistresses and their children.[35] In other words, some couples, though unmarried, believed their unions entailed financial and emotional obligations, and the courts tacitly agreed.

Before 1753, the precedents were inconsistent. Most of the actions involved the heirs of an estate suing to be relieved from having to redeem bonds given to 'kept' women. In general, the courts found for women whenever they seemed to be victimised by seducing males. In *Spicer v. Hayward* (1700), the plaintiff 'had seduced his wife's sister, and had several children by her'. He gave her bonds to keep her and the children, but then sued to have them returned. The judge insisted that Spicer pay his sister-in-law the full amount 'and said it was a pity he could do no more'.[36] The exception to this leniency was any sexual aggression on the part of the woman. In *Priest v. Parrot*, in 1751, the defendant was a woman of a good family who had been 'induced' to live with a well-off man. But in this case, the man was married, she was a companion of his wife, and the two of them had broken up the marriage. These factors altered the case, and the court voided the bond.[37]

In the hundred years following the Marriage Act in 1753, the courts refined their dealings in cohabitation contracts. The deciding factor of the cases centred around the well-known legal tenet that contracts that tended to immorality were void.[38] That is, if a man promised money to a woman in order to persuade her to live with him, the courts would not enforce the contract. A good example of this was *Walker v. Perkins* in 1764.

William Perkins and Sarah Walker had agreed to cohabit, and he promised to support her while they did so and to pay her an annuity of £60 if he left. Lord Mansfield found against Walker, because 'if she becomes virtuous, she is to lose the annuity.' An even clearer example was *Franco v. Bolton* in 1797. In May 1793, Jacob Franco met Elizabeth Bolton and the two began an affair. Early on, Bolton asked Franco to give her an £100 annuity in return for her living with him. At first he agreed, but he soon discovered she was unfaithful and refused to pay. When Bolton sued, Lord Chancellor Loughborough found against her.[39]

Nevertheless, in many circumstances cohabitation contracts were valid. For instance, if the bond were given at the end of the cohabitation, in order to compensate for the wrong done to the woman, the contract stood. In *Gibson v. Dickie* in 1815, the couple had lived together for years, and the woman had even given £200 to her paramour. The two quarrelled frequently, and Gibson (the woman) asked for some protection in case the relationship failed. Dickie obliged, agreeing to pay her £30 a year, but only if she did not marry or live with any other man. Once the couple separated, Dickie reneged on his promise. Gibson's barristers argued that this contract encouraged her to virtuous living, since she only got payment if she cohabited with no one, and she won her case.[40] Not surprisingly, in later cases women invariably argued that the bonds did not encourage illicit arrangements, while men asserted the opposite. If the woman could convince the court, she could recover, even if she was not pure. In *Friend v. Harrison*, in 1827, the plaintiff was a 'common prostitute', who lived with the defendant for two years before he promised her an annuity of £50. Still, the jury and judge agreed that the money was a voluntary gift, despite the sexual experience of the plaintiff, and enforced the bond.[41]

For the courts, the key to the matter was if the bonds were voluntary. Courts upheld them as long as the contract was not *expressly* written to encourage immorality. In *Turner v. Vaughan* (1767), Catherine Turner sued Thomas Vaughan for repayment of a £30 annuity he had promised while they lived together. The defence tried to argue that the contract was 'executed and given upon an illegal, flagitious consideration of having cohabited with the plaintiff,' but the judges disagreed. Chief Justice Clive retorted: 'If a man has lived with a girl, and afterwards gives her a bond, it is good.'[42] In *Hill v. Spencer* (1767), the defendant was a prostitute before she lived with the plaintiff, Thomas Hill, an oil-shopkeeper. Furthermore, she apparently had another lover named Perry. Hill argued that she should not have the £50 annuity because the law 'presumes that common prostitutes are full of arts and designs'. But Lord Camden found for the defendant, and the Lord Chancellor upheld the decision on appeal because 'every person who has a hand may receive a gift.'[43] In *Gray v. Mathias* (1800), William Jamison executed two separate bonds to Jane Mathias in 1796, one of £700 and another of £1000. After his death, his daughter sued; her barristers argued that Jamison was 'a man of weak understanding, and given to excessive drinking', while Mathias was 'a very loose woman', adding that the law should protect men from the influence 'which artful women may acquire through the medium of the passions.' The defence argued, predictably, that both bonds were voluntary gifts. Despite the plaintiff's rather sensational language, the court agreed with the defence.[44] In short, on the whole, the law of cohabitation contracts from 1750 to 1850 worked on the side of female cohabitees.

Though the Victorian period was sometimes one of rigid morality, the courts continued to uphold cohabitation contracts if worded correctly. For example, the Chancery Court heard two similar cases in 1874 and 1884. In *Ayerst v. Jenkins*, the couple had been unable to marry because Isabella Buckton was the sister of William Hardinge's deceased wife. They lived together for four months until Hardinge died in January of 1862. In his will, Hardinge set up a trust fund for his pseudo-wife. This money sustained Isabella for years until she remarried in April 1870. After her marriage, the executor of the estate sued to revoke the trust, arguing that it was immoral. Lord Chancellor Shelborne found for Isabella; he believed that the gift had been voluntary, so he found no reason to set it aside.[45]

The court was also on the side of the female cohabitee in the case of *Re Vallance* (1884). The couple in this action had cohabited for many years until the death of the testator in 1881. Vallance left his lover £6000, because 'he considered that she was entitled to it'. Though the other heirs of the estate argued that the contract was invalid, Justice Kay disagreed. He insisted that there was no proof that Vallance gave the bond in order to induce his lover to remain. Indeed, it was far more likely that he was simply trying to take care of her.[46] These examples show a distinct set of assumptions on the part of the court. Men and women could make private arrangements, and, indeed, a man had the duty to do so when he had 'ruined' a woman. Though the judges could have voided all of these contracts on the assumption that they were 'against public policy', they chose to uphold them instead.

The clearest statements about the duties of male cohabitees emerged in those cases that dealt with illegitimate children. Two well-documented actions from mid-century made this plain. In *Smith v. Roche*, the couple had lived together and had two children by 1853. Roche did not want to marry Smith, and so he arranged to pay her £50 a year to care for the children, a girl and a boy. A few years later, the daughter died, and Roche discontinued his payments, arguing that the death of one of the children voided the contract. Smith sued in the Court of Common Pleas. Chief Justice Cockburn ordered Roche to continue the payments, declaring, 'a woman has a right to call on the father of her illegitimate child for its support if she is unable to maintain it'.[47]

The justices undermined the bastardy clause of the New Poor Law by their decision in this case, but the reason may have been the seeming 'innocence' of the woman involved, since Smith's barristers painted her as a seduced maiden. Nevertheless, such passivity was not a requirement for winning the case. The best example of this was the second mid-century case, *Keenan v. Handley*, in 1864.[48] Ellen Keenan met Captain Henry Edward Handley in 1859. She had no stated occupation (suspicious in itself), while Handley was an army officer. The two lived together, and Ellen had a daughter, Lucy, in 1860. Handley was uninterested in marriage, since Ellen had already lived with two other men and had children with both of them. He broke off the connection in the autumn of 1861, but he volunteered to give Keenan and their daughter £150 a year. However, Henry soon stopped paying, probably because of his marriage in April 1862, and Ellen sued him for repayment. In 1864, the Vice-Chancellor found for Keenan, so Handley appealed to the Court of Chancery, but to no avail. Lord Justice J. L. Knight Bruce, in concurrence with the other judges, insisted that 'the whole mass of evidence' supported the plaintiff.[49]

The courts' reactions to these cases had class implications. All of the cases concerned the middle class, even if sometimes they were only the lower-middle class (no estate, no case for recovery). For the most part, the women were lower class than the men, which explained their difficulties in achieving permanent relationships. Indeed, the class of the men may be one reason the courts insisted that they hold to their agreements; a gentleman should not take advantage of an inferior (in class and gender) without offering reparation. Over and over the justices carped on the 'moral obligation' and 'conscience' that demanded payment of the bonds. In a way, the justices were the upholders of the old church and community sanction that a man do right by a woman he has 'ruined'.[50]

In fact, the gender aspects were crucial to judges. Some female cohabitees played on the sympathy of the court as hapless, innocent virgins, seduced by the machinations of wily men. In *Gray v. Mathias*, Mathias's lawyers painted her as a pitiful creature, 'reclaimed' by her love of a good man, and the language of 'being kept' also gave the impression of passivity. In these cases, one could argue that the patriarchal courts were rewarding women for patient, long-suffering, if not exactly chaste, behaviour. All the same, the defendant in *Hill v. Spenser* was no shrinking violet – a prostitute, a cohabitee with Hill, and the lover of Perry at the same time – yet the

Barons of the Exchequer and, on appeal, the Lord Chancellor, upheld her claim. The opposition pointed out the moral deficiencies of these women, referring to them as 'common prostitutes' or 'strumpets'. Yet, in most cases, this unchastity did not mean that the women lost; the courts did not punish them for not conforming to 'proper' womanly behaviour.

One explanation for this fact may be that before 1850, the construction of gender was fluid enough to accommodate some irregularities on the part of women. Another was the early nineteenth-century insistence on contractual obligations, a tenet that only became more powerful by 1900. Hand in hand with their emphasis on morality went judges' obsession that men who made agreements keep them. A man had an obligation to keep promises and provide for dependents.[51] As for the 'immorality' of the woman involved, the rule of caveat emptor prevailed; a man should make sure of the character of his associates before signing contracts with them. In short, upholding individual responsibility was more important than punishing a few errant women. A third possibility is that the courts insisted on romanticising the women involved. Particularly when one of the cohabitees was a well-off man and the other a lower-class woman, the melodramatic idea of the 'aristocratic' seducer would have sprung to mind; sympathy in such cases usually went to the woman.[52] And, of course, the state also had a financial stake in seeing that men supported their children; otherwise, the ratepayers had to foot the bill.

Cohabitation contracts were not the only way women found to get compensation for years of faithful, if unlegalised, devotion; they could also sue for breach of promise of marriage. The sexual activity of cohabitees made them less than ideal plaintiffs, but they could sometimes sway a jury if they appeared 'more sinned against than sinning'. In *Daniel v. Bowles*, in 1826, the plaintiff had run away with a much older general. They lived together until she discovered that he was already married. She then left him and sued, and the jury found for her, with damages of £1500.[53] Often cases with large differences in class resulted in generous verdicts. In *Berry v. Da Costa* (1866), a well-off gentleman lived with the daughter of a milliner for several months. When he married another woman, the jury gave her £2500.[54]

Naturally, not all cohabitees collected damages. Women had to offer at least some proof that the man intended marriage, and women with irregular pasts, though not automatically excluded, had to counter accusations of immorality. In *Irvine v. Vickers*, the plaintiff was a prostitute with a police record for violent behaviour; with such a background, she could not convince the jury of the existence of an engagement, and she lost her case. Furthermore, the contemplated marriage had to be legal, or the plaintiff could not sue. Hannah Rowlands sued her deceased sister's husband; she worked as his housekeeper and had eventually become his lover. Baron Pollock dismissed the case, saying 'A man could no more marry his deceased wife's sister than he could marry his grandmother.'[55] All the same, breach of promise cases often allowed female cohabitees to get some provision for themselves and their children. Though women did not have a perfect winning record, they did make impressive gains and established in the minds of judges and juries that a man had a moral obligation to support a woman he treated as a wife. One should not overstate these legal advantages, but these cases show that courts believed in men keeping their promises, with or without marriage.

Supporting the family: illegitimacy and wills

The courts, then, were surprisingly friendly to 'kept' women throughout the nineteenth century, which was probably, at least in part, a strategy to provide for children of these unions. Illegitimate children became wards of the parish if the JPs could not find anyone to maintain them, so enforcing bonds made financial sense. Middle-class and upper-class couples also worried about supporting children, but they relied on bequests in wills. Men and women had to write these carefully; courts assumed that the word 'children' referred to legitimate ones only, with rare exceptions. In addition, the common law assumed that a contract given to support future illegitimate children was against public policy (encouraging the birth of illegitimates) and was therefore void. Only settlements written after the birth of children, and specifically mentioning those children, stood. A good example was *Wilkinson v. Adam* in 1812. John Wilkinson left his property to Ann Lewis 'who now lives with me' and to their children, whom he carefully listed in a ledger. When he died in 1808, his nieces and nephews sued to get the estate. The court decided that since Wilkinson had specifically called them the 'children which I may have by the aforesaid Ann Lewis', whom he could not marry legally (he had a wife living), he must have meant the children in the ledger. Also, only those children born at the time of the will could inherit, since an illegitimate child had to acquire 'the Reputation of being such Child' to be included. All three of Ann's children fitted this description, so they inherited the estate.[56]

Unfortunately, the fine lines laid down by the courts meant that many who desired to provide for their children failed to do so. In *Swaine v. Kennerly* in 1813, James Swaine left his estate to his son, Thomas Swaine, and then to his grandchildren. Only one of his grandsons was legitimate, though, so only he inherited.[57] In *In re Ayles' Trusts* (1876), a man left his money to his daughter Ann 'and all the children of my daughter Ann'. At the time of the will, Ann lived with James Hicks outside of wedlock and had three children. She and James wed in 1845 and had one child after the marriage. When Ann died, the legitimate child inherited everything, because Ann's father had simply said 'children' in his will.[58]

Judges recognised that the parents intended their illegitimate children to inherit, but did not feel that they could overturn the law. In 1851 a Mr Pratt had married his deceased wife's sister, Susan Broom. He made a will in 1852 when she was about to give birth to his son, leaving a trust to his 'wife' and 'all and every my children hereafter to be born'. Pratt died in 1853, and Susan soon discovered that the wording in his will was too vague. Sir John Romilly, the Master of the Rolls, upheld Susan's right to the trust, but not her son's. The wording could possibly refer to legitimate children of a subsequent marriage, so these phantom children got the right to the trust rather than Pratt's actual offspring. Romilly gave the decision 'with much regret,' but it stood.[59] In *Howarth v. Mills* in 1866, a woman who married her brother-in-law after the death of her sister made a will at the birth of her first child. By the time she died, she had four more children, but because she had failed to make a new will, specifically naming them, they were all cut out of the inheritance. Sir W. P. Wood explained that 'to hold that the after-born illegitimate children could take would be a direct encouragement of an unlawful cohabitation.'[60] The problems also occurred when wider kin tried to include illegitimate children. In 1883, an aunt left property to her nephew's illegitimate children, but the court disinherited the youngest, because she was born after the making of the will. Like Romilly, Lord Justice James expressed his opinion 'with regret,' but felt that he had no choice.[61]

Another problem in inheritance was that illegitimate children without wills forfeited their entire estates to the crown. *Brook v. Brook*, in 1861, illustrated this danger. The grandchildren of the couple involved, a man and his deceased wife's sister, could not inherit because their father was illegitimate and died intestate, so the crown took the property.[62] Nor could the parents inherit from their illegitimate issue if the latter died without a will. In 1818, David Don, a Scot, had a son with his cohabitee. He later married the mother of his son; in Scotland this marriage legitimated the boy. The son settled in Newcastle and bought some land there; unfortunately, he died without a will. His father was unable to inherit the property, because in England, the son was illegitimate.[63]

Similarly, children suffered because the English courts would not accept Scots divorces for English marriages. In two cases in 1859 and 1865, English courts ruled that since the Scots divorces were collusive, they were invalid in English law. Thus, the children of subsequent (bigamous) marriages were illegitimate and could not inherit.[64]

Illegitimate children could prevail in some instances, because many judges tried to find ways to uphold parents' intentions. In *Beachcroft v. Beachcroft* (1813), Samuel Beachcroft, a long-time inhabitant of India, left his estate divided between 'my children' and 'the mother of my children' before he died in 1806. Beachcroft's companion was an Indian woman, and they had five children. Beachcroft's natal family contested the will, but the court declared in favour of the children. Though they were not specifically named in the will, they had attained the reputation of being Samuel's children. Since Beachcroft also left money to 'the mother of my children', this was another point in the children's favour. Thus, the Indian cohabitee and her children succeeded to the property.[65]

Nor was the above case an isolated instance. In the early nineteenth century, Nathaniel Wright cohabited with Mary Lomas and had four children with her. In October 1811, Wright created a trust for Mary to care for her and 'his four natural children by her, and also of any after-born child that *Mary Lomas* might have by him.' Mary did have another child before he died in 1818, so she had five children to care for alone. Nathaniel's legitimate son John refused to confirm his father's settlement, so Mary sued. The Chancery Court found in favour of Mary and her children, judging that Nathaniel's wording had been specific enough to uphold.[66] A similar instance was that of *Gabb v. Prendergast* in 1855. In this case, the five children of Felix and Elinor Rolland, all of whom were born before their parents' marriage, inherited from their aunt, Mary Parry, since she called them in her will 'all and every the child or children then already born or thereafter to be born ... of Felix Rolland and Elinor his wife'. Into the late Victorian period, the courts fulfilled the intentions of those who left legacies to illegitimate children if they could find a way to do so.[67]

The oddities of the law of illegitimacy meant that illegitimate siblings sometimes fought each other over the inheritance. In these cases, the courts tried to find a way to be equitable. In *In Re Goodwin's Trust* (1874), Mary Goodwin had married her brother-in-law and had two children who survived her, one born after she wrote her will and one before. In her will, she left her property in trust 'equally between and among all and every my children and child by the said Richard Perkins'. Goodwin died in 1860, and her elder son sued to get the estate away from his brother, since the second son had not been born when she wrote her will. The Court of Chancery, however, found for the younger son, Sir G. Jessel arguing that 'before the death of Mary Goodwin, William Harry Perkins had acquired the reputation of being her child by Richard Perkins'.[68] Thus, by the end of the century, the courts were more generous towards illegitimate children, though the children often had to fight lawsuits to gain their legacies.

As confusing and difficult as these decisions often were, the children involved and their relatives at least had some hope for maintenance. This was not true for those in the working classes, where the consequences of cohabitation might be destitution. Cohabiting couples dealt with the Poor Law at several points, and the strictures of the law meant that the women involved were 'fallen', no matter how long-standing the relationship, and any children were illegitimate, taking their mothers' birth parishes. Sometimes mothers could affiliate the fathers, but this was not always possible. Parishes had particular difficulties when cohabitees' marital status was complex. The New Poor Law assumed single women bore all bastards. Thus, married women who left their husbands and had children with other men were in a grey area. If the husband had access to his wife, the law assumed all children of a married woman were his. If the husband did not have access, the woman could make an order of maintenance against the natural father. Broken and reconstituted marriages, though, complicated the process.

For instance, G. W. D. asked the editors of *Justice of the Peace* about the following case. A woman's husband was transported for a crime in 1840; she lived with another man during her husband's ten-year absence, having his child in 1846. In 1850, the husband returned and the wife went to live with him again. She asked the justices to make an order of maintenance against the father of her illegitimate child. Could this be done, considering that she had not made the order before the child had reached twelve months old? The editors thought it could, since the putative father had maintained the child, but the JPs would have to prove non-access of her husband.[69] In another case, a woman left her husband to live with another man and had three children with him. After her cohabitee died, she returned to her husband, with whom she had another child. When the husband deserted her, all four children went on relief. The justices could not compel the husband to support the three illegitimate children, despite his 'condoning' her adultery by taking her back. They could, though, sue him to maintain his wife and legitimate child.[70]

In fact, no matter how badly the husband had behaved, he could not be forced to support an adulterous wife. In 1842, a couple married and lived together for three to four years. The wife then discovered that her husband had been unfaithful. She left him, and he lived with his lover for the next forty years. The wife, in the meantime, lived with another man in a different town. In 1882, the wife's cohabitee died, and she became a pauper. The JPs tried to get the husband to support her but failed. According to the law, it made 'no difference that her adultery has been committed while she has been living apart from him in consequence of his own misconduct.'[71] In short, because of these limitations, women cohabitees often lost support. Moreover, because they were not married, they could not stay with their mates even when both were willing to do so. In 1860, a couple went to the workhouse, and the magistrates prepared to remove them to the man's settlement (the place where he had established residency, either by birth or by residing there a certain number of years). The authorities in the husband's parish then discovered that the two were not legally married. They separated the couple, and the woman took her own birth settlement.[72]

When families were broken and reconstituted, then, the children involved could be left out of the equation. In 1853, *Justice of the Peace* reported the story of a couple who had married and lived together for slightly over a year. The wife then began a sexual relationship with her employer, one that lasted seven years. She had a child but failed in her attempt to affiliate it. The JPs were unable to force the husband to maintain the child, and since the only evidence of non-access of the husband was the word of the husband and wife – neither of which was admissible – they could not prove the responsibility of the employer either. Thus, the child was legitimate in law, but the husband did not have to support it.[73] Another example, in 1865, concerned a married couple with two children. The husband, a soldier, left England, and the wife lived with another man and had a child with him. Her cohabitee died, so when the husband returned, she lived with him again. The husband took his wife and his own children back, but would not support the illegitimate child. As a result, the mother left the child behind when the family moved. The magistrates could do nothing, since the husband did not have to support a child not his own, and the mother, as a married woman, could also not be compelled to do so (all her property was her husband's). The luckless child went to the workhouse.[74] At times, then, mothers as well as fathers avoided supporting their children; little wonder that Poor Law officials were frustrated. In both the upper and working classes, children could suffer the most from cohabitation.

Clearly, the legal position of cohabiting women and their illegitimate children made their condition challenging. Nevertheless, none of these consequences stopped informal unions or women's determination that men should honour their irregular relationships. The state made marriage more difficult in 1753, and left cohabiting women and their children with limited options. In response, most people made the effort to marry in the prescribed manner. But a distinct minority chose to ignore the legal definition of marriage and to create their own, and these couples caused difficulties from the parish level to the House of Lords. This challenge continued into the criminal courts; the Victorian state had to find a way to cope with cohabiting couples in both branches of law. In neither part was the state's role easy or consistent.

Notes

1   L. Stone, *Uncertain Unions: Marriage in England, 1660-1753* (Oxford: Oxford University Press, 1992), p. 31.

2   J. Gillis, *For Better, For Worse: British Marriages, 1600 to the Present* (New York: Oxford University Press, 1985), pp. 140-2; R. Outhwaite, *Clandestine Marriage in England, 1500-1850* (London: The Hambledon Press, 1995), pp. 75-144; S. Parker, *Informal Marriage, Cohabitation and the Law, 1750-1989* (New York: St Martin's Press, 1990), pp. 29-47; D. Lemmings, 'Marriage and the law in the eighteenth century: Hardwicke's Marriage Act of 1753', *Historical Journal* 39 (1996), 339-60.

3   Outhwaite, *Clandestine Marriage*, pp. 112-21; 145-67; Parker, *Informal Marriage*, pp. 50-61; S. Cretney, *Family Law in the Twentieth Century: A History* (Oxford: Oxford University Press, 2003), pp. 3-11.

4   J. Cookson, *Thoughts on Polygamy* (Winchester: J. Wilkes, 1782), pp. 44-5.

5   *Munro v. De Chemant* (1815), 171 *English Reports* 69; 'Presumption in favour of marriage', *Justice of the Peace* 45 (1881), 711-12.

6   Outhwaite, *Clandestine Marriage*, p. 144.

7   *Justice of the Peace* 6 (1842), 429.

8   Outhwaite, *Clandestine Marriage*, p. 144; 'The law relating to marriage as it affects the law of settlement', *Justice of the Peace* 2 (1838), 65-7; quote on 65; W. Hooper, *The Law of Illegitimacy* (London: Sweet and Maxwell, 1911), pp. 122-31.

9   U. Henriques, 'Bastardy and the new poor law', *Past and Present* 37 (1967), 103-29.

10   C. Tomalin, *Mrs Jordan's Profession: The Actress and the Prince* (New York: Alfred A. Knopf, 1995), pp. 64-7.

11   J. B. Atlay, *The Victorian Chancellors* 2 vols (London: Smith, Elder, & Co., 1906), I: 444-6; Cretney, *Family Law*, p. 545, note 4.

12   *Reddall v. Leddiard* (1820), 3 *Phillimore's Reports* 256-7; quote from p. 256.

13   *Wiltshire v. Prince, otherwise Wiltshire* (1830), 162 *English Reports* 1176-7. See also *Pouget v. Tomkins* (1812), 1 *Phillimore's Reports* 499-506.

14   National Archives (hereafter NA), HO 45/O.S. 1300.

15   *The King v. The Inhabitants of Tibshelf* (1830), 109 *English Reports* 758-60; Outhwaite, *Clandestine Marriage*, pp. 151-2.

16   *Cope v. Burt* (1809), Lambeth Palace Archives (hereafter LPA), Court of Arches Records, D475, Case #2266.

17   *Wakefield v. MacKay* (1808), LPA, Court of Arches Records, H 142, D2161, 1-19.

18   Outhwaite, *Clandestine Marriage*, pp. 151-2; see also *Chichester v. The Marquess and Marchioness of Donegal* (1822), 1 *Addams's Reports* 5-29.

19   *Diddear, falsely called Faucit, otherwise Savill v. Faucit* (1821), 3 *Phillimore's Reports* 580-3; *Dormer, falsely called Williams v. Williams* (1838), 163 *English Reports* 301-4.

20   *Gompertz v. Kensit* (1872), 36 *Justice of the Peace* 548-9, quote from 548; *The Times*, 25 January 1872, p. 10.

21   R. Mitchison and L. Leneman, *Girls in Trouble: Sexuality and Social Control in Rural Scotland, 1660-1780* (Edinburgh: Scottish Cultural Press, 1998), p. 42.

22 *Watson and Watson v. Faremouth and Others, Annual Register* 53 (1811), 136–7, quote from 137. See also LPA, Court of Arches Records, H 151/20, Case #9682.

23 *Ware v. Ware* (1765), LPA, Court of Arches Records, D 2185, Case #9614.

24 'False declaration of marriage', *Justice of the Peace* 65 (1901), 428 (for quote); *The Times,* 7 July 1901, p. 9.

25 Outhwaite, *Clandestine Marriage,* pp. 149–50.

26 HO 45/O.S. 7953, Letter from J. D. Powles to the Foreign Secretary (re-routed to the Home Office), 14 May 1867. The undersecretary wrote back on 19 June 1867.

27 *Middleton v. Janverin* (1802), 161 *English Reports* 797–801; quote from 801.

28 Cretney, *Family Law,* pp. 161–95.

29 L. Leneman, *Alienated Affections: The Scottish Experience of Divorce and Separation, 1684–1830* (Edinburgh: Edinburgh University Press, 1998), pp. 218–31; *Conway v. Beazley* (1831), 162 *English Reports* 1292–8.

30 *Fenton v. Livingstone* (1859), 23 *Justice of the Peace* 579–81; Mitchison and Leneman, *Girls in Trouble,* pp. 67, 98.

31 Leneman, *Alienated Affections,* pp. 223–31.

32 *Justice of the Peace* 3 (1839), 680; 32 (1868), 477.

33 *Justice of the Peace* 5 (1841), 598–9; 21 (1857), 814; 46 (1882), 571.

34 *Justice of the Peace* 16 (1852), 799.

35 C. Barton, *Cohabitation Contracts: Extra-Marital Partnerships and Law Reform* (Aldershot: Gower Publishing Company, 1984), pp. 38–42.

36 24 *English Reports* 55 (1700). See also *Harris v. Marchioness of Annandale* (1727), 24 *English Reports* 801–2; and *Cray v. Rooke* (1735), 25 *English Reports* 713–14.

37 28 *English Reports* 103–4 (1751).

38 A. R. Cleveland, *Woman Under the English Law* (London: Hurst and Blackett, 1896), pp. 222–4; W. Eversley, *The Law of Domestic Relations* 6th edn (London: Sweet and Maxwell, 1951), pp. 111–18.

39 97 *English Reports* 985 (1764); 30 *English Reports* 1058–60 (1797).

40 105 *English Reports* 684–5 (1815).

41 172 *English Reports* 265–6 (1827).

42 95 *English Reports* 845–7 (1767); quotes from 846.

43 27 *English Reports* 416–17 (1767); first quote on 416; 27 *English Reports* 524–5 (1767); second quote on 525.

44 31 *English Reports* 591–5 (1800), quotes from 592.

45 *Justice of the Peace* 38 (1874), 37–8; *The Times,* 8 July 1872, p. 11.

46 *Justice of the Peace* 48 (1884), 598.

47 *Justice of the Peace* 23 (1859), 312–13, quote from 313; *The Times,* 28 April 1859, p. 9.

48 *Justice of the Peace* 28 (1864), 660; and *The Times,* 11 July 1864, p. 11.

49 Quote from *Justice of the Peace* 28 (1864), 660.

50 F. M. L. Thompson, *The Rise of Respectable Society: A Social History of Victorian Britain, 1830–1900* (London: Fontana, 1988), pp. 307–8; J. Weeks, *Sex, Politics, and Society: The Regulation of Sexuality Since 1800* 2nd ed. (London: Longman, 1989), pp. 60–4.

51 L. Davidoff and C. Hall, *Family Fortunes: Men and Women of the English Middle Class, 1780–1850* (Chicago: University of Chicago Press, 1987); J. Tosh, *A Man's Place: Masculinity and the Middle-Class Home in Victorian England* (New Haven, CT: Yale University Press, 1999), pp. 53–101; K. McClelland, 'Masculinity and the "representative artisan" in Britain, 1850–1880', in M. Roper and J. Tosh (eds), *Manful Assertions: Masculinities in Britain since*

1800 (London: Routledge, 1991), 74–91.

52 P. Brooks, *The Melodramatic Imagination: Balzac, Henry James, Melodrama, and the Mode of Excess* (New Haven, CT: Yale University Press, 1976); J. Walkowitz, *City of Dreadful Delight: Narratives of Sexual Danger in Late-Victorian London* (Chicago: University of Chicago Press, 1992).

53 *The Times,* 19 December 1826, p. 3.

54 *The Times,* 15 January 1866, p. 11; 1 *Law Reports, Common Pleas Division* (1866) 331–6.

55 NA, ASSI 1/65; *Berkshire County Chronicle,* 17 July 1869, p. 5; *Liverpool Mercury,* 10 February 1882, p. 8; *Illustrated Police News,* 18 February 1882, p. 3 (for quote); *Gibson's Law Notes* 1 (1882), 75. For more cases, see G. Frost, *Promises Broken: Courtship, Class, and Gender in Victorian England* (Charlottesville, VA: University Press of Virginia, 1995), pp. 111–13, 130, 134.

56 *Wilkinson v. Adam* (1812), 35 *English Reports* 163–82; first quote from 164; second from 175; 1 *Vesey and Brames Reports* 422–69.

57 *Swaine v. Kennerley* (1813), 35 *English Reports* 182.

58 *In re Ayles' Trusts* (1875), 40 *Justice of the Peace* 181.

59 *Pratt v. Mathew* (1856), 52 *English Reports* 1134–9; first quote from 1137, second from 1139.

60 30 *Justice of the Peace* 759–60 (quote from 759); *The Times,* 30 May 1866, p. 11. See also *Meddowcroft v. Huguenin* (1842–43), 163 *English Reports* 771–78.

61 *In re Du Bochet, Mansell v. Allen* (1901), 2 *Law Reports, Chancery Division* 441–50; quote from 450.

62 *Brook v. Brook* (1858–61), 21 *Justice of the Peace* 21 (1857), 804–5; 22 (1858), 272–4; 25 (1861), 259–62; *The Times,* 17 March 1857, p. 11; 21 November 1857, p. 10; 23 November 1857, p. 8; 25 November 1857, p. 10; 26 November 1857, p. 8; 19 April 1858, pp. 11–12; 26 February 1861, p. 10; 4 March 1861, p. 10.

63 *In re Don's Estate* (1857), 21 *Justice of the Peace* 694; *The Times,* 6 July 1857, p. 10; 3 August 1857, p. 10.

64 *Dolphin v. Robins and Another* (1859), *The Times,* 6 August 1859, p. 11; *In re Wilson's Trust* (1865), 30 *Justice of the Peace* 163–4; *The Times,* 15 November 1865, p. 11. See also *In re Wright's Trust* (1856), 20 *Justice of the Peace* 675–6; *The Times,* 8 May 1856, p. 11.

65 *Beachcroft v. Beachcroft* (1816), 56 *English Reports* 159–64; quote from 162.

66 *Lomas v. Wright* (1835), 2 *Mylne and Keen's Reports* 769–79; quote from 769.

67 *Gabb v. Prendergast* (1855), 1 *Kay & Johnson's Reports* 439–43; quote from 440. For a later case, see *Hill v. Crook* (1873), 6 *Law Reports, House of Lords* 265–86 and *Crook v. Hill* (1877), 41 *Justice of the Peace* 228–9.

68 *In re Goodwin's Trust* (1874), 38 *Justice of the Peace* 500.

69 *Justice of the Peace* 14 (1850), 165.

70 *Justice of the Peace* 20 (1856), 621.

71 *Justice of the Peace* 46 (1882), 301–2; quote from 302.

72 *Justice of the Peace* 24 (1860), 717; see also *Justice of the Peace* 39 (1875), 92. Parliament restricted removals to those who had lived in an area less than five years in 1846, later reduced to three years (1861) and then one (1865). This couple had either not lived in the area long, or were victims of the poor wording of the law, which allowed for some exceptions even late in the century. M. Rose (ed.), *The Poor and the City: The English Poor Law in its Urban Context, 1834–1914* (Leicester: Leicester University Press, 1985), pp. 9–10; P. Thane, 'Women and the poor law in Victorian and Edwardian England', *History Workshop Journal* 6 (1978), 36.

73   *Justice of the Peace* 17 (1853), 351.
74   *Justice of the Peace* 29 (1865), 12.

2

Violence and cohabitation in the courts

L IKE THE CIVIL LAW, criminal courts showed ambivalence about, rather than simple disapproval of, irregular unions. In fact, the juries and especially judges focused as much on the men as the women in the cases, and did not allow middle-class status to excuse violence. This fact complicates the traditional view of English criminal justice as patriarchal, class-biased, and moralistic. Though Victorian justice could be all of those things, it was not invariably so, and even when it was, the results were not predictable.

This chapter focuses on cases of violence within cohabiting families, based on a collection of 217 violent incidents culled from the *Yorkshire Gazette, Lancaster Guardian,* and *The Times* between 1850 and 1905. [1] Analysis of the data by region did not disclose any clear regional differences in motives for murder or outcomes in the cases. In fact, the reaction of the couples and the courts were remarkably similar across England.

In civil courts, the difference in status between married and unmarried couples was considerable, which was why Hardwicke had so much impact. In criminal cases, the situation was complicated, since courts tended to see cohabitees as 'practically married' at the same time as 'fallen'. On the one hand, cohabitees' relationships mirrored those of married couples, and judges and juries expected them to carry out spousal duties. On the other hand, the fact that the two were not married sometimes changed the motives for violence and the courtroom dynamic. In particular, judges saw concubinage as a strand in working-class pathology that needed elimination. These contradictions led to disagreements within the courtroom and also to conflicts between different branches of the law.

The majority of these cases involved the poor; of the 212 where the newspapers mention class or occupation, 197 cases (93 per cent) were working-class. Only 15 cases (7 per cent) had even one partner in the lower-middle or middle classes. [2] Similar studies of marital violence have yielded more middle-class cases, so the predominance of the poor reflects the fact that fewer middle-class people cohabited. In other words, domestic violence existed in all classes, but those above the working class struggled with this problem while legally wed.[3] In addition, of the 189 violent incidents between cohabitees, the man was the aggressor 161 times (85 per cent), the woman, 28. Of the 20 cases involving children, men were the aggressors 9 times, women 6, and both 4.[4] Men also resorted to suicide more frequently, with 19 cases of male suicide and 19 attempted suicide. Women committed or attempted to commit suicide in only 5 cases. Though women could sometimes hold their own in scuffles, then, men were more deadly.[5]

Statistically, the trial results favoured victims. Of the 155 cases with recorded verdicts, 105 resulted in a guilty verdict, 21 were acquittals or discharges (4 for insanity), 25 had a dead or escaped perpetrator, and in 4 the defendant was bound over to keep the peace. If one removes those with a dead perpetrator and those bound over, the prisoner was convicted in 105 of 125 cases, a rate of 84 per cent. This statistic is misleading, though. Many incidents did not make it to trial; in those that did, juries often lessened the charge, as from murder to manslaughter. Not all of my cases have a clear charge and verdict, but of the 82 which do, 31 cases (38 per cent) were reduced from the original charge, including 15 reduced from murder to manslaughter and 4 reduced from attempted murder to attempt to do grievous bodily harm.[6]

Furthermore, many times coroners' inquests had already reduced the charges before the defendants went to trial. Of the 34 full inquest reports in my group of cases, 13 (more than one-third) reduced the charge, usually from murder to manslaughter. Thus, though juries often convicted defendants, the sentences were not always severe. Especially in magistrates' and police courts, penalties could be fines or being bound over to keep the peace. The police courts, in particular, tried to reconcile the parties, knowing that women needed breadwinners.[7] In these ways, as well as many others, cohabitees showed little distinction from those legally wed.

Cohabitees as husbands and wives

In addition to these statistical similarities, judges and barristers at all levels emphasised the way that cohabitees matched the experience of married couples. Robert Cooper's barrister defended him from the charge of murder by appealing to the jury's sympathy for a man whose 'wife' had left him: 'the defendant was not legally married to the prisoner, but ... the prisoner always looked upon her as his wife,' he explained. Nor was such rhetoric limited to defence barristers. In 1878, the police court magistrates gave James Stubbs six months at hard labour for kicking his cohabitee, Ann Bullock, since, Mr Bridge insisted, 'she was equally entitled to protection as if she were his wife.'[8] In essence, these judges and lawyers semantically erased the difference between cohabiting and married partners, expecting those who had made no vows to fulfill marital obligations.

The similarities to married couples often worked in women's favour, but such ideas could also hurt women who had not shown 'wifely' obedience. As historians have found, courts disapproved of women who cursed, fought back, or drank, because they failed in their domestic duties and upset the middle-class ideal of the helpless victim of the brutal working-class man.[9] Ann Perry called William Burke an 'Irish bugger' and stabbed him when he beat her and pushed her out of their home. At her trial, the Common Serjeant insisted that 'The man whom she destroyed, although not legally her husband, was to be regarded in the same light. It was true that he had struck her; but the language that the Court had heard that she had used … had provoked him'.[10] In short, he ignored the fact that Perry had made no vow to obey, treating her as a wife. Similarly, John Abbot beat Hannah McKay with a coal rake in 1876 in Yorkshire, justifying it because she had been out drinking all night. The jury found him guilty of the unlawful wounding, a lesser offence, and the judge agreed, considering the 'great provocation'. Abbot got only eight months. In 1893, Job Taylor, a labourer, beat Emily Twiggs to death over some money, but also because 'he was exasperated by the conduct of the woman and the language she made use of.' The jury reduced the charge to manslaughter, and Justice Mathew 'was satisfied they had adopted the right course.'[11]

By expecting cohabitees to fulfil spousal duties, judges and juries agreed with most couples' views of their cohabitation. The vast majority of these couples saw themselves as married. They shared the same name, registered their children as legitimate, and followed the gender roles of working-class marriage. As we will see, the motives for violence were the same as married couples – sexual jealousy and money squabbles. The courts' reactions to their quarrels, then, supported these couples' wider definition of the institution. In other words, judges and juries elided the differences between married and non-married couples, believing men and women could expect their partners to behave as spouses simply by assuming these roles. The court did this in part because the couples themselves did so, and judges and juries followed suit. Indeed, judges and juries probably could not imagine a coupling that did not involve traditional gender roles, with or without a ceremony. In addition, if the couple were 'married', the cases fell into predictable patterns that made decisions easier for all. And both defence and prosecution barristers had reasons to support the confusion at different times; 'unwifely' behaviour might mitigate the man's offence, for instance. Whatever the reason, both the law and society reinforced each other in pretending that an open, negotiable relationship was in fact a marriage.

'Fallen' couples

Nevertheless, in many cases the fact that the couples were unmarried changed the approach of those in the courtroom. First, cohabiting couples had some motives peculiar to themselves. At times female cohabitees left or planned to leave precisely because the men had not married them. Women often entered 'tally' arrangements hoping they would lead to marriage. When the men did not follow through, the women decided to try their luck elsewhere; though they were technically free to do so, their partners often objected. Ellen Marney threatened to leave George Mulley in 1855 'because he has not kept his promise and married me.' His response was to cut her throat and then stab her several times. When a woman found a new man, the ex-lover was even more enraged. Amelia Blunt lived with Francis Wane in 1864, but she left him and became engaged to another man. Wane begged her to return, but she replied: 'No, Francis; you had a chance for me to be your lawful wife.' In response, Wane cut her throat.[12]

Another issue peculiar to cohabitees was the question of children; because they were illegitimate, fathers had no legal rights to them. John Hannah, for instance, attacked Jane Barnham when she left because she took the children with her. Richard Sabley, similarly, left Sophia Jackson when his wife returned, but he still wanted to adopt his child with Jackson. He did not succeed though, since 'the deceased refused to part with the child.'[13] These men could not assert control precisely because they had not married the mothers of their children. Married couples also battled over custody when they separated, but in those cases the women did not have the legal upper hand. In cohabiting relationships, the mother was the legal parent and could even refuse visitation rights. Though few women went this far, many insisted on keeping their children, with fatal results.

More generally, at times the issue at stake was the man's inability to head the household. In Shani D'Cruze's words, Victorian men 'wished to be "masters in their own house"', and used violence if they could not achieve mastery any other way.[14] Cohabitation complicated this already contested terrain. Particularly if the woman owned her home, a male partner did not control her finances and this led to tensions. Mark Turner lived with a widow, Mrs McCrea, in Lancaster in 1900. He got into a scuffle with her married daughter, Elizabeth King, and a lodger, Annie Bowles, because he had spread rumours about their sexual probity. Turner tried to force King and Bowles out of the house, and King threw a pot at him. He then hit her with a poker. Bowles, in giving evidence, insisted, 'It was not defendant's house and he had no authority to order her to leave.' Turner, for his part, 'appealed to the Bench to support him in conducting his house properly.' The Mayor was unimpressed, well aware that it was not actually Turner's house, and fined him 5s.[15]

As many of these cases indicate, the motives were bound up in men's desire to assert their masculinity. Legally, an unmarried woman had every right to disobey a man not her husband, to leave an unsatisfactory partner, or to keep her children, but the poorest classes often did not make distinctions between marriage and cohabitation. Both Andrew Davis and John Carter Wood have explored working-class men's violence as a way to assert their 'honour' and community standing. The men in my sample were very poor, so physical strength was one of the few ways they could impose themselves. Men also saw 'disciplining' wives as an acceptable part of marriage. The fact that in these instances the men did not have legal right on their side made little difference.[16] In fact, in a few cases, men's anxiety about proving their 'mastery' was the main motive. Henrietta Corn left Joseph Fountain in 1870 to go with another man. In April, Joseph urged her to come back to him; when she refused, he slit her throat. In his defence, he explained that 'the woman had been persuaded to leave him twice by a man who was a fellow private in a regiment of Militia. He did not intend to have anything more to do with her, but she came while the regiment was training and threatened to show him up in it.' Fountain's fear of being 'shown up' in front of the men of the regiment led him to attack Henrietta, to prove that neither she – nor the other private – could better him.[17]

As well as these distinct motives, the reaction of the judges and juries also distinguished cohabiting couples' violence. Especially, some judges took the position that if a man did not choose to marry a woman, he could not expect her to behave like a wife and so had little excuse for violence. In other words, the women, no matter how impure or drunk, were not to blame for the illegality of their relationships. These findings contradict those of other historians who have found that unchaste, assertive, and drunken women would not receive sympathy from the courtroom. Since all of my cases involve women who were unchaste by definition, and were often entirely disorderly, these findings indicate that Victorian justice was highly complex.

Indeed, judges and coroners castigated violent men even when their partners were drunk or worked as prostitutes. In 1863, the Commissioner of the London police court had scant sympathy with George Shields, who beat Jane Dixon, a prostitute, with a bedpost. Both were drunk and they lived in a brothel, and he concluded, 'The prisoner was living in a state of concubinage with a known prostitute, in a house inhabited by other women of loose character; they were all drinking to excess, and what but violence among them could be expected?' Shields got two years at hard labour for unlawful wounding, a long sentence for that charge. Justice Brett, similarly, disdained Thomas McDonald, who had beaten Bridget Welch, a prostitute, to death. After the jury found Thomas guilty of murder, Brett concluded: 'She was a bad and wicked woman; you were a bad and wicked man, and of all people on this earth you had no right to judge her for her wickedness.'[18]

In short, judges, at times, insisted on policing male behaviour as much as female. Men who did not marry legally, drank, and were violent were just as much of a problem as unruly women. In fact, sometimes judges were biased against defendants precisely because they had not married their lovers. In 1866, Justice Martin summed up strongly against John Banks, who had killed Ann Gilligan over money quarrels. When the jury found him guilty of murder, Martin gave him the death sentence and lectured him: 'You had been drinking all day; you went with this woman to a public house and although she was the wife of another man you were living with her as your wife … you were guilty of the most barbarous violence towards her.' Banks drank to excess, lived 'in sin', and could not control his temper; he had only himself to blame when the situation became deadly.[19]

The courts were most sympathetic to women when they were the victims of violence. As Perry's case demonstrated, women received less sympathy when they perpetrated violence. Mary Turner, who shot her ex-lover because he taunted her with his upcoming marriage, pleaded that she was not in her right mind, and the jury convicted her of attempting to cause grievous bodily harm rather than attempted murder, and recommended mercy. Justice Williams, though, disliked her use of a gun. Insisting that she had 'an implacable spirit of revenge', he gave her eighteen months. Judges had a bias against any use of deadly weapons, as opposed to using fists or boots, since the former appeared premeditated. This disadvantaged women, since they were unlikely to wound or kill by beating or kicking.[20] All the same, women rarely received the capital charge, and their sentences for violence were shorter than those of men. Emily Mason, who stabbed and killed her cohabitee, William Rae, in a drunken fury in 1856, was indicted for manslaughter rather than murder, to which she pleaded guilty at the trial. Sarah Burch, a prostitute, killed John Williams by fracturing his head with tongs in 1885, but the jury found her guilty of manslaughter only. She had used a blunt instrument, was drunk, and was hardly pure, but Justice Hawkins agreed with the jury, giving her ten years. Though this was a lengthy sentence, it could easily have been longer. Tom Dixon, who beat Mary Wilson with a poker in 1860 while 'beastly drunk', was also convicted of manslaughter, but he got penal servitude for life.[21] The Victorian courts, especially judges, primarily blamed men for cohabitation and violence.

Judges with juries: controlling male violence

Martin Wiener has argued that Victorian judges tried to improve working-class male behaviour through the courts, particularly from the 1860s. Work by early modern historians has shown that concern with male violence began before the nineteenth century, but in the Victorian period the issue was politicised, since working-class men themselves started criticising domestic violence. The decisions of judges, then, gained added resonance and also became more consistent.[22] Judges wanted to shape working-class masculinity to be 'respectable'. Thus, they supported harsher penalties and disagreed with juries who took a more merciful view. My research supports Wiener's view that some judges castigated violent male defendants as 'unmanly'. In my cases, the brutality of working-class cohabitees offended the judges in part because the men asserted control over women without having married them.

Though lower courts had the well-earned reputation of being unsympathetic to abused wives, some coroners did their part to 'civilise' male behaviour. The coroner in Newcastle in 1856 influenced the jury to commit William Fleming to trial for wilful murder instead of manslaughter, since he had beaten his cohabitee Ann for five years. The coroner insisted that 'his conduct towards her has been most unmanly, and his usage of her most savage and brutal.' Similarly, the coroner in Thomas Brown's case supported the jury's decision to indict him for wilful murder of Elizabeth Caldwell; Brown had sawn off Caldwell's head when both were drunk. The coroner exclaimed, 'a more deliberate and brutal thing I never heard of. I cannot think how you could go and inflict a wound of this kind upon a woman you profess to love so much.'[23]

The main impetus for reforming male behaviour, though, came from high court judges. Justices had much latitude in the nineteenth century, so their treatment of violent offenders varied. In her study of criminal justice in Victorian Kent Conley gives several examples of justices who supported lower charges and short sentences against men who killed their wives or cohabitees. But Conley also documents a growing tendency to be harsher on working-class male violence over time.[24] And some justices cracked down on domestic violence as early as the 1850s. Justice Martin, in sentencing George Mulley, a porter, for stabbing his cohabitee in 1855, insisted 'they [the judges] had come to the determination of passing the fullest sentence allowed them by law, in the hope of making an example to deter others from similar acts of brutality.' Martin then transported Mulley for life.[25] In that same year, Justice Wightman made a similar speech at the trial of Maurice Hearn, who was found guilty of manslaughter after beating and kicking Jane Kelly to death. Though Kelly was no angel, Wightman insisted that Hearn 'had been convicted of a most unmanly and brutal act,' and sentenced him to seven years.[26]

Neither of these judges made any distinctions between lawful and unlawful wives in their desire to protect women, and this was typical. Justice Denman, in 1890, heard the murder trial of George Bowling who had beaten Eliza Nightingale to death with a hammer. Denman made a long speech about domestic violence when he sentenced Bowling to death:

> Over and over again, nowadays, we see the terrible state of things which indicates a sort of belief on the part of men who are living with women either as their wives or as you are living with the deceased, they have a power of life and death over them, that if the woman ... makes herself disagreeable to the man, that the man, who is unworthy of the name of brute – it would be an insult to the brute to say that he was like a brute – thinks himself justified at once in ... acting as her executioner.[27]

Like the magistrate in Stubbs's case, Denman thought Eliza deserved the protection of a wife, despite her illegal status.

Indeed, judges did not limit themselves to speeches after the trials were over; they also influenced juries to find defendants guilty of murder rather than manslaughter. In two trials in 1862 and 1866, Baron Martin dismissed the extenuating circumstances of the killings and persuaded the juries to hang the defendants.[28] In 1877, Justice Grove refuted Caleb Smith's attempt to plead manslaughter by pointing out that he had used a knife (showing premeditation) and had no immediate provocation. Grove repeated his opinion to the Home Secretary, pointing out that Smith killed his lover from 'an excessive fondness ... & a jealous fear that she should leave him', and Smith hanged on 14 August 1877.[29] Judges were also suspicious of pleas of 'excited feelings'. Justice Hawkins, in a murder trial in 1878, rebutted the defence barrister's attempt to have the charge reduced because of the defendant's passion. Hawkins insisted, 'No man was excused by the law from the consequences of his act because he did it in a moment of excitement.' Like Grove, Hawkins later insisted to the Home Office that there was 'no palliation of the crime' in the evidence. Numerous judges also rejected drunkenness as an excuse; a man could not excuse his inebriated actions if he had voluntarily put himself in such a state.[30]

Insanity pleas also received short shrift. Earnest Southey murdered his three sons with his cohabitee, Mrs White, and then murdered his legal wife and daughter in August of 1865.[31] Southey's barrister, E. T. Smith, pleaded insanity, and since Southey made many wild accusations and suicide threats, the defence had merit. Justice Mellor, however, stated flatly that Southey had showed 'sense and sanity of mind' while in prison. Not surprisingly, the jury found him guilty. Henry Poland, the prosecuting barrister, expressed the difficulties of meeting the legal definition of insanity when he described Southey as 'probably half brute, and half mad in the popular though not in the legal sense.' Though Southey's case was unusually brutal, other defendants had equally poor success with pleas of temporary insanity. Justice Denman demolished Thomas Smithers's attempt to plead insanity due to his epilepsy, insisting to the Home Office that he was 'not of *entirely* sound mind', but still knew 'the nature & quality of his act'. Not surprisingly, only four defendants in my sample were acquitted for insanity, two men and two women.[32]

The gender dynamic evident in the reaction of judges to male violence fused the two contradictory impulses in the criminal courts towards cohabitation. These judges held the men responsible both for the cohabitation and the violence. A man who did not marry a woman could not expect her to behave well nor to run an orderly home. If he so forgot himself as to add violence to his sins, he deserved the highest punishment. By focusing on fallen men, judges and juries ignored a counter-argument that cohabiting women did not deserve to be treated as spouses; on the contrary, they extended the need for husbandly protection to such women. In these instances, judges and juries agreed.

Judges v. juries: class and gender differences

All the same, juries dissented from the judges' opinions on occasion. Most jurors were lower-middle or middle-class men who saw little difference between regular and irregular unions.[33] They also understood more clearly why many couples cohabited and did not assume that the men chose it. In addition, they may well have sympathised with the defendants' wider range of justifiable 'correction'. Thus, conflicts between judges and jurors occurred. For one thing, judges did not always support juries' recommendations to mercy. The jury in William Abigale's case recommended mercy 'on account of the prisoner's youth' (he was twenty). Baron Pollock, though, told the

Home Office that Abigale's murder of his pregnant lover was without 'any excuse that I can see.' Abigale was hanged in May 1882.[34] In 1893, George Cooke, a policeman, beat Maud Merton, a prostitute, with his truncheon and then asphyxiated her; she had 'pestered' him after their relationship ended. The jury recommended mercy, but Justice Hawkins disagreed, telling the prisoner, 'yours is a case in which peculiar atrocity is manifested.' Hawkins was just as emphatic when he wrote to the Home Secretary: 'this recommendation to mercy astonished me ... This was one of the most cruel murders I ever heard of'. The Home Office eventually agreed, and Cooke hanged on July 25.[35]

For another thing, juries found lesser charges more often than judges preferred. Since judges had discretion over sentencing, they gave longer sentences than usual to demonstrate their disapproval. Joseph Fountain, the man who attacked his cohabitee over 'showing him up' in front of his militia, had badly wounded her when he slit her throat with a razor. The jury convicted him of intent to do grievous bodily harm rather than attempted murder. Nevertheless, Justice Blackburn gave him fifteen years, because, he insisted, 'it was a very bad case indeed'. In 1895, Justice Grantham presided over the trial of John Foster, who had killed Mary Johnson by hitting her with a coal rake. When the jury found him guilty of manslaughter rather than murder, Grantham lectured him on how fortunate he had been, before giving him twenty years. Justice Quain was even blunter, telling an 1875 jury that they were being 'extremely stupid' when they wavered over whether to convict for murder or manslaughter. When they finally settled on the latter, he gave the defendant fifteen years.[36] These courtroom disagreements indicated a difference in opinion over gender roles, but also over class, for judges found no justification for working-class domestic violence.

The jurors may well have been right in their take on these relationships; judges were unrealistic in expecting men always to 'make honest women' of their partners. Some couples did indeed choose to remain unmarried, but in ninety-two of the cases, the newspaper reported that one or both of the partners were married to other people. Many of these couples, then, probably would have married if they could. Thus, the judges' insistence that the men were responsible for 'living in sin' was incorrect; the strict law of divorce, and its high expense, kept many of these couples from marrying. In fact, one could look at it another way and be impressed that these couples stayed together at all. But such sympathy rarely occurred from the bench. The defendants' violence and drinking marked them out as unrespectable, so judges assumed that their choice to cohabit was part of their general disorderliness. Juries, however, understood the circumstances better, which might in part explain their more merciful approach.

This conundrum points up several contradictions in Victorian law about the issue of cohabitation, marriage, and violence. On the one hand, the domestic laws in England supported marriage and discouraged cohabitation, giving irregular unions no legal recognition and illegitimising the children. At the same time, the criminal courts often saw the similarities between marriage and cohabitation in the working class and expected men to provide and women to obey, with or without vows. This, seemingly, supported cohabitation by regarding it as practically the same thing as marriage. In short, the civil law said they were not married, but the criminal law (at times) treated them as if they were. But it was not this simple, either. The civil law, with its limited divorce, forced some couples either to part or live in illegal unions. Cohabitation was a perfectly rational choice with such restricted options. But the criminal law, particularly late-Victorian judges, punished couples for this behaviour, regarding them as irrational. In other words, the civil law helped to create a pathology which the criminal law then punished when violence erupted. The contradictions in the legal system make the Victorian anxiety about marriage and divorce reform understandable, particularly in its effect on the working class.

Middle-class 'fallen' men

Though the majority of cases were committed by working-class men, a minority involved the middle classes, either as one or both of the parties. Such cases were uncommon and garnered extensive press coverage. Though rare, these cases destabilised the comforting equation between cohabitation, drinking, and unruly working-class masculinity. Middle-class men were well-educated, comfortably funded, and exemplars to others. When middle-class and upper-class men forgot themselves to the extent that they not only took part in irregular liaisons, but also committed violence, judges and juries could be doubly severe. Thus, though high class status was usually an advantage at the Victorian courts, this was not always the case. A man who had 'fallen' lost his immunity in the eyes of the court.

Because of the wide press coverage and the small number of cases, I will centre on two high-profile cases that illustrate the interplay of class, gender, and cohabitation. Both involve men accused of violence towards a cohabitee, and the criminal justice system's reaction to their behaviour shows the uneasiness of the courts with men who sacrificed their respectability for their passions. The best example of the problems for middle-class men was the 1859 case of Thomas Smethurst.[37] Smethurst, a doctor, lived in a boarding house in Bayswater with his wife Mary, who was twenty years his senior. Smethurst made enough money from medicine to retire at the age of forty-nine, and the two lived comfortably until Isabella Bankes also came to the boarding house in 1858. Bankes was a forty-two-year-old spinster of independent means; within weeks, Bankes and Smethurst ran away together, married bigamously, and lived under assumed names in Richmond.

In April of 1859, Bankes became quite ill. She had always been subject to bilious attacks, but these were worse than normal. When she realised the seriousness of her condition, she wrote a will leaving her property to Smethurst, partly under his urging. Smethurst eventually consulted two other doctors, both of whom became suspicious, and they called in the police. When Bankes died in May, Smethurst was charged with her murder. Despite the circumstances, the evidence of murder was weak. The authorities found no poison in Smethurst's possession, and the autopsy revealed only slight traces of antimony in Bankes's body. Furthermore, Isabella was seven weeks pregnant when she died, which may have fatally worsened her usual ill health. Smethurst also did not have a strong motive. Bankes did not leave much money, and her income from an annuity stopped at her death. Thus, the matter might not even have gone to trial had the police surgeon not blundered by claiming he found arsenic in Smethurst's possession when he had not (the doctor had added in the arsenic himself while doing the tests). Nevertheless, the jury convicted Thomas of murder at his trial in 1859.

The main reason for this result was the attitude of Chief Baron Frederick Pollock (the first of this name). Pollock was seventy-six at the time of the trial and was thoroughly against the defendant from the beginning; indeed, in his lengthy summation to the jury, he re-prosecuted the case. Since the evidence was weak, Pollock did not dwell on it; instead, he harped on the doctor's immorality. Pollock mentioned six times that Smethurst had committed a felony (bigamy) and three times that he had run away with a younger woman. His language was sensational; when discussing the bigamous marriage, Pollock stressed 'the iniquity, the sin, and the crime of that act'. Pollock even theorised that Bankes was not a willing partner in the bigamy, since an educated and well-off woman would not commit a crime. Thus, Pollock surmised that Bankes had believed that Smethurst's marriage to Mary was invalid; only when she made her will did she find out she was still single. Since she was pregnant, she pressured Smethurst to prove that their marriage was the real one. Smethurst could not do this and so killed her.[38] Though the prosecution had made no attempt to prove this theory during the trial, Pollock crafted it for them, and the jury found it convincing.

Smethurst's conviction was wrong to most medical men, and they persuaded the Home Secretary to issue a pardon in November of 1859. Even then, Pollock insisted that the murder may have been an attempt at abortion, but it was still murder.[39] Though unwilling to give him the death penalty, the government wanted Smethurst punished, so the attorney general arranged a rare public prosecution for bigamy. Smethurst was rearrested, convicted, and sentenced to a year at hard labour by Baron Bramwell.[40] One must conclude the juries convicted Smethurst more for his 'immorality' than on the evidence. Especially to Pollock, Smethurst, a professional man, was at fault when he committed adultery and bigamy. Bankes, on the other hand, was innocent because Pollock could not believe that a middle-class woman would willingly 'live in sin' or participate in a felony.

Like in the murder trial, Smethurst's position hurt him in his bigamy case. His sentence was unusually long, considering that Bankes was a willing partner in the fraud. Bramwell, in contrast to Pollock, told the court that he believed Bankes 'knew the prisoner was married when she went through the ceremony with him'. He gave Smethurst a long sentence, then, because he had deserted his wife and because he had committed perjury, and 'he, as a man of education, must have known what he was doing'.[41] In other words, this trial was another occasion where Smethurst's class hurt him. Even more ironic was the partnership of Bramwell and Pollock in punishing Smethurst. In August 1858, Pollock wrote to Bramwell, a younger judge, insisting, 'a legal sentence is not a punishment for moral sin ... its object is to deter others with as small an amount of human suffering as will answer that end.'[42] Smethurst could be forgiven for thinking that neither judge had followed this precept in his two criminal trials.

In some ways, Smethurst's case is the reverse of the Florence Maybrick murder trial (in 1889), in which a middle-class woman was convicted of poisoning her husband more because of her adultery than from the evidence.[43] In that case, too, a large number of people pressured the government to release her, though it took ten years. Like Maybrick, Smethurst's adultery and willingness to commit a crime wiped out the advantages he should have had from his position. Instead, his status hurt him; a bigamous marriage was not such a disgrace in the working class and so would not constitute a motive for murder. In addition, as we will see, few working-class men served a year for an 'honest' bigamy, even though they, too, took false oaths. Smethurst discovered that the courts were not always sympathetic to male sexual freedom; the idealisation of the middle-class woman meant that the blame for irregular relations fell on the men.

Smethurst's alleged victim was in his own class. But even with cross-class relationships, the middle-class man might be censured for immorality; after all, a man with both class and gender superiority should be especially chivalrous. Nevertheless, these cases usually meant that both partners faced character tests. These points are well illustrated in a murder trial in 1875. Henry Wainwright, the owner of a brush business and a married man with five children, took Harriet Lane as his mistress in 1871. Harriet was the youngest child (of eleven) of John Lane, a labourer, and she was a milliner's apprentice when she met Wainwright. They had two children and lived together under the name 'Mr and Mrs Percy King' in the early 1870s. By 1874, relations had cooled between them, because Wainwright went bankrupt that year and could not continue to support her. Harriet's financial difficulties were severe, and she pawned many possessions, including her 'wedding' ring.

On 11 September 1874, Henry gave Harriet £15 to clear her debts, and she went off to new lodgings, while her children lived with a close friend, a Mrs Wilmore. After that date, Lane disappeared. When she had not communicated for several days, Wilmore and Lane's family questioned Wainwright. Wainwright told them she had run away with a friend of his, a man who insisted that she stay away from her family. When Wilmore received a letter supposedly from Harriet's new lover, her family accepted this story. A year later, on 11 September 1875, police caught Wainwright transporting Lane's partially decomposed body across town. The autopsy revealed that Lane had been shot in the head three times and had her throat cut. The police soon discovered the grave in the cellar of Wainwright's warehouse where she had lain for the past year, and they arrested him for murder.[44]

During the trial, the prosecution amassed an impressive case against Wainwright for murder and against his brother Thomas as an accessory. Most of the evidence was factual, but the trial also turned on the characters of Wainwright and Lane. According to the prosecution, Lane was like a poor heroine in a melodrama, 'seduced' by an older, wealthier man. Though she had been weak, she was also a fond mother and good friend. Attorney-General Holker insisted that such a loving mother and daughter would not suddenly leave with a strange man and never write again.[45] In contrast, to the defence, Lane was frivolous and promiscuous; she refused to support herself, drank too much, and left the care of her children to servants. Thus, she might well run off with a virtual stranger, which was probably what she had done. Lane was vulnerable to these criticisms because of her class. Middle-class women rarely worked outside the home and employed servants as a matter of course. Lane, a milliner, was different. In addition, her affair with a married man left her open to accusations of promiscuity;

indeed, Henry later insisted that she had been a prostitute and had an affair with Thomas as well as himself.[46]

Historians have noted that working-class female victims of violence had to pass character tests. Thus, the prosecutors had a problem, since Lane was not pure and had been publicly drunk at least once. Fortunately for them, the defence had a bigger problem, since Wainwright's character was also badly flawed. The defence barrister, Mr Besley, tried to mitigate the circumstances by calling Harriet a prostitute and saying she initiated the affair. He also argued that the defendant had decided to end the relationship, in deference to his wife and family. Moreover, Henry supported Lane as long as he could, but she was never satisfied, bleeding him for money and threatening him with exposure.[47] Besley ended by asserting Henry's middle-class credentials. As Wainwright himself later put it, he was a model citizen – a school manager and a church-goer – ruined by his obsession with a worthless woman.[48]

The prosecution did not allow this interpretation to go unchallenged.[49] Primarily, Holker stressed that Wainwright was an utter failure. He was promiscuous, keeping a mistress and also picking up girls at ballet halls. He was bankrupt, and his money woes were his own fault; he was a gambler and had produced two families to support despite his shrinking resources. His financial failure meant that he could not provide for Lane, much less make things right by marrying her. Furthermore, he had blackened her name to her family. These were not the actions of an honourable man, but of someone capable of a horrific crime.

Chief Justice Cockburn's attitude was complex. In his summation, he described Lane as 'an angry, clamorous woman, for whom he [Henry] had probably ceased to care' and who was a 'constant source of danger'. But Harriet's failings did not excuse the crime. In fact, Cockburn summed up the evidence firmly against the defendant and his brother; the jury could have had little doubt about Cockburn's views of each man's degree of guilt. After a complicated trial of nine days, the jury took less than an hour to convict Henry of murder and Thomas as an accessory after the fact. Wainwright hanged on 21 December 1875. Cockburn gave Thomas, who had apparently written the fake letters and helped Henry move the body, seven years. Cockburn, in sentencing Henry, approved of the jury's decision: 'There can be no doubt that you took the life of this poor woman, who had been on the closest and most intimate terms of familiarity and affection with you, and who was the mother of your two children … It was a barbarous, cruel, inhuman, and cowardly act.'[50] Cockburn agreed with the prosecution that Wainwright was a failure in every important respect – as a husband, provider, and protector.

Though the double standard in Victorian England allowed men more latitude in extra-marital affairs, such leeway had limits. A man who beggared his legitimate family by keeping another could not make a convincing case that he was provoked to violence by a cunning woman. Lane was working-class and possibly both drunken and promiscuous, but her sins paled in comparison. As in Smethurst's case, the criminal justice system punished the middle-class man in part for his sexual irregularity. Henry could not blame Lane, since he was equally, if not more, at fault. Thus, he went on trial for the capital charge, not manslaughter, and the Home Secretary found no reason to extend mercy.

Whatever the class, then, the attitude of the Victorian state towards cohabitation was ambivalent. The civil and criminal laws did not always work in tandem, and judges and juries could also disagree about the appropriate response to domestic violence. The criminal courts increasingly cracked down on violent cohabiting men, confusingly treating these couples as married and unmarried at the same time. On the one hand, judges blamed the men for irregular unions, despite the fact that many could not marry. Juries were more sympathetic, but, overall, male cohabitees faced increasing sentences for their 'irrational' behaviour. On the other hand, the court agreed that the couples should follow the gendered expectations of marriage: men should provide, and women should obey. In other words, these cases exposed the difficulty in adjudicating a status – common-law spouse – that had no legal standing.

Cohabitees were, of course, a minority of those who came into the courts, civil or criminal. All the same, their cases indicate that large numbers of couples lived outside of legal matrimony in the nineteenth century. Who were these couples? And why did they ignore the laws? The rest of this book explores these questions. Those who lived together without marriage had a wide variety of motives, and their relationships with each other, their families, and the larger community were closely related to their reasons for flouting the law. If the couple had no choice, they were more likely to get sympathy for their plight. Not surprisingly, then, the first group, those who could not marry, was by far the largest one, and included people from all classes. They were 'victims' of the Hardwicke regime, the limited access to divorce, and the tightening of laws against marriage within the prohibited degrees. As we will see, the courts frequently had to contend with hard cases and obdurate juries with these couples as well, but the couples' main concern was with reconciling their friends and themselves to their choice to live outside the law.

Notes

1 I read the *Lancaster Guardian* for regular five-year intervals (1850, 1855, etc.). The years I used in the *Yorkshire Gazette* were 1850, 1855, 1865, 1870, 1876, 1882, 1885, 1892, 1895, and 1899. Those in *The Times* were 1853, 1856, 1863, 1866, 1872, 1878, 1884, 1891, and 1893. To find this sample, I read through all the issues of the *Yorkshire Gazette* and the *Lancaster Guardian* (both weeklies) in ten separate years between 1850 and 1905, collecting police, assize, and magistrates' court reports. For *The Times*, I read the police, assize, and Old Bailey reports for four months (March–April and August–September) in nine separate years between 1853 and 1893. I used two local papers to avoid having London-centred history, and I chose Lancaster because it was a good example of an industrial area (with high levels of women's labour) and because I could supplement its records with the Elizabeth Roberts's Oral History collection at Lancaster University. I added Yorkshire in order to get a more rural area. After assembling the cases, I looked at the Old Bailey Sessions papers and Home Office records of the trials.

2 Many reports listed the men's jobs, but in some cases, the reports said simply 'poor' or 'residing in a low part of town'. If the preponderance of evidence pointed to the working class, I counted it as such.

3 A. J. Hammerton's sample in Preston had 25 per cent middle-class cases, *Cruelty and Companionship: Conflict in Nineteenth-Century Married Life* (London: Routledge, 1992), p. 37; S. D'Cruze's had 8.8 per cent, *Crimes of Outrage: Sex, Violence and Victorian Working-Class Women* (DeKalb, IL: Northern Illinois University Press, 1998), p. 65.

4 The remaining case involved the murder of a male cohabitee by his partner's two sons.

5 V. Bailey, *This Rash Act: Suicide Across the Life Cycle in the Victorian City* (Stanford, CA: Stanford University Press, 1998), pp. 125–30; C. Conley, *The Unwritten Law: Criminal Justice in Victorian Kent* (Oxford: Oxford University Press, 1991), pp. 70–1.

6 R. Chadwick, *Bureaucratic Mercy: The Home Office and the Treatment of Capital Cases in Victorian Britain* (New York: Garland Publishing, 1992), p. 242.

7 G. Behlmer, *Friends of the Family: The English Home and Its Guardians, 1850–1940* (Stanford, CA: Stanford University Press, 1998), pp. 181–229; Conley, *The Unwritten Law*, pp. 75–81; J. Davis, 'A poor man's system of justice: The London police courts in the second half of the nineteenth century', *Historical Journal* 27 (1984), 309–35.

8 *The Times*, 30 October 1862, p. 11; *The Times*, 5 July 1878, p. 12.

9 Conley, *The Unwritten Law*, pp. 72–5; Behlmer, *Friends of the Family*, pp. 198–213; Hammerton, *Cruelty and Companionship*, pp. 46–52; D'Cruze, *Crimes of Outrage*, p. 79; A. Ballinger, *Dead Woman Walking: Executed Women in England and Wales, 1900–1955* (Aldershot: Ashgate, 2000), pp. 204–21.

10 National Archives (hereafter NA), CRIM 10/52, pp. 508–9 (first quote on p. 508); *The Times*, 3 August 1863, p. 11; 17 August 1863, p. 11; 22 August 1863, p. 11 (for second quote).

11 Abbot in *Yorkshire Gazette*, 5 August 1876, p. 4; 16 December 1876, p. 4 (for quote); Taylor in *Tonbridge Telegraph*, 12 August 1893, p. 5. See also *The Times*, 7 July 1902, p. 3.

12 NA, PCOM 1/69, pp. 681–3; Mulley in *Lancaster Guardian*, 26 October 1855, p. 9 (for quote); 3 November 1855, p. 2; Wane in *The Times* 15 December 1864, p. 10. See also *The Times*, 19 April 1869, p. 6; 20 April 1869, p. 9.

13 Hannah in *The Times*, 13 September 1856, p. 7; *Leeds Intelligencer*, 13 September 1856, p. 8; Sabley in *Northampton Daily Chronicle*, 29 June 1893, p. 4.

14 D'Cruze, *Crimes of Outrage*, p. 68.

15 *Lancaster Guardian*, 14 April 1900, p. 6.

16 J. C. Wood, *Violence and Crime in Nineteenth-Century England: The Shadow of Our Refinement* (London: Routledge, 2004), pp. 37–8; 56–69; A. Davis, 'Youth gangs, masculinity and violence in late Victorian Manchester and Salford', *Journal of Social History* 32 (1998), 349–69.

17 *The Times*, 9 June 1870, p. 11. See also NA, HO 144/248/A54672; *The Times*, 29 September 1892, p. 7; *Gloucestershire Chronicle*, 1 October 1892, p. 5; 8 October 1892, p. 7.

18 Sheilds in PCOM 1/84, pp. 647–8; *The Times*, 7 March 1863, p. 12 (for quote); MacDonald in HO 45/9366/36100; *Devonport Independent and Plymouth and Stonehouse Gazette*, 4 July 1874, p. 7; 1 August 1874, p. 3 (for quote).

19 *Lancaster Guardian*, 28 July 1866, p. 3.

20 *The Times*, 6 August 1860, p. 10; *Warwick and Warwickshire Advertiser*, 4 August 1860, p. 2 (for quote). See also Chadwick, *Bureaucratic Mercy*, pp. 338–9.

21 Mason in *The Times*, 11 December 1856, p. 9; Burch in CRIM 10/75, pp. 60–6; *The Times*, 25 April 1885, p. 6; Dixon in *The Times*, 27 July 1860, p. 11; *Yorkshire Gazette*, 14 July 1860, p. 4. R. Smith, *Trial by Medicine: Insanity and Responsibility in Victorian Trials* (Edinburgh: Edinburgh University Press, 1981), p. 153; D. Bentley, *English Criminal Justice in the Nineteenth Century* (London: The Hambledon Press, 1998), p. 18; Chadwick, *Bureaucratic Mercy*, pp. 289–315; G. Frost, '"She is but a woman": Kitty Byron and the English Edwardian criminal justice system', *Gender and History* 16 (2004), 538–60.

22 M. Wiener, 'The sad story of George Hall: Adultery, murder and the politics of mercy in mid-Victorian England', *Social History* (1999), 174–95; and *Men of Blood: Violence, Manliness and Criminal Justice in Victorian England* (Cambridge: Cambridge University Press, 2004), pp. 123–69; E. Foyster, *Marital Violence: An English Family History, 1660–1857* (Cambridge: Cambridge University Press, 2005), pp. 115–22.

23 Fleming in *Newcastle Chronicle*, 5 September 1856, p. 8 (for quote); *The Times*, 16 September 1856, p. 6; Brown in *The Times*, 23 May 1881, p. 12; *Nottingham and Midland Counties Daily Express*, 23 May 1881, p. 3; 24 May 1881, p. 3 (for quote).

24 Conley, *The Unwritten Law*, pp. 79–81.

25 PCOM 1/69, pp. 681–3; *Lancaster Guardian*, 3 November 1855, p. 12; *The Times*, 26 October 1855, p. 9 (for quote).

26 PCOM 1/68, pp. 367–70; *The Times*, 2 February 1855, p. 10 (for quote); Chadwick, *Bureaucratic Mercy*, pp. 309–13.

27 HO 144/236/A51714; *Surrey Advertiser and County Times*, 12 July 1890, p. 2 (for quote); *The Times*, 14 July 1890, p. 6. See also *The Times*, 24 September 1874, p. 5; 29 October 1874, p. 11; *Devonport Independent and Plymouth Gazette*, 26 September 1874, p. 6.

28 *The Times*, 30 October 1862, p. 11; *Lancaster Guardian*, 9 June 1866, p. 8.

29 HO 45/9441/66322; *The Times*, 28 July 1877, p. 11; 16 August 1877, p. 6; *Croydon Journal*, 19 April 1877, p. 3; 26 April 1877, p. 3; 26 July 1877, p. 3. Grove's letter, dated 7 August 1877, is piece six in the Home Office file.

30 HO 45/9464/75868; *Nottingham and Midland Counties Daily Express*, 29 July 1878, p. 3; Hawkins's letter, dated 10 August 1878, is piece three in the file. For a case with

drunkenness, see HO 144/85/A7411; *The Times*, 29 July 1881, p. 10.

31 *The Times*, 10 August 1865, p. 12; 11 August 1865, p. 9; 15 August 1865, p. 3; 21 December 1865, p. 11; 22 December 1865, pp. 9–10; 12 January 1865, p. 10; 13 January 1865, p. 9. See also Chadwick, *Bureaucratic Mercy*, pp. 239–45; and Smith, *Trial by Medicine*, pp. 124–42.

32 E. Bowen-Rolands, *Seventy-Two Years at the Bar: A Memoir* (London: Macmillan, 1924), pp. 64–7; quote from p. 67. Smithers in HO 45/9466/67890; *The Times*, 19 September 1878, p. 9; Denman's letter is piece five in the file.

33 Jurors had to be £10 householders or £20 leaseholders in most places. Bentley, *English Criminal Justice*, pp. 92–3; Chadwick, *Bureaucratic Mercy*, p. 90; M. Wiener, 'Judges v. jurors: Courtroom tensions in murder trials and the law of criminal responsibility in nineteenth-century England', *Law and History Review* 17 (1999), 467–506.

34 HO 144/98/A16400; *The Times*, 9 May 1882, p. 7; 24 May 1882, p. 10. Clerk's notes are in piece one of the file.

35 HO 144/250/A55024; *The Times*, 8 July 1893, p. 16; 10 July 1893, p. 12; 24 July 1893, p. 9; quote from 10 July. Hawkins's letter is in piece four in the file.

36 Fountain in PCOM 1/98, pp. 139–41; *The Times*, 9 June 1870, p. 11; Foster in *Durham Chronicle*, 27 November 1895, p. 7; Quain in *Shrewsbury Free Press and Shropshire Telegraph*, 27 March 1875, p. 2.

37 L. Parry (ed.), *Trial of Dr. Smethurst* (London: William Hodge & Company, 1931); *The Queen against Thomas Smethurst* (London: Butterworths, 1859); R. Altick, *Victorian Studies in Scarlet* (New York: W. W. Norton and Company, 1970), pp. 160–9; and B. Cobb, *Trials and Errors* (London: W. H. Allen, 1962), pp. 144–62.

38 Parry, *Trial of Dr. Smethurst*, pp. 113–22, quote from p. 116.

39 *Ibid.*, p. 194.

40 *Ibid.*, pp. 235–59.

41 *Ibid.*, pp. 235–40; quote from p. 240.

42 C. Fairfield, *Some Account of George William Wilshere, Baron Bramwell of Hever* (London: MacMillan and Co., 1898), p. 33, letter dated 7 August 1858.

43 G. Robb, 'Circe in crinoline: domestic poisonings in Victorian England', *Journal of Family History* 22 (1997), 176–90.

44 The Wainwright case based on HO 144/19/48007; NA, MEPO 3/121; TS 18/1; *The Times*, 6 October 1875, p. 11; 7 October 1875, p. 11; 13 October 1875, p. 11; 14 October 1875, p. 11; 15 October 1875, p. 9; 18 October 1875, p. 6; 20 October 1875, p. 6; 23 November 1875, p. 10; 24 November 1875, p. 10; 25 November 1875, p. 10; 26 November 1875, p. 8; 27 November 1875, p. 10; 29 November 1875, p. 10; 30 November 1875, pp. 10–11; 1 December 1875, p. 10; 2 December 1875, pp. 5–7; 4 December 1875, p. 10; 6 December 1875, p. 5; 8 December 1875, p. 6; 9 December 1875, p. 6; 10 December 1875, p. 6; 13 December 1875, p. 6; 17 December 1875, p. 5; 18 December 1875, p. 10; 20 December 1875, p. 6; 21 December 1875, p. 5; 22 December 1875, p. 11; 23 December 1875, p. 11. See also L. P. Curtis, *Jack the Ripper and the London Press* (New Haven, CT: Yale University Press, 2001), pp. 101–4; Altick, *Victorian Studies in Scarlet*, pp. 210–19.

45 *The Times*, 1 December 1875, p. 10.

46 HO 144/19/48007/15; Chadwick, *Bureaucratic Mercy*, pp. 46, 48.

47 *The Times*, 29 November 1875, p. 10.

48 HO 144/19/48007/16; Chadwick, *Bureaucratic Mercy*, p. 313.

49 W. Foulkes, *A Generation of Judges* (London: Sampson Law, Marston, Searle &

Rivington, 1886), p. 124; Bowen-Rowlands, *Seventy-Two Years at the Bar*, p. 175.
50 *The Times*, 2 December 1875, p. 7. Thomas was released from prison in 1881.

3

Affinity and consanguinity

ENGLISH LAW did not permit marriage between those too closely related by blood or marriage. These prohibitions followed Leviticus 18, which banned marriages with kin of the first and second degrees. For example, a woman could not marry her uncle or stepfather, nor the husband of her deceased granddaughter or niece; a man could not marry his stepaunt or his grandniece.[1] The most controversial issue during the Victorian period was the prohibition over marriage to a deceased wife's sister, but unions between other relatives were common, including women and deceased husbands' brothers, uncles and nieces, and several which crossed generational lines. Other historians have studied the reform movements to change the laws, so I will centre on the affinal and consanguineous relationships themselves and how neighbours, families and society reacted to them.[2]

Although the law made no distinction between marriages between blood relatives and those between in-laws, most of the people involved did. Few cohabitees were blood kin, and such cases involved public disapprobation. In addition, relationships with a man in a position of a father to a younger woman (such as stepfather) were problematic. Both of these types of relationships could be frankly exploitative and shameful, though the Victorian state rarely dealt effectively with them. In contrast, many people in all classes saw no harm in marriages between in-laws.[3] Unsurprisingly, then, most cases of 'incest' were affinal, even in the 'low dens' of the working class.

Prohibited degrees and the working class

Most middle-class Victorians assumed the incest was primarily a problem for the poor, though they were short on specifics. Henry Mayhew reported some instances of blood incest in the London working class, including that of a well-known street patterer who 'had lived in criminal intercourse with his own sister, and his own daughter by one of his wives.' Hugh Shinman, a journalist, surveyed families in the poor part of Liverpool. He found a widower who allegedly had a child with his own daughter; in the same house was a brother 'cohabiting' with his sister.[4] Yet actual evidence, rather than suspicion on the part of hostile observers, is difficult to obtain, since England had no criminal penalty for incest until 1908. Carolyn Conley's study of criminal justice in Kent uncovered only five fathers, four stepfathers, and three uncles accused of incest; almost all were discharged or acquitted.[5]

The number of blood relatives who had sexual unions in the working classes was probably low. Anthony Wohl has argued that historians must take the testimony of middle-class observers seriously, since those friendly to the working class (like Friedrich Engels) also believed incest was common. Even when blood incest occurred, though, most cases involved intermittent incidents rather than cohabitation.[6] In addition, the respectable working classes disapproved of blood relatives marrying or cohabiting. Robert Roberts, in *The Classic Slum*, explained that the neighbours in Salford condemned the few households with incestuous unions, seeing them as 'the ultimate disgrace.'[7] J. B. Aspinall, a barrister who gave evidence before the Royal Commission on Marriage in 1848, surveyed several northern cities. He reported on an uncle and niece marrying in Doncaster, but he added that it 'was looked upon with a degree of horror and disgust'. W. C. Sleigh, another barrister, heard rumours of a village 'in which uncles and nieces cohabited', as well as an uncle/niece union in Wakefield, but admitted he found no 'well authenticated cases'. Their testimony was supported by other investigators in London and Staffordshire.[8]

Legal cases also indicate that most such marriages were between in-laws. All the removal cases involving incestuous marriages were those of affinity. Typical cases include one in 1847 where a woman had married her deceased sister's husband, or a case in 1861, in which a man had married his deceased wife's niece.[9] In addition, in criminal desertion cases, the incest defence almost always was one of affinal ties. At the Hertfordshire assizes in 1904, James Brown escaped conviction for neglecting to maintain his wife because she was his aunt by marriage, and church cases tell a similar story.[10] Moreover, letters to the editor of *Justice of the Peace* show that JPs dealt with a variety of marriages of affinity but few of blood ties. Between 1850 and 1914, JPs asked questions about the following: deceased wife's sister (thirteen); uncles and nieces (ten: four affinal, six by blood); deceased husband's brother (six); and one each for the following: half-sister and brother, granddaughter of an uncle's wife, father-in-law and daughter-in-law, and nephew and aunt-in-law.[11] In short, most unions within the prohibited degrees were between in-laws, though a minority of others might occur, especially uncles and nieces.

Men and women married relatives for a number of reasons, the most important of which was the issue of housekeeping. A widower with children turned to his children's aunt for help, and the close quarters led to romantic attachments. Wider kin supported these unions because they preferred to have young children in the care of someone closely interested in their welfare. Childless widowers or bachelors also needed housekeepers, so chose them from kin. Since the women involved were doing all the duties of the wife – cooking, cleaning, childcare – they easily slipped into sexual duties as well, as Leonore Davidoff's work on landladies has shown.[12] After all, how could a man be just an employer when his housekeeper was also his relative? And if the woman became pregnant, a relative felt added pressure to 'make things right' and marry her.

According to several sources, the results of such marriages were generally positive. W. C. Sleigh interviewed affinal working-class couples in 1846–47. One man, a widower with four children, explained, 'My wife's sister was extremely kind to them. I thought I should like her, and she thought she should like me; we married, and we have been as happy as man and wife could be ever since.' Indeed, most witnesses before the Royal Commission emphasised the happiness of these homes. J. F. Denham speculated that the parties were more likely to know 'each other's real character and disposition' before they wed and so had a better chance for a successful union. Considering these cheering prospects, working-classes couples ignored the law, or at least assumed it did not apply in their particular cases. A publican in Maidstone explained, 'My wife was dead, and I could not be so well suited in my house as to marry her sister; therefore, I do not recognize any law that says I shall not.'[13]

These couples insisted that their marriages were morally correct even in the face of religious and state opposition. Annie Bailey, twenty-three, was a servant in Revd S. W. Mangin's household in the late 1880s. Her uncle-in-law (he had married her mother's sister), William Clapp, lived nearby. The two decided to marry and first tried to do so in the church, but Mangin told them he could not marry them because of their affinity. In response, in September of 1889, the couple married at the Registrar's Office. When arrested, both Annie and William argued that though they could not be married in the church, they assumed they could still have a civil ceremony. Annie went further, asserting that 'She searched the Bible through, but could not find such a marriage anywhere forbidden.' Justice Stephen summed up against Bailey, but the jury acquitted her anyway.

Stephen, annoyed, lectured Bailey, 'whatever she or others might think … she was not married in the least.' One suspects that she paid no more attention to the judge than she had to the vicar.[14]

As this case indicates, most of these couples 'went through a form of marriage' at some point. These ceremonies gave legitimacy to the couple and their family and friends. The desire for a ceremony was particularly acute if the woman became pregnant, but the latter was not always necessary. One commentator guessed that a small trader had married his wife's niece 'to avoid scandal' even though they had no children. Most of the time, the two had lived together first and then tried to regularise the relationship. A couple in 1852, for example, a niece and uncle, lived 'in concubinage' for a few weeks, but then 'went to a large town some distance from their residence' and married by licence.[15] Fortunately for these couples, marrying illegally was quite easy. Most of the clergymen who gave evidence to various Royal Commissions of Marriage complained that they could not stop such marriages. Revd J. F. Denham testified that banns were useless: 'I find that people go out of the parish continually to be married'. Revd John Hatchard agreed; every time he refused to marry a couple, they went to London and returned married.[16]

The clergy were conflicted about these unions, for if the couple did not marry illegally, they often lived 'in sin' together. One clergyman in the Potteries had two couples in his parish who cohabited because they were in-laws, and he testified that he would much prefer them to marry, especially as they preferred this themselves, but did not wish to break the law. John Garbett seconded this, pointing out that 'when notorious cases of concubinage have occurred, and the parties have been spoken to, they have pointed to these persons and said, "He is no more married than I am, in law." I think it has a bad moral effect'.[17] In addition, couples forced to cohabit unmarried blamed the church or the state, not themselves. A Devonport farmer tried to marry his deceased wife's sister, but his vicar refused him. He then lived with the woman and 'threw the responsibility of the refusal upon the clergyman', and his neighbours supported him. In fact, not even all clergymen disapproved of affinal marriages. Several testified for removing the prohibition on at least some of the degrees. Dissenters particularly wanted reform; some of these ministers had married their deceased wives' sisters themselves.[18] In addition, the Catholic church offered dispensations for special cases. If a couple received one, they did not hesitate to marry, ignoring the Anglican rules.[19]

As these examples indicate, the Anglican clergy disapproved more than the wider community. Especially in affinal unions, neighbours and friends were generally supportive. In 1864, Tom Mann's father married

Mary Ann Grant and had four children with her before she died in 1858. Five years later, Mann married Harriet Grant, Mary Ann's sister. None of the neighbours objected, and Tom got five more half-siblings over the next few years.[20] Arthur Stanbra, a farmer in Oxford, took in his older brother Richard's daughter, Mary, as his housekeeper in the 1880s, and the two eventually shaded into an intimate relationship. When Mary became pregnant, Arthur married her out of the parish by licence. The record of the case does not indicate who prosecuted Arthur – perhaps the vicar. Whoever did so, though, was in the minority. His neighbours defended him at the trial, and the jury 'very strongly' recommended mercy. Justice Cave agreed, sentencing Arthur to one day.[21] Arthur had seduced his niece, but he tried to 'do the right thing' when she became pregnant. Thus, his neighbours ignored his perjury and incest.

Still, occasionally these unions led to strong intra-family disagreements. The cases that provoked more opposition were those with much older men and young women and blood ties. In 1894, a Primitive Methodist minister at Guernsey married a man named John Matthews (fifty-six) to Louisa Carré (twenty-four), the daughter of his sister. The ceremony was in the minister's house without a registrar, so the minister was sentenced to six months at hard labour, while Matthews got twelve months. The local community thought the punishment too severe and petitioned the Home Secretary for clemency. Though the Methodist community sympathised, Thomas Carré, the girl's father, bitterly resented Matthews's conduct. Carré had allowed his brother-in-law to live with the family when Matthews had returned to England after a twenty-year absence. In return, Matthews pursued his niece and ignored Thomas's warnings that marriage with her was illegal. When the couple eloped, Thomas, furious, prosecuted everyone involved. Nonetheless, her father's ire did not influence Louisa, who stood by her decision. Eventually, the minister was pardoned and released. Matthews's fate was uncertain, but his family's disapproval almost certainly meant the end of his 'marriage'.[22]

Matthews's difficulties were in part the result of Louisa's natal family's hostility to the marriage. In addition, the age difference was large in this case, so the marriage seemed less natural. Still, the fact that the local reaction was divided between the disapproving jury and the forgiving petitioners indicates support for some consanguineous marriages (again, an uncle and a niece). Many could not understand why these marriage were illegal, perhaps because they were not far removed from cousin marriages, which were legal (even, on occasion, actively encouraged). One could say the same about aunts and nephews, but there the age difference was more of a bar. At any rate, laws against these marriages did not discourage all couples, though some cases caused controversy.

The reaction of authorities to these marriages was mixed. By marrying illegally, the couples faced the threat of arrest and trial, usually for perjury or making false statements to a registrar. Interestingly, the church was often readier to prosecute than the state. In 1861, the vicar of Longbridge Deverill wrote to the Home Secretary about a man and his sister-in-law who had gone to a different parish, lied about their residency and their relationship, and married. The vicar demanded the Home Secretary prosecute them, supported by the General Registrar of the area. Nevertheless, the secretary refused, since 'I am afraid we shall be laughed at if we prosecute this old couple … What harm have they done?' The in-laws, then, were left in peace, yet another example of the law's flexibility when faced with marital dissent.[23] Indeed, when cases got to court, juries usually acquitted defendants or recommended mercy (as with Stanbra). William Perry, mentioned in Chapter 1, was tried for falsifying his marriage licence to his half-niece in 1901. Despite testimony from the vicar, the jury acquitted him because 'the witnesses were very illiterate.'[24]

Juries' attitudes undoubtedly made officials reluctant to prosecute, despite pressure from the church. In 1875, a Welsh vicar wrote to the Home Secretary about a case in Llanelly. John Hopkins, sixty, a carpenter, had married his stepdaughter, Jane Francis, thirty. The vicar had refused to marry them, saying that '*marrying her was quite out of the question* as it would be contrary *to the law* of the land, of the *church* and of the *Bible*'. Shortly afterwards, the reverend left the parish, and Hopkins persuaded the curate to marry them. The vicar, incensed, tried to get the police to prosecute, but they refused. He then appealed to the Home Office, arguing they should make an example because '*incestuous marriages are becoming common in this neighbourhood*, and that in some cases marriage licenses are obtained for this purpose *which cannot be had without perjury*'. The Home Office could not agree about a prosecution, since most of the officials doubted they could get a conviction.[25] Given these conditions, the working class's determination to ignore both the laws and the advice of the Anglican clergy was understandable.

Though the official silence worked in favour of many couples, it had negative consequences as well, since it extended to abusive relationships. This was particularly the case with stepdaughters and stepfathers, whose relationships could be frankly exploitative. Sarah Anne Scott lived with a man named John King whom she had always regarded as her father. In 1844, King's cohabitee died, so Sarah took over the household. In December, John began trying to induce Sarah into a sexual relationship. John saw Sarah as his cohabitee's successor, since she was doing other wifely duties.

Sarah fought him off and then prosecuted him, but she was fortunate to have a neighbour's support. Susan Mumm also found cases of abuse in her study of Anglican penitentiaries; one woman, aged twenty-four, had been sexually abused by her stepfather since the age of nine. When she arrived, she had four children and another on the way.[26]

Lack of sympathy for incest victims was common in Victorian courts; Carolyn Conley, in her study of Kent, found that men charged with incest with their stepdaughters, unless the girl was under the age of twelve, were all acquitted. Judges assumed that young girls consented to sexual relations, ignoring the power differences between fathers and their dependants. Louise Jackson's findings about child sexual abuse also showed that the Victorian courts rarely prosecuted incest cases with older girls as victims, and such cases had a low conviction rate.[27] At any rate, these incidents point up, again, the difficulty of knowing how much cohabitation went on within families; with the courts so hostile, few girls complained. Thus, disapproving clergymen or, on occasion, neighbours, were the only help for many victims of incest.

With the criminal courts largely indifferent, the more serious consequence for working-class affinal and consanguineous families was when they needed assistance, especially with the death or desertion of the breadwinner. At that point, women and children came into contact with the poor law. Since none of these marriages were valid, the women were single and their children illegitimate. The women, then, were 'undeserving' and went to the workhouse. This happened to a woman in 1884, whose husband had died. He had been her former father-in-law, so the JPs denied her outdoor relief.[28] Second, deserting 'husbands' could ignore their responsibilities for providing, a circumstance that frustrated many magistrates. Robert Clarke, a JP in the Wincanton union, complained about a man in his parish who married his deceased wife's niece in 1846 and had nine children with her. He then deserted her in 1862, and his children and their mother went to the workhouse. Clarke warned that women should beware such marriages; an illegally-wed man could leave his family 'to the tender mercies of the parish, and continue to enjoy himself as if nothing had happened.' Clarke's anger echoed in other sources. J. S. Thorburne testified in 1848 that he knew of 'three or four cases where the law was taken advantage of, and made the means of great cruelty by the wilful desertion of the second wife.'[29] Whether or not they had intended to desert their families from the beginning, men pled 'nullity of marriage' quickly when arrested for non-support.

Magistrates fought court cases to remove unmarried mothers and their children to the mother's birth parish in an effort to avoid the expense of a pauper family; though this power was restricted in 1846, 1861, and 1865, parishes used it when they could. Mary Burrin married the husband of her deceased sister, Hannah. When William died in 1844, he left Mary and a daughter destitute, and the JPs successfully sued to have her marriage declared invalid so she and her child could be removed.[30] A similar case was that of Elizabeth Jones, who married John Morgan, her uncle-in-law, in 1843. After he died, Elizabeth went on relief and at first took the settlement of her 'husband'. However, the parish authorities soon learned that her marriage was invalid. Though Elizabeth's mother was only a half-sister (because illegitimate), the laws of consanguinity held, and Elizabeth went back to her home parish, her marriage declared void in a very public manner.[31]

Still, if the families could avoid the Poor Law, they might live together (or even marry) without serious consequences. Most couples in affinal unions – and even some consanguineous ones – remained part of their communities. Denham, in a typical passage from the 1848 Commission, insisted such marriages were not considered immoral by 'intelligent and well-informed people.'[32] In addition, the reluctance of juries to convict for perjury shows support, or at least indifference, to the legal position. Cases with close blood relations or large age differences might excite disapproval, but affinal marriages would not. In other words, popular self-marriage persisted through the Victorian era. Indeed, judges' and juries' leniency indicated that working-class behaviour influenced the state to mitigate the punishments for illegal unions.

Middle-class marriages of prohibited degrees

Middle-class people also married within the prohibited degrees, but they had a smaller range of acceptable partners. The overwhelming majority of the records concern in-laws. Of the twenty-seven legal cases that show marriages of too close proximity in the middle class, twenty-five were affinal (the two exceptions were a half-nephew/half-aunt and an uncle/niece). The disgust for blood marriages in higher life was evident in the uncle/niece case; the judge who voided that marriage called it 'exceedingly revolting to the opinions and feelings of mankind.'[33] In addition, the range of acceptable affinal marriages was small, since eighteen of the affinal cases involved marriage with a deceased wife's sister. Only one other category, that of marriage with a deceased husband's brother, got more than one case, and there were only two of these, both before 1850. Though the sample is small, it indicates that the middle classes had more taboos about consanguineous and affinal unions than the working class, and that the ban against such unions increased over time. Of the seven affinal cases not involving the sister of a deceased wife, only two occurred after 1816.[34]

The witnesses before the Royal Commission in 1848 gave slightly more variety in their examples, but the vast majority were still affinal, usually of a deceased wife's sister or niece, and occasionally of a deceased husband's brother. Thomas Campbell sent out investigators to all areas of England, and each diligently searched for affinal marriages. The total came to 1,648 cases, and of these 1,501 were marriages with a deceased wife's sister, and a further 147 were with a deceased wife's niece or another affinal relative. There were six cases of men marrying their blood nieces, but these cases were dwarfed by those with in-laws.[35]

Before 1835, these marriages at least had the chance of remaining valid at law. In *Elliott and Sugden v. Gurr* in 1812, for instance, the marriage in question was that of Sarah Lester and her deceased husband's nephew, William Gurr. Sarah's brother and sister sued to get her estate from William after she died intestate, but the courts rejected their attempt: since the marriage had not 'been declared void in the lifetime of the parties[,] the husband remained husband to all civil purposes'.[36] All such couples, though, ran a risk of a hostile party suing within their lifetimes. Anne and David Williams were aunt and nephew-in-law; their marriage was upset when James Bryant brought an incest case against them in 1769, most likely to protect the property for the children of the first marriage. As indicated in Chapter 1, too, the nature of the unions could be an advantage to a spouse who wished to leave. Charlotte Aughtie married her brother-in-law, William, fourteen months after the death of her husband. She sued to be relieved of the marriage in 1810, apparently to protect her inheritance. Judges increasingly disapproved of these kinds of suits, though. In a case in 1888, a woman who married her deceased sister's husband sued to get a declaration of nullity. The judge granted the request, but refused costs, since he thought it 'odd, when two people choose to go through a ceremony which they both of them know to be illegal and void, that either of them should be entitled to come here and ask for a decree of nullity'.[37] In the working classes, the ability to walk away from such unions primarily benefited men, but in the middle classes, both sexes took advantage of the loophole, which was perhaps what concerned the judge.

As these cases indicate, the middle classes preferred to have a marriage ceremony, but they did not have to risk prosecution. Because of their means, they could go abroad to one of the countries that permitted affinal marriages, including Switzerland and many German states. Though such marriages were not valid at English law, the marriage certificate and ceremony gave public sanction to the union. Many, in the first few decades after the 1835 act, even hoped that the laws would soon change or at least that their children might be legitimised. One barrister testified that he had married his deceased wife's sister in Holstein. Though he knew the marriage was void in England, he hoped that the English courts would uphold his conveyance of his property to his children.[38]

Considerable disadvantages came with contracting a marriage that was not recognised at English law. Why, then, did so many couples do so? Most participants insisted that the first wife wanted her sister to marry her husband and care for their children, a reason that echoed the concerns of the working class. A stockbroker who married his wife's sister in Denmark in 1844 claimed that his wife had said, 'she should die happy' if he did so. A Manchester businessman testified that he married his sister-in-law because his wife had 'expressed a very strong desire' for it. Such concerns lasted well past mid-century. John Pettifer wrote to the Home Office in 1907 to lobby for a change in the law because, he explained, his dying wife 'begged of me to have her sister to mother & care for her children out of respect for her & her family.'[39] Aunts were natural caregivers for children, and their maternal duties put them in the place of a wife. William Holman Hunt, the Pre-Raphaelite painter, lost his first wife, Fanny Waugh, in childbirth. The maternal family took charge of the baby, Cyril, as a matter of course, particularly Fanny's younger sister, Edith. In time, Hunt became attached to her as well, and they married a few years later in Switzerland.[40]

Many men preferred women they already knew and who would cause minimal disruption. Thomas Franklyn grew up with both of his future wives, two of eleven sisters. After his wife's death, he turned to a woman he 'knew ... to be virtuous and good'. The larger community also understood these reasons; when Lord George Hill married his deceased wife's sister, his tenants said 'how wise George had been not to bring a stranger into his family.' In addition, men did not want to part their sisters-in-law from children they loved. Richard Cobden's sisters both married William Sale, and Cobden supported the second union. His younger sister had acted as a second mother, and Cobden believed 'it would have been almost the death of my sister if she had been obliged to part with the child.'[41]

Because of the illegal status of these unions, families could react negatively to them. Waugh's parents were furious when she announced her engagement to Hunt and forbade the match. Hunt's mother disinherited him, and Edith also lost all hope of a marriage settlement by the terms of her father's will. The feud estranged two branches of the family for decades.[42] Nor were the Waughs unique in their concern. Henry Thornton, a prominent mid-century banker, married his deceased wife's sister in 1852. His siblings opposed the marriage vehemently. Only his eldest sister,

Marianne, remained in contact with him; the rest refused to receive them. They would not even refer to his wife, Emily Dealty, by her married name, always styling her 'E. D.' in letters.[43]

Several of the witnesses to the Royal Commission also mentioned family opposition in their testimony. James Brotherton testified that when one Independent minister married his sister-in-law, it 'gave rise to much family bickering'. An anonymous barrister who married his deceased wife's sister in Holstein admitted that some of his relatives disapproved. The woman's family objected more often, knowing that she would bear the brunt of social and legal disabilities. Another barrister who married his deceased wife's sister admitted that her father opposed the marriage at first, though he later relented. His father-in-law explained, 'it was his duty to oppose it, because he considered it illegal.'[44]

All the same, many families were warmly supportive. At times, maternal families promoted the marriages because they did not want an unmarried sister-in-law living with a now-widowed man, as many witnesses in 1848 attested.[45] At other times, relatives were simply happy to keep congenial in-laws in the family fold. John Crook married two sisters, first Sarah Ann Hill, who died in 1851, then Mary Hill. John Hill, the women's father, showed no disapproval of the second marriage, leaving his property to Mary and John and their children. A similar case was that of John Harrison, who had continued to associate with his daughter and son-in-law, James Higson, despite the fact that James had first married John's sister. He, too, left his daughter his property, and he always referred to Anne as James's 'wife'.[46]

Most of the siblings in these families apparently managed to blend together, at least as well as any of the stepfamilies that were common in an age of high mortality. In the case of marriages with a deceased wife's sister, the children from first and second marriages were both half-siblings and cousins, which may have made them closer. In the Hunt family, Cyril got along well with his half-sister and brother, Gladys and Hilary. Gladys was jealous of her full sibling, but adored Cyril.[47] Some families had large age differences, so older siblings might resent sharing the estate with a new family, but the majority of the legal cases over incestuous marriages did not involve legitimate siblings trying to disinherit their half siblings. Most will disputes occurred when extended kin tried to get the estate or when the crown claimed it.[48] Unsurprisingly, the harmony was not unanimous. Some of those testifying before the Royal Commission argued that such marriages led to tensions. Revd Joseph Owen, a vicar in Staffordshire, knew a family who quarrelled over property. During the argument 'one of the children of the first marriage ... cast into the teeth of the children of the second marriage their illegitimacy.'[49] Still, though this case was not unique, it was not the norm.

Tensions were greater between the generations than between siblings. One man testified that his eldest daughter was jealous of her aunt's position in the house; he hoped by marrying his sister-in-law, the daughter would be more reconciled to sharing housekeeping.[50] The close relationship between fathers and daughters in middle-class homes would have made the transition to a new stepmother hard for some daughters. In addition, when the second wife had children herself, she might show preference to her own. Waugh became jealous of her stepson, Cyril, after her marriage to Hunt, so she favoured her own son and daughter.[51] Ironically, too, the success of the maternal aunt might mean that paternal ones suffered. Marianne Thornton had tended her nieces since their mother's death, but lost them when they left the country with their father and new step-mother. She was broken-hearted at their 'exile'.[52]

Though tensions within the nuclear family circle existed, the majority of testimonies indicated positive reactions of extended family and friends. The attitude of the wider middle-class society was more problematic, since the middle class had strict standards about sexuality. And, equally important, the participants in these marriages felt uneasy themselves. Diana Holman-Hunt argued that Hunt and Waugh 'imagined slights where none were intended' during their engagement. The stockbroker who married his wife's sister warned his friends about his marriage before they called so they could decide if they still wanted to do so. Indeed, some couples moved to new cities where no one knew them to avoid possible slights.[53] Not all these fears were unfounded. When Edith Waugh called on the Rosettis after her marriage, for instance, Christina Rosetti refused to receive her. Problems were particularly acute for those couples whose vicars disapproved; a surgeon in Shropshire lost almost all his friends when his marriage to his wife's sister offended his clergyman.[54]

The disapproval became more serious after mid-century. Henry Thornton made an all-out effort to have the prohibition against marriage with deceased wives' sisters removed in 1850. The ecclesiastical party in Parliament defeated the bill, but they were alarmed by the attempt and became less tolerant as a result. Thornton's own brother-in-law, Revd Charles Forster, approved of his Bishop's attempts to punish affinal matches. Forster's bishop told the clergy to 'treat the man as excommunicate and to reject him from the Communion; to refuse to church the woman; and to register the children as illegitimate.'[55] At the least, no middle-class person could remain ignorant of the illegality of these unions after the Royal Commission of 1848 and the defeat of the 1850 bill. Thus, anyone who lived in a parish with a disapproving vicar could find themselves socially snubbed.

As a result, the couples' lives were subject to various disruptions. J. S. Thorburne reported of a woman and her brother-in-law who were members of the Society of Friends. When they married, they had to leave the Society, since Quakers insisted that 'members of the Society of Friends must respect that law of which they claim the benefits.'[56] In addition, the legal necessity of regarding a 'wife' as a single woman galled many men. The Indian army officer complained, 'I am obliged to make a will leaving whatever property I give to my wife to her in her maiden name. I feel that to be exceedingly grievous.' A man in Norfolk had the same problem, having to refer to his second wife as a 'reputed Wife' in his will. The dry legal terms do not indicate the distaste the men and women felt about being semantically 'unmarried' in these documents. And the legal disabilities went further; any man who did not plan carefully could leave his spouse without support. A Norfolk woman could not get maintenance from her husband's estate when he went insane, since she was not his legal wife.[57] All of these issues must have separated the couple from those around them, especially the women.

Still, many affinal couples insisted that the dominant reaction of their friends was supportive. The businessman in Manchester testified that 'I have never found any possible inconvenience arising from it … I have rather had commendation'. When asked specifically about his wife, he insisted that she found no difference either. The stockbroker who wrote to all of his friends and acquaintances to warn them about his remarriage claimed that he did not receive a single snub.[58] Despite an occasional problem, Edith and Hunt had support from their friends, including Dinah Craik, who travelled with Edith to Switzerland for the ceremony. Indeed, Lucy Rosetti was 'quietly outraged' by her sister-in-law's snub of Edith, indicating that differences of opinion could be strong within families.[59] Some people even managed to remain successful in their careers. A clergyman in the Church of England went to Switzerland to marry his sister-in-law. The pair remained there some years until the wife's health required a return. Since they had lived in Switzerland several years, they had established a domicile, and thus could argue that they were legally married. Though he had to wait through a three-year probation, the man eventually got a licence to preach again. Similarly, James Low won election to the Corporation of London both before and after his affinal marriage.[60]

The majority of the time, the wider community accepted the marriage as valid. In other words, they did not support cohabitation, but instead had a wider definition of marriage than the law. As a vicar wrote to the Royal

Commission about a couple in his parish: 'their friends and neighbours regard it as a legal marriage'.[61] One woman who wrote a letter during the 'Is Marriage a Failure?' controversy in 1888 admitted that she had married her brother-in-law seven years before. She insisted that their friends saw them as 'legally married in our Maker's sight'. The attitude only grew stronger as the century went on, since more people believed in marriage as a relationship rather than an institution.[62] This growing acceptance probably helped mitigate the greater intolerance of the church.

These couples had reasoned out their defiance of the law. First, since scripture did not forbid the marriage, the law had no right to do so. The Manchester businessman, like Annie Bailey, said he had searched the Bible, but found no prohibition in the scriptures. Similarly, Samuel Watson asked four ministers for advice before going through with the ceremony with his deceased wife's sister. All 'told him there was no harm in it, but it was contrary to law.' Not surprisingly, Watson did as he wished.[63] Second, because such marriages were not against God's law, any act to ban them was tyrannous and unreasonable. The Indian army officer insisted that 'I consider such prohibition an infringement of my natural liberty.' Several of the witnesses warned that the laws were so far out of balance with popular views that they were bound to cause problems. As Garbett put it, 'I think the argument, "You ought not to set the law at defiance," is one which is very difficult to urge upon people when their affections are deeply interested … I do not think the law should put persons in such a position.'[64] The couples involved, then, were not hurting marriage; the law itself was the problem. The law of affinal marriages undermined marriage, since normally conventional couples went outside the law to marry – or worse, did not marry at all. Since the law defied both scripture and natural emotions, many people ignored it. This attitude would emerge again with adulterous and bigamous couples.

Those who worked in the law also had divided feelings. Many judges and lawyers supported the ban. Baron Bramwell, though he sympathised with those who married irregularly, nevertheless castigated men for doing so, since it put their wives and children at risk. Chief Justice Coleridge was firmly against such unions and fought legalisation, as did Lord Hatherley, a mid-century Lord Chancellor.[65] In contrast, others within the tight legal community supported repeal of the ban. Edward Clarke, a barrister, came out in favour of repeal in 1884, and Frederick Pollock, the third generation of the legal dynasty, was one of Hunt's strongest supporters.[66] Thus, those who wanted to marry within this prohibited degree could count on some high-profile support even within the conservative legal establishment.

All the same, the defiance of most middle-class people went only so far. Part of the reason for the support for these unions was that the majority *had* gone through a marriage ceremony, even though the English courts did not recognise them. Those few middle-class couples who chose not to marry were in more tenuous situations. In his testimony in 1848, T. C. Foster reported that of the 1,648 affinal unions he found, 88 did not marry because of the law; of these, 32 resulted in 'illicit cohabitations'. Though most of these were working-class, Foster did not make any distinctions, which indicates he included all classes.[67] Also, many couples may simply have announced that they were married without actually going through the ceremony, since a trip to the continent was expensive and made no legal difference. Though many women wanted some sort of ceremony, others were less insistent.

Several of the investigators in 1848 discussed middle-class cohabitees. Respectable people with no wedding at all could fall into serious difficulties. A Staffordshire widower with four children had his sister-in-law living with the family after his wife's death. After a time, they wanted to marry, but the local clergyman refused them. When the woman became pregnant, the two knew marriage was impossible, so instead they procured an illegal abortion. Unfortunately for them, they were discovered and tried at the assizes in 1844. Though acquitted, 'the effect upon their social position, which had hitherto been respectable, is, of course, a total blight.'[68] In other words, respectable people faced a dilemma; they had to be nonconformist one way or the other, and some chose to abide by the marriage laws, but to live 'in sin'. J. S. Thorburne reported a case of 'a man of wealth' who lived with his sister-in-law. He said 'he would gladly marry but for the uncertain state of the law.' According to Thorburne, 'though he is living in open concubinage, his neighbours sympathize [sic] with him'.[69] The choice to cohabit openly was out of step with the general middle-class solution to the problem, but perhaps these couples had a better grasp of the legal situation. If the marriage would be invalid, why go to the expense?

In addition, any couple outside the narrow parameters of acceptable affinal unions had severe difficulties. Robert James was a 'clerk in holy orders' in Wales in the 1870s. When his wife died, he lived in a cottage with his stepdaughter, Emma Alice Hamer. The neighbours insisted that they 'lived at a cottage in the village in every respect as man and wife', and the rumours became rampant when Emma had a child and the two shared a hotel room when they went to register the birth. The Archbishop of Canterbury sent a commission to investigate, and the commission uncovered the fact that James had lied about his relationship to the child on the birth certificate. The authorities prosecuted him for putting false information on the register (he called himself the father, the cousin, and the uncle of the child at different times). The jury convicted him, and Chief Justice Coleridge gave him five years in prison. Since few working-class men who perjured themselves got much punishment, this case indicates that, as in violence cases, a middle-class man who went too far outside the norm could suffer grave consequences.[70]

With such examples before them, few middle-class or upper-class women agreed to cohabit; the vast majority of middle-class women insisted on a ceremony. Because so few economic opportunities for women existed, they were particularly vulnerable if the relationships failed. Most open cohabitees, then, were working-class, who had a more elastic definition of marriage and less to lose. Still, even with a ceremony, middle-class affinal couples had many challenges. This was one reason that they worked so hard to legalise their unions, and, in this instance, they worked in tandem with poorer couples.

Conclusion

Both the working and the middle classes engaged in 'incestuous' unions during the nineteenth century. Often the couples went through some sort of wedding, despite the fact that this did not change their legal status. Working-class couples persisted in these ceremonies in the face of possible prosecution for perjury; many assumed, correctly, that juries would sympathise with them. On this issue, then, the legal definition of marriage was out of line with many Victorians' views. Too close relationships by blood provoked disapproval and disdain, but marriages with in-laws seemed not only acceptable, but even desirable, to a large number of people.

The preference for in-laws indicates several things, especially the importance of proximity. In the working class, related women and men became intimate because the women served as housekeepers and stepmothers. The woman performing the roles of wife was often the key; she had already 'tried out' for the position. Men, women, and children all benefited, as well as the extended family, which preferred a second marriage that kept the family circle intact. These factors also influenced the middle classes and are good examples of the importance of siblings to the middle-class family.[71] The grandmother might well be dead or still caring for her own young children, so when married daughters became ill, sisters were their mainstays. In addition, keeping a son-in-law in the family was important to the maternal kin, to protect the rights of the children. With so many advantages, these marriages often seemed the best solution to homes broken up by death.

For the most part, couples wanted to go through a ceremony; the vast majority did not dislike marriage itself. In fact, they were willing to go to considerable expense and risk to have a wedding. The marriage law, on the other hand, was another thing. If marriage laws defied reason and scripture, couples need not follow them. Indeed, flouting the law of marriage was so common that the police declined to prosecute most cases. Eventually, in the case of marriages with a deceased wife's sister, Parliament changed the law, a result that shows the limitations of a view of law as emanating from the top-down alone. These unions also point out that all classes in Victorian society might ignore the marriage laws, not just the poor. This attitude would also be true of those who could not marry due to previous unions, as the next two chapters make clear. Divorce laws were so far out of line with the needs of many couples that they defied them. As a result, the Victorian criminal justice system faced yet another dilemma in dealing with irregular unions.

Notes

1 Atlay, *The Victorian Chancellors*, pp. 115–16; A. Kuper, 'Incest, cousin marriage, and the origin of the human sciences in nineteenth-century England', *Past and Present* 174 (2002), 163–5. For the prohibited degrees, see *Reports From Commissioners on the Laws of Marriage and Divorce with Minutes of Evidence Appendices and Indices. Vol. I. Marriages and Divorce* (Shannon, Ireland: Irish University Press, 1969), 'Appendix of Evidence', p. 159.

2 N. F. Anderson, 'The "marriage with a deceased wife's sister bill" controversy: Incest anxiety and the defense of family purity in Victorian England', *Journal of British Studies* 21 (1982), 67–86; E. R. Gruner, 'Born and made: Sisters, brothers, and the deceased wife's sister bill', *Signs: Journal of Women in Culture and Society* 24 (1999), 423–47.

3 P. Morris, 'Incest or survival strategy? Plebeian marriages within the prohibited degrees in Somerset, 1730–1835', in J. C. Fout (ed.), *Forbidden History: The State, Society, and the Regulation of Sexuality in Modern Europe* (Chicago: University of Chicago Press, 1992), 139–69; J. Ayers (ed.), *Paupers & Pig Killers: The Diary of William Holland, A Somerset Parson, 1799–1818* (Stroud: Sutton Publishing, 1984), pp. 77–8; 190.

4 H. Mayhew, *London Labour and the London Poor* 4 vols (New York: Dover, 1968), I, 219; J. K. Walton and A. Wilcox (eds), *Low Life and Moral Improvement in Mid-Victorian England: Liverpool Through the Journalism of Hugh Shinmin* (Leicester: Leicester University Press, 1991), p. 110.

5 Conley, *The Unwritten Law*, pp. 121–2.

6 A. Wohl, 'Sex and the single room', in A. Wohl (ed.), *The Victorian Family: Structure and Stresses* (New York: St Martin's Press, 1978), 197–216.

7 R. Roberts, *The Classic Slum: Salford Life in the First Quarter of the Century* (London: Penguin Books, 1973), p. 27.

8 *Reports from Commissioners on the Laws*, 'Minutes of Evidence', pp. 6, 7, 32, 74, quotes from pp. 6–7.

9 *Reg. v. St Giles in the Field* (1847), 11 *Law Reports, Queen's Bench Division* 173–204; *The*

Times, 15 June 1847, p. 7; *Reg. v. Brighton*, 30 *Law Reports, Magistrates Cases* 197–201.

10 *Justice of the Peace* 68 (1904), 521; Morris, 'Incest or survival strategy', 149.

11 *Justice of the Peace, passim*, 1850–1914; Wohl, 'Sex and the single room', 209.

12 L. Davidoff, 'The separation of home and work? Landladies and lodgers in nineteenth-and twentieth-century England', in S. Burman (ed.), *Fit Work for Women* (New York: St Martin's Press, 1979), 68–92.

13 *Reports from Commissioners on the Laws*, 'Minutes of Evidence', pp. 7, 32, 82.

14 *The Times*, 25 February 1890, p. 12; *Devizes and Wiltshire Guardian*, 27 February 1890, p. 6; first quote from *Guardian*, second from *The Times*.

15 *Justice of the Peace* 12 (1848), 644; 16 (1852), 799.

16 *Reports from Commissioners on the Laws*, 'Minutes of Evidence', pp. 34 (for quote), 59; see also pp. 96–7.

17 *Ibid.*, pp. 12, 96.

18 *Ibid.*, pp. 16, 97; for clergy marrying within the prohibited degrees, see pp. 8–9; 12; 15–16; 77–9.

19 *Justice of the Peace* 68 (1904), 188; and *Reports from Commissioners on the Laws*, 'Minutes of Evidence', p. 10.

20 D. Torr, *Tom Mann and His Times* (London: Lawrence & Wishart, 1956), pp. 23, 41; C. Tsuzuki, *Tom Mann, 1856–1941: The Challenges of Labour* (Oxford: Clarendon Press, 1991), p. 8.

21 *Oxford Chronicle and Berks and Bucks Gazette*, 5 July 1890, p. 7; *The Times*, 3 July 1890, p. 7.

22 NA, HO 45 9978/X51597; *The Times*, 20 November 1902, p. 14.

23 NA, HO 45/7026, 15 January 1861.

24 *The Times*, 7 July 1901, p. 9; *Justice of the Peace* 65 (1901), 428.

25 NA, HO 45/9393/49503; emphases in original.

26 *The Times*, 20 December 1844, p. 8; S. Mumm, '"Not worse than other girls": The convent-based rehabilitation of fallen women in Victorian Britain', *Journal of Social History* 29 (1996), 530.

27 Conley, *The Unwritten Law*, pp. 121–2; L. Jackson, *Child Sexual Abuse in Victorian England* (London: Routledge, 2000), pp. 36–50.

28 *Justice of the Peace* 48 (1884), 92.

29 R. Clarke, 'Marriage within the prohibited degrees', *Justice of the Peace* 26 (1862), 334; *Reports from Commissioners on the Laws*, 'Minutes of Evidence', p. 13. See also 'A marriage of affinity', *Justice of the Peace* 68 (1904), p. 521.

30 11 *Law Reports, Queen's Bench Division* (1848) 173–204; *The Times*, 15 June 1847, p. 7.

31 30 *Law Reports, Magistrates Cases* (1861) 197–201.

32 *Reports from Commissioners on the Laws*, 'Minutes of Evidence', p. 32.

33 *Woods v. Woods* (1840), 163 *English Reports* 493–8, quote from p. 497.

34 One was a bigamy case involving marriage with a deceased wife's niece in 1872; *Reg. v. Allen*, 1 *Law Report, Crown Cases Reserved* 367–77; 36 *Justice of the Peace* 820–2. The other, in 1894, involved the marriage of a nephew with his aunt, which had taken place in 1843; *Re Shaw, Robinson v. Shaw* 2 *Law Reports, Chancery Division* 573–75; 71 *Law Times* 78–81.

35 *Reports from Commissioners on the Law*, 'Minutes of Evidence', pp. 3–5.

36 161 *English Reports* 1064–6; quote from 1066. See also Cretney, *Family Law in the Twentieth Century*, p. 43, note 37.

37 *Williams v. Bryant* (1769), LPA, Court of Arches Reports, D291, Case #10003, 70–85; D 293, Case 10004; *Aughtie v. Aughtie* (1810), 161 *English Reports* 961; *Andrews v. Ross* (1888), 59 *Justice of the Peace* 900–1; quote from p. 900. See also *Women's Suffrage Journal* 16 (1885), 93.

38 *Reports from Commissioners on the Laws*, 'Minutes of Evidence', p. 24.

39 Ibid., pp. 24, 67; NA, HO 45/B2853.

40 D. Holman-Hunt, *My Grandfather, His Wives and Loves* (London: Hamish Hamilton, 1969), p. 261.

41 *Reports from Commissioners on the Laws*, 'Minutes of Evidence', pp. 82, 28, 76.

42 Holman-Hunt, *My Grandfather*, pp. 277–82; A. Clark Amor, *William Holman Hunt: The True Pre-Raphaelite* (London: Constable, 1989), pp. 211–14.

43 E. M. Forster, *Marianne Thornton: A Domestic Biography, 1797–1887* (New York: Harcourt, Brace and Company, 1956), pp. 189–217.

44 *Reports from Commissioners on the Laws*, 'Minutes of Evidence', pp. 8, 23, 22.

45 *Ibid.*, pp. 10–11, 68.

46 *Hill v. Crook* (1873), 6 *House of Lords Appeals Cases* 265–86; *In re Harrison* (1894), 1 *Law Reports, Chancery Division* 561–8.

47 Clark Amor, *William Holman Hunt*, p. 227.

48 See, for example, *Pawson v. Brown* (1880), 44 *Justice of the Peace* 233; *The Times*, 6 November 1879, p. 4; and *Brook v. Brook*, Chapter 1.

49 *Reports from Commissioners on the Laws*, 'Minutes of Evidence', pp. 74–5; quote from p. 74.

50 *Ibid.*, p. 10.

51 Clark Amor, *William Holman Hunt*, pp. 240–1; D. Holman-Hunt, *My Grandmothers and I* (New York: W. W. Norton & Company, 1960), pp. 100–1.

52 Forster, *Marianne Thornton*, pp. 206–7; 211.

53 Holman-Hunt, *My Grandfather*, p. 283; *Reports from Commissioners on the Laws*, 'Minutes of Evidence', pp. 25–6, 65.

54 S. Weintraub, *Four Rosettis: A Victorian Biography* (New York: Weybright and Talley, 1977), p. 210; *Reports from Commissioners on the Laws*, 'Minutes of Evidence', p. 9.

55 Forster, *Marianne Thornton*, p. 196.

56 *Reports from Commissioners on the Laws*, 'Minutes of Evidence', p. 13.

57 *Ibid.*, pp. 71, 2.

58 *Ibid.*, pp. 67–8, 26.

59 Holman-Hunt, *My Grandfather*, pp. 283–4; Weintraub, *Four Rosettis*, p. 210.

60 *Reports from Commissioners on the Law*, 'Minutes of Evidence', pp. 9, 81–2.

61 *Reports from Commissioners on the Law*, 'Appendix', p. 145.

62 H. Quilter, *Is Marriage a Failure?* (New York: Garland, 1984), p. 27.

63 *Reports from Commissioners on the Law*, 'Minutes of Evidence', p. 68; *Watson and Watson v. Faremouth and others*, Annual Register 53 (1811), 136–7.

64 *Reports from Commissioners on the Law*, 'Minutes of Evidence', pp. 70; 97.

65 Lord Bramwell, 'Marriage with a deceased wife's sister', *Nineteenth Century* 20 (1886), 403–15; Lord Coleridge, Tract #13 in 'What the Liberals say', *Tracts Issued by the Marriage Law Defence Union* (London: Marriage Law Defence Union, 1884), 10–13; Atlay, *Lives of the Lord Chancellors*, II, 355.

66 E. Clarke, *The Story of My Life* (London: John Murray, 1923), pp. 232–3; W. H. Hunt, et.al., *Deceased Wife's Sister Bill: Letters from William Holman Hunt, Sir Frederick Pollock, and*

Others (London: Marriage Law Reform Association, 1901), pp. 26–9.

67 *Reports from Commissioners on the Law*, 'Minutes of Evidence', pp. 4–5.

68 *Ibid.*, p. 9 (for quote); *The Times*, 14 December 1844, p. 8; 21 December 1844, p. 6; 23 December 1844, p. 7; *Staffordshire Advertiser*, 21 December 1844, p. 2.

69 *Reports from Commissioners on the Law*, 'Minutes of Evidence', p. 14.

70 *The Times*, 3 June 1875, p. 7; 26 July 1875, p. 10.

71 L. Davidoff, *Worlds Between: Historical Perspectives on Gender and Class* (London: Polity Press, 1995), pp. 206–26.

4

Bigamy and cohabitation

ECAUSE OF THE strict divorce law in England, few unhappy couples could end their unions legally. Thus, many couples lived apart, either by mutual consent or because of desertion. These separations could be long standing, and sometimes one or both of the partners wished to remarry. Such marriages were bigamous and a felony at English law. Most couples would not open themselves up to these charges and so cohabited or parted, but others took the risk, apparently a substantial number.[1] According to the *Judicial Statistics of England and Wales*, bigamy trials occurred 5,327 times between 1857 and 1904, an average of 98 per year. As the population rose, bigamy cases also increased, but not as quickly. The average number in the 1850s was 85; in the 1890s, 103; and in the early twentieth century, 112. Either bigamies declined, or the authorities ignored more cases by the end of the century. All the same, almost every assize saw one or two bigamy trials.[2]

Though these numbers are not huge, bigamy remained one of the largest category of 'offences against persons' each year. And these were only the bigamies that the authorities prosecuted; far more often, bigamists faced no penalty. Gail Savage has found that in divorce cases using bigamy as a grounds, only one in eight was prosecuted.[3] Anecdotal evidence backs up this statistic. John Skinner, a rector in Somerset in the early 1800s, recorded the story of a man who went to the East Indies, leaving his wife behind. She was about to remarry, having had three children with her lover, when he returned. After an unsuccessful attempt at reconciliation, the man 'married a Timsbury woman by licence at Bristol'. Though Skinner admonished the wife for cohabiting, he did nothing about the husband's bigamy. At the other end of the century, Guy Aldred's estranged parents both married bigamously after his father deserted the family in 1889, and neither faced criminal charges.[4]

In other words, a small minority of bigamies, possibly one in five, made it to the courts. Still, the historian has little choice but to use criminal cases to study bigamy. Thus, this chapter is based on 304 bigamy cases between 1760 and 1914, most between 1830 and 1900, from newspapers and law reports.[5] I was unable to uncover any strong regional differences in the treatment or reasons for bigamy. Undoubtedly, local communities did have variations, but they do not emerge in the often brief reports of bigamy trials. As a result, this chapter will deal with overall patterns of behaviour, using the trials as a window into attitudes towards marriage, cohabitation, and the law.

Judges and juries assessed the causes and consequences of cohabitation through these cases. Unlike in violence trials, the actors in bigamy cases agreed on both 'bad' and 'good' bigamies, as did the wider community. All were convinced that happy bigamous marriages were preferable to miserable, legal ones. The couples defied the strict divorce laws but still regarded marriage as better than cohabiting, risking prison sentences to be 'man and wife'. Unfortunately, since the marriages were illegal, they could not avoid the problems of unwed cohabitation, especially when the families were poor.

Bigamy and criminal law

Bigamy, a criminal offence since the reign of James I, did not receive statutory attention until the Offences Against the Person Act of 1828, which made marrying another person while a first spouse was alive a felony. A revision of the penal code in 1861 included necessary changes due to the Divorce Act of 1857 (remarrying divorced persons could not be convicted of bigamy) and guidelines for sentencing. To succeed, a charge of bigamy had to have proof of both marriages, preferably the marriage registers. The first marriage could not be proved simply by the testimony of the spouse, since spouses could not testify against each other in a criminal trial.[6] However, others could testify to the wedding, and prosecutors preferred to have both the registers and witnesses as evidence.

Bigamy prosecutions had a good chance of success. The conviction rate between 1857 and 1904 was almost 80 per cent, slightly higher in the mid-Victorian years and slightly lower at the end of the century. If the state had both licences, defendants had difficulty refuting the charges, but exceptions existed. The most important of these, enacted in 1828, was that a bigamy charge failed against anyone who had not heard from her or his spouse for seven or more years. The second marriage was invalid if the first spouse was alive, but the defendant was not criminally guilty. In addition, the invalidity of the first marriage (for instance, if within the prohibited degrees) was a successful defence, but not that of the second marriage, since it was invalid by definition.[7]

Over time, juries and judges accepted other defences. For instance, if the bigamist had honestly believed that her or his first spouse was dead, juries often acquitted. And, even if found guilty, defendants used this plea to mitigate the punishment.[8] Eventually, judges began to argue that intent was one of the factors in determining guilt. In a case in 1869, the Appeals Court overturned a conviction of a female bigamist, because they insisted that the question of intent should be left to the jury.[9] All the same, the point did not become settled law until 1889, in *Reg. v. Tolson*. In this case, the High Court of Justice quashed the conviction of Mary Ann Tolson for bigamy, on the grounds that juries had every right to consider intent when reaching their verdicts.[10]

Despite these helps to the defence, most defendants were convicted in the nineteenth century. I have verdicts in 280 of my 304 cases. Juries convicted in 225 and acquitted in 55, a conviction rate of 81 per cent. Defendants were largely male – 249 of 304 cases (82 per cent). Both of these figures agree with the *Judicial Statistics*, though men are slightly over-represented in my group; men made up almost 79 per cent of the defendants overall in the period 1857–1904.[11] In addition, juries convicted men at a higher rate. Of the 208 cases with male defendants and a verdict, 177 were convictions and 31 were acquittals, a conviction rate of 85 per cent. Of the 54 female defendants, 37 were convictions and 17 acquittals, a 68 per cent conviction rate. Women also had lower sentences than men. In the 1840s, eight men were transported, and three received sentences of a year or more, while the three women got two months or less. By the 1860s, men's punishments had diminished but were still higher than women's. Five men received three to seven years; six got six to twelve months; nine got one to three months; and three received sentences of two weeks or less. In the same decade all nine guilty female defendants received sentences of two months or less. In the 1880s, twelve men received one to ten years in prison, while all six of the women defendants served only a few days. Obviously, bigamy was a much more serious crime when the defendant was male.

The *Judicial Statistics* show that punishments for bigamy were usually mild. Throughout the 1850s and 1860s, only a minority of defendants spent more than a year in prison for bigamy, an average of 15 per cent of those convicted between 1857 and 1869. This percentage grew slightly larger over the course of the Victorian period; between 1885 and 1900, 19 per cent of bigamists received a year or more. At the same time, those who got no punishment or short sentences also increased. Those who received a month or less were almost 25 per cent of the defendants in the 1860s, 29 per cent in the 1870s, 39 per cent in the 1880s, and 37 per cent in the 1890s. Thus, the punishments bifurcated over the course of the century. Serious bigamies, usually those involving fraud, received long sentences, but the majority received lesser punishments.

As these statistics indicate, circumstances were crucial to verdicts and sentencing; the courts pondered a number of factors before giving out punishments. The first consideration was the prosecutor in the case; someone had to bring the matter to the attention of the authorities. Most of the time, the prosecutor was the first or second spouse of the defendant. Of the 167 cases in my selection with a named prosecutor, the first spouse did so forty-five times (twenty-nine wives and sixteen husbands). When the first spouse prosecuted, the court considered her or his motives. If the first spouse were a woman who had been unjustly deserted, the court was sympathetic, but judges and juries would not support vindictive prosecutions.[12] First husbands who prosecuted were even more suspect, since they could support themselves. For instance, Joseph Morant left his wife in 1859 after six years of marriage. Caroline remarried in 1864, and when Morant reappeared in 1872, he had her arrested. The jury acquitted her, and Morant then asked if he could have her back. Commissioner Kerr snapped, 'Certainly not. How can a fellow like you have the face to complain seeing that you suddenly leave your wife and remain away from her for 13 years...? It is preposterous to make such a request.'[13]

Second spouses far outnumbered first ones as prosecutors. Of the 167 cases with identified prosecutors, 61 were second wives, 8 were second husbands, 13 were members of the second wives' families, and 4 were members of second husbands' families. Thus, almost 45 per cent of the prosecutors were second wives or their relatives. The key to the court's reaction here was the information available to the second spouse. If she had been tricked into an invalid marriage, the court would be severe; if she knew the connection, the sentencing was light. Justice Lush believed that Ebeneezer Derby had told his second wife that he was already married so gave him only one day. In contrast, Justice Denman fumed at Robert Steventon in 1880. Judith Killen, his second wife, did not know that he was married, and he had also sold up her property after they 'wed'. Denman complained, 'this was not an ordinary case of bigamy but one of cruel deception.' He gave Steventon five years.[14]

If neither spouse prosecuted, family members usually did. Brothers, in-laws, cousins, aunts, and uncles, as well as parents, got involved. Martha Blaney's parents instituted the arrest of her husband, William Johnson, in 1830. Johnson had sent Blaney to the hospital with his violent behaviour, and Blaney's parents used his previous marriage in 1828 to free her. Men's families also intervened, especially in the few cases involving well-off people. Annabella Robertson had become a governess after her first marriage had failed, due, she claimed, to the cruelty of her husband. She worked for the Radermacher family and fell in love with the oldest son, and the couple married in 1854. The elder Mr Radermacher discovered her previous marriage and prosecuted her 'to shield his son from the consequences of the illegal contract'.[15]

Public prosecutions were rare, totalling 19 cases, and fall into two main categories. First were 'serial' bigamists, those who used marriage to defraud people. Twenty-seven defendants had married three or more times, and ten of these resulted in public prosecutions. Most serial defendants (89 per cent, or 24 of 27) were men. A typical case was that of Robert Taylor, who had married six women by 1840 by pretending to be the heir to a large fortune. He was convicted three times and finally received fourteen years, so at least he did not marry anyone else for awhile. These men had found an easy way to make money by fraud, and some were probably professional con men. A bigamist in prison with R. M. Fox during the First World War bragged that 'his offense was better than stealing', though an indignant pickpocket disputed this.[16]

In contrast, only two women in my study made a career of marrying, and one was in the late eighteenth century. Sarah Lane pleaded guilty to bigamy in 1764; she had married four men and was branded on the hand. Anne Wood, who was tried in 1870, was also a serial bigamist. She had already married three men when she went through another ceremony with George Wood. Wood testified that 'she acted most improperly, obtaining money under false pretenses from his friends'. She also opened his letters and helped herself to any money they contained. The Common Serjeant gave her twelve months in prison.[17] The only other woman with three husbands was Margaret Milton. Despite her multiple spouses, she was not a 'professional' bigamist; her case is discussed in the section on 'acceptable' bigamy, below.

The second major type of public prosecution involved men who deserted their wives and left them chargeable to the parish. For example, in 1880 Edward Prince was arrested for deserting his wife and three children. By the time the police caught him in January 1880, he had already remarried. The police added a charge of bigamy to the original charge, and he served three months. Other men tried to get out of supporting their second wives by proving they were not legally married; the authorities retaliated by bringing bigamy charges. In 1895, James Coaley deserted his first wife, then had two children with a second. He deserted the second wife as well, and the JPs ordered him to support her. He refused and produced his first marriage certificate to demonstrate why. He was promptly arrested for bigamy, convicted, and sentenced to twelve months at hard labour.[18]

Class, gender, and 'acceptable' bigamy

The majority of bigamous families were from the working class. Of the 187 cases where the newspapers mention a specific occupation, 144 were working-class, 31 were lower-middle, middle-class or upper-class, and 12 involved mixed class pairings.[19] Over three-quarters of the cases, then, were entirely in the working class, and 84 per cent had at least one working-class partner. Most of the middle-class cases involved lower-middle class families who meshed well with the working-class people around them. An example was Maria Humphries, who owned a lodging house; her second husband was Edwin Fisher, a navvy, who boarded with her. Though she was of a higher class, the difference was small.[20]

The few with large class differences interacted with gender in complex ways. Some men married bigamously in an effort to gain control of women's money fraudulently, but most were simply trying to better themselves. James Foster married Ada Tucker, the daughter of the an admiral, in 1889. Foster had been in the navy and did odd jobs around Tucker's home, and they courted for seven months. When she learned he had already married in 1864, she prosecuted him for bigamy, annoyed that she had 'raised him' only to be 'ruined'. Judges and juries were dubious about men who used women to make their fortunes, and Foster received twelve months in prison.[21]

The other major category of cross-class cases involved women who married men of higher class. Women using marriage in this way was far more acceptable to judges and juries, though women who were 'adventuresses' did not get much sympathy. Eliza Manley married Thomas Archer, a wealthy man, in the 1850s. The two lived extravagantly for some months until Archer tried to divorce her, at which point he discovered she was already married. At her trial in 1860, the Recorder gave her two months at hard labour. More typically, the women were servants, and the marriages were of doubtful legality. Richard Dames was an officer in the militia and the son of a sugar refiner. At the age of nineteen, in 1879, he secretly married a servant in his mother's house, Elizabeth Pace, by making false statements to the registrar. When he married a more suitable woman in 1882, Pace unsuccessfully prosecuted him for bigamy.[22] Despite their press coverage, these cases were a minority; most bigamies occurred within the working class.

Whatever their class, these couples shared reasons for marrying and for 'self-divorce', and their communities accepted bigamous families under certain conditions. Historians have noted the influence of neighbours on working-class families; they often served as alternative authority structures on social and domestic issues.[23] Most historians have centred on neighbours' roles as enforcers of certain levels of family harmony, cleanliness, and sexual conformity. In contrast, bigamy cases, like affinal marriages, show that communities could be flexible; a strict adherence to the law was not always necessary.

The major circumstance that made bigamy acceptable was if the bigamist had a good reason for leaving her or his first spouse. Not surprisingly, then, bigamists explained their desertions by highlighting the 'misbehaviour' of their husbands/wives, a highly gendered term. When applied to wives, it usually meant sexual misconduct. Benjamin Griffiths left his wife when she had an affair with his nephew. Similarly, William Trouse's wife 'had become an abandoned woman'. Both men argued at their trials that their desertions of such women were justified. Their arguments were persuasive, because neither had neighbours testify against them, and the judges in the trials (Platt and Huddlestone) gave them nominal sentences (Griffiths paid a fine of one shilling, and Trouse served one day).[24] Since few poor men or women could afford a divorce, courts kept this in mind. James Mitchell's wife left him for another man, so he remarried; at the trial in 1854, Justice Erle asserted 'if the prisoner had been in a higher rank of life, he would have been divorced, and then he could have legally married to the second person.' He gave Mitchell only three days.[25]

Men were also reluctant to remain in marriages in which the wives were too assertive. Joseph Ainley, a peddler, ran away from his wife, Sarah, after only one week because, he said, she had 'taken upon herself to become a tyrant in the house', including throwing him out after an argument. Charles Matthews, an accountant in Bristol, characterised his first wife, Elizabeth, as a 'woman of very violent temper'. When arrested, he remarked that 'he would rather go to prison than go back to his wife.'[26] Whether or not their tempers had been provoked, these women had stepped over the bounds of acceptable behaviour, so their husbands felt free to find happiness elsewhere. In fact, one detective testified that Matthews's neighbours supported his version of events. Matthews was lower-middle class, so his community's flexibility was particularly noteworthy.

Money was also often a bone of contention. Husbands might accuse wives of 'misbehaviour' if they did not share property or earnings. Jane Bristow, the second wife of Peter Collen, a labourer, claimed that as soon as Peter married her, he became abusive: 'he demanded her money, and when she refused him, said, "What do you suppose I married you for except your money?'" Jane might have been overstating the case to excuse herself, but some husbands confessed that money led to trouble. George Galway, a traveller, admitted that he and his wife, married since 1825, had serious problems after she inherited property in 1843. That acquisition led to arguments, and he soon left.[27] With resources chronically short, conflicts over money were bitter. Because providing was one of the linchpins of Victorian masculinity, especially after 1850, men reacted badly to any challenges to it.[28]

Finally, men felt justified in refusing to live with women who were not successful housekeepers. First, women should balance the family's budget; men could not live with women who squandered their pay. George Braidwood accused his first wife of such reckless spending that she 'caused the home to be broken up'.[29] Second, women were to be nurturing and caring. John Calvert said he had been unhappy with his first wife, because she 'had left him twice when he was seriously ill', a dereliction of wifely duty. Patrick Leach, an Irishman in York, summed up these expectations when he explained why he had separated from his wife: she 'treated him very ill, neglected his children, and sold him up, on account of which he imagined that he was justified in taking another wife.'[30]

Women had their own meanings for 'misbehaviour'. Primarily, the term meant violence, and these claims elicited mercy in bigamy trials. Eliza Gallivan had particularly bad taste in husbands. Her first husband went to prison for gouging out one of her eyes and stabbing her. She then remarried but had to run away again when her second husband threatened to gouge out her remaining eye. Although most women did not have such horror stories, many claimed that 'ill-treatment' or 'disgraceful' behaviour had forced them from their homes.[31] Stephen Aldhouse's first wife left him due to his ill treatment. He then married Hephzibah Roberts in 1837; though she had two children with him, she, too, left him for abusing her. Roberts, unlike Frances, was able to free herself from his threats by prosecuting him for bigamy, and he was transported for seven years.[32] Violence may have been an accepted part of working-class marriage, but not all women tolerated it.

Second, 'misbehaviour' for men included failure to provide. James MacDonald, a clerk, married three women between 1847 and 1863. His first wife, who had four children with him, tracked him down and prosecuted him. According to the court reports, 'He had treated all three wives with the grossest neglect'. Not surprisingly, the judge gave him seven years.[33] On the other hand, many times, women justified their illegal remarriages by the need to find a provider. Like MacDonald, Margaret Milton had married three times by 1872. Unlike him, though, Milton pleaded the need for support to explain her actions. Her first husband, Henry, 'had ... been imprisoned for neglecting to support her and her children.' Her second husband stayed only a short time, since he lost his job. Her third, James Foggart, finally proved to be a provider. Henry prosecuted her, but Justice Denman gave her only five days; apparently, he agreed that she needed a breadwinner.[34] The emphasis on providing was so great that some men continued to support their children, even if their wives had 'misbehaved'.[35]

Working-class marriage, then, could be a strife-torn experience, as many historians have found.[36] Youthful choices often proved disastrous, and some people could not find a congenial partner even with second and third choices. Although most couples stayed together, a minority refused to continue in poisoned relationships. Historians of nineteenth-century working-class marriage have justifiably concentrated on the majority of couples who continued to live together, despite violent conflicts. But the evidence of bigamy cases partially revises the argument that working-class people expected little more than dogged companionship in marriage.[37] Obviously, several modes of behaviour wrecked working-class marriages. Poor husbands and wives accepted more sexual infidelity and violence than middle-class couples, but they had limits. Unhappy spouses divorced with their feet for drunkenness, adultery, violence, and even incompatibility.

These 'self-divorces' did not show a contempt for matrimony. On the contrary, bigamies were strong evidence of people's attachment to marriage. Despite miserable experiences, many risked prison to create new ties. Often, the illegal unions were more successful. For neighbours, bigamous unions had advantages as well, because they provided stable families in the place of those with constant bickering. Examples of happy second unions abound in the records; in fact, second wives sometimes refused to prosecute, forcing the magistrates or police to do so.[38] Some people needed a first mistake to find a congenial mate, but the law did not allow for such experimentation. As Justice Lawrance remarked, 'He could never countenance the doctrine that if a man could not live happily with his wife he was entitled to ... commit bigamy. At that rate, a great many men would be leaving their wives and marrying some one [sic] else.'[39] The judge's discomfort was palpable; when an illegal union was more successful than a legal one, judges had to deal with the consequences.

Wider kin and community

The attitude of family members towards bigamous unions varied by circumstances. The relatives of wronged spouses were usually hostile, either to defend a deserted spouse or to protect a second one. As stated above, families of either the first or second wives instigated many cases. Even when they did not start the prosecution, they testified for their relatives.[40] A father, in particular, would take any chance to punish a man who had 'ruined' his daughter, as many examples attest.[41] Though parents predominated, siblings were also important. Anna Campbell's brother prosecuted her bigamous husband; Mary Greene's sister was the main force in the prosecution of William Sheen.[42]

Nevertheless, some family members actively supported bigamous unions, depending, again, on circumstances. Edward Jones's daughter defended her father's decision to remarry illegally, since her mother had refused to return to him despite his appeals. Some family members even participated in fooling second spouses. Robert Green, a carman, was married when he courted Alice Gabbetie. Alice heard that Robert was already married shortly before the wedding, so she went to Green's mother's house to find out the truth. Green denied it, and his mother told her 'he was single, and could, therefore, do as he liked.' When Annie discovered the truth, she was so angry that she prosecuted both Greens, though the authorities dropped the charges against the mother.[43]

The most difficult and conflicted situation for families were bigamies within the family fold. These cases could lead to bitter divisions with extended kin, showing the limitations of family forbearance. Joseph Moran, an engineer, married his sixteen-year-old cousin in 1854, though he was already married to Rebecca Bridger. 'After the second wife's relatives found out that prisoner had a wife then alive, and spoke to him about it, he said they might do their worst – they could only give him three months.' This response made a private settlement impossible, so the case went to court, and Moran received nine more months than he expected. John Curgenwen married his first cousin in 1852. They lived together only a year before she returned to her father's house, and Curgenwen shipped out to the Crimea in 1854. She did not see him for the next ten years; clearly, the family members had little desire to meet again. Curgenwen remarried in 1862. When he was posted to Cornwall, his extended kin discovered his marriage and prosecuted him. Despite the long passage of time, the bitterness remained.[44]

Still, the case of Benjamin Toombs of Surrey shows that marriages within the same families did not always lead to predictable divisions. Toombs married Letitia Rudge in 1814 after lodging in her parents' house for some time. Benjamin apparently became attached to many of the members of Letitia's family, including wider kin, during his marriage. He soon left Rudge (apparently for sexual misconduct). In May 1830, he married Mary Ann, Letitia's first cousin. Obviously, Mary Ann knew that

Benjamin was already married, yet she did not hesitate, nor did her father protest. Only her brother objected, which was why Benjamin ended up in court.[45] This kind of support was unusual, but it does indicate that families disagreed about how best to deal with failed relationships. Mary Ann's father preferred to keep Benjamin, an in-law, in the family, over Letitia, a blood relative, whom he forbade Mary Ann to see. Letitia's 'base' behaviour made her a less desirable family member than her estranged husband, and, indeed, Letitia did not object to the new arrangement, since Benjamin continued to support her. These tangled family alliances made for a difficult court case.

As with families, neighbours and friends considered the reasons for the separation before they condemned bigamy. 'Misbehaviour' of the first spouse was crucial, and neighbours expected the man to provide for the first spouse as well as his new family, as many of the above cases indicated.[46] Also, the bigamist must be honest about her or his past. In fact, if the bigamist did not volunteer the information, someone else often did. In Leeds, Elizabeth Gillson's neighbours told her that her fiancé, Alfred Windsor, a labourer, was a married man, though she married him anyway. In Dalton, John Jessop, a hay dealer, married Kate Boucher, even though his wife was alive. At the trial, Kate claimed she knew nothing of his first wife when they married, but two witnesses testified that they had told her the truth, with the warning that 'she would be a fool to marry him'. Even in the arguably more anonymous realms of London, neighbours intervened, if in indirect ways. Jane Willis received an unsigned letter after her wedding to Samuel Potling, warning her that he was already wed.[47] On this issue, in fact, community standards were stricter than the letter of the law; one case in 1838 led to a near riot by outraged female neighbours after the dishonest male defendant got off the bigamy charge.[48]

In short, notions of 'right' behaviour did not follow those of the legal system. In some cases a legally innocent defendant was distinctly unpopular. Far more often, a guilty defendant earned public sympathy. Put another way, popular definitions of marriage and divorce were wider than the law allowed. Similarly to affinal marriages, many people did not see any harm in bigamy as long as all the parties were informed about and satisfied with their relationships. Annie Waterton told neighbours in Leeds that it did not matter that her fiancé, Charles Scoltock, was already married because 'there would be no bother about it as she had asked the first wife's permission.' This reasoning was particularly popular when both spouses remarried; Scoltock argued that since his first wife had a new spouse, he assumed he could do the same. James Young had a similar defence in London in 1907; both of his previous wives had remarried by the time he was arrested. The magistrate, unimpressed, insisted 'Bigamy by both parties will not improve his position.'[49] But often such mutual partings did make a difference to neighbours and kin.

Defining marriage and divorce

Most of these couples thought of themselves 'as husband and wife', and even the newspaper records called multiple spouses 'the first wife' or 'the second wife'. Judges, witnesses, prosecutors, and defendants did the same.[50] These couples resisted legal definitions of marriage and divorce, a phenomenon that many historians have explored, though most have argued that the age of marital nonconformity was the first half of the century.[51] Bigamy cases prove that many people had their own definitions of marriage and divorce until at least the twentieth century. Nevertheless, Victorian bigamists combined a challenge to the marriage laws with a desire for the ritual. Couples, especially women, wanted a wedding to validate their unions, echoing affinal and consanguineous couples. Paradoxically, they defined 'marriage' loosely, defying the authorities, yet at the same time, they craved the formality of marriage, thereby seeking the approval of those authorities. Especially to women, marriage was still 'better', conferring status and security.[52]

Examples abound of women who insisted on going through the ceremony even though they knew it was invalid. Rhoda Byrne married Joseph Courtney, a gardener, in 1900, though she knew he was married. She explained, 'it was better to marry than merely to live with him, and therefore he consented.' John Calvert testified that he told Hannah Metcalfe that he was already married, but they had a wedding 'in order to satisfy her scruples'. Women's insistence on a ceremony showed up in other sources as well. Sir William Cobbett told the Royal Commission on Divorce in 1912 that the limited nature of divorce led to bigamies because women would not live with men without a wedding. Cobbett knew of two men who 'took the risk' so they could live with the women they loved.[53]

Sometimes men initiated the second weddings themselves. William Weaver was a former comedian who had reformed into a travelling preacher. His first wife was unfaithful, and Weaver lived with Mary Drinkwater until his conversion. At that point, he was reluctant to continue cohabiting and so married bigamously. In other words, to him, committing a felony was less sinful than cohabitation; ironically, his religious scruples justified his law-breaking. Nor was Weaver unique. William Goode was a clerk in holy orders who had married first in 1860 and then married Isabella Vickery in 1876. Isabella found out in 1878 that he was married; when she confronted him, he replied, 'what he had done might appear wrong in the sight of man, but it was right in the sight of God.' The two had lived together for two years before they wed, and even a felonious marriage was superior to living 'in sin'.[54]

Part of the preference for marriage came from families, especially if the woman was expecting a child. James Garden, a surgeon's assistant from Bromley, married Caroline Smith because her father insisted on it when Caroline became pregnant. In the same way, the married John Arthur Rogerson, from Stafford, committed bigamy with a Miss Shekell to 'save her from shame'.[55] In short, to avoid one legal stigma, the couple incurred another. Nothing could legitimate their children, but the couples did not always know this and, even if they did, they still wanted the ceremony, since it conferred public validity. As Elizabeth Hutton explained in 1884, she married an already wed man 'because I loved him and to save my name with my friends; I did not want to live with him without being married'.[56]

Bigamy cases also indicate that self-divorce persisted beyond the first half of the nineteenth century.[57] The simple act of desertion could be enough for some men and women; the fact that they lived apart for several years, they insisted, invalidated their ties. This belief persisted in the face of repeated official denials, because of the confusion over the seven-year rule; people mixed up the idea that they could not be convicted of bigamy with the idea that they could remarry legally. In addition to the trials, other sources hint at this confusion; Guy Aldred's mother believed she could remarry legally because her second marriage took place more than seven years after her husband's desertion; she clung to this belief despite her son's exasperated denials.[58]

A number of factors constituted a self-divorce. At times, a long separation was accompanied by the permission of the first husband or wife. Annie Birkhead and Michael Jessop consulted her husband before they married, 'and he told her she was at liberty to get married again'. She was apparently telling the truth, since both of her husbands stood bail for her. Other times, the couples assumed that if their first spouse had remarried, they could do so as well.[59] Such couples were most unwilling to accept that these remarriages were not valid. Thomas Bevan, a plasterer, married Catherine Wilson in 1848, though his wife was still alive. Catherine defended Thomas at his trial and said she would live with him again when he was free. The judge protested, '"he don't belong to you, he belongs to his first wife." The witness shook her head, seeming very much to doubt his Lordship's authority as to her right and title'.[60] Similarly, Alice Mary Currey told the judge in Albert Durrant's trial that 'he has been a most kind and loving husband to me ... after this is all settled I am going to live with him again.[61]

For many bigamists self-divorce involved quasi-legal sanctions. Several pleaded that their first marriages were not valid, for example, that they were under-age. Others denied that civil marriages were binding, since they were not 'real'. When George Stiffle was tried for bigamy, a man named Green was a witness to the first marriage, a civil ceremony. Green sniffed, 'he never saw such a marriage – it was not at all like his – there was no minister, nor any ring.'[62] Of course, most of the defendants were trying to find an excuse for breaking the law, but they may also have convinced themselves that one of the marriages was not 'real' in order to justify their behaviour to themselves.

English marriage laws also had numerous loopholes. For example, in Ireland, a Protestant who married a Roman Catholic by a Roman Catholic priest had to have been in the country and converted for a full year or the marriage was invalid. Both William Dwyer and Thomas Fanning used this provision to defend themselves (successfully, in Fanning's case).[63] Others assumed that if they had grounds for an annulment, the marriage was not legal even if they had not gone through the process. Richard David said his first wife had 'some physical malformation' which he assumed voided the marriage; after his sentencing, the judge told him he should have the marriage annulled. Others argued that the first marriage was not real because they had not lived together. Annie Stephens married Alexander Stephens in 1854, but she insisted 'he was not her husband, he left her on coming home from church.'[64]

In addition, some couples thought the marriage was legally over when the wife or husband had been deserted for someone else. In the 1850s, Thomas Barnes's first wife left him for another man. When she applied to the parish for relief, the Leicester magistrates called him up to know why he did not support her. Barnes explained his reasons and left; his cost for the summons was thirty shillings. Barnes believed that because the workhouse had taken over supporting his wife, he was free to remarry, especially considering his monetary outlay. Indeed, his wife's brother testified, 'Barnes paid thirty shillings to be divorced.' More often, couples drew up formal deeds of separation in an effort to make the divorce official. Both Edward Green and John Nield separated from their wives with formal documents which included clauses allowing remarriage.[65] Judges were never impressed with these papers. Justice Mellor lectured Nield sternly, 'As for the agreement made between the prisoner and his first wife that was perfectly absurd. It was quite ridiculous to suppose that he believed he was enabled by that to marry again during her life.' But some couples obviously did think so – or at least chose to tell themselves that they could.

Wife sales also came up in bigamy trials throughout the century. Betsy Wardle insisted that she could marry George Chisnall in 1882 because her husband 'sold her for a quart of beer'. Two of her female neighbours took part in the second wedding because she had a 'paper' that ceded her husband's rights, and Chisnall confirmed that he bought Wardle for 'Sixpence'. Justice Denman grew increasingly exasperated as witness after witness argued the transaction was legal: 'Everybody has committed bigamy in this case as far as I can make out', he opined. When he sentenced Wardle to a week at hard labour, he told the court, 'a man has no more right to sell his own wife than to sell his neighbour's wife, or cow, or ox, or ass, or any other thing that was his.' Despite judicial incredulity, such defences persisted; as late as 1895, a plasterer claimed to have sold his wife for 3s 6d.[66] In fact, some defendants believed that the bigamy trial was a sort of divorce. These confusions, too, occurred throughout the century, including a coal porter in 1850 and a machinist in 1880. In both cases, the defendants asked the judges if they could remarry after serving their time, only to receive exasperated negatives.[67]

Clearly, the men and women involved in bigamous marriages were not invariably ruined. Friends, neighbours, and even wronged spouses tolerated this sexual nonconformity. Second spouses often said they would continue to live with already-married spouses. Dinah Taylor, although she had known nothing about labourer Jeremiah Thomas's first wife, said 'she was quite ready to continue to live with him.' Nor were the tolerant spouses only women; Caroline Morant's second husband testified on her behalf, saying 'she had been a very good wife to him.'[68] First spouses also sometimes forgave bigamies. Robert Frost, a shoemaker, had heard that his first wife was dead. So he married Elizabeth Long, a street hawker. When his first wife returned, he went back to her, and they lived happily together. Annie Gibbon's first husband also took her back after she married another man during his six-year absence, saying 'he did not consider himself aggrieved.'[69] Nor did women necessarily lose their attractiveness by allying themselves with bigamists. In Dorchester, George Wells, an iron moulder, married Bertha Maidment in 1891 and Susan Broom in 1893. Broom prosecuted him, but by the time of the trial, she had already married someone else. Justice Kennedy, amused, gave Wells only five days.[70] In short, bigamous marriages were tolerated – or even approved – in many communities; the strict marriage laws meant that most neighbours and friends had to be practical when marriages broke down.

Judges and bigamy

Another indication of a limited acceptance of bigamy was the conflicted attitude of many judges. Their reactions, much like those of neighbours and kin, depended on the circumstances. As Justice Erle put it, 'there are no cases which differed so much in their character as those of bigamy'. The main way that judges adapted the law was in sentencing, where they had maximum control. As Chief Justice Cockburn explained in 1865, 'In a case where the woman knew the whole state of things, and went through the ceremony of marriage merely to satisfy her conscience, the offence was comparatively small; but where a woman was betrayed, believing that she was contracting a valid marriage, the offence was most atrocious.'[71] Historians of Victorian justice have long recognised the biases of the courts along class and gender lines. On this issue, bigamy trials, like violence cases, offer a complicated pattern. On the one hand, the cases were overwhelmingly brought against working-class men. On the other, many of the men escaped harsh penalties for their crimes, and almost all of the women did so. Because men were four-fifths of the defendants, one could argue that the judges' leniency showed a bias against working-class women, but since women defendants received even gentler treatment, this will not suffice. Instead, judges pondered a complex array of circumstances to come to their decisions.

Judges' collective sentencing decisions varied over time. First, because of the change in the law, transportation applied only before 1850; in addition, sentences were longer on average in the early part of the century. Of the thirty-nine cases with a sentence of five years or more, fifteen (almost 40 per cent) occurred before 1850; the rest were spread over the remaining sixty-four years fairly evenly. In addition, of the sixty-seven cases which had sentences of a month or less, sixty-three were after 1850. To some extent, then, judges relaxed their standards as time went on. Partly this was a result of the discussions of sentencing and changes in the law throughout the Victorian period. The 1861 Offences Against Persons Act put the maximum sentence for 'aggravated' bigamy at three to six years (later changed to seven), with lesser sentences for those without aggravation.[72] However, judges decided how to regard the bigamy (aggravated or not) and also had leeway within each category.

Thus, punishment was contingent on numerous factors. Judges always gave long sentences to serial bigamists. In addition, anyone who lied to her or his second spouse, thus contributing to the fall of a pure man or (especially) woman, received harsher penalties. Men of higher classes sometimes also got longer sentences, because they set a bad example. In

1860, Justice Blackburn was disgusted with Henry Bickerstaffe, a clergyman, calling his bigamy 'an outrage to society' before giving him three years.[73] Other factors that lengthened sentences included a very young deceived spouse or a mercenary motive for the marriages. James Malcolm combined a number of these factors: he was a meat salesman, so lower-middle class; he tricked a young woman into a fraudulent marriage; he attempted to ruin another a few months later; and then, at his trial, he impugned the women's characters. Justice Field, as a result, called Malcolm 'cowardly', 'disgraceful' and 'dastardly' in an impassioned speech from the bench and gave him the maximum sentence of seven years.[74]

On occasion, as well, judges considered the public danger. The indissolubility of marriage was, after all, the law, and people should not break the law lightly. In an Old Bailey trial in 1840, the Common Serjeant argued that 'an example must be made in order to protect the public' in giving an 'honest' bigamist six months. Such sentiments survived into the twentieth century. Sir F. Jeune, a Divorce Court judge, was appalled when he heard that Evan Powell had received only a day in jail after pleading guilty to bigamy. He fumed, 'I have noticed several times that light sentences are given in bigamy cases, and I very much regret to see it.'[75] All the same, these judicial voices were the minority. As many of the above cases showed, judges agreed with juries about what made bigamy acceptable, giving short sentences to those with good reasons to leave their first spouses and who were honest with everyone involved.

The clearest indicator of this latitude was judges' reactions to public prosecutions. Judges considered prosecution by neighbours or even relatives illegitimate if none of the spouses were unhappy. Justice Blackburn disallowed the costs of the prosecution in Ann Birkhead's case in York in March 1860, complaining that '[i]t looked like the ignorant meddling of some malicious person.' That same year, Blackburn did the same in Ellen Calverly's case, since it was not prosecuted by either of her husbands, but by a man named Wood who was feuding with her father. Even if public prosecutions had good reasons, judges gave lesser sentences. John Calvert was prosecuted by the Excise authorities. He had retired with a pension; apparently, the authorities wanted to avoid paying it and so had him arrested. As both wives were aware of the situation, Baron Parke considered it a 'venial' case and gave him two months.[76]

Judges objected more strongly when they felt that the authorities should have intervened to stop, rather than encourage, prosecutions. In March 1860, Mary Hannigan was tried before Justice Hill at the Liverpool Assizes. Her first husband, Edward Hannigan, had lived with her only two months and then enlisted in the army and left her pregnant. After five years, she married John Collin; when Hannigan returned, he turned her in. Hill gave Mary one week 'served', meaning that she could count the time spent in jail awaiting trial, with the result that she went home immediately. He complained, 'witnesses ought not to have been bound over to prosecute in such a case', and he also denied the costs of the prosecution. The magistrates appealed to the Home Secretary; they were, after all, bound by law to bring a case when the evidence was clear. Though this argument was right in theory, judges believed that the authorities should show discretion in practice.[77]

Indeed, nothing excited the contempt of the justices more than prosecutions brought by public authorities. Justice Willes was outraged by the case of William Brightman, a Lincoln labourer, and his wife, Martha. By 1860, they had been married twenty years and had four children. Brightman became ill that year, so the family appealed to the parish for support. The Poor Law officials soon discovered that both William and Martha had been married before. To save the cost of supporting the family of six, they prosecuted both for bigamy. Willes complained, 'One might have thought … that after the lapse of so long a time no one who had the commonest feelings of man would have ventured to prosecute such a case.' Martha's trial provoked another tirade, in which Willes branded the Poor Law commissioners as 'indiscreet, ill-informed, and most unfeeling'. He gave William and Martha a one-day sentence each and refused to allow the costs. Again the commissioners appealed to the Home Secretary, although they came away empty-handed. Their MP then appealed to the House of Commons, but in vain.[78]

To modern readers, the magistrates who prosecuted poverty-stricken couples come across as cruel and rapacious. On the other hand, they were frustrated by the provisions of the New Poor Law as regards illegitimates, just as when affinal marriages broke down. Men who married bigamously and had children did not have to support their offspring; the temptation to make them pay with a prison term was strong. A woman who married bigamously was an equal problem; her legal husband could not be compelled to support her, nor could her illegal spouse.[79] Though the magistrates might have preferred to punish the absconding father, they may have settled for the satisfaction of punishing the mother. In the case of the Brightmans, the JPs had a strong motive for having her four children declared illegitimate, since this way Martha and her children might be shifted back to her birth parish.[80] In contrast, judges, unconcerned with these local problems, considered these cases 'frivolous', unfairly crowding the assize calendar. Public prosecutions of bigamy cases show an interesting divide within the ruling class for dealing with working-class irregularities, one that worked in the favour of poor defendants.

Judges disdained public prosecutions so regularly, in fact, that in 1894, a chief constable and a commissioner complained to the Home Secretary. The commissioner, in fact, insisted he would not prosecute any more bigamy cases. Both were motivated by a trial in Staffordshire during the winter assizes. The defendant, Rosannah Owen, had been married to William Owen, who, she testified, had ill-treated her and then thrown her out of their home. Justice Mathew stopped the trial there, asking who had prosecuted. A local police constable had done so; furthermore, Rosannah had a good character in her town. At that point, Mathew discharged her with no punishment. The chief constable admitted that this case was not heinous, but argued that 'there may arise some future question of legitimacy of children, so ... there are strong reasons for punishing such offences.' Since most bigamists were working-class, the constable's remarks about property were beside the point to most judges. In contrast, most of them believed, as Justice Hawkins put it in 1898, that couples who had hurt no one should be 'free from the vexatious interference of the law.'[81]

Eventually, the Director of Public Prosecutions came up with a set of guidelines for prosecution. In 1901, when the question of trying Lord Russell for his second marriage, made in America, arose, R. B. Finlay delineated them:

> Firstly, whether the case is in itself a bad one, e.g., where, as not infrequently happens, persons have been in the habit of going through a ceremony of marriage with young women in order, either to obtain possession of their persons or possession of their money; (2) where the circumstances of the case are such as to occasion serious injury either to the wife or the person with whom the second marriage ceremony was gone through.

In Finlay's opinion, Russell's case met neither of these criteria, so he recommended against prosecution. The fact that the Attorney General insisted on the prosecution was more a case of Russell's personal unpopularity than the norm in bigamy trials by the end of the century.[82] Public prosecutions, except in rare instances, did not pay.

If even the legal community could not agree on the desirability of prosecuting bigamy cases, the public's ambivalence is not surprising. In fact, one could argue that these cases are another example of the legal system being influenced from the bottom up. The actions of thousands of ordinary people to expand the marriage law – and the support they received from neighbours, kin, and, eventually, the courts – limited the effectiveness of an entire type of criminal prosecution. These cases, like the violence trials, also partially revise notions of the biases of the Victorian judicial system.

Although their reasoning could be flawed and inequitable, judges did take many circumstances into account in sentencing, which mitigated the conventions of class and gender. In addition, bigamies again emphasised the difficulties of the criminal justice system in dealing with a status with no legal standing. As a result, judges did not impose middle-class standards of morality, nor did they favour men over women; if anything, they did the opposite. Judges' leniency was such, in fact, that they came into conflict with local authorities rather than presenting a united front in favour of legal marriage.

The judges were perhaps more supportive of marriage by their flexibility than by a rigorous execution of the law. They realised that most of the people involved in bigamous unions did not intend to subvert matrimony. For one thing, they wanted to have a ritual and the support of the state. For another, their second, happier unions were better advertisements for marriage than their first, unhappy ones. In fact, reformers argued that the laws meant to support marriage instead undermined it by forcing people to remain in empty unions. As a result, some unhappy couples took little notice of the law. As long as certain rules were followed, most people accepted these bigamous unions.

Though this usually remained unstated, bigamous marriages were, by definition, adulterous. At least one marriage had been broken up, and sometimes both partners had formed second unions. The fact that communities accepted these couples as married anyway disturbed conservatives, but at least bigamists agreed that a marriage ceremony was vital. Not all couples made that choice. Some instead lived together without any wedding at all, openly cohabiting in adultery. Such partnerships offered another, and in some ways, stronger critique of marriage and divorce laws and a redefinition of marriage as a relationship and idea. Not surprisingly, then, they also provoked more disapproval from their families and the wider community.

Notes

1 S. Colwell, 'The incidence of bigamy in 18th and 19th century England', *Family History* 11 (1980), 92; Justice Ridley, 'Increase in bigamy', *Justice of the Peace* 74 (1910), 125.

2 *Parliamentary Papers: Judicial Statistics of England and Wales* (London: Her Majesty's Stationery Office, 1857–1906).

3 G. Savage, 'Defining the boundaries of marital sexuality: Bigamy, incest, and sodomy in the divorce court, 1857–1907', Mid-Atlantic Conference on British Studies Annual Meeting, New Brunswick, NJ, 22 March 2003.

4 J. Skinner, *Journal of a Somerset Rector, 1800–1834*, eds H. Coombs and P. Coombs (Oxford: Oxford University Press, 1984), p. 35; G. Aldred, *From Anglican Boy-Preacher to*

Anarchist Socialist Impossiblist (London: Bakunin Press, 1908), pp. 48–52.

5 I amassed this group of cases from the same newspapers as the violence trials. The years I used were the same in the two provincial newspapers; for the *Times*, I looked at every bigamy case in the index at five-year intervals beginning in 1830 and ending in 1900. I also included cases from law reports and the *Annual Register*. The chronological breakdown was as follows: before 1830: ten cases; 1830–39: eighteen cases; 1840–49: thirty-nine cases; 1850–59: forty-six cases; 1860–69: forty-eight cases; 1870–79: thirty-four cases; 1880–89: forty-eight cases; 1890–99: thirty-three cases; 1900 and after: twenty-eight cases.

6 See, for example, *The Times*, 17 May 1845, p. 8; *Justice of the Peace* 72 (1908), 90; 9 (1845), 624; and 15 (1851), 711. Bentley, *English Criminal Justice*, p. 164.

7 G. W. Bartholomew, 'The origin and development of the law of bigamy', *Law Quarterly Review* 74 (1958), 259–71; see also Bartholomew, 'Polygamous marriages and English criminal law', *Modern Law Review* 17 (1954), 350–4. For the defence of invalidity of first and second marriages, see *Reg. v. Chadwick* (1847); 11 *Justice of the Peace* 140–3; 829–40; and *Reg. v. Allen* (1872); 1 *Law Reports, Crown Cases Reserved* 367–77; 36 *Justice of the Peace* 356–7; 820–2; *The Times*, 6 May 1872, p. 13.

8 See *Yorkshire Gazette*, 16 March 1850, p. 7; *The Times*, 17 July 1850, p. 8.

9 1 *Law Reports, Crown Cases Reserved* (1872), 196–9; *The Times*, 26 April 1869, p. 11; L. Radzinowicz and R. Hood, 'Judicial discretion and sentencing standards: Victorian attempts to solve a perennial problem', *University of Pennsylvania Law Review* 127 (1979), 1288–1349. I thank Dr Stephen White for this reference and for Bartholomew's articles, above.

10 23 *Law Reports, Queen's Bench Division* (1889), 168–203; 54 *Justice of the Peace* (1890), 4–7; *The Times*, 28 January 1889, p. 3.

11 T. J. Gilfoyle, 'The hearts of nineteenth-century men: bigamy and working-class marriage in New York City, 1800–1890', *Prospects* 19 (1994), 135–60; Colwell, 'Incidence of bigamy', p. 95.

12 52 *Justice of the Peace* (1888), 808; *Lancaster Guardian*, 7 March 1868, p. 3.

13 *The Times*, 26 August 1872, p. 9.

14 Derby in *Warwick and Warwickshire Advertiser*, 15 November 1879, p. 3; *The Times*, 17 November 1879, p. 11; Steventon in *The Times*, 20 April 1880, p. 13 (for quote); *Liverpool Mercury*, 20 April 1880, p. 6. See also Colwell, 'Incidence of bigamy', 96.

15 Johnson in *The Times*, 13 July 1830, p. 4; Robertson in *The Times*, 8 May 1855, p. 11.

16 *Annals of Our Time* (1840), p. 70; R. M. Fox, *Drifting Men* (London: The Hogarth Press, 1930), p. 92. Fox was in prison for refusing to fight in World War I. See also *Annual Register* 85 (1843), p. 116; Colwell, 'Incidence of bigamy', 102.

17 *Annual Register* 7 (1764), p. 113; *Lancaster Guardian*, 17 December 1870, p. 2.

18 Prince in *Leeds Daily News*, 24 January 1880, p. 4; Coaley in *The Times*, 11 May 1895, p. 16.

19 Anyone with a job that required work for wages was working class, as well as criminals and those described as 'poor'. Small business owners and clerks were lower-middle class, and those with larger concerns or in the professions were middle class. The small upper class included those with independent incomes or 'gentlemen'. Both Gilfoyle's and Colwell's samples were also overwhelmingly working class, 'Hearts of nineteenth-century men', 137; 'Incidence of bigamy', 101.

20 *Yorkshire Gazette*, 13 June 1885, p. 6.

21 NA, PCOM 1/138, p. 1064; *The Times*, 28 August 1890, p. 11; 12 September 1890, p. 10.

22 Manley in *The Times*, 19 December 1860, p. 9; Dames in *The Times*, 22 April 1885, p. 10;

Western Times, 22 April 1885, p. 3.

23   E. Roberts, *A Woman's Place: An Oral History of Working-Class Women, 1890–1940* (Oxford: Basil Blackwell, 1984); E. Ross, '"Not the sort that would sit on the doorstep": Respectability in pre-World War I London neighbourhoods', *International Labor and Working-Class History* 27 (1985), 39–59; Gillis, *For Better, For Worse*, pp. 248–52; M. Tebbutt, *Women's Talk? A Social History of 'Gossip' in Working-Class Neighbourhoods, 1880–1960* (Aldershot: Scolar Press, 1995); and E. P. Thompson, *Customs in Common: Studies in Traditional Popular Culture* (New York: New Press, 1993), pp. 442–52.

24   Griffiths in *The Times*, 16 March 1850, p. 8; Trouse in *The Times*, 8 August 1885, p. 6; *East Sussex News*, 7 August 1885, p. 5. See also Gilfoyle, 'Hearts of nineteenth-century men', 139–42.

25   *The Times*, 30 March 1854, p. 9; M. L. Shanley, *Feminism, Marriage, and the Law in Victorian England* (Princeton: Princeton University Press, 1989), p. 37.

26   Ainley in *The Times*, 15 July 1840, pp. 6–7 (quote from p. 6); Matthews in *The Times*, 30 November 1900, p. 11 (first quote) and *Bristol Mercury Supplement*, 1 December 1900, p. 6 (second quote).

27   Collen in PCOM 1/43, pp. 284–7; *The Times*, 17 December 1840, p. 7; Galway in PCOM 1/59, p. 505; *The Times*, 8 March 1850, p. 7; see also *The Times*, 3 April 1845, 7; and *Liverpool Mercury*, 4 April 1845, p. 117 (bound).

28   P. Ayers and J. Lambertz, 'Marriage relations, money, and domestic violence in working-class Liverpool, 1919–39', in J. Lewis (ed.), *Labour and Love: Women's Experience of Home and Family, 1850–1940* (Oxford: Basil Blackwell, 1986), 195–219; and E. Ross, '"Fierce questions and taunts": Married life in working-class London, 1870–1914', *Feminist Studies* 8 (1982), 575–602.

29   *Lancaster Guardian*, 10 November 1900, p. 3.

30   Both cases in *Yorkshire Gazette*, 10 March 1855, p. 7; Colwell, 'Incidence of bigamy', 99–100.

31   *The Times*, 10 May 1865, p. 11. See also Emma Hill/Hall in CRIM 10/69, p. 20; *The Times*, 25 March 1880, p. 4.

32   *Annual Register* 84 (1842), 143.

33   *The Times*, 21 November 1865, p. 9.

34   *The Times*, 11 December 1875, p. 11; *Durham County Advertiser*, 10 December 1875, p. 7 (for quote).

35   See *The Times*, 10 December 1870, p. 11; *Hampshire Advertiser and County Newspaper*, 10 December 1870, p. 8; and CRIM 10/2, p. 365; *The Times*, 11 July 1850, p. 7.

36   E. Ross, *Love and Toil: Motherhood in Outcast London, 1870–1918* (Oxford: Oxford University Press, 1993), pp. 84–6; Hammerton, *Cruelty and Companionship*, pp. 34–67; Conley, *The Unwritten Law*, pp. 74–81; A. Clark, *The Struggle for the Breeches: Gender and the Making of the British Working Class* (Berkeley, CA: University of California Press, 1995), pp. 67–87; and Behlmer, *Friends of the Family*, pp. 181–229.

37   Gillis, *For Better, For Worse*, pp. 251–3; Ross, *Love and Toil*, pp. 69–86; Clark, *The Struggle for the Breeches*, pp. 259–63.

38   *The Times*, 21 March 1860, p. 11; *Justice of the Peace* 22 (1858), 454–5; 63 (1899), 795; Gilfoyle, 'Hearts of nineteenth-century men', 150.

39   *The Times*, 12 November 1900, p. 11.

40   See, for instance, *The Times*, 8 February 1850, p. 7; 9 May 1845, p. 14; 13 March 1865, p. 11; *Staffordshire Advertiser*, 11 March 1865, p. 5; 18 March 1865, p. 6.

41 *The Times*, 30 July 1860, p. 11; 12 December 1860, p. 9; 18 December 1860, p. 11; and *Warwick and Warwickshire Advertiser*, 15 November 1879, p. 3; *The Times*, 17 November 1879, p. 11; *Women's Suffrage Journal* 11 (1880), 6.

42 Bickerstaffe in *The Times*, 14 March 1860, p. 12; *Yorkshire Gazette*, 17 March 1860, p. 4; Greene in PCOM 1/60, pp. 471–73; *The Times*, 22 August 1850, pp. 6–7.

43 Jones in *The Times*, 24 August 1850, p. 7; Green in *Illustrated Police News*, 2 July 1898, p. 2.

44 Moran in *The Times*, 26 October 1855, p. 9; Curgenwen in *The Times*, 7 August 1865, p. 9; *Cornish Times*, 5 August 1865, p. 4; 1 *Law Reports, Crown Cases Reserved* (1872), 1–4; 29 *Justice of the Peace* 820–1.

45 *The Times*, 9 June 1830, p. 6.

46 *Leeds Daily News*, 31 March 1890, p. 3; PCOM 1/138, pp. 957–9; *The Times*, 1 August 1890, p. 10; and 30 March 1854, p. 9.

47 Windsor in *Leeds Daily News*, 6 August 1875, p. 6; Jessop in *Lancaster Guardian*, 5 March 1870, p. 3; Potling in *The Times*, 22 April 1830, p. 3.

48 *Annual Register*, 'Chronicle', 81 (1838), 122–3.

49 Scoltock in *The Times*, 22 March 1890, p. 5; Young in *Justice of the Peace* 71 (1907), 401.

50 For judges, see *The Times*, 12 July 1845, p. 8; and 20 April 1880, p. 13; for newspapers' terms see *The Times*, 8 March 1850, p. 7; and 19 December 1855, p. 11.

51 Gillis, *For Better, For Worse*, p. 229; Clark, *Struggle for the Breeches*; and S. Rose, *Limited Livelihoods: Gender and Class in Nineteenth-Century England* (Berkeley, CA: University of California Press, 1992).

52 Thompson, *Customs in Common*, p. 430.

53 Courtney in *The Times*, 16 November 1900, p. 10; *Western Times*, 15 November 1900, p. 3; Calvert in *Yorkshire Gazette*, 10 March 1855, p. 7; Cobbett in *Royal Commission on Divorce and Matrimonial Causes* 3 vols [Vols. 18–20 of *Parliamentary Papers* of 1912] (London: His Majesty's Stationery Office, 1912), I, 403.

54 Weaver in *The Times*, 13 March 1865, p. 11; Goode in PCOM 1/118, p. 687 and *The Times*, 20 October 1880, p. 4 (for quote).

55 Garden in *The Times*, 17 March 1845, p. 8; Rogerson in *The Times*, 12 December 1900, p. 14.

56 *The Times*, 19 August 1884, p. 3; 28 August 1884, p. 3; quote from 19 August.

57 Gillis, *For Better, For Worse*, pp. 190–228; B. Taylor, *Eve and the New Jerusalem: Socialism and Feminism in the Nineteenth Century* (London: Virago, 1983), pp. 47–53.

58 Aldred, *From Anglican Boy-Preacher*, p. 48. See also PCOM 1/43, pp. 284–7; *The Times*, 17 December 1840, p. 7; 31 July 1861, p. 1; and CRIM 10/86, pp. 77–8 (1895).

59 *Yorkshire Gazette*, 14 January 1860, p. 9. See also *The Times*, 22 March 1890, p. 5.

60 PCOM 1/59, p. 391; *The Times*, 6 February 1850, p. 7 (for quote).

61 PCOM 1/138, pp. 959–60; trial on 31 July 1890.

62 PCOM 1/60, p. 221; *The Times*, 15 June 1850, p. 7 (for quote). For other examples, see *The Times*, 26 October 1855, p. 9; 26 November 1840, p. 6; and *Yorkshire Gazette*, 17 March 1860, p. 4.

63 Dwyer in *The Times*, 8 December 1860, p. 9; Fanning in *The Times*, 28 October 1865, p. 11; and 10 *Cox's Criminal Cases* (1864–7), 411–15.

64 David in *The Times*, 8 January 1840, p. 7; Stephens in *The Times*, 21 March 1860, p. 11; *Lewes Times*, 21 March 1860, p. 1 (for quote).

65 Barnes in *The Times*, 3 March 1865, p. 12; *Leicester Chronicle*, 4 March 1865, p. 8 (for quote); Green in *The Times*, 10 March 1830, p. 7; Nield in *Lancaster Guardian*, 11 March 1865, p. 2.

66 Wardle in *Women's Suffrage Journal*, 14 (1883), 222; Gibbons in *The Times*, 30 July 1895, p. 5. S. P. Menefee, *Wives for Sale: An Ethnographic Study of British Popular Divorce* (Oxford: Basil Blackwell, 1981); Thompson, *Customs in Common*, pp. 404–66.

67 PCOM 1/60, p. 221; *The Times*, 15 June 1850, p. 7; and *Swansea and Glamorgan Herald and the Herald of Wales*, 28 April 1880, p. 4.

68 Thomas in *The Times*, 9 August 1855, p. 11; Morant in *The Times*, 26 August 1872, p. 9.

69 Frost in *The Times*, 23 August 1850, p. 6; Gibbon in *The Times*, 1 August 1872, p. 10.

70 *The Times*, 8 June 1900, p. 6; *Dorset County Chronicle and Somersetshire Gazette*, 7 June 1900, p. 9.

71 Erle in *The Times*, 30 March 1854, p. 9; Cockburn in *The Times*, 3 March 1865, p. 12.

72 Colwell, 'Incidence of bigamy', 102. See also Gilfoyle, 'Hearts of nineteenth-century men', 151–2.

73 *The Times*, 14 March 1860, p. 12; Conley, *The Unwritten Law*, p. 174.

74 For a very young woman, see *The Times*, 26 October 1855, p. 9; for a mercenary motive, see *The Times*, 21 May 1845, p. 8. Malcolm in *The Times*, 20 October 1885, p. 3; 21 October 1885, p. 3; 22 October 1885, p. 3; 23 October 1885, p. 3; 25 October 1885, p. 8; 26 October 1885, pp. 3, 9 (quote on p. 3).

75 Gore in *The Times*, 7 July 1840, p. 4; Jeune in *Justice of the Peace*, 64 (1900), 42.

76 Birkhead in *Lancaster Guardian*, 24 March 1860, p. 6; *Yorkshire Gazette*, 17 March 1860, p. 10; quote from *Lancaster Guardian*; Calverly in *Yorkshire Gazette*, 17 March 1860, p. 4; Calvert in *Yorkshire Gazette*, 10 March 1855, p. 7.

77 *Lancaster Guardian*, 31 March 1860, p. 6; NA, HO 45/O.S. 6995; TS 25/1100. Hill's letter dated 25 June 1860 in Home Office file. The magistrates did get the costs back, about £12.

78 HO 45/O.S. 6999; for the MP's appeal, see *Yorkshire Gazette*, 2 June 1860, p. 3.

79 *Justice of the Peace* 31 (1867), 718.

80 Thane, 'Women and the poor law', 35–38.

81 Constable in HO 45 9744/A56594; Hawkins quoted in *Adult* 2 (1898), 61.

82 NA, DPP 1/6; R. B. Finlay to the Attorney General, 24 April 1901. E. L. Russell, *Though the Heavens Fall* (London: Cassell and Company, 1956), pp. 58–82. I thank Dr Gail Savage for the DPP reference.

5

Adulterous cohabitation

MOST COUPLES who could not marry because of previous unions did not go through another ceremony. Middle-class couples, in particular, avoided breaking the law, but many working-class couples were also cautious. Though they escaped criminal sanctions, these couples' relationship with the state was not severed, but, in some ways, more vexed. They also faced social difficulties; open adultery was a much more serious offence than affinal unions, especially for women. The social stain did not convince such couples that they were in the wrong, though; many, to the contrary, argued that their cohabitation was a true marriage, unlike the broken unions they had fled. They questioned the meaning of marriage openly, refusing to accept that legal and religious rituals defined it.

Nonetheless, these relationships were not the same as marriages, as most of the participants were well aware, since adulterous unions had great legal and social consequences. Thus, those in them were touchy about their social position, and the women, especially, worried about the future. Though the middle class railed against the laws of marriage, then, they regularised their unions whenever they could. In short, these unions had special tensions, awkward beginnings, and even more problematic endings. The experience also differed by class, as the middle class concentrated on justifying their decisions, while the working class focused more on the financial strains. In addition, as with bigamy cases, the working-class community was more supportive of marital nonconformity. All in all, adulterous cohabitees experienced great ambivalence in their family lives and at law.

Motives and means

Marital breakdown was complex and varied, but the law recognised only adultery as grounds for divorce, and women had to prove an additional offence as well. Parliament had compromised between those who wanted to uphold the indissolubility of marriage and those who wanted several grounds, as well as those who wanted only men to be able to divorce and those who wanted equal grounds between the sexes. The result was a bill that accepted the idea of marriage as a relationship, but narrowly limited the ways to end it. All the same, Parliament had secularised divorce, endangering marriage's sacramental character. Because of that, future governments could, in theory, expand the grounds for divorce to include many other offences. This was especially tempting to those who emphasised the importance of love and respect to any 'real' marriage.[1]

Those few middle-class couples who chose to live in adultery in the nineteenth century, then, fell into the latter group. Nevertheless, to justify their actions, they had to convince themselves that the first marriage was irretrievably dead and for good reason. They also had to believe that the law of divorce was out of date with the realities of married life. In practice this usually meant two things. First, the second union occurred some time after the breakdown of the legal marriage, so that the cohabitees would not be 'homewreckers'. Second, the participants were in professions that had wider sexual norms, such as art, acting, or literature, and were more willing to challenge marriage laws.

Couples justified cohabitation on causes that mirrored the list of suggested divorce reforms in the late nineteenth century. First, those with mentally ill spouses argued that they should be able to find happiness elsewhere. Novelist Mary Braddon lived with John Maxwell, her publisher, for years because his wife was insane. Her case is famous, but such problems existed more broadly. An infanticide case in 1872, for example, revealed that the respectable Mrs Morrall had been forced to take in lodgers after her husband went to the insane asylum in 1871. She eventually cohabited with one, having his child in September 1872.[2] A second reason was desertion, especially for women. In the early part of the century, Jane Cleveland justified two cohabiting relationships, one to Edward Williams and one to Jefferson Hogg, because her army officer husband had ill-treated and deserted her.[3] Third, violence and drunkenness destroyed marriages, though these show up less often in the middle classes than in the working classes. Still, some men and women refused to stay with brutal or alcoholic partners, as Cleveland's case demonstrates.

Most observers of such hard cases agreed that the wronged spouses were victims. They might not approve of the solution, but they could still recognise the problems such spouses faced. A much more troubling situation was that of couples who were simply incompatible. The middle-class emphasis on the centrality of the love relationship between spouses meant that those with differences of temperament and interests could argue that their unions were not 'true'. One writer during the 'Is Marriage a Failure?' controversy from 1888 blamed the age difference with his much older wife for the end of his marriage. He and his wife separated after ten years, and he now lived happily with 'a worthy girl some five years my junior.'[4] Others just had different interests. Henrietta Hodson, an actress, left her solicitor husband to return to the stage, stultified by her life as a lawyer's wife. She fell in love with Henry Labouchere, and they lived together until her husband divorced her.[5] The English courts did not recognise incompatibility as grounds to end a marriage, but for those in uncongenial unions, the alternatives were bleak.

'Incompatibility' was a vague term, but one problem appeared repeatedly. Professional men often claimed that their wives did not support their work. In other words, many middle-class men wanted wives who could share in their interests. Few women were both domestic angels and professionals, especially if they had children, so the marriages ran into difficulties. Thomas Southwood Smith and his second wife Mary became estranged early in their marriage. Years later, in the 1830s, he set up a household with Margaret Gillies. In contrast to his legal marriage, Thomas and Margaret built relationship by collaborating on his reform work.[6] Similarly, novelist George Gissing separated from his mercurial wife Edith in March 1898, due to their contrary temperaments. He met his eventual cohabitee, Gabrielle Fleury, in July. Gissing's happiness with Fleury led to a renewed enthusiasm for writing, and he considered her intelligence one of her main attractions.[7]

In all these examples, the partners had not begun the second union until the first had irrevocably ended. In other cases, though, the unhappy spouses did not end the marriage until a new partner had come along. The consequences were so serious in marital break-ups that many people only faced up to it when they could look forward to a happier union. W. J. Fox, a Unitarian minister and social reformer, married Eliza Florence in 1820. The marriage was unhappy; Fox complained that he wanted only 'a moderate share of comfort, a disposition to help me in my exertions … and economy in the management of their fruits', but his wife failed him. He did little to resolve the situation, however, until he had fallen in love with Eliza Flower in 1829; he separated from Mrs Fox in 1832.[8] Again, the need for someone to 'help me in my exertions' was crucial; Flower was Fox's intellectual equal. But Fox only left his wife when he had hope for a better situation.

The most disapproved adulterous union was one that broke up a surviving, if not flourishing, marriage. 'Coming between man and wife' was a serious wrong, and the social stigma had long-lived effects. If the adulterous partner was a man, he probably would have preferred to keep both mistress and wife rather than make the break. T. E. Lawrence's father, Thomas Chapman, ran off with the family governess in 1887. He only did so, though, because his wife gave him an ultimatum, forcing him to choose between his families. If wives were accommodating, or ignorant, the man could keep both. Roger Ackerley, a businessman, kept two mistresses with two separate families in the *fin-de-siècle*. Though he married one of the women in 1919, he never entirely broke his connection with his other family.[9]

Indeed, discretion was the key to a successful *ménage à trois*. William Bell Scott, an associate of the Pre-Raphaelite movement, stayed married to his wife of twenty years after falling in love with Alice Boyd in 1859. In the summer and early autumn, he went to Alice's family home; in mid-autumn, the two returned to London for the winter. Scott made no break with his wife and carefully described his relationship with Boyd as a 'perfect friendship' in his memoirs.[10] Such cases point out the much greater sexual freedom of men in the Victorian period; I have no examples of women who lived with two men or had separate houses with a husband and lover. In contrast, some wives tolerated adultery as long as the situation remained discreet; indeed, with their legal and economic disabilities, they had little choice.

Such cases demonstrated that conservatives' concern about the consequences of secularising marriage and divorce had some basis in fact. If individual love and happiness were the primary points of marriage, incompatibilities of various kinds justified separations. Still, the supporters of divorce reform could have replied that denying all divorce did not stop separations from happening; if anything, wronged spouses lived 'in sin' more often when they had no possibility for remarriage. The compromise of the divorce bill was the result of these two points of view; like all compromises, it satisfied neither side.

A 'real' marriage?

Because of the seeming irrationality of the divorce law, adulterous couples argued that theirs were 'true' marriages of heart and soul. Most of the couples took each other's names, called each other husband and wife, and considered themselves married. Belief in the purity of the bond was necessary to continue living in what was otherwise simple adultery. Marian Evans eloped with the married George Henry Lewes in 1854. She took his name, called him her husband all of her life, and believed the union to be 'a sacred bond.' Similarly, Gissing considered Fleury his wife, and she took his name. They also went through some sort of marriage ceremony, probably a simple exchange of rings.[11] Violet Hunt always insisted that she and Ford Madox Ford, who lived together in the Edwardian period, had gone through a ceremony in France, though it did not stand up to scrutiny in court.[12] Most of these couples did not wish to criticise marriage – in fact, most wanted to marry – so they acted out the roles as much as possible.

Despite their resemblance to marriage, these unions challenged the Victorian marital regime broadly, since they had no religious or legal sanctions. The couples justified their decisions by blaming the law rather than themselves. The rigidity of English marriage law received scorn, since it shackled unhappy spouses together for life. Gissing, for example, raged, 'What vile, what an insensate law, is the law of divorce in England. A man is moulted, outraged, ill-used day after day, month after month, year after year … finally, he is *driven from home*, with every brutality that can be uttered – and the law refuses to break such a marriage!'[13] Gissing's cry was common to those unhappily yoked; since the law was unjust, rebellion was the only moral choice.

As Gissing's anger shows, most cohabitees would have preferred to marry; similarly to all the cohabitees in this section, they did not revolt against marriage per se. In fact, most tried to find ways to marry before settling for cohabitation. Evans and Lewes explored the option of divorce in 1860, though they found that they could not do so (because Lewes had 'condoned' his wife's adultery).[14] Ford went to Germany to obtain German citizenship so that he could divorce his wife, ignoring his lawyers' opinion that the English courts would not accept it. Gissing tried for months to find a way to marry Fleury, though he had the same problem as Ford.[15] Moreover, when couples became free to marry, they did so readily, including Labouchere and Hodson and Braddon and Maxwell. They were thrilled to be able to regularise their unions, despite their claims that they were 'already' married in every important sense. Clearly, they contradicted themselves with this reaction, but it was, in part, the result of the legal and social, rather than emotional, benefits of marriage.

Consequences

However much these relationships resembled a 'true' marriage, they were legally null, and the consequences were considerable. Adulterous cohabitees experienced the difference from the start. When a couple married, they sent out wedding invitations and a public announcement. When a couple lived together, they had to be more discreet. They wrote to friends and family first, an anxiety-producing experience, especially for the women. Most received mixed responses; some friends stayed loyal, while others refused to see them again. Marian Evans lost touch with her family, especially her censorious brother Isaac. He did not communicate with her again until she married legally after Lewes's death, twenty-five years later.[16] Braddon's brother disapproved of her union with Maxwell and so naturally snubbed Mary and John, but he also ostracized his own mother, who had accepted it. Hunt's sisters never approved of Ford. When their relationship became a scandal, her sister Sylvia forbade her daughter to visit her aunt, and she also sued Violet over the care of their mother.[17]

The women's families were the most dismayed, knowing that the main scorn would fall on them. Women who chose to accept the social costs, then, tended to be unusually independent. In fact, many middle-class women involved in free unions had lost their fathers, including Flower, Evans, Hunt, Fleury, and Boyd. The loss of their fathers meant that these women had to make their own ways in the world, but also that they were freer to make their own decisions. Women who supported themselves were also more liberated, even if their fathers were alive. For instance, Gillies had left home to become an artist when she met Southwood Smith. These women had more negotiating room for setting up unconventional households, though they still took the brunt of disapproval from kin and society.

Men's families might be more sympathetic than women's, since men had more sexual freedom. Unless the family was religious or had close ties to the first wife, they were not devastated. In addition, many men already had children with the first wife, so issues of inheritance did not occur. Gissing's siblings were generally pleased when he told them about his relationship with Fleury. One brother wrote, 'I can't enough rejoice that you have had this solace ... Pray give my sincerest greetings to your good, brave more-than-wife.'[18] The sexual double standard also meant that kin might blame the wife more than the husband for marital collapses. H. G. Wells delayed telling his family that he was leaving his first wife, his cousin Isabel, for Amy Catherine Robbins until the divorce was in progress. But his relatives did not cut him, because, he claimed, his mother 'was so amazed at Isabel "letting me go," and so near indignation about it that she quite forgot to be shocked at the immorality of my situation.'[19]

More often, though, men's families were appalled, and this could have financial consequences for the couple. Thomas Chapman (T. E. Lawrence's father) had to sign over his estate to his brother in order to support his second family and never saw his four daughters again. In addition, because his sons were all illegitimate, his title passed out of his branch of the family.[20] Jefferson Hogg's family refused to accept his cohabitation with

Jane Williams, though the two lived together from 1826 until Hogg's death in 1862. He had to leave his work as a barrister and instead get a position as a professor, and he was financially insecure for years.[21]

Economic woes were particularly a problem for those with two households. Harold Frederic, an American novelist, had grown apart from his wife Grace when the family moved to England in the 1880s. He met Kate Lyon in the early 1890s, and persuaded her to live with him, but he did not leave his wife. Instead, he lived with his wife in the suburbs at weekends, and spent the rest of the week with Kate and, eventually, their three children. Keeping up two wives and seven children cost him £1400 per year, an amount he could ill afford.[22] Frederic was not alone in his money worries. The cost of eloping could get men into serious trouble. John Griegg, the married surveyor for Blackpool in 1860, fell in love with a boarding-house keeper. They eloped, but they were soon apprehended, since Griegg had embezzled money to pay for the escape.[23]

Since few men could afford to keep up two establishments, one of the families usually suffered, especially after the man's death. The cohabiting family was the most likely to face hardships, as they had few legal rights. Linn Boyd Porter visited the Lyon/Frederic household in 1899 and foresaw the problems for Lyon's brood: 'had they been mine I could never have closed my eyes in slumber ... any moment might plunge them into an Inferno'. These concerns were not illusory. After Frederic's death, friends took up a collection of £270 for the legitimate family, and Frederic's family took them in. Lyon's children received only £50 when Stephen and Cora Crane tried to raise money for them. Similarly, Roger Ackerley had drained his finances by the time of his death in his efforts to support two families. His legal wife and children got a pension, but his irregular family struggled on alone.[24]

In addition to economic worries, couples faced severe social sanctions, especially the women. Flower, who always insisted that her relationship with Fox, though emotionally intimate, was sexually pure, was hurt when her friends did not believe her. One of them told her 'she is determined ... to shew by deed and word that she no longer associates with me', Flower wrote to a more loyal friend, Harriet Taylor.[25] Williams had almost no social life, due to Hogg's family's hostility, and this made her separations from him much more difficult. Similarly, Evans had years of isolation before her standing as a novelist (as George Eliot) and her wealth allowed her more leeway. Lewes lost some of his friends, but he largely went out as he always had. In contrast, Evans remained at home, though her isolation was, in part, self-imposed, due to her fear of snubs.[26] The only way to avoid this social consequence was to hide the adulterous connection. T. E. Lawrence's parents went under assumed names ('Mr and Mrs Chapman') and moved frequently to avoid detection. Ironically, though, this method still left them isolated, since they were afraid to develop intimate friendships, for fear of exposing their secret.[27]

Social ostracism was only one possible negative response to adulterous unions. Middle-class men needed contacts and references to be successful; in other words, Victorian professional life depended on reputation. As a result, marital scandals could be disastrous. Clergymen faced particular difficulties, for obvious reasons. In 1860, Revd W. Prosser, a married curate in Durham, ran away with his lover, a servant, when their 'improper intimacy' came to light. Unsurprisingly, he had lost his curacy as soon as the scandal broke, and his chances of advancement in his profession were slim indeed after such an episode. In the 1880s, William Ross, the rector of Belfast, fell in love with the wife of the Commissioner of Emigration, a Mrs Foy. When she became pregnant, they ran away together. Two years later, Mr Foy discovered Ross giving a public lecture in Plymouth. The outraged husband disrupted the talk, denouncing Ross and causing a near riot. Mrs Foy stood by her second mate, but Ross was convicted of unlawful wounding and fined £50. Similarly, a married doctor in Lancashire, Thomas Wardleworth, sold up all of his property and his practice and ran away with Miss Bell, the daughter of a Wesleyan minister. He was unable to practice long, however, since he was traced by journalists and forced to flee again.[28]

Legal difficulties also abounded. In both 1864 and 1874, Maxwell misrepresented his marital situation to the press, saying he and Braddon were married. Both times his brother-in-law, Richard Knowles, contradicted him publicly, causing great humiliation, and, in 1874, the resignation of their entire domestic staff.[29] Ford (then known as Hueffler) told a reporter that he had divorced his wife in Germany and married Hunt, when, in fact, he done neither. Violet then changed her name to Hueffler, and other publications repeated the falsehood, most notably the *Throne*. Hueffler's wife Elsie promptly sued for libel. The case not only bankrupted the *Throne*, but destroyed Violet's reputation. Her godfather cut her out of his will, and her society friends snubbed her.[30]

Because of these difficulties, couples were touchy and saw slights where they were not intended, just as some affinal couples did. Charles Matthews invited Maxwell and Braddon to a party and sent them separate invitations; Maxwell immediately wrote a reproving letter. Matthews pleaded ignorance, but the incident showed the sensitivity of many couples.[31] Though it was frustrating to cohabitees to have to assert their respectability at every turn, one can have some sympathy with confused friends, since pseudo-wives made for unusual social problems. Hunt's name situation, for instance, caused considerable anxiety. Douglas Goldring, a close friend, did not know what to call her: "'Miss Hunt" sounded unfriendly … while "Mrs. Hueffer" might lead to further reprisals from the successful litigant.' As Mr Wild, the defence barrister for the *Throne*, put it, 'when a woman passed as a man's wife … What on earth were they to call her?' Most of Violet's friends wrote her as Mrs Hueffler, ignoring the risks. Friends of cohabitees would be baffled by similar social dilemmas throughout the period.[32]

Adulterous unions had other, more serious, legal problems. Any mother who lived in adultery risked losing her children. In a case in 1899, a widow living with a married man lost her five younger children to her husband's brothers, since an adulteress was not a 'proper' person to rear children.[33] Even without issues of custody, couples faced difficult legal choices. Fleury was unwilling to sign documents in her maiden name, so she gave all of her property to her mother, including her house. She thus risked losing half of her property to her brother when her mother died.[34] The issue of wills was particularly vexed. As with affinal unions, men had to call women by their maiden names, which they hated doing. And disputes over inheritance could be ugly. Frederic left the American copyrights of his novels and their house to Lyon. He left his legal wife their home as well as the English copyrights, but the latter were heavily mortgaged. Grace tried to get Kate to turn over the American copyrights, but Kate refused. Grace retaliated by prosecuting Lyon for manslaughter, since, as a Christian Scientist, she had refused medical attention for Frederic when he was dying. Though she was acquitted, the trial was so traumatising that the children would not speak of it decades later.[35]

Despite social and legal slights, one should not overstate the women's isolation. Women who shared irregular pasts stuck together, while broad-minded friends remained loyal. Williams was close friends with Mary Shelley after their return to England. Barbara Smith and Bessie Raynor Parkes remained friends with Evans, in defiance of their families' wishes, as did the Bray family. In fact, some women may have preferred life in the demimonde to a stultifying respectability, particularly if they had an alternate social group, and better-off couples could also go abroad where social life was laxer. Mary Costelloe left her husband, a lawyer, for artist Bernhard Berenson in the 1890s; they lived in Italy most of their lives.[36] In short, ostracism was serious, but rarely unanimous.

Successes and failures

The difficulties of making adulterous 'marriages' were many; those who agreed to make them, then, were unusual. Many of the prominent cohabitees were from circles which retained a tinge of unrespectability (such as the theatre). In addition, some couples, like Gillies and Southwood Smith, disdained orthodoxy; I will explore their opinions in the final two chapters of this book. All the same, most were normally conventional, yet lived in breach of the law. Why? Of first importance was the emotional attachment. Leaving with a lover was romantic and exciting, and many women and men made the decision while still in the first flush of happiness and rebellion. In addition, as in bigamous unions, most partners believed that the first marriage was a failure. Women accepted men's characterisations of their first wives as adulterous, bad-tempered, or unhelpful; they, then, could redeem the men's lives. As Hunt put it, 'I was full, not of Love, but of Loving-kindness, and obsessed by the permanent illusion of all women that they can Save.'[37] For their part, men felt protective towards women who had been deserted or brutalised, also accepting the women's explanations for the failures of their first unions. The combination of emotional attachment and a desire to save led most to believe that the first marriage was a legal shell.

As in bigamy cases, some of these second 'marriages' were spectacular successes. Gissing insisted that Lyon 'saved' Frederic: 'But for his true companion, his real wife, this work would never have been done … she saved him & enabled him to do admirable things.'[38] Another example was Gissing himself; biographers agree that his last years with Fleury were the happiest of his life. Other unions showed their success by their longevity. Boyd and Bell Scott remained a couple for thirty-one years. Their relationship was so well known that his friends sent condolences to Alice rather than Letitia when Scott died.[39] Williams and Hogg lived together for thirty-six years, and Gillies and Southwood Smith did so for over twenty. Evans and Lewes, the most famous example, stayed together twenty-four years with no outward sign of discontent. Biographers disagree about whether they were actually perfectly happy, but few contemporaries doubted it.[40]

These couples were not only good for each other, but often for other family members as well. Flower was a successful stepmother to Fox's oldest daughter as well as his deaf son, and she was also close to his mother and sister. Gillies acted as an aunt/stepmother to Gertrude Hill, Southwood Smith's adopted grandchild.[41] Evans got along with Lewes's three sons, though biographers debate how much she wanted this responsibility. Still, she supported them with her earnings, and she left her estate to Lewes's surviving child, Charles. Mary Braddon's five stepchildren loved her, and the family was both busy and happy, particularly after she added six more children to the brood.[42] These stable families made a strong argument for divorce reform, since they had few bad consequences and numerous good ones. Rather than destroying families, they strengthened them.

On the other hand, some of these unions failed spectacularly. As in legal marriages, the reasons were as various as the people involved, but some commonalities appear. First, many of the men, such as Wells and Ford, had well-established patterns of unfaithfulness. The decision to live with a man who had already deserted his wife, then, was risky. Second, the difficulties of some of these unions came out of the strong wills of both of the partners; women independent enough to choose a free union were also unwilling to sublimate their desires to men. In fact, such women resented their partners' comparative freedom. Whatever the reasons, the ends of free unions were fraught with difficulties. Since the couple had never been married, they could not divorce, so neither partner knew how to achieve closure.

An example of these difficulties was the case of H. G. Wells and Rebecca West, who first became lovers in 1913 when Wells was married to his second wife. From the beginning, West resented Wells's freedom, which was even more noticeable after she had his child in August 1914. She was stuck in the country with no one for company, and she also resented the interruption to her career. Their serious problems surfaced in 1919; West wanted Wells either to marry her or give her an allowance (for the child) and let her go, but he resisted. Then, in 1921, Wells became ill and expected West to nurse him; he was also unfaithful. Since he did not visit West when she was ill in 1920 and was as jealous of her as if they were married, West saw few reasons to stay in a union that gave her all the duties of a wife without the advantages. She initiated the break in March 1923. A combination of infidelity, two strong wills, and West's independence led to a long succession of quarrels.[43]

Facing up to the failure of a free union was difficult, particularly for women, since they were often economically dependent. In addition, they were socially isolated already; being a deserted fallen woman was one of the few situations that was worse. The pattern for cohabiting break-ups, then, was one of desertion (usually by the man), but not quickly or cleanly. As stated above, West and Wells had serious problems as early as 1919, but the relationship dragged on until West went to America in 1923.[44] Hunt and Ford drew apart as the First World War loomed, when Ford enlisted in the army. All the same, Ford only left Violet for Stella Bowen, an Australian painter, after the war. Even after he was gone, Violet could not let go, insisting that her years of cohabitation gave her the right to stay in his life.[45] Unsurprisingly, Ford did not agree, and he moved to France to be sure of a complete break.

In short, unless one of the partners was ruthless, cohabiting unions died a slow death. Men felt guilty, and women faced major economic and social difficulties. Having insisted their unions were 'truer' than many marriages, couples were chagrined to discover their free unions also fell apart. This was the danger of defining marriage by emotional attachments alone, since the latter could change rapidly. Problems also developed because of couples' confusion about what they wanted from these unchartered relationships. Most of these men wanted intellectual companions, but they also wanted women who would take care of domestic matters and consider their careers secondary to men's. Successful relationships tended to be like that of Flower, who ran Fox's home, did secretarial work for him, and was a stepmother to his children, to the neglect of her musical career.[46] Unions that mirrored Victorian gender roles, then, were more likely to survive, though at a cost for the women.

A few rare relationships were happy with independent women, though only when the women's careers did not challenge domestic roles. Braddon and Maxwell had a successful marriage with Braddon continuing to write her novels, though she also ran the house. The same could be said of Evans and Lewes; Lewes strongly encouraged her writing, but he did not take over domestic duties. Gillies and Southwood Smith lived together for twenty years, and she had a successful painting career. In fact, when Southwood Smith lost his job on the Board of Health, she was the main breadwinner. He did not object to her work; on the contrary, he helped her get some of her commissions. As a result of this equality, as well as their shared beliefs in Unitarianism and social reform, theirs was a happy home, lasting until Southwood Smith's death in 1861.[47] Some adulterous unions, then, were both happy and relatively equal, but these were the exceptions.

In addition, even in a successful union, the woman knew that her position was delicate. Though without the legal advantages of marriage, male cohabitees still had more power. Thus, any separation or quarrel was magnified. Williams suffered from Hogg's frequent absences, and wrote to him, in 1833 that her 'health has suffered so cruelly by this abominable absence, that I can bear nothing.' Rather than reassuring her, Hogg's reply scolded her for making him feel guilty, a letter that must have been hard to bear. All relationships had ups and downs, but for a cohabiting woman, the down periods were especially frightening.[48] Women cohabitees had good reason to fear desertion, especially if the men had already left their wives. In addition, female cohabitees were wary of hostile family influence. Fleury left Gissing in London after a brief trip and returned to France to care for her ailing mother in 1901. Gissing's friends persuaded him to stay in England for medical care, which alarmed Gabrielle. She wrote several letters, worried that his family would try to get him to go back to his second wife.[49] She summarised her fears in a letter: 'I should have very much preferred to have all these people living *with* us, *beside* us, rather than *between* us'. Gissing returned to France after his treatment, so Fleury had underestimated him, but her fears were not unrealistic. Like most cohabitees, she had anxieties unknown to wives.[50]

Middle-class adulterous cohabitation showed both the possibilities and limitations to marital rebellion. These couples defined marriage broadly, but only so they could marry themselves. As usual with the middle class, rebellion was limited, and the fallout redounded more on the women than the men. Despite having financial resources, these couples had severe economic strain, and they handled both the beginnings and ends of their unions awkwardly. Still, for some of these couples, the happiness of their unions mitigated the worst of the social disapprobation, and their isolation was not total even at the height of Victorian respectability.

Working-class adulterous cohabitation

The restrictions of the divorce law hit the working class harder than better-off couples, since few could afford the process even with legal grounds. Working-class women, especially, faced an uphill battle. Unsurprisingly, then, numerous sources indicate that working-class adulterous cohabitation was widespread. At the Royal Commission on Marriage and Divorce in 1912, John Palin, a police missionary, gave typical testimony when he stated that in his district in Yorkshire, one neighbourhood had seven cohabiting couples, four of which were adulterous. Appendix XI of the report included 160 cases of separated married couples; in 47 of these, at least one of the partners was already living with someone else.[51] In 1911, the Women's Cooperative Guild surveyed its members about divorce reform, and the report included stories of 76 couples with marital problems. Of these couples, 30 had at least one of the partners living with someone else after the marriage ended.[52]

Historians' work on self-divorce also indicates a large number of adulterous unions. S. P. Menefee and E. P. Thompson have shown that wife sales continued into the nineteenth century. Menefee identified approximately 270 wife sales between 1800 and 1900, though most were in the first half of the century. Thompson's sample included 42 cases between 1760 and 1800, 121 between 1800 and 1840 and 55 between 1840 and 1880. Wife sales were not the norm in self-divorce, and these numbers are small. But since the majority of self-divorces would have been unrecorded, they indicate acceptance of separations followed by irregular cohabitation.[53] In addition, in my cases involving violence, over 40 per cent of the couples

(92 of 217) had at least one partner married to someone else. In short, such couples were a significant portion of working-class cohabitees, probably half. If one factored in bigamy cases, the percentage of those who lived together because they were already married was a clear majority of working-class adulterous cohabitees.

Though they avoided criminal sanctions for bigamy, these couples had legal problems, primarily due to the expense of keeping two families. Few working-class men could afford to do so, and they often found themselves charged with neglecting to support a wife or affiliated for illegitimate children. Their relations with the state, then, remained contentious. In addition, their reasons for second unions were similar to those of the middle classes. When they could not live compatibly in early marriages, they refused to submit to an unhappy or celibate future. The working-class community, though, was more tolerant of marital irregularity, since they knew that divorce was costly.

Motives and means

I have already discussed working-class justifications for leaving unhappy marriages in the previous chapter, and many of these were the same in adulterous unions. They also matched the motives of middle-class couples. Illnesses, both mental and physical, justified finding comfort elsewhere, as a wide variety of sources make clear. Mrs T4P, one of Elizabeth Roberts's interviewees in Preston, discussed one of her neighbours, who lived with a married man, since '[h]is wife was a chronic invalid in a chair and they wouldn't be able to live a normal married life'.[54] Mental illnesses could be even more difficult. Ellen Lanigan had to support four children with a small shop after her husband went insane in 1873. She cohabited with a lodger, though he was just as unreliable, leaving her the mother of twins. Mrs S7P, born 1914, also knew a couple who lived together in the early twentieth century because the woman had a 'mentally deranged' husband. She added, 'they lived together until she was 84 but she wasn't promiscuous'.[55]

Infidelity was also a cause, though women tolerated adultery more readily than men. Many of the people who wrote to the Royal Commission of 1912 about infidelity were working-class men, often those who had to be away from home for their jobs or who had lodgers. A good example of both was a man who complained of having come home from a business trip to find his wife in bed with their lodger. She eventually ran away with him, and her husband could not afford to divorce her.[56] Conversely, husbands also deserted wives for other women. Francis Fulford, a rector in Cambridgeshire, had such a situation in his parish. He tried to shame

Thomas Pestill, a shoemaker, into returning to his wife in the 1840s, but with no success. Pestill preferred his new lover.[57]

Working-class couples, too, had incompatibilities which were only compounded when new partners came along. In some marriages, in fact, conflict was endemic. Sarah Cook married William Cook in 1859 and they lived together until 1875. By that time, both became jealous of other people, Sarah of a Miss Clegg and William of a shoemaker named Wyatt. The two quarrelled bitterly, so Sarah left to live with Wyatt until his death in 1879; William lived with Clegg. He was still cohabiting when Sarah became a pauper, and the JPs demanded that he support her. Cook appealed, and the High Court concluded that the couple had lived 'in a state of discomfort, having constant bickerings.' Given these problems, it tacitly approved of the separation by relieving William of his responsibility for Sarah.[58]

Some class differences do emerge from the evidence. Cases of drunkenness and brutality were more common in poor couples. Dr Ethel Bentham, a Fabian, told the 1912 Commission about an artisan who left his drunken wife and hired a housekeeper who soon became his cohabitee. Similarly, Dr Samson Moore, the Medical Superintendent for Huddersfield, sympathised with a woman who left her drunken, violent husband and later lived in a happy irregular union. In addition, women expected men to provide for them or they had the right to leave and find a man who would do so. Elizabeth Lidgett, a member of the St Pancras Board of Guardians, knew a woman who left her husband because he could not find work. When he and their children went to the workhouse, she began living with someone else. She complained when the board would not let her see her children. Lidgett told her the reason was that she was living in adultery, but the woman said 'he was no husband for her, and the one that worked for her she respected.'[59]

As in affinal unions, the interdependence of poor men and women repeatedly comes through. Men needed housekeepers and women needed providers, and neither could live well without the other. Thus, the disappearance or desertion by a spouse was often decisive in causing new unions. Throughout the century, husbands emigrated, went to the army, or got transported or imprisoned for crimes. In all these cases, the wives had to find new breadwinners. These cases point up John Tosh's recent argument that emigration – forced or voluntary – was 'hugely significant', in Victorian England, both because of population decreases and 'socially in terms of the drastic realignments of family and community.'[60] In fact, any long absence could lead to adulterous cohabitation, even if it were temporary, as with sailors. Several women lived with other men while their husbands were at sea. And, in this class, the result of adultery was often two cohabiting couples rather than one. For example, William Simpson, a Leicester solicitor, testified in 1912 that he had many sailor clients who came home to find their wives with new partners. Most could not afford divorce and so they, too, cohabited with new lovers.[61]

In addition, broken marriages in this class were not always bitter. If both partners found new loves, they often agreed to give each other freedom, as many bigamy cases showed. Other sources also have examples of this phenomenon. Charlie Chaplin's parents, both actors, married in 1885, but the marriage effectively ended in 1890. Hannah later lived with another performer, while Charles Senr. lived with a woman known as Louise until his death in 1901. Hannah evinced little jealousy and visited Louise's son in the workhouse after Louise died young.[62] Poor people did not have the luxury of standing on principle. If the first spouse did not work out, they got another, whether the law recognised them as spouses or not.

Consequences

Adulterous unions were not illegal, but the participants still faced intervention from the state. The crux of the matter was that a poor man had to be able to support both families; if he could not, he had to deal with poor law guardians who might arrest a man as a 'vagrant' if he did not support his legal family. The police court in Clerkenwell sentenced Charles Cornell, a gold beater, as a 'rogue and vagabond' when he deserted his wife for another woman in 1863. The new lover had a private income, and Cornell nevertheless had the nerve to plead that he was unemployed and thus unable to support his wife. Mr Barker, the judge, sentenced him to fourteen days at hard labour, considering this conduct 'disgraceful'. Later in the century, after revisions to the poor law in 1868, the magistrates had even more power to compel husbands to maintain their wives and children, since that act allowed summary courts to punish any parent who did not support children under fourteen. Magistrates did not hesitate to use this power. A typical example was Joseph Duffin, who came before the police court in Lancaster in 1890 for neglecting to support his family. His wife testified that for the past three months, Duffin had stayed away 'every Saturday night' and finally left altogether. The reason was his cohabitation with another woman, which the Paisley guardians soon discovered. The magistrate gave him a month in prison, insisting that 'he was a disgrace to manhood.'[63]

If a man wanted to avoid going to jail, he had to accept responsibility and pay a set weekly amount to his legal family, which meant that his new family often had very little money. One man complained to the 1912

Commission that he earned only 18s per week. Out of this, he had to pay his wife 5s, leaving very little for his new family of cohabitee and three children. He feared falling behind on his payments since 'if I cant [sic] pay back arrears I have to go to prison for one month ... while the woman who is one of the best in the world to me has to starve with her three children'.[64] In addition, the legal wives had to go to the workhouse first before they could get help from their erring husbands. In 1888, Agnes Battersby and her husband Matthew had been married fifteen years and had five children when he deserted her for another woman. When she went on relief in 1890, the authorities ordered him to pay 15s per week; how he did this as well as supporting his cohabitee is a mystery. Because of these problems, men sometimes went to elaborate lengths to avoid financial ruin, though their schemes did not always succeed. John Chapman circulated a false report of his death to his wife when he left her for another woman. All the same, she discovered the deception and tracked him down, at which point he told her bluntly that he needed his money to support his new lover and her children. The police court ordered him to pay 10s a week to Mrs Chapman, 'struck with the heartlessness of the defendant'.[65]

Interestingly, legal problems also dogged adulterous wives. Wives who eloped with new lovers had to be careful about what they took with them; otherwise they could be arrested for theft, since the wife's property belonged to her husband. In 1858, the wife of David Kimpton, an upholsterer, ran away with the seventeen-year-old lodger, John Budgin, 'taking with her furniture and wearing apparel to the value of nearly 60l.' Kimpton prosecuted them both for robbery. Husbands were not assured of a victory; judges eventually determined that a mother could take her children's clothing legally. Still, some angry husbands put their wives' lovers behind bars. Robert Elliott successfully prosecuted William Berry, since Berry not only took Mrs Elliott and the couples' three children with him to Leeds, but also 'a bed, two boxes, four pairs of blankets, six sheets, two dresses, and two carpets'.[66] Though most of the problems fell on the husband and wife, some of them spread through divided families. Frank Rowland, a Lancashire solicitor, told the 1912 Royal Commission about one of his clients, whose wife had left him for a lover. The client had five children, and almost all of them got into trouble with the police. Rowland concluded, 'He did whatever he could, but he really could not look after the children as well as working'.[67] Such stories again show how crucial both partners were in a home. Working-class men without wives had either to break up the home, sending their children away, or to take on a housekeeper, who frequently became a de facto wife.[68]

Though men had to provide for two families, social and economic consequences also fell heavily on adulterous women. As in the middle classes, a man who had already left his wife was not always reliable. Given a choice between affiliation proceedings and a prison sentence for neglecting to maintain a wife, most men preferred the former. Hannah G. lived with her aunt in London, and fell in love with the aunt's lodger, Meyer L., a fifty-year-old wine agent. The aunt discovered that Meyer was married, and so sent her niece, who was only eighteen, to work as a nursery maid. Meyer sought Hannah out, and she ran away with him. When Hannah became pregnant, though, he went back to his wife. Similarly, when the woman was the married party, the man could leave her with few anxieties, since he had no legal obligation to her. Frances S. was married, but 'during the Absence of her husband', lived with Samuel H., a baker. Unfortunately, after she became pregnant, Samuel disappeared.[69]

A woman who lived in adultery could expect little help from the disapproving middle class. The authorities were unsympathetic to 'homewreckers', men or women, though they were harder on the latter. For instance, the Foundling Hospital rejected all petitions from adulterous applicants (including those of Hannah and Frances, above). Women who were already married themselves, even if deceived by their deserting partners, also got rejected. Louisa A., a needlewoman, was married to a man who had been transported for a felony, but the Hospital rejected her child with Henry W., a smith, all the same (Henry was also married). In fact, the investigators rarely accepted claims of ignorance. Jane R., a lady's maid, stated that she married a groom, James C., not knowing he was already wed. They stayed together eight months, but he deserted her when she became pregnant. The investigators could find no record of a marriage between Jane and James, so believed Mrs C.'s contention that 'the Petitioner is the principal cause of C---- deserting his Wife & family'. Jane's petition was also rejected.[70]

Moreover, most state agencies would not deal with any adulterous couples no matter what their reasons. Charles Barker, a solicitor in Sunderland, told the 1912 Royal Commission about a pair of unhappily married people who decided to live together. Both their spouses were also living with other people, so their union broke up no homes. Still, when they fell on hard times, the magistrates refused them 'because they were living in adultery'. Nor would private charities help. Dr William Evans, the Chief Medical Officer for Bradford, told the 1912 commissioners about a man whose wife left him and became a prostitute. The man persuaded a servant to live with him, with whom he was happy: 'Yet when ill, no charitable society would come to their assistance, because they were not married.' In order to avoid rewarding immorality, most charities also rejected illegitimate children, and many London crèches would not take them either.[71]

Given this situation, married women were reluctant to cohabit. Several of the witnesses in the 1912 Royal Commission testified that husbands found new partners more quickly after the break-up of a marriage than wives.[72] But women's situation left them vulnerable; though they delayed, they too eventually lived with new mates. A divorce case in 1904 illustrates this point. A woman's husband was violent and unfaithful, and she worked for three years to earn the money for a divorce. Yet the Divorce Court refused her when they found she lived with a 'young gentleman' after she had become ill and lost her job. The judge did not consider her economic plight an adequate excuse for adultery.[73] Because of these problems, many working-class men and women gave up on the idea of divorce and cohabited. Frank Rowland, a Lancashire solicitor, testified about a woman whose unfaithful husband had given her a venereal disease. She had met someone new and wanted a divorce, but Rowland warned her it would cost a minimum of £25 to £30. After eighteen months, she gave up trying to save the money and lived with her new lover. Indeed, even if a woman could resist a new love, she often struggled to live on the maintenance she received from her husband – if she got it at all. One woman who wrote to the Royal Commission had separated from her husband and received maintenance, yet she had to send her two sons to a state home because she could not support them. She was now considering a bigamous marriage proposal because she was 'so longing for my two little lads to be with me again'.[74] With so many incentives, only the strongest-willed women could live for decades, eking out an existence with no hope for remarriage.

Family and friends

The reaction of wider families to adulterous cohabitation varied. Though some families reluctantly accepted it, many were unhappy. In particular, women's families opposed the adultery, seeing only ruin for their daughters. Hannah G.'s aunt, who sent her away from the married lodger, was one such example. Anne Barnham's parents persuaded her to leave Robert Cooper, even though she had two children with him, because he was already married. Similarly, Caroline Woodhead's parents always disliked her relationship with John Brookes, a lacemaker, since she was still married to a printer. After two years, her mother wrote to say that if she would give up Brookes, she could return home. She promptly did so, to Brookes's fury.[75] Though working-class standards were laxer, most families preferred marriage, or at least the hope of one; a man married already could not offer security. Significantly, though, all of these examples indicate that the families did not cut themselves off from erring daughters. On the contrary, they tried to help; disapproval in the working class did not necessarily mean ostracism.

The ambivalence and tensions within the family were mirrored in the attitude of friends and neighbours. Most neighbours were sympathetic if the cases were hard.[76] By 1900, poor couples understood all too well their class disadvantages as regards divorce. A typical letter to the Royal Commission was one from a servant who had separated from her brutal husband. He lived with another woman, but she had no hope for a divorce: 'It seems such hard lines that he should spoil my life and go free.'[77] In 1911, the Women's Cooperative Guild, which represented upper working-class women, surveyed their members about divorce reform, finding a majority in favour of it. Particularly, women wanted equal grounds between men and women and lower costs. Some of the members also asked for wider grounds, including cruelty, insanity, and desertion, and a small majority supported divorce by mutual consent. As one secretary put it, 'All our branch members … were most emphatic that where the husband and wife could not live happily together it was no real marriage.'[78] These responses helped to balance out views of working-class women as unvaryingly conservative about marriage; by 1912, leaders in the working class also defined 'true' marriages differently from the law.

Since most sources privilege the artisan class, the attitude of the rest of the working class is harder to determine. Evidence from the violence cases indicates that many adulterous couples were regular members of their neighbourhoods. When John Banks killed Ann Gilligan (married to a soldier) in 1866 in Lancaster, four female neighbours testified to his ill-treatment of her, and John Walsh, a weaver, had intervened when the two argued in a pub. Banks and Gilligan lived 'in sin' and drank heavily, but their neighbours, all employed and married, tried to help them. Similarly, in 1895 in Nottingham, Edward Kesteven, a framework knitter, lived with Sarah Oldham, a dressmaker whose husband had deserted her. They lived in a row of houses among three sets of married couples. After Edward killed Sarah, all the neighbours testified, and their evidence made clear that the irregular union made no difference to the daily interplay among them.[79] Numerous other examples show the same kind of mixing; the working class had to accept wider sexual parameters, since they relied on each other for survival.

The working class was not monolithic, so not all neighbours were supportive. Particularly in the respectable, artisan class, such couples tried to be discreet. Also, I have few rural cases of violence among cohabitees, which may indicate that the rural poor were less tolerant of sexual immorality. Self-consciously respectable families might also be censorious, no matter how poor. John Gillis points to working-class families like that of Richard Hoggett, who were frankly horrified by any breach in the moral code. Gillis, in fact, gives several examples of families who felt so disgraced by various scandals that they moved away. In addition, a minority of witnesses in 1912 insisted that a woman 'living in adultery' would be 'drummed out of the neighbourhood'.[80]

This disapproval did not mean that adulterous unions did not occur, but that such couples tried to pass as married. Herbert Wrigley, a Manchester solicitor, pointed out in 1912 that most such couples simply moved to a new neighbourhood and lived 'as husband and wife'. If the method failed, however, the couple could face serious consequences. Dr Ethel Bentham cited a case where a married man and his second partner lived together discreetly. After a few years, the man's wife turned up, demanding custody of her three children; she was so disruptive that the couple emigrated to America.[81] All the same, as bigamy cases make clear, only some irregular unions provoked neighbourly unease. Neighbours condemned 'homewreckers', but not all adultery. And those who were able to keep their secret lived among their respectable friends with no one the wiser.

Despite this flexibility, women felt guilty about their position, as did some of the men. Norah M., who lived with her lodger, knew that she was not the same as a married woman: 'people look down on a woman so if she lives as I am doing.' Though they bowed to necessity, these couples preferred marriage. One woman, whose husband was in prison, eventually lived with her lodger. Though she was 'generally respected' by the neighbours, she knew the church would disapprove. Still, she insisted, 'God couldn't blame any poor woman for giving her children a chance whatever the parson might say.'[82] Again, the marital rebellion, because it was from necessity rather than choice, was limited. These couples wanted to marry and blamed the law and the church for their defiance.

Successes and failures

Since many of my sources on the working class are cases of violence, stories of disastrous second unions are more common than in the middle class. After all, a man or woman whose alcoholism or brutality wrecked her or his first marriage was not a good marital risk. All the same, many second unions were happy. Dr Scurfield, for instance, annexed twenty cases for the Royal Commission to support his testimony. In each, an unhappy marriage had been followed by a happy free union. Cases from the Cooperative Guild survey also included many happier, though illegal, second unions.[83] In addition, even in some of the cases of violence, happier times in these unions appear. Thomas Pagden and Caroline Burton lived together for ten years, apparently content, though her earlier marriage had failed. They would probably have continued had she not become mentally ill. George Nicholson deserted his first wife shortly after their marriage. In 1880, he went to live with a new lover. Nicholson's unemployment and alcoholism eventually ruined the relationship, but it was successful for fifteen years.[84]

As in the middle class, most adulterous working-class cohabitees saw themselves as married. Cohabitees fulfilled spousal duties, called each other husband and wife, and only exposed the nature of their unions when forced. Frederick Hinson adored Maria Death, though he was married to someone else. According to a witness, 'He always called her his wife, and treated her with just as much respect as if she was.'[85] Also, the emotional attachment of many of these relationships was as strong as in marriages. John Snape lived with Rachel Taberner after having left his wife and four children. He killed her because of jealousy, confessing, 'People said I was out of my reason in thinking so much about her.' *The Times* concluded that Snape's 'passion for her appears to have run to a mad and ridiculous extreme', but his story was common. Violent incidents indicate strong attachments; the leading reason for violence was jealousy (81 of 149 cases). Robert Cooper, for instance, was already married when he committed bigamy with Annie Barnham. When she left him upon discovering the truth, he became distraught and obsessive. He wrote to her, 'Annie, my dearest, dear, sweet Annie, how I love you' (and much more in the same vein) before he shot her.[86] In other words, the relationship was the critical factor, not the legal status. Though both partners were free to leave, this did not always reconcile the deserted partner to the separation. Most adulterous couples considered themselves married, stayed together in the face of grave problems, and suffered emotional trauma when the unions failed.

Again, as in the middle class, the marital rebellion was muted. These couples were committed to each other and passed as married; in addition, most of them mirrored the expectations of husbands and wives. Those who could articulate it stressed the need for divorce reform rather than disdain for the institution and regretted that they could not marry. Like the middle class, they made 'marriages' by assuming the roles of husbands and wives. In this, they challenged the strict marital laws of their time.

Conclusion

Adulterous cohabitees overall shared many similarities. Couples in both classes suffered from not being able to divorce and yet refused to accept their position. They faced many penalties for their decisions, though the working class had to deal with the intervention of the state more often. Both groups experienced family opposition; moreover, women suffered more than men in both groups. All were insistent that theirs were 'true' marriages, as opposed to their moribund first unions, but would almost certainly have preferred marriage. Authorities criticised the working class for supposedly ignoring marital ties, but they did not see the desire for marriage that stands out to the historian. Like bigamists and those who practiced affinal marriages, these couples were firmly in favour of marriage.

Their attitude put them at odds with others in the working class who could not see the point of the ceremony, whose class differences made marriage impossible, and who openly disdained marriage as an institution. These groups were a different type of threat to marriage, seeing it as irrelevant or even pernicious. In theory, they could have married legally, so they had more trouble justifying their sexual irregularity to family, friends, and society. On the other hand, they also often lived among groups which tolerated or even encouraged marital dissent, and this mitigated the social scorn. In addition, because they had no legal impediments, they dealt with the state less directly, moving outside its parameters. In a different way, though, they too challenged the Hardwicke regime and 'Victorianism', especially those in the parallel social systems of the very poor and the demimonde.

Notes

1 Shanley, *Feminism, Marriage and the Law*, pp. 39–44; M. Poovey, *Uneven Developments: The Ideological Work of Gender in Mid-Victorian England* (Chicago: University of Chicago Press, 1988), pp. 51–88.

2 R. Wolff, *Sensational Victorian: The Life and Fiction of Mary Elizabeth Braddon* (New York: Garland, 1979), pp. 80–102; *Lancaster Guardian*, 6 March 1880, p. 2.

3 W. Scott, *Jefferson Hogg* (London: Jonathan Cape, 1951), p. 136; S. Norman (ed.), *After Shelley: The Letters of Thomas Jefferson Hogg to Jane Williams* (London: Oxford University Press, 1934), p. xiv.

4 Quilter, *Is Marriage a Failure?*, p. 174.

5 H. Pearson, *Labby: The Life and Character of Henry Labouchere* (New York: Harper and Brothers, 1937), p. 63.

6 J. R. Guy, *Compassion and the Art of the Possible: Dr Southwood Smith as Social Reformer and Public Health Pioneer* (Cambridgeshire: Octavia Hill Society & Birthplace Museum

Trust, 1994), p. 11; C. Yeldham, *Margaret Gillies RWS: Unitarian Painter of Mind and Emotion, 1803-1887* (Lewiston, NY: Edwin Mellen Press, 1997), pp. 11-33.

7   J. Halperin, *Gissing: A Life in Books* (Oxford: Oxford University Press, 1982), pp. 272-83; M. Collie, *George Gissing: A Biography* (Folkstone, Kent: William Dawson and Sons, Ltd, 1977), pp. 152-5; P. Coustillas (ed.), *The Letters of George Gissing to Gabrielle Fleury* (New York: The New York Public Library, 1964), pp. 90-2.

8   F. E. Mineka, *The Dissidence of Dissent: The Monthly Repository, 1806-1838* (Chapel Hill: University of North Carolina Press, 1944), pp. 192-5; R. Garnett, *The Life of W. J. Fox: Public Teacher and Social Reformer, 1786-1864* (London: John Lane, 1909), pp. 43-5; 156-66, quote from p. 43.

9   M. Asker, *Lawrence: The Uncrowned King of Arabia* (London: Viking, 1998), pp. 7-12; J. E. Mack, *A Prince of Our Disorder: The Life of T. E. Lawrence* (Boston, MA: Little, Brown, and Co., 1976), pp. 1-13; J. R. Ackerley, *My Father and Myself* (London: The Bodley Head, 1968), pp. 11-28; 49-52; 150-76; P. Parker, *Ackerley: A Life of J. R. Ackerley* (New York: Farrar Straus Giroux, 1989), pp. 7-14; 40-1.

10   W. Fredeman (ed.), *The Letters of Pictor Ignotus: William Bell Scott's Correspondence with Alice Boyd, 1859-1884* (Manchester: John Rylands University Library, 1976), pp. 4-13; *A Pre-Raphaelite Gazette: The Penkill Letters of Arthur Hughes to William Bell Scott and Alice Boyd, 1886-97* (Manchester: John Rylands University Library, 1967), pp. 6-9; W. Minto (ed.), *Autobiographical Notes of the Life of William Bell Scott* 2 vols (New York: Harper and Brothers, 1892), II, 293.

11   G. Haight (ed.), *George Eliot Letters* 7 vols (New Haven, CT: Yale University Press, 1954-55), II, 349; Eliot to Vincent Holbeche, 13 June 1857; Hughes, *George Eliot*, pp. 55, 190-2; Coustillas, *Letters of George Gissing to Gabrielle Fleury*, p. 75; letter from Gissing to Fleury, 29 October 1898; R. Gettman, *George Gissing and H. G. Wells: Their Friendship and Correspondence* (Urbana, IL: University of Illinois Press, 1961), pp. 229-33.

12   B. Belford, *Violet: The Story of the Irrepressible Violet Hunt* (New York: Simon and Schuster, 1990), p. 185; J. Hardwick, *An Immodest Violet: The Life of Violet Hunt* (London: Andre Deutsch, 1990), p. 105; D. Goldring, *South Lodge: Reminiscences of Violet Hunt, Ford Madox Ford and the English Review Circle* (London: Constable & Co., 1943), pp. 97-8.

13   Coustillas, *Letters of George Gissing to Gabrielle Fleury*, pp. 102-3; letter dated 4 February 1899; Halperin, *Gissing*, p. 287.

14   Haight, *George Eliot Letters*, III, 366, note 5; Eliot to Barbara Bodichon, 26 December 1860, pp. 365-6; Ashton, *George Henry Lewes*, p. 211; Hughes, *George Eliot*, p. 252.

15   Belford, *Violet*, pp. 175-87; A. Mizener, *The Saddest Story: A Biography of Ford Madox Ford* (New York: Carroll & Graf Publishers, 1971), pp. 209-12; Coustillas, *Letters of George Gissing to Gabrielle Fleury*, pp. 41-4; 68-70; 90-5; 101-6; Halperin, *Gissing*, pp. 281-3.

16   F. Karl, *George Eliot: Voice of a Century* (New York: W. W. Norton, 1995), pp. 249-54; 301-5; Hughes, *George Eliot*, pp. 192-3; 340; Ashton, *George Henry Lewes*, pp. 120-39; Haight, *George Eliot Letters*, II, 331, 341-2, 346-50; III, 23-30.

17   Wolff, *Sensational Victorian*, p. 226; Belford, *Violet*, pp. 152-3; 159; 169-70; Goldring, *South Lodge*, pp. 92-3; 120-1; V. Hunt, *I Have This to Say: The Story of My Flurried Years* (New York: Boni and Liveright, 1926), pp. 108-9; 144.

18   Coustillas, *Letters of George Gissing to Gabrielle Fleury*, p. 150; quoted by Gissing in his letter to Fleury, 26 January 1902.

19   H. G. Wells, *Experiment in Autobiography: Discoveries and Conclusions of a Very Ordinary Brain (Since 1866)* (New York: Macmillan, 1934), pp. 329, 355-6; quote from p. 356.

20 Asker, *Lawrence*, p. 14; J. Wilson, *Lawrence of Arabia: The Authorised Biography of T. E. Lawrence* (London: Heinemann, 1989), pp. 29–30.

21 Scott, *Jefferson Hogg*, pp. 149; 189–91; 198–202; 217–19; 272.

22 R. M. Myers, *Reluctant Expatriate: The Life of Harold Frederic* (Westport, CT: Greenwood Press, 1995), pp. 18–19; 92–105; B. Bennett, *The Damnation of Harold Frederic: His Lives and Works* (Syracuse, NY: Syracuse University Press, 1997), pp. 45–52; P. Coustillas (ed.), *London and the Life of Literature in Late Victorian England: The Diary of George Gissing, Novelist* (Hassocks, Sussex: The Harvester Press, 1978), p. 413.

23 *Lancaster Guardian*, 8 September 1860, p. 5.

24 Bennett, *Damnation of Harold Frederic*, pp. 8–9, 50 (for quote); S. Wertheim and P. Sorrentino (eds), *The Correspondence of Stephen Crane* 2 vols (New York: Columbia University Press, 1988), II, 402–3; Ackerley, *My Father and Myself*, pp. 154–7.

25 British Library of Political and Economic Science. Mill-Taylor Collection. Vol. 27, #32, fol. 60. Eliza Flower to Harriet Taylor, n.d.

26 Scott, *Jefferson Hogg*, pp. 189–204, 212–13; Ashton, *G. H. Lewes*, pp. 116, 155–9; Haight, *George Eliot Letters*, V, 7; Karl, *George Eliot*, pp. 441–2; Hughes, *George Eliot*, pp. 150–5; 163–6, 213–24.

27 Mack, *A Prince of Our Disorder*, p. 4.

28 Prosser in *Lancaster Guardian*, 11 February 1860, p. 2; Ross in *Lancaster Guardian*, 14 November 1885, p. 2; *Western Daily Mercury*, 6 November 1885, p. 8; 7 November 1885, p. 2; 11 November 1885, p. 3; 2 January 1886, p. 3; Wardleworth in *Lancaster Guardian*, 23 November 1850, p. 2; 7 December 1850, p. 2. See also LPA, Court of Arches Records, *Schultes v. Hodgson* (1822), Eee18, H319/1–9; *Oliver & Toll v. Hobart* (1827), H 381/1–7. Both these cases involved vicars removed from their positions due to cohabiting unions.

29 Wolff, *Sensational Victorian*, pp. 104, 249–51.

30 Hunt, *I Have This to Say*, pp. 225–42; Goldring, *South Lodge*, pp. 87–114; Belford, *Violet*, pp. 175–210; 238–9; Hardwick, *Immodest Violet*, pp. 172–3; Mizener, *The Saddest Story*, p. 305.

31 Wolff, *Sensational Victorian*, p. 105.

32 Goldring, *South Lodge*, pp. 108, 114 (for first quote); *The Times*, 8 February 1913, p. 3 (for second).

33 A. S. Holmes, "'Fallen mothers': Maternal adultery and child custody in England, 1886–1925', in C. Nelson and A. S. Holmes (eds), *Maternal Instincts: Visions of Motherhood and Sexuality in Britain, 1875–1925* (New York: St Martin's Press, 1997), 49.

34 R. Selig, *George Gissing* (New York: Twayne Publishers, 1995), p. 17; Halperin, *Gissing*, p. 355.

35 Myers, *Reluctant Expatriate*, pp. 157–60.

36 B. Strachey and J. Samuels (eds), *Mary Berenson: A Self-Portrait from Her Letters and Diaries* (London: Hamish Hamilton, 1983), pp. 42–93.

37 Hunt, *I Have This to Say*, p. 73.

38 Myers, *Reluctant Expatriate*, p. 94.

39 Halperin, *Gissing*, pp. 295–351; Selig, *George Gissing*, pp. 16–18; Fredeman, *A Pre-Raphaelite Gazette*, pp. 8; 25–6.

40 Karl, *George Eliot*, pp. 409; 427; 584; Hughes, *George Eliot*, pp. 221–2; 273–4.

41 Garnett, *Life of W. J. Fox*, pp. 168–76; Yeldham, *Margaret Gillies RWS*, p. 45.

42 Haight, *Letters of George Eliot*, V, 66; VII, 268, n.7; Hughes, *George Eliot*, pp. 250–2; 274–6; Wolff, *Sensational Victorian*, p. 107.

43 C. Rollyson, *Rebecca West: A Life* (New York: Scribner, 1996), pp. 65–6; 87–92; H. G. Wells, *H. G. Wells in Love: Postscript to an Experiment in Autobiography*, ed. G. P. Wells (London: Faber and Faber, 1984), pp. 97–107; G. Ray, *H. G. Wells and Rebecca West* (New Haven, CT: Yale University Press, 1974), pp. 96–166.

44 Rollyson, *Rebecca West*, pp. 69–94; J. R. Hammond, *H. G. Wells and Rebecca West* (New York: Harvester/Wheatsheaf, 1991), pp. 120–43.

45 Goldring, *South Lodge*, pp. 110–15; 127; Belford, *Violet*, pp. 217–50; Hardwick, *An Immodest Violet*, pp.137–42; Mizener, *The Saddest Story*, pp. 278–313; A. Judd, *Ford Madox Ford* (Cambridge, MA: Harvard University Press, 1991), pp. 254–6; 273–8; 311–16; 321–7.

46 Mineka, *The Dissidence of Dissent*, p. 192; Garnett, *Life of W. J. Fox*, pp. 166–76.

47 Yeldham, *Margaret Gillies RWS*, pp. 74–84; 87; F. N. L. Poynter, 'Thomas Southwood Smith – the man (1788–1861)', *Proceedings of the Royal Society of Medicine* 55 (1962), 390; 392; M. Howitt, *An Autobiography* 2 vols (London: William Isbister Ltd, 1889), II, 30–1; 311–12; Lady Lindsay, 'Some recollections of Miss Margaret Gillies', *Temple Bar* 81 (1887), 265–73.

48 Norman, *After Shelley*, pp. 82–4, quote from p. 82; Scott, *Jefferson Hogg*, pp. 217–19.

49 Gettmann, *George Gissing and H. G. Wells*, pp. 165–6.

50 *Ibid.*, pp. 171–2; letter from Gabrielle Fleury to H. G. Wells, 24 June 1901, all emphases as in original.

51 *Royal Commission*, II, 248,252; III, 74–90.

52 A. Martin, *Working Women and Divorce* (London: David Nutt, 1911), pp. 49–73.

53 Menefee, *Wives for Sale*; Thompson, *Customs in Common*, p. 409.

54 Lancaster University, Centre for Northwest Regional Studies, Elizabeth Roberts Collection (hereafter ERC), Mrs T4P, p. 46.

55 HO 144/31/75877; *The Times*, 2 August 1878, p. 4; ERC, Mrs S7P, p. 9.

56 *Royal Commission*, III, 173–4.

57 F. Fulford, *The Rector and His Flock: A View of the Cambridgeshire Village of Croyden in Early Victorian Days*, ed. D. Ellison (Bassingbourn, Cambridge: Bassingbourn Booklets, 1980), p. 13.

58 *Justice of the Peace* 47 (1883), 116–18; quote from 118.

59 *Royal Commission*, III, 31, 121; II, 309 (for quote).

60 J. Tosh, *Manliness and Masculinities in Nineteenth-Century Britain: Essays on Gender, Family and Empire* (London: Pearson/Longman, 2005), p. 174; O. Anderson, 'Emigration and marriage break-up in mid-Victorian England', *Economic History Review* 50 (1997), 104–9. For examples, see *Rex v. Twyning* (1819), 2 *Barnewall & Alderson's Reports* 386–91; 106 *English Reports* 407–9; Martin, *Working Women and Divorce*, pp. 64–6; London Metropolitan Archives, Foundling Hospital Rejected Petitions (hereafter LMA), A/FH/A8/1/3/44/1, Petition #63, 7 June 1837; A/FH/A8/1/3/60/1, Petition # 151, 8 October 1853.

61 *Royal Commission*, I, 447. See also *The Times*, 28 July 1866, p. 12; *Lancaster Guardian*, 9 June 1866, p. 8; 28 July 1866, p. 3; *The Times*, 10 December 1887, p. 6; *Portsmouth Times and Naval Gazette County Journal*, 10 December 1887, p. 3.

62 C. Chaplin, *My Autobiography* (New York: Simon and Schuster, 1964), pp. 20–59; D. Robinson, *Chaplin: His Life and Art* (London: Collins, 1985), pp. 4–36.

63 Cornell in *The Times*, 24 March 1863, p. 11; Duffin in *Lancaster Guardian*, 13 September 1890, p. 3.

64 *Royal Commission*, 'Appendix', III, 183.

65 Battersby in *Lancaster Guardian*, 28 June 1900, p. 2; Chapman in *Lancaster Guardian*,

17 August 1895, p. 5. See also *Yorkshire Gazette*, 30 July 1870, p. 10; and *Women's Suffrage Journal* 13 (1882), 119.

66 Kimpton in *The Times*, 26 April 1858, p. 11; Elliott in *Justice of the Peace* 23 (1859), 117. See also *Lancaster Guardian*, 29 July 1865; 22 October 1870, p. 4; 29 October 1870, p. 6; 3 July 1880, p. 7.

67 *Royal Commission*, II, 228.

68 See, for example, *Royal Commission*, II, 95; Martin, *Working Women and Divorce*, p. 72; Charles Booth, *Life and Labour of the People of London*, 17 vols (London: William & Norgate, 1891–1904 [Reprint edition: New York: AMS Press, 1970]), II, 53.

69 LMA, A/FH/A8/1/3/51/1, Petition #70, 3 April 1844; A/FH/A8/1/3/41/1, Petition #36, 11 June 1834.

70 LMA, A/FH/A8/1/3/44/1, Petition #63, 7 June 1837; A/FH/A8/1/3/39/1, Petition #31, 4 April 1832.

71 *Royal Commission*, I, 429; III, 126; Sir John Kirk, 'The creche and the ragged school union', *Progress, Civic, Social, Industrial: The Organ of the British Institute of Social Services* 2 (1907), 184; A. Davin, *Growing up Poor: Home, School and Street in London, 1870–1914* (London: Rivers Oram Press, 1996), p. 93.

72 *Royal Commission*, I, 324; II, 308; III, 126.

73 Cretney, *Family Law*, pp. 189–90.

74 *Royal Commission*, II, 227; III, 174 (in 'Appendix'); see also II, 311; and A. August, *Poor Women's Lives; Gender, Work, and Poverty in Late-Victorian London* (London: Associated University Presses, 1999), p. 48.

75 Barnham in *The Times*, 30 October 1862, p. 11; Woodhead in NA, HO 45/9454/70865; *The Times*, 18 December 1877, p. 7; *Nottingham and Midland Counties Daily Express*, 15 December 1877, p. 4.

76 *Royal Commission*, II, 388; 383; III, 122; 31.

77 *Ibid.*, III, 182 (in 'Appendix'); for other examples, see III, 171–89. See also Quilter, *Is Marriage a Failure?*, pp. 238–40.

78 Martin, *Working Women and Divorce*, pp. 1–26; quote from p. 21.

79 Banks in *The Times*, 28 July 1866, p. 12; *Lancaster Guardian*, 9 June 1966, p. 8; 28 July 1866, p. 3; Oldham in *Nottingham Evening Post*, 5 March 1895, pp. 3–4; 26 March 1895, p. 3.

80 Gillis, *For Better, For Worse*, pp. 256–9; *Royal Commission*, I, 383 (for quote); II, 82.

81 *Royal Commission*, II, 82; III, 31. Being able to 'pass' as married, of course, contrasts with the experience of gay couples. See Brady, *Masculinity and Male Homosexuality*, pp. 200–6; Vicinus, *Intimate Friends*, pp. 61–84.

82 *Ibid.*, II:391; III:33.

83 *Ibid.*, II:389–93; Martin, *Working Women and Divorce*, pp. 49–74.

84 Padget in *Yorkshire Gazette*, 3 December 1870, p. 7; Nicholson in *Lancaster Guardian*, 19 October 1895, p. 5; 26 October 1895, p. 2; 31 October 1895, p. 2; *Lancaster Standard*, 8 November 1895, p. 8.

85 CRIM 10/59, pp. 26–32, quote from p. 30.

86 Snape in *The Times*, 26 July 1865, p. 6 (for quote); and *Lancaster Guardian*, 29 July 1865, p. 3; Cooper in *The Times*, 30 October 1862, p. 11.

6

The 'other Victorians': the demimonde and the very poor

THE MAJORITY OF PEOPLE who cohabited in the nineteenth century did so because they could not marry, but some couples lived together by choice. These fall into four categories: the very poor, the 'criminal' classes, the demimonde, and, finally, cross-class couples. This last category is the subject of Chapter 7. This chapter concentrates on the first three of these groups, with the most emphasis on the first, since the second and third groups have received more historical attention. What these couples had in common was their unrespectability, due either to poverty or their professions. They made up two major segments of the 'other Victorians': the undeserving poor and the demimonde. These couples were in more marked dissent from the marital regime than those who could not marry, and had less interaction with the law as a result. They did not seek reforms, nor did they challenge gender roles. In fact, the power relations in these groups showed that the sexual double standard was universal, since the preference for cohabitation was not equal between the genders.

Cohabitation and the poor

The largest category of those who chose not to marry was that of the poor. Most of the poor married legally, of course, but a significant minority did not. Determining the number of such couples is difficult, since many passed as husband and wife; in addition, the numbers changed over time and varied by region. Historians have argued that cohabitation was more common early in the century. G. N. Gandy, in his study of Culcheth, Lancashire, found that common-law marriages peaked between 1829 and 1842, when the economy was most depressed. Gandy estimated that 10 to 20 per cent of all couples were in free unions between 1780–1840, but over 30 per cent in the 1830s. Similarly, J. R. Gillis argued the period between 1750 and 1850 was an age of marital nonconformity, with large numbers of irregular unions, though differentiated by region. Areas with cottage industries, in which women and children could contribute to the family economy, had higher levels of cohabitation. Anna Clark's work also revealed many common-law marriages in the first half of the nineteenth century, particularly in weaving communities in Scotland and Lancashire.[1] In short, cohabiting couples were a normal part of the landscape between 1800 and 1850, with some regional variations.

Later in the century, the numbers dropped, though many cohabitees probably just concealed their status more successfully. Maude Davies, who surveyed families in a rural village in Wiltshire in the early 1900s, found no cases of cohabitation out of 130 families. Either they were not willing to make their situation public, or villagers would not tolerate unmarried couples in their midst. Still, the acceptance or disapproval of cohabitation varied by region. Barry Reay's research in Kent revealed several examples of long-term irregular unions after 1850, as much as 10 to 15 per cent of his couples. In other words, people called themselves married, and their neighbours went along with it. Though they did not advertise their free unions, the high number of such couples is significant, particularly for the late nineteenth century and a rural area.[2]

Large cities had a wider scope for marital nonconformity. Middle-class observers of urban poverty, such as Charles Booth, surveyed poor neighbourhoods, recording the number of unmarried couples. Despite his diligence, Booth probably undercounted; many families refused to speak to him, and others may have misled him. Booth's researches showed that in the poorest districts, the number of unmarried couples was the highest, but still only around 10 per cent. B. Seebohn Rowntree's survey of York yielded even fewer examples; only one family out of 103 in the lowest two income groups admitted to living outside marriage and none at all in the top two income groups.[3] As Rowntree's conclusions indicate, as one went up the social scale, the emphasis on respectability grew, and couples were more likely to be married – or at least less likely to admit to being unmarried. Some neighbourhoods may have had as high a concentration as 20 per cent unwed couples, but overall the number was probably half that, especially in the late nineteenth century.

Despite their small numbers, such couples worried middle-class and upper-class observers. Charles Tijou, the bailiff of Bow County Court, complained that East End cohabitees freely admitted their status and met little disapproval from neighbours. Andrew Mearns, writing about the slums of London, asserted, 'Ask if the men and women living together in these rookeries are married, and your simplicity will cause a smile. Nobody knows. Nobody cares.' Similarly, George Sims asked cohabiting couples in the poorest parts of England why they did not marry, and they replied that they 'never gave it a thought'.[4] These observers melded together their fears of an uncontrolled lower class with sexual freedom, assuming that those who could live happily 'in sin' were also idle, drunken, and criminal. The elision between these categories was almost universal, perhaps because such couples were more threatening than those who could not marry. As we will see, these worries were largely unfounded, though deliberate cohabitees did expand the definition of marriage beyond its legal borders.

Reasons

Rather than being pathological, many cohabitees had sensible reasons for living 'in sin' and saw clearly the difference between cohabitation and marriage. For instance, cohabiting couples kept their privacy. Both the 1848 and 1894 Royal Commissions on Marriage and Divorce reported that many couples resented the publicity of the banns. This was one reason, too, for the beginnings of civil marriage in 1836, and its further simplification in 1856.[5] Also, cohabitation was economically flexible. Particularly in the first half of the century, some men and women cohabited to guard against economic disaster; should things go wrong, they could go back to their natal homes. Both Gandy and Gillis credit women's earning power in weaving with a more relaxed view towards marriage, and unmarried women did not have to go to the workhouse if their partners became unemployed or ill.[6]

As cottage industry declined, these types of economic motives disappeared, but others emerged. James Greenwood reported that for poor London couples 'the expense attending the process ... makes matrimony the exception and not the rule'. Similarly, a witness in Frederick Andrews's murder trial admitted that he and his 'missus' were cohabiting, but insisted 'we shall get married when we can afford the money.' Some cohabitees particularly resented the church taking fees. Henry Mayhew interviewed a street buyer who claimed he 'really couldn't afford to pay the parson ... If it's so good to go to church for being married, it oughtn't to cost a poor man nothing; he shouldn't be charged for being good.' Mayhew also found anti-clericalism among street-sellers; they argued that marrying 'is only to put money into the clergyman's, or as these people say the "parson's," pocket.'[7]

All the same, many in the clergy removed the financial impediments and this did not always result in more weddings. A clergyman's wife in East London persuaded a young cohabiting couple to marry by paying for the expenses and getting her husband to cancel his fees. When the wedding day came, though, the two did not show up. The man explained that he was offered a job at the last minute and 'I couldn't lose five bob just for the sake o' getting married.' Mary McCarthy, who worked as a Methodist missionary in London, was equally disillusioned when she and James Yeames, a clergyman, provided clothing, a ring, and a wedding breakfast for a cohabiting couple only to have them disappear, probably having pawned the dress and ring. Yeames concluded, 'We have been grievously deceived and disappointed.'[8]

Thus, other reasons were important, and these were heavily gendered. Though sometimes both partners were uninterested, more often the man was reluctant. Men faced few disadvantages and gained many advantages from cohabiting. For example, if a woman did not prove satisfactory, a cohabitee could desert her with few consequences. In contrast, as a London man told Charles Booth, 'If I married my woman I should never be sure of my tea'. Mayhew also interviewed a coster girl who disapproved of cohabitation, because, she claimed, 'if he can turn a poor gal off, as soon as he tires of her, he begins to have noises with her, and then gets quit of her altogether.'[9] Ironically, because of men's economic power, women who had not vowed obedience sometimes had less room to manoeuvre. The upper classes had changed the law of marriage in 1753 and the Poor Law in 1834 to make women insist on marriage, but because women's economic opportunities were so limited, they often took support without a wedding.

Women entered free unions in order to parlay the sexual relationship into a more permanent bond; unfortunately, many were disappointed. Susan Mumm's work on Anglican penitentiaries revealed many such women, and Foundling Hospital records also include instances of men eloping with lovers, without long-term intentions. Once the women had left with them, they were vulnerable to desertion, having cut themselves off from their friends.[10] In other cases women left home or work because they became pregnant. With nowhere else to go, the women agreed to live in lodgings with the men as their wives. These cases particularly point up women's economic weakness. Harriet B. was a needlewoman, living with her mother. She courted a lodger, George M., in 1851. When she got pregnant, she lived with him until two weeks before the birth of the baby, at which point he disappeared. When her landlady questioned her, 'she acknowledged that she was not married'. As this last case indicates, couples had to pass as married, since most landladies would not accept unmarried tenants. Mary B. lived with Isadore S., a black sailor, for some months and 'passed as Mrs S.' with their landlady. Only after he had lost his job and left did Mary admit she was not married.[11]

Men could indulge in such unions without losing their jobs or marriageability. They 'tried out' women as wives, but could change their minds if they did not find what they wanted. The women, often in poor professions, gambled with their attractiveness to find a provider. One young tramping woman told Mayhew that she had lived with her father, a gardener, in great poverty, making shirts from the age of twelve. When she was seventeen, she met a carpenter who 'told me if I'd come to London with him he'd do anything for me.' She finally agreed, but he soon abandoned her. She confessed, 'I knew it was wrong to go away and live with him without being married; but I was wretched at home, and he told me he would make me his wife, and I believed him.'[12] The dangers for poor women in cohabitation could not be clearer. Yet many women took the chance, mainly because their jobs were such poorly-paid drudgery.

Marriage conferred a legal obligation for the husband to support his wife, but a cohabitee had no such right. And even when men did not purposely desert women, they left their families in tenuous positions when they died. Mary Ann L. lived with James C. for seventeen years, and they had ten children. When he died in 1849, the Foundling Hospital authorities refused to help a woman who had lived 'in a state of Concubinage'. The hospital also rejected Elizabeth N., who had lived with James S. for seven years and had two children when he died in 1836. She was so confused about her marital status that at first she put 'widow' on her application, but her assertion of respectability made no difference to the Hospital.[13] Some of the women who appealed to religious charities were also long-time cohabitees. Susan Mumm sums up the problem well when she quotes the casebook of an Anglican penitentiary: 'Nurse in private family – got entangled by promise of marriage. Lived with man 11 years. Had 4 children. He deserted her. Work House.' These clipped phrases contained years of struggle and a downward spiral for mother and children.[14]

Men refused to marry for a number of reasons. Occasionally small class differences were enough to give a man pause. Joseph Tonge, a publican, lived with Sarah Langford, a millhand, for many years and they had five children together. He nevertheless married the landlady of a prosperous inn in 1886. Sarah had no inheritance, and his freedom to leave her meant that he could do better. At other times, the issue was the woman's sexual impurity. In other words, having 'fallen' with their lovers, these women ruined their marriage chances. Mary Turner lived for three months with William White, she claimed because he promised to marry her, but his feelings changed when she had sex with him. White had no problem with marriage in general; he got engaged to another woman soon after he broke up with Mary.[15] Whatever the reason, men without legal ties were able to find more congenial partners.

In close-knit communities, women sometimes found allies to help urge marriage; clergy and landlords were highly disapproving of irregular unions. In 1843, Revd Francis Fulford remonstrated with one of his Cambridgeshire parishioners, a man named Nash, for living with Mary Newman. Fulford knew Nash was the reluctant party, since 'The woman would marry gladly'.[16] Later in the century, Francis Kilvert was scandalised by the cohabitation of Stephen Davies and Myra Rees in 1870. Kilvert wrote in his diary, 'People are very indignant about this affair ... But what is to be done?' Less than two months later, Kilvert reported that the landlord visited Davies, and, 'finding him living in open concubinage ... gave him notice'. Though the landlord hurt both Stephen and Myra with his decision, sometimes the stories had happier endings for the women. Kilvert brought equal pressure on another couple who were living together, finally getting them to wed fourteen months later. He was also relieved when Edward Morgan and his cohabitee married in 1871, again blaming the groom for the delay, since the woman 'begged and prayed her lover to marry her before he seduced her and afterwards'.[17] In these cases, the interference from authorities helped get the man to the altar. Thus, the reaction to such interventions differed between the genders, with women more welcoming to – perhaps even grateful for – religious pressure. But these instances were limited to smaller communities with energetic clergymen.

Obviously, the double standard of sexuality benefited men, but some women also refused to marry. They, too, sought the main advantage of cohabitation – that they could change their minds. Indeed, the most common reason for women was that they wanted to be able to leave if a partner 'misbehaved'. A charity worker insisted in 1881, 'the dread of granting absolute power over her to any of her lovers is *one* cause for women preferring *free love*'. Dr Ethel Bentham testified to the 1912 Royal Commission about two women who eschewed marriage altogether, since they 'preferred to be able to "get shut of him if he does not behave himself"'. The Foundling Hospital records also sometimes indicate that women feared being linked to violent men. Harriet B. lived with Robert I. for eighteen months, but 'she would not marry him on account of his dreadful Temper'.[18] Though women might have been mistaken in thinking they could leave without incident, they believed they had a better chance of escape if unmarried.

In fact, some women wanted economic and sexual independence, just like men. Widows with property had much to lose with remarriage. Harriet Stallion refused to marry Leonard Tillett, though they lived together in her lodging house, since she preferred to keep her annuity under her own control. Other women, particularly younger ones, wanted to be able to find better partners. A scavenger told Mayhew that he had offered to marry his cohabitee, but 'she went to the hopping ... and never came back. I heered [sic] that she'd taken up with an Irish hawker'. Rather than being ruined, this young woman used her unmarried state to find a man she liked better.[19] Nonetheless, these women were the minority, because of economic limitations and childcare concerns. In the poorest classes, as in the rest of Victorian society, the sexual double standard worked in men's favour.

Age, race, family, occupation

In addition to gendered motives, couples had other reasons to prefer cohabitation. Most commentators insisted that age was important. Booth argued that even in the roughest neighbourhoods, most young people married, but older couples often did not bother. Reay's examples of common-law unions included several that occurred after the woman had already borne illegitimate children or had become widows.[20] My violence cases indicate that many couples cohabited after having been legally married or in middle age. In 92 cases out of 217, at least one partner was married to someone else and 17 more had a widow/er. In another 23, the couple began living together when at least one partner was over forty. Over half of the cases (132), then, involved people who had already had a major relationship or were middle-aged. Of course, some of these couples could not marry, but these numbers indicate that age was a factor.

Mature couples may have had bad experiences they did not wish to repeat, or they may simply have grown old enough not to worry as much about public opinion. For instance, they had less concern about bearing illegitimate children. One of Reay's examples, Harriet Lees, had eight illegitimate children between 1858 and 1879. The father of three of them was Alfred Tong, who eventually lived with her, probably after her father died in 1873 (when she was thirty-nine). Clearly, after eight illegitimate births, Harriet was not concerned about her reputation, so did not insist on marriage. Even if they did not want to marry, older couples wanted a companion for their later years, and needed someone to help with any children. Women, especially widows without property, needed economic help. Johanna Nevin was a widow with two children when she began living with James Flynn, a factory operative. He was violent and threatening, but she stayed with him for two years, probably because of her children.[21]

Another factor that could affect both people in the relationship was race and ethnicity. For one thing, Mayhew insisted that some nationalities (such as Irish and Jewish couples) were less prone to cohabitation than others. A second way that race could be a factor was when there were mixed relationships. Although mixed-race partners do not appear in the records often, they certainly existed, and racial barriers may have inhibited couples from marriage. Mayhew interviewed a prostitute whose father was a black seaman. Her mother, who was white, would not marry him even when she became pregnant; instead, she married a white boxmaker.[22] Laura Tabili has shown that port towns had many mixed-race marriages, at least by the early twentieth century, but the difficulties of reconciling family and friends to the matches may have discouraged some legal unions. And sometimes the black partner was not enthusiastic, as in the case of sailors like Isadore S. Indeed, since many male Afro-Britons were at sea, they clustered in a profession that had more cohabitation.[23]

Other factors, while not decisive, could influence the couples' choice. If the couples' families disdained marriage, they were likely to do the same. Some of Reay's examples had multiple common-law unions within the same kin group. Booth's cases also showed how free unions ran in families. Martin and Eliza Rooney had three children, and all cohabited; in addition, both of Eliza's sisters and one of her nephews did as well. In other instances, the neighbourhood as a whole influenced the couple. If most of the families who lived on a street did not marry, new couples did not do so either. A Mrs B— told Mayhew that she and her husband had lived in three different places, all associated with rubbish carters. In two of them, most of the couples married, but Paddington was different: 'I don't know why, for they seemed to live one with another, just as men do with their wives.' In part, these were self-selected neighbourhoods, since cohabiting couples chose streets where they felt comfortable.[24]

In addition, some occupations tended to cohabitation more than others. Gillis identified shoemakers, costers, sweeps, and dustmen as having high levels of cohabitation. In mid-century, Mayhew listed costers, street patterers, sailors, tramps, and scavengers. Cohabitation was a rational choice for couples in these professions, since they either involved long periods of separation and/or extreme poverty. Those who were gone for long periods, especially, needed flexibility, which was why sailors and soldiers were prone to it.[25] Often the women involved with sailors or soldiers were full-time or part-time prostitutes, another reason for not regularising the relationships. George Thomas, a black sailor in Liverpool in the 1880s, lived with Margaret Askin, a prostitute, when he was in port. He resented her demands for money and her unfaithfulness, and he eventually killed her. Nonetheless, he insisted she was 'driving me backwards and forwards so as to marry her, but I did not want to marry.' George did not see her as an appropriate wife, even for a poor sailor of colour, despite his strong feelings for her.[26]

Tramps, too, had little reason to marry, since they were constantly on the move and very poor. Though some tramping pairs stayed together for years, others wanted temporary unions. J. W. Rounsfell, a tramping printer in the 1880s, described meeting a beggar named Kitty while on the road. Her previous partner was in prison, so Kitty tried to get Rounsfell to take his place, an offer he declined.[27] Mayhew also heard stories from tramping women about these unions. One woman went haymaking and a tramping haymaker 'ruined' her, so 'I belonged to him. He didn't say I was his wife. They don't call us their wives.' The haymaker left her after a few years, taking advantage of his legal freedom. These women could not hold out for marriage, since they needed protection on the road. Mary Higgs, an Edwardian social investigator, reported: 'A destitute woman once told me that if you tramped, "you had to take up with a fellow." I can well believe it.'[28] Though tramps' reasons for cohabiting were gendered, they were not irrational.

As Gillis's and Mayhew's lists showed, poor settled couples also eschewed the ceremony. Indeed, many of them did not marry because it was not different enough from cohabitation to be worth their while. Several things distinguished them from the often temporary unions of soldiers or tramps. First, many of them went through their own versions of weddings, indicating a desire for ritual. Throughout the century, clergymen complained about couples who came to other people's weddings, mouthed the words, exchanged rings, and then left. Other couples, particularly in the early nineteenth century, used folk rituals, such as 'jumping the broom'. Couples also exchanged rings, or, in the case of shoemakers, made 'tack' marriages by saying 'If thee tak, I tak thee.'[29] Middle-class observers insisted that the poor had no regard for marriage, but the desire for a ritual showed support for a public bond, even if the couple did not want to pay for a ceremony.

Second, these unions began at young ages, the couples stayed together for years, and they expected fidelity. Mayhew had several examples of these kinds of unions. The costers treated their 'wives' badly, but the women remained faithful. Similarly, he estimated only one in twenty dustmen married, but they 'remain constant', because 'the woman earns nearly half as much as the man.' Because of the similarity to marriage, these couples saw a ceremony as pointless. The neighbours of Mrs B—, the wife of the rubbish carter, argued that 'there was no good wasting money to get their "marriage lines" all for no use.'[30] Sims quoted London couples who said 'it's a lot of trouble and they haven't the time.' And women as well as men demurred. Booth discussed a couple who lived together for forty years. When asked why they did not marry, the woman explained, 'He would have married me again and again … but I could never see the good of it.'[31] The wedding did not give enough benefits to justify the expense, and living together lessened – though did not eliminate – interference from the church and state.

The resemblance of stable cohabitation to marriage comes out most clearly in the violence cases. As stated before, jealousy was overwhelmingly the motive for attacks. Forty-two times, the victim had ended the relationship; in thirty-five more cases, the victim had aroused the attacker's jealousy while they were still together; and in six more cases, the victim had threatened to leave. This adds up to 83 of 149 cases with stated motives – almost 56 per cent.[32] Moreover, as with married households, money was a significant factor in conflicts; arguments over funds were the main problem in thirty-two cases (21 per cent). Just as if she were wed, a woman cohabitee managed the household budget on whatever pay the man gave her. If she did not, she had failed her main duty, and any woman who took more of the pay packet than the man offered was 'stealing' from him. A typical case was that of John Banks, who murdered Ann Gilligan in 1866, because, he claimed, '[s]he has taken three shillings out of my pocket.'[33]

For their part, women insisted that men support them and any children, even after the end of the union. Though the state limited men's responsibilities for illegitimate children, women recognized no difference, using affiliation when possible and demanding support in other ways when it was not. Louisa Jenkins insisted that William Bennet support their two children, even after he had left her. Bennet, unwilling to give her more money, broke her neck. Similarly, Thomas Carter, a police constable, beat Hermoine Taylor with a hammer when she asked him for money for their baby daughter.[34] One of the supposed advantages to men in cohabiting relationships was the lack of financial responsibility; men were, then, exasperated when cast-off women refused to accept this. But the resemblance to marriage led women to insist on men providing, whether their children were legitimate or not.

In their reasons for conflict, then, many poor cohabitees resembled spouses, fighting over resources and infidelity. In fact, some of these relationships were so unhappy that one cannot help wondering why they did not separate, since they were free to go. Contemporaries also found this puzzling. Martha Truss, a pub landlady, told John Wiggins about Agnes Oaks: 'if you cannot be happy and comfortable together you had better part; you are not compelled to live with her if you are not married'. Unfortunately, Wiggins ignored the advice, and he was not unique. Job Taylor and Emily Twiggs tramped together, and, over time, Taylor became enraged with her drinking and infidelity. Rather than leaving her, he murdered her in a rage. They were relatively young (Taylor was thirty-three), had been together only eighteen months, and were in a profession that often had temporary unions. Yet Taylor considered her his wife and could not break away from her.[35]

Some reasons for refusing to leave were obvious. Women needed economic support, especially if they had children, and they may also have feared retaliation if they left. But why did the men stay? In part, the men did not like to be separated from their children, as we saw in Chapter 2. Also, cohabitees who had settled into a relationship found starting again difficult. Isaac Townend lived with Ruth Hollings for years; both were in their forties, and both were bickering alcoholics by 1872. Rather than leave her, he strangled her and hanged himself. The key point, though, was the level of commitment, that is, if the couple felt 'married'. Some couples, like Townend and Hollings, cemented their ties with years of cohabitation, but others did so more quickly. William Abigale (twenty) killed his pregnant cohabitee because he could not provide for them. In his confession, he claimed, 'We were not married but we had drawn up & signed an agreement – that we were to live together as husband and wife and be faithful till death should part us.' Moreover, most of those who murdered their partners struck out in moments of fury but did not intend to kill. Like adulterous cohabitees, these couples called each other 'husband' and 'wife', and the woman took the man's name, and their emotional pain at the end of their relationships was clear.[36] They were married in all but name. Because they were too poor to interest the state, their decisions, in a sense, created a 'marriage' by taking its roles and making a public statement, and the bonds endured. They were, then, supportive of marriage as a concept, but challenged its legal and religious definition, though not its gender roles.

Family and neighbours

As with adulterous unions, wider kin were unenthusiastic about cohabitation. As usual, the women's family preferred marriage, especially as there were no legal impediments. Ellen Marney lived with George Mulley, a porter, in the 1850s. When she left him for refusing to marry her, she had the firm support of her mother. Similarly, James Gobey, who had three children with Mary Ann Chalmers, complained that her 'mother and sister enticed her away'.[37] All the same, as these examples show, families did not ostracise women cohabitees. Siblings, especially, kept close contact and tried to help. Eliza Nightingale, for instance, lived in her sister's lodging house with her lover, George Bowling, and both her sister and a sister-in-law defended her reputation after George murdered her. The man's natal family could intervene to break up these unions, too, but this was less common.[38]

The reaction of neighbours to this kind of cohabitation differed little from those of adulterous cohabitees; if anything, those in poor, rough neighbourhoods were even more indifferent to it. Since the divide between respectable and rough was seldom clean, though, the relationship with neighbours was complex. Many cohabiting couples in the poorest classes lived side by side with married couples and interacted with them often. The tolerance for them is nevertheless hard to determine, since most of the evidence about them is in violence cases. Newspapers sensationalised the coverage of crime and tended to divide the working class into a respectable/rough dichotomy that was far too simplistic.[39] The historian must look carefully at these sources to determine the acceptance of cohabitation among England's poorest subjects.

Many times the newspapers highlighted the 'indifference' of the neighbours to the frequent quarrels of unrespectable couples, and neighbours' intervention certainly had limits. Neighbours would not enter another person's home unless they heard sounds indicating that the altercation was life-threatening. Where to draw that line depended on many factors, including the woman's respectability, partly indicated by her marital status.[40] All the same, one can easily overstate the reluctance of neighbours to intervene. For one thing, many of the poor lived in boarding houses where privacy issues were less clear-cut. For another, the evidence from my cases indicates that neighbours were often the mainstays of those involved in domestic violence; in particular, women neighbours aided each other. Neighbours were the primary witnesses to the violence in 74 of the cases, and in 32 more they intervened to assist the victim but did not give evidence. Since I have detailed trial data for 196 of my cases, a large number of incidents (54 per cent) involved neighbourly help. In part this is because many of my cases involve the deadly violence that brought in outside assistance. But these numbers also indicate that these cohabitees were regular parts of their neighbourhoods. Most of these female witnesses were respectably married, but this fact did not lead them to ignore cohabiting couples in distress.

A case in the 1876 *Birmingham Daily Mail* illustrates this point. Two of the neighbours heard violent noises from the home of Mary Boswell and George Elwell and did nothing. The newspaper concluded that since the fights were common, the neighbours were 'indifferent'. Yet the inquest showed that the neighbours, though reluctant to invade another family's home, were heavily involved. On the night in question, Boswell and her children took refuge with neighbours on two separate occasions. The second time, a married neighbour volunteered to keep the children for the rest of the night. In addition, both men and women neighbours were key witnesses precisely because they did not ignore the violence.[41] Neighbours might disapprove of sexual irregularity, but they still pulled together in times of trouble. Numerous examples attest to both men and women trying to lessen the violence or rescue victims.[42]

One should not build too much on this evidence, since cases of violence were, by definition, unusual. Other sources, such as the evidence from the Royal Commission of 1912 and Mayhew and Booth, record neighbours who disliked unmarried couples in their midst. Mrs B—, who complained about the cohabiting rubbish carters, offers one example. In addition, working-class autobiographies have evidence that marriage certificates conveyed added status; Robert Roberts recalled a Salford woman who won disputes by 'bearing her "marriage lines" aloft like a banner'.[43] Also, since these couples chose not to marry, they could not appeal for sympathy by blaming the law as did adulterous or bigamous couples. Over all, though, since rough and respectable often lived side by side, the married working class had to cooperate with cohabitees on a regular basis. In fact, despite the moral strictures of his Salford neighbourhood, Roberts admitted that cohabitees did not suffer discrimination: 'those who dwelt together unmarried – "livin' tally" or "over t' brush", as the saying went – came in for little criticism'. Roberts thought this exception 'strange', but it does point up the careful calculations made in assessing respectability in the working classes.[44]

Prostitutes, 'criminals', and the demimonde

As the above discussion made clear, most of the poor who lived in cohabiting unions lived among and interacted with their married neighbours. They, then, were not part of the 'criminal classes'. Those who made a living solely from crime, as well as full-time prostitutes with their 'fancy men' or 'bullies', made up this category. They had little respect for the law, and, because of the dangers of prosecution, they had good reason to keep their relationships open-ended. Though many of these couples probably moved in and out of criminal life, the authorities and middle-class observers did not make many distinctions in dealing with them, seeing them as unstable and irrational. Like tramps and soldiers, though, these couples had logical reasons for cohabiting.

Prostitutes and their bullies made up one segment of this population. Historians disagree about the degree to which prostitutes were separated out from the regular working class.[45] The evidence I have collected indicates a continuum in the working class, rather than a strict divide between criminal, rough, and respectable. Prostitutes sometimes associated with labouring men, living in the same neighbourhoods as the respectable poor, or with criminals in 'low' districts, or they moved between these groups. Unless a keen observer, a middle-class reporter would not see where one strata shaded into the other. For example, three of the five women killed by Jack the Ripper, identified as prostitutes, were either in cohabiting relationships or had been so in the past; John Kelly, who lived with Catherine Eddowes, insisted she was not a prostitute at all. These women were examples of the movement between streetwalking, cohabitation, and marriage that many poor women experienced.[46]

That prostitutes lived with lawbreakers was the firm opinion of many observers. Robert Broughton, a London police magistrate, told the Select Committee on Drunkenness in 1834 that all prostitutes in his part of London lived with thieves.[47] Mayhew, writing in mid-century, identified such men as 'fancy men' or 'bullies'. The former were part-time criminals who acted as companions to prostitutes, 'loose characters, half thieves half loafers.' Bullies, on the other hand, he associated with brothels. At the end of the century, at least in port cities, bullies were more likely to be with a single prostitute or small groups of them, since the women needed protection once the brothels closed. Bullies helped rob unwary clients and enforced payment for the prostitutes' services.[48]

Though they did not articulate them, these couples had many reasons for not marrying. Few men, even criminal ones, wanted to wed a woman who regularly had sex with other men. In Shrewsbury, Emma Marston, a prostitute, lived with Henry Dorricott, a man with thirteen criminal convictions. The two lived a life of constant violence, and Emma also drank too much. Despite this, Emma told a neighbour that she stayed with him because he said he would marry her. He had not, however, fulfilled this promise by the time he killed her.[49] Perhaps, too, the women were uneasy about marrying such violent men, thus giving the latter even more power. According to Arthur Harding, 'Spuds' Murphy 'lived off of and terrorized a succession of women' in the East End of London in the Edwardian period; he hardly made an ideal husband. Often, though, the choice made little difference. Despite putative 'freedom', few women broke free from bullies, and they remained faithful and handed over their earnings. Booth, in fact, called the relationship 'something of the character of a marriage – the tie a lasting one, and the woman often devoted to the man even though very roughly treated'.[50]

As this last remark indicates, observers tended to sentimentalise prostitutes, perhaps equating them with Nancy from Charles Dickens's *Oliver Twist*. Though some women matched this stereotype, these relationships were often more complex than this characterisation allowed.

Some men who lived with prostitutes had jobs, for example, and others footed the couples' bills.[51] Since many working-class women were only part-time prostitutes, they lived with working-class men in the short or long term, whether or not the latter were 'bullies'. Confusions came from the middle-class tendency to call any woman who lived with a man outside of marriage a prostitute. For example, in reports on a violent incident in 1884, one newspaper called Rosina Squires a charwoman, while another called her a prostitute. George Townsend, her cohabitee, was both a farrier and a 'fancy man'. Probably the two subsisted on varying combinations of activities, but newspaper writers did not understand the survival strategies of the poor, and the authorities could be equally obtuse. John Jenkinson was arrested in Lancaster in 1910, accused of pimping for Ann Hornby, a 'well-known prostitute'. Jenkinson claimed their income came a variety of sources (a lodger, for example), but the magistrates did not believe him. Ann had been convicted of prostitution, and he lived with her, so he must be her bully. He got two months at hard labour.[52]

Prostitution was not illegal, but vagrancy, public drunkenness, and violence were. As a result, local and national authorities intervened between prostitutes and bullies regularly. As with other violence cases, the authorities blamed the men for the problems; a local magistrate, Mr Slade, when sentencing a bully for violence in 1884, called him 'a cowardly, worthless fellow'. The state became further entangled in these relationships when Parliament passed a law in 1898 that empowered the police to arrest for vagrancy any man living from the earnings of a prostitute. In a Lancaster case in 1905, the police court sentenced Thomas Lafferty to two months for doing so. The presiding magistrate lectured him, 'He was not a man but an apology for one ... When he came out he must try to be a man.' Interestingly, this view of pimps crossed class lines, since working-class men despised pimps as well. Mayhew claimed that cabmen who lived with prostitutes were known by a 'very gross appellation' by other drivers. Similarly, Arthur Sullivan, a long-time petty criminal in the East End of London, saved his deepest contempt for such men, despite his general indifference to moral issues.[53]

These relationships involved more mutuality than commonly believed, even in violence. Though some prostitutes were bullied, others were tough and pugnacious. Emma Marston, though she eventually died from a beating, 'was a violent woman when drunk' and often held her own against Dorricott.[54] In addition, some of the men, even those in the criminal classes, became attached to their prostitute cohabitees. Victor Bailey details two examples of men who lived with prostitutes and killed themselves when the women rejected them or appeared to have done so. The women also were not always attached solely through fear. Ellen Greenwood, an eighteen-year-old prostitute in London, tried to commit suicide in 1861 over her live-in lover, who had left her for another woman.[55] Women also willingly shielded their lovers from the law, though this was partly a fear of retaliation or losing economic support. In Lancaster, Charity Platt, an 'unfortunate', gave an alibi for her cohabitee, John Nesbitt, for a mugging, even though he had apparently bloodied her nose. Her behaviour demonstrates a common dynamic: many working-class women identified more with men in their own class – even violent ones – than with men or women who wanted to 'save' them.[56]

A similar type of relationship were those women who lived with men in the 'criminal' classes but did not resort to prostitution. These couples probably moved in and out of criminal behaviour, depending on opportunity, but when doing illegal activities, they worked together. Most avoided marriage, since they would likely have spells in prison. Mayhew told several stories of pairs of thieves who lived together and then separated as circumstances dictated. Female pickpockets, for instance, often lived with 'pickpockets, burglars, resetters, and other infamous characters', changing partners as necessary. An advantage to staying unmarried was that the man could put stolen property in the name of his paramour; with no legal tie between them, the courts could not prove she had no right to it. However, a disadvantage was that cohabitees could testify against their lovers in court as wives could not.[57] At any rate, many sources showed 'criminal' women and men working together, and the women sometimes went to prison for 'abetting' the crimes.[58]

The constant intervention of the state in the 'criminal' classes was a given, and certainly the courts disapproved of men living with prostitutes and arrested lawbreakers when they could. But Victorian courts could be surprisingly sympathetic to cohabiting relationships even in this class. Edward Agar, the mastermind behind the 'Great Bullion Robbery' of 1855, lived with Fanny Kay, a barmaid, and they had a child by the time of the heist. Agar was arrested on an unrelated charge some weeks later. He asked William Pierce, one of his partners, to give Fanny his share of the money, but Pierce did not do so. Fanny told Agar about it, and he turned state's evidence, resulting in the arrest and conviction of all the robbers. Despite Agar's theft, Justice Martin was most incensed by Pierce, lecturing him, 'A greater villain than you are, I believe, does not exist.' Even more ironically, Agar's money was not subject to seizure, since Agar was not convicted of burglary. So the English courts awarded it to Kay and her child.[59] The relationship of these couples to the state was usually antagonistic, but, as in violence cases, the justice system sometimes gave left-handed support to cohabiting unions.

A further complication is the danger of overstating the 'free and easy' sexuality of these couples. Criminal men expected fidelity; though the relationships were temporary, they were exclusive (at least for the women) while they lasted. Mayhew interviewed a burglar who lived with an Irish coster-girl for a time, but he left her after she flirted with another man.[60] And the number of violent incidents due to jealousy indicates that men (and some women) in this class did not accept changes of allegiance indifferently. In addition, these couples often argued over the same things – money, drink, and fidelity – as the rest of the working classes. For all these reasons, the difference between the very poor and the 'criminal' classes was often a fine line, hard for the middle classes to see.

Deliberate cohabitation

Most of those who chose not to marry were working class, but a small minority were not. These lower-middle-class and middle-class cohabitees divided into two groups. First, some were in professions that skated on the bare edge of respectability, such as performers (actors, singers, dancers), or bohemian occupations such as writers and painters. These groups, along with professional mistresses/courtesans (explored in the next chapter), made up the demimonde, a parallel, unrespectable social system. The most prominent of these groups were performers. Cohabitees in the theatre continued to work freely despite the implications of their living arrangements, since both men and women performers had enough social and economic support to flout convention.

Again, though, the degree of choice in cohabitation differed between the genders, since women preferred marriage. Dora Jordan, at the end of the eighteenth century, lived for four years with Richard Ford (1786–90). Both were actors and continued to work, and they had four children. Most of Jordan's biographers agree that she would have preferred to marry, but Ford postponed matrimony because of his father's disapproval. When Jordan finally gave him an ultimatum, he refused outright.[61] Though the Regency stage was notoriously lax, the acting profession continued to see irregular relationships throughout the nineteenth century. Ellen Terry lived with Edward Godwin from 1868 to 1875. Since she was already married to Frederick Watts, they could not regularise the relationship, though Terry could have asked Watts to divorce her. Godwin and Terry apparently made no effort to marry, perhaps because Godwin really wanted a housekeeper as a wife. He later married Beatrice Philip, a young student. In contrast, Terry later married Charles Wardell, another actor.[62] Terry was independent and successful, like West and Hunt, and she thus shared their difficulties in building a lasting relationship with any man who wanted a domestic mate. On the other hand, because of her salary, she was not 'ruined' by the end of her free union.

At the lower end of the performing scale, the likelihood of cohabitation was greater. These couples had the same lax attitude as sailors or tramps, in part because actors were also highly mobile. William Compton, a comic singer, was charged with abducting Mary Ann Malbon in 1885 in Nottingham. They met at the music hall, and when his engagement ended, she offered to go with him. They lived as a married couple until her family tracked them down. The problem for women was that those who were most likely to cohabit were also the poorest, causing economic distress if the relationship failed. Louisa T., who performed at the Queen's Theatre in London, lived with Charles B., another performer. When he deserted her in 1853, she appealed to the Foundling Hospital to take the younger of her two children, without success.[63]

The family experience of such couples was similar to that of the middle-class professionals who could not marry. Families, especially those of the women, opposed such arrangements, and were only reconciled by subsequent marriages. Terry's children, for example, did not meet their extended family until she married legally for the second time (after Watts divorced her). Nevertheless, stage life had its peculiarities. First, the theatre offered an alternative social group that compensated for alienated friends or family. Second, some actresses earned comparable salaries to men and so survived the end of partnerships. Terry, in fact, did not lose her income or her marriageability. More importantly, audiences separated the lives of performers from their roles. As Theresa Davis put it, despite her past, 'Terry still evoked the consummation of "womanliness" in her roles and could command universal respect and admiration'. This bifurcation allowed women in this profession to live unconventionally and still succeed. William Holand, the Somerset vicar, demonstrated this double vision. He saw a play with Jordan in 1811 and had mixed feelings: 'Mrs Jourdan [sic] acted her part very well and made us laugh much … I hate to be pleased with a bad character such as Mrs Jordan has tho she makes me laugh.'[64] The stage both condemned women as potentially 'fallen', and offered them a way to overcome the stigma, something few other professions did.

The second major group of those non-poor couples who chose not to marry were made up almost entirely of couples in which the man was reluctant to do so. These cases were the clearest examples of the sexual double standard in this group. Women in the lower-middle and middle classes had the most to lose if they agreed to an irregular union, so the majority did so only because the men refused to marry. For instance, the few lower middle-class women who appealed to the Foundling Hospital entered cohabiting relationships hoping a marriage would follow. This choice was risky, since they could easily slide into poverty if deserted. Sarah Ann D., a music teacher, inherited £200 from a relative. Charles C., a scrivener, persuaded her to live with him for two years 'much against the wishes of her Mother and Friends'. The relationship was not long-lived; when the money was gone, so was Charles.[65]

Women who either agreed to or were forced into sexual relations could often not get the men to marry them afterwards, but felt compelled to stay, since they were now 'fallen'. Caroline W. lived for three years with Joseph D., a French Master and clerk, in the 1840s. She claimed he was the son of a gentleman and 'forced her' to have sex. The two then lived together until he left in 1848. Men in tenuous, lower middle-class positions were not ready for marriage, but they still wanted companionship. Jessie H., who was 'of respectable connexions', lived with Alexander M., a clerk, for five months in 1854. When she became pregnant, he 'suddenly deserted her'. Considering Alexander's slender hold on respectability, his decision was not surprising. But she was, according to the Foundling Hospital investigator, 'now utterly ruined'.[66]

The sexual double standard played out in many different ways. At times, the men were simply not monogamous, since they did not have to be. Gordon Craig, Ellen Terry's son, was notoriously unfaithful to his wives and lovers. He married May Gibson in 1893, but left her in 1898 to live with actress Jess Dorynne. Dorynne became pregnant in 1901, and Craig deserted her. Shortly afterwards (in 1902), he ran away with Elena Meo, the daughter of an artist. Although May divorced him in 1904, he never married Elena, and continued to have affairs. Similarly, the painter Augustus John fell in love with other women even when he was living with both his wife Ida and his mistress Dorelia McNeill. After Ida's death, he lived off and on with Dorelia but had numerous affairs. Like Craig, he was simply not a good marital risk.[67]

At other times, the men did not regard women who would live with them as suitable marriage material. Men could enter sexual relationships and remain desirable marriage partners, but women could not. This was, in fact, probably more likely to happen in the middle and upper classes, where standards of sexual propriety were strict. Once having had sex with a man, a woman had to stay with him or admit to the world that she was 'ruined'. Felix Spicer, a restaurant owner, lived with Mary Palin for seventeen years. Palin wanted to marry, but Spicer would not do so, and the couple had seven children. In 1890, Spicer told their landlord the truth about their relationship. Palin left him at once, writing, 'You mean, contemptible scrub, did you think of my tears when, before Felix was born, I asked you to marry me out of my shame'?[68] Mary had little choice but to live with Felix as long as he pretended to be married to her. Once he let people know the truth, she left him in disgust.

Though men were overwhelmingly less willing to marry, a few rare women also preferred to be free. Octavia S., only seventeen, told the Foundling Hospital that she declined to marry Thomas E., a gentleman, because he was going to Ceylon and would have to leave her behind. She was reluctant to tie herself to a man who might not return.[69] But such women were a minority; middle-class women needed marriage. They had few employment opportunities that would allow them to care for their children in the style of a middle-class home. In addition, since respectable women avoided telling their families about their shame, they were even more isolated than most unwed mothers. One can only speculate about the fate of Octavia S. after the Foundling Hospital refused to aid her, since she feared telling her family the truth. In the end, these cases again show the difficulties of women in every class and every type of cohabitation in comparison with men.

Conclusion

Couples who chose not to marry challenged Victorian norms more than those who would have married if they could have done so. Especially in the working class, some men and women saw few reasons to go through a ceremony that made no difference to them. The couple avoided expense and the interference of the state, and they might hope that strictures on providing and obedience would be looser, though this often did not prove true in practice. Also, sometimes their unions were necessarily temporary, as with sailors or tramps; the advantages of cohabitation were clear to couples with frequent separations.

Nevertheless, most of these unions were curiously conservative, particularly the stable cohabiting unions of the poor. The majority did not advertise their status; on the contrary, they went by the man's name and called each other husband and wife. Furthermore, such couples kept traditional gender roles. If cohabitation resembled marriage in every way except the legal ritual, it was a fairly tepid rebellion against it. One might argue instead that these couples had expanded the definition of marriage to include long-term cohabitees well before the state did so.[70] Whatever their reasons, people found their own ways to form families, ones that could be as emotionally demanding and hard to dissolve as legal relationships.

Though the state largely stayed out of these unions, it intervened in those of prostitutes and bullies or in violence cases. At times, the courts recognised long-term unions as marriages, as in the case of Fanny Kay; in others, the courts harshly punished men for the irregularity, as with bullies. Like the courts, neighbours and kin reacted in a wide variety of ways, but sharp divisions between married and unmarried couples were not often possible. Though not unanimous, the primary response of neighbours in the working class was, at the least, tolerance. Voluntary cohabitees were, though, more often pressured to marry by authorities and their families, since they had no impediments to marriage.

In addition, gender and class differences were starker in these groups. Men were the reluctant party more often than women, since they had less to gain from legal marriage and paid fewer of the costs of cohabitation. Women, with restricted economic horizons and the responsibility for childcare, preferred marriage. Many cohabiting couples lived comfortably together, passing as husband and wife, but those who ran into difficulties showed the disproportionate burden for women. The only exception were women who could earn a good living, such as actresses. Women accepted free unions, but seldom as a first choice. A similar dynamic would be at work in cross-class relationships, which were overwhelmingly those of a poor woman and a better-off man. The complications of gender and class were even more tangled in those cases, as we shall see.

Notes

1 G. N. Gandy, 'Illegitimacy in a handloom weaving community: Fertility patterns in Culcheth, Lancashire, 1781–1860', (D.Phil. dissertation, Oxford University, 1978), p. 381; Gillis, *For Better, For Worse*, pp. 190–228; Clark, *The Struggle for the Breeches*, pp. 42–62; 177–96.

2 M. Davies, *Life in an English Village: An Economic and Historical Survey of the Parish of Corsely in Wiltshire* (London: T. Fisher Unwin, 1909), pp. 156–84; B. Reay, *Microhistories: Demography, Society, and Culture in Rural England, 1800–1930* (Cambridge: Cambridge University Press, 1996), pp. 185–97; 209.

3 Booth, *Life and Labour of the People in London*, II, 45–85; B. S. Rowntree, *Poverty: A Study of Town Life* (London: Macmillan, 1901), pp. 32–70; the one cohabiting couple was on p. 49.

4 *Royal Commission*, I, 112; A. Mearns, *The Bitter Cry of Outcast London*, ed. A. Wohl (Leicester: Leicester University Press, 1970), p. 61; G. Sims, *How the Poor Live and Horrible London* (London: Chatto & Windus, 1883), pp. 24–6, quote from p. 26.

5 *Irish University Press Series of British Parliamentary Papers: Reports, Returns, and Other Papers Relating to Marriage and Divorce with Proceedings and Minutes of Evidence, 1830–96* (Shannon, Ireland: Irish University Press, 1971), I, 44; III, 6; O. Anderson, 'The incidence of civil marriage in Victorian England and Wales', *Past and Present* 69 (1975), 50–87.

6 Gandy, 'Illegitimacy in a Handloom Weaving Community', pp. 406–8; Gillis, *For Better,*

For Worse, pp. 116–30.

7   J. Greenwood, *The Seven Curses of London* (London: Stanley Rivers & Co., 1869), p. 20; Andrews in PCOM 1/151, p. 501; Mayhew, *London Labour and the London Poor*, II, 112; I, 475.

8   Sims, *How the Poor Live*, pp. 26–27; J. Yeames, *Life in London Alleys, with Reminiscences of Mary McCarthy and Her Work* (London: F. E. Longley, n.d.), p. 141.

9   Booth, *Life and Labour of the People of London*, I:49; Mayhew, *London Labour and the London Poor*, I, 45.

10 Mumm, '"Not worse than other girls"', 527–47; LMA, A/FH/A8/1/3/63/1, Petition #63; Barret-Ducrocq, *Love in the Time of Victoria*, pp. 125–7.

11 LMA, A/FH/A8/1/3/59/1, Petition #143, 13 November 1852; A/FH/A8/1/3/39/1, Petition #6, 11 January 1832.

12 Mayhew, *London Labour and the London Poor*, III, 404.

13 LMA, A/FH/A8/1/3/56/1, Petition # 90, 16 June 1849; A/FH/A8/1/3/44/1, Petition #16, 22 February 1837. The Hospital did not take widows' children, so Elizabeth would not have received help in any case.

14 Mumm, '"Not worse than other girls"', 532. See also A. Higginbotham, 'Respectable sinners: Salvation Army rescue work with unmarried mothers, 1884–1914', in G. Malmgreen (ed.), *Religion in the Lives of English Women, 1760–1930* (Bloomington, IN: Indiana University Press, 1986), 227.

15 For Langford, see ASSI 54/5; *Manchester Examiner and Times*, 28 January 1887, p. 3; for White, see *The Times*, 6 August 1860, p. 10; *Warwick and Warwickshire Advertiser*, 4 August 1860, p. 2.

16 Fulford, *The Rector and his Flock*, p. 32.

17 W. Plomer (ed.), *Kilvert's Diary, 1870–79: Selections from the Diary of the Rev. Francis Kilvert* (London: Penguin Books, 1977), pp. 27; 41; 43; 141; 145, first quote from p. 27, second from p. 43, third from p. 145.

18 C. Rose, *European Slavery; or Scenes from Married Life* (Edinburgh: Andrew Elliot, 1881), p. 46; *Royal Commission*, III, 31; LMA, A/FH/A8/1/3/37/1, Petition #29, 1830.

19 *The Times*, 19 April 1869, p. 6; 20 April 1869, p. 9; Mayhew, *London Labour and the London Poor*, II, 225.

20 Booth, *Labour and Life of the People of London*, XVII, 41; Reay, *Microhistories*, pp. 186–8.

21 Reay, *Microhistories*, pp. 186–7; HO 45/9315/14967; *Manchester Weekly Times*, 20 April 1872, p. 7; 4 May 1872, p. 3; *The Times*, 1 May 1872, p. 12; 3 August 1872, p. 6.

22 Mayhew, *London Labour and the London Poor*, II, 119; III, 384–5.

23 L. Tabili, *'We Ask for British Justice': Workers and Racial Difference in Late Imperial Britain* (Ithaca, NY: Cornell University Press, 1994), pp. 143–58.

24 Reay, *Microhistories*, p. 196; Booth, *Labour and Life of the People of London*, IV, 317–22; Mayhew, *London Labour and the London Poor*, II, 294.

25 Gillis, *For Better, For Worse*, p. 204; Mayhew, *London Labour and the London Poor*, IV, 226–36.

26 HO 144/161/A41540 (for quote); *Liverpool Mercury*, 17 November 1885, p. 3; 9 December 1885, p. 7.

27 J. W. Rounsfell, *On the Road: Journeys of a Tramping Printer*, ed. A. Whitehead (Horsham: Caliban Books, 1982), pp. 19–20.

28 Mayhew, *London Labour and the London Poor*, III:403; M. Higgs, *Glimpses into the Abyss* (London: P. S. King & Sons, 1906), p. 94.

29 Gillis, *For Better, For Worse*, pp. 201–5; quote from p. 204.

30 Mayhew, *London Labour and the London Poor*, I, 20–2, 34–40; II, 177 (for first quote), 294 (for second quote).

31 Sims, *How the Poor Live*, p. 26; Booth, *Labour and Life of the People of London*, XVII, 42.

32 See Hammerton, *Cruelty and Companionship*, p. 45; Conley, *The Unwritten Law*, pp. 72–3.

33 *The Times*, 28 July 1866, p. 12; *Lancaster Guardian*, 9 June 1866, p. 8 (for quote); 28 July, 1866, p. 3. See also Ross, *Love and Toil*, pp. 72–8; Ayers and Lambertz, 'Marriage relations, money, and domestic violence', pp. 195–219; A. Clark, 'Domesticity and the problem of wife beating in nineteenth-century Britain: working-class culture, law and politics', in S. D'Cruze (ed.), *Everyday Violence in Britain, 1850–1950* (New York: Longman, 2000), 27–40.

34 Bennet in *The Times*, 18 August 1854, p. 10; *Gloucestershire Chronicle*, 19 August 1854, p. 3; Carter in PCOM 1/106, pp. 438–42; *The Times*, 29 October 1874, p. 11.

35 Wiggins in PCOM 1/92, p. 511; Taylor in *The Times*, 12 August 1893, p. 3; *Tonbridge Telegraph*, 12 August 1893, p. 5.

36 Townend in *The Times*, 11 July 1872, p. 12; *Leeds Mercury*, 11 July 1872, p. 7; Abigale in HO 144/98/A16400/11; confession dated 21 May 1882. For striking out, see *Yorkshire Gazette*, 23 May 1885, p. 9; *Leeds Mercury*, 20 May 1885, p. 8; for taking each others' names, see *Norwich Mercury*, 3 December 1892, p. 5; *Lancaster Guardian*, 27 October 1860, p. 2.

37 Mulley in *Lancaster Guardian*, 3 November 1855, p. 2; *The Times*, 26 October 1855, p. 9; Gobey in CRIM 10/58, pp. 602–5, quote from p. 603. See also *Lancaster Guardian*, 17 March 1880, p. 7.

38 Bowling in HO 144/236/A51714; *The Times*, 14 July 1890, p. 6; *Surrey Adverstiser and County Times*, 12 July 1890, p. 2. For men's families intervening, see Plomer, *Kilvert's Diary*, p. 27; and ASSI 75/2; *South Wales Daily News*, 7 April 1876, p. 6.

39 D'Cruze, *Crimes of Outrage*, pp. 176–80; Hammerton, *Cruelty and Companionship*, p. 49; and J. Knelman, *Twisting in the Wind: The Murderess and the English Press* (Toronto: University of Toronto Press, 1998), pp. 35–42.

40 D'Cruze, *Crimes of Outrage*, p. 72; C. Chinn, *They Worked All Their Lives: Women of the Urban Poor in England, 1880–1939* (Manchester: Manchester University Press, 1988), p. 159.

41 *Birmingham Daily Mail*, 6 March 1876, p. 3 (for quote); 9 March 1876, p. 3.

42 For women intervening, see HO 144/85/A7411; *Nottingham and Midland Counties Daily Express*, 23 May 1881, p. 3; 24 May 1881, p. 3; *The Times*, 23 May 1881, p. 12; for men, see *Nottingham Evening Post*, 18 May 1885, p. 4.

43 R. Roberts, *A Ragged Schooling: Growing Up in the Classic Slum* (London: Fontana Paperbacks, 1984), p. 83.

44 Roberts, *The Classic Slum*, 47.

45 J. Walkowitz, *Prostitution and Victorian Society: Women, Class and the State* (Cambridge: Cambridge University Press, 1980), pp. 192–213; F. Finnegan, *Poverty and Prostitution: A Study of Victorian Prostitutes in York* (Cambridge: Cambridge University Press, 1979); L. Mahood, *The Magdalenes: Prostitution in the Nineteenth Century* (London: Routledge, 1990); P. Bartley, *Prostitution: Prevention and Reform in England, 1860–1914* (London: Routledge, 2000), pp. 12–18.

46 Curtis, *Jack the Ripper and the London Press*, pp. 20–4; 152.

47 British Library. Francis Place Papers ADD 27,830, Vol. XLII, 'Minutes of Evidence Taken

Before the Select Committee on Drunkenness', 5 August 1834, fol. 91, p. 16.

48 Mayhew, *London Labour and the London Poor*, IV, 253; Finnegan, *Poverty and Prostitution*, p. 122; Mahood, *The Magdalenes*, p. 44.

49 *The Shrewsbury Free Press*, 26 September 1874, p. 2; 27 March 1875, p. 2.

50 R. Samuel, *East End Underworld: Chapters in the Life of Arthur Harding* (London: Routledge and Kegan Paul, 1981), p. 108; Booth, *Labour and Life of the People of London*, XVII, 123.

51 *The Times*, 7 July 1862, p. 5.

52 Squires in PCOM 1/126, pp. 721–4; *The Times*, 4 July 1884, p. 3; 26 July 1884, p. 6; 4 August 1884, p. 3; 16 August 1884, p. 3; 19 September 1884, p. 10; Jenkinson in *Lancaster Guardian*, 12 February 1910, p. 3.

53 Slade in *The Times*, 8 September 1884, p. 3; Lafferty in *Lancaster Guardian*, 25 November 1905, p. 8; Mayhew, *London Labour and the London Poor*, III, 351; Samuel, *East End Underworld*, p. 130. See also *The Times*, 24 October 1898, 14.

54 *Shrewsbury Free Press*, 27 March 1875, p. 2.

55 Bailey, *This Rash Act*, pp. 174–5; *The Times*, 20 July 1861, p. 11.

56 *Lancaster Guardian*, 20 December 1890, p. 2; 8 November 1890, p. 2.

57 Mayhew, *London Labour and the London Poor*, IV, 308–9; 324; 344; quote from p. 308.

58 For example, see *The Times*, 25 October 1860, p. 9.

59 D. Thomas, *The Victorian Underworld* (New York: New York University Press, 1998), pp. 204–29, quote from p. 228.

60 Mayhew, *London Labour and the London Poor*, IV, 354.

61 Tomalin, *Mrs Jordan's Profession*, pp. 72–8; 113–20; C. Jerrold, *The Story of Dorothy Jordan* (New York: Benjamin Blom, 1914), pp. 105–16; 156–65.

62 N. Auerbach, *Ellen Terry: Player in Her Time* (New York: W. W. Norton, 1987), pp. 132–86; D. Harbron, *The Conscious Stone: The Life of Edward William Godwin* (New York: Benjamin Blom, 1971), pp. 66–76; 89–92; 116–19; J. Melville, *Ellen and Edy: A Biography of Ellen Terry and her Daughter, Edith Craig, 1847–1947* (London: Pandora, 1987), pp. 47–80. For another example, see J. Coleman, *Charles Reade as I Knew Him* (London: Treherne & Co., 1903); M. Elwin, *Charles Reade: A Biography* (London: J. Cape, 1931); and E. Smith, *Charles Reade* (Boston: Twayne Publishers, 1976).

63 *Yorkshire Gazette*, 19 December 1885, p. 9; LMA, A/FH/A8/1/3/60/1, Petition #83, 28 May 1853.

64 Auerbach, *Ellen Terry*, pp. 183–4; T. Davis, *Actresses as Working Women: Their Social Identity in Victorian Culture* (London: Routledge, 1991), pp. 105–6, quote from p. 106; Ayres, *Paupers and Pig-Killers*, p. 223.

65 LMA, A/FH/A8/1/3/33/1, Petition #4, 4 October 1826.

66 LMA, A/FH/A8/1/3/56/1, Petition #62, 28 April 1849; A/FH/A8/1/3/62/1, Petition #134, 11 August 1855.

67 Auerbach, *Ellen Terry*, pp. 367–436; Melville, *Ellen and Edy*, pp. 45–7; 169; 185–7; 217–20; E. Craig, *Gordon Craig: The Story of His Life* (New York: Alfred A. Knopf, 1968), pp. 102–8, 116–32, 143–6, 156–9, 180–99, 214–24, 248–64, 300–4; M. Holyroyd, *Augustus John: A Biography* 2 vols. Vol. I: *The Years of Innocence* (London: Heinemann, 1974), pp. 273, 285–90; 326–7; 335–6; 346–8; Vol. II: *The Years of Experience* (London: Heinemann, 1975), pp. 1–10; 25–7; 49–53; 89–94; 131–3; 149–52; 190–3.

68 HO 144/235/A51593; quote from piece 7; *Lancaster Guardian*, 31 May 1890, p. 5; 7 June 1890, p. 3; *The Times*, 2 August 1890, p. 10; 23 August 1890, p. 10; *Chester Guardian and*

Record, 2 August 1890, p. 5; 6 August 1890, p. 6.

69 LMA, A/FH/A8/1/3/52/1, Petition #120, 11 October 1845.

70 B. M. Ratcliffe, 'Popular classes and cohabitation in mid-nineteenth-century Paris', *Journal of Family History* 21 (1996), 316–50; and L. Abrams, 'Concubinage, cohabitation and the law: Class and gender relations in nineteenth-century Germany', *Gender and History* 5 (1993), 81–100.

7

Cross-class cohabitation

IN *MARY BARTON,* Elizabeth Gaskell offers a depiction of Victorian cross-class liaisons through the character of Mary's Aunt Esther, who ran away with an army officer and lived with him for three years. They had a little girl, but he left her when his regiment was called away. In rapid succession, her business failed, her daughter died, and she became an alcoholic prostitute.[1] Gaskell assumed that cross-class matings were between wealthy men and poorer women, that they were temporary, and that the lower-class woman paid the price for her 'fall'. In some ways, this portrait was accurate. The vast majority of such unions were between better-off men and working-class women. In addition, many of these women gave birth to children and were abandoned with little compensation. The opposite situation, that of a well-off woman with a poorer man, was rare because such women were all but unmarriageable after cohabitation. They might *marry* into a lower class, but were unlikely to 'live in sin' at all, much less with a man who had lower status. Indeed, I have only four examples of better-off women with poorer men, and two of these involved women in feminist/socialist circles (discussed in Chapter 9). Of the remaining two, one had only a slight class difference; in the other, the man was already married, so the couple had no choice about marrying.[2] Because of the rarity and peculiarity of these cases, this chapter will deal only with the more common cross-class pattern.

Overall, these unions offer another example of women's bleaker prospects in cohabitation. Middle-class and upper-class men regarded their working-class lovers as temporary, there only until a 'real' marriage came into view. All the same, these relationships were complex. The men did not want to marry, but many felt a sense of responsibility towards their lovers; records show such men leaving bonds and inheritances to them. Moreover, the women did not always end up degraded and dead. The life of a mistress was precarious, but its financial rewards could be high, especially for any children. Nor did all men despair of marrying lower-class lovers. The myth of Pygmalion tempted some men to train their cohabitees to climb the social ladder. Cross-class unions, then, combined exploitative and advantageous elements for men and women, both defying and deferring to class and gender expectations.

Kept mistresses

The participants in most cross-class cohabiting relationships expected them to be temporary. These cohabitees broke into two groups. The first involved professional mistresses; in these instances, women negotiated terms for cohabitation and moved from protector to protector during their careers. Some mistresses preferred to stay with the same man, and others had their own careers (particularly in bohemian professions), but all understood that they might someday lose out to a wife. The second group includes poor women who preferred to marry, but chose to live with better-off men rather than lose them; these relationships usually ended when the men married 'suitable' women. In neither of these groups were the women entirely passive, but those in the second group were more likely to fall into poverty when their lovers left.

Because middle-class and upper-class men had years of schooling and work before they could marry, they either had to be celibate or find other outlets for their sexual energies. Though Victorians worried most about prostitution, another option was a mistress. Kept women were several steps above common prostitutes; they lived with a succession of men and could receive handsome incomes. Henry Mayhew argued that these women were an entirely separate set of prostitutes, usually faithful to their keepers. He pointed out that many 'confirmed bachelors' were 'already to all intents and purposes united to one who possesses charms, talents, and accomplishments'. He claimed men who kept such women included merchants, army officers, and members of Parliament.[3]

Professional mistresses earned a good living. Early in the century, Harriette Wilson made fabulous sums of money from a succession of prominent men. The most famous Victorian courtesan, Catherine Walters ('Skittles'), had a long, prosperous career, beginning in 1859; she died in 1920 in comfortable retirement.[4] Skittles was unusually successful, but women at the lower end of the spectrum could also prosper. Mayhew wrote about the daughter of a tradesman who went away with a 'young gentleman' to begin her career. She had since lived with four different men and had no worries for the future: 'What do I think will become of me? What an absurd question. I could marry to-morrow if I liked.' Many working-class women saw the life of a mistress as more alluring than their other options – domestic service, the sweated trades, factory work, or marriage to a poor man. Women had so little economic power that the sex trade was a rational choice.[5]

Indeed, at times, the women were already prostitutes when they met their future cohabitees. The men became regulars, and eventually monopolised the women's time and shaded into cohabitation. Men with property did not want to marry prostitutes, but they did sometimes feel responsible for them. Thomas Hill, a London oil-shop owner, lived with a prostitute named Chamber for two years, and he gave her two guineas a week. He never wanted to marry her, but he left her £50 a year in his will. The plaintiff in *Friend v. Harrison* was also 'a common street walker' who settled into a cohabiting relationship with a wealthy man. He, too, gave her £50 a year at his death.[6] Clearly, these women had every reason to prefer the status of mistress to that of prostitute.

Nevertheless, a mistress was not a wife. Olive Schreiner, the South African novelist, wrote to Karl Pearson in 1886 about a destitute young woman she tried to help. The woman had been a prostitute, but 'for seven years she has been living with one man ... He had promised to leave her provided for: now he has died suddenly & left no will. Of course the son won't give her anything.' The young woman felt she had no choice but to return to the streets. This circular career path was typical; women frequently moved from respectable jobs to prostitution to kept status, then back to respectable employment or prostitution. Françoise Barret-Ducrocq's study of the Foundling Hospital disclosed many such examples. Sarah T., a servant, lost her job due to 'bad' behaviour and was a prostitute for six months until she met a lawyer who took a fancy to her. She was his mistress for six months, during which she lived well. However, the lawyer broke off the connection when she had a child, and Sarah had to appeal to charities for help. She hoped to go back into domestic service, thus completing the circle.[7]

Sarah was only a part-time prostitute, but she still saw being 'kept' as a step up. Many poor women agreed that they could have more comfortable lives with wealthy men. They made more money than most working women, and they moved with apparent ease from one man to another. Ellen Keenan, mentioned in Chapter 1, first lived with a baronet and had a child with him, then with another man, and both gave her allowances. She then lived with Captain Handley and had a daughter, earning her an annuity of £150.[8] Not all women were this fortunate, but certainly many tried to make a living out of protection. Elizabeth Irvine lived with the wealthy Austen Vickers in 1868. Vickers did not marry her, but told her to '[a]sk me for as much money as you like, and you shall have it'. When he ended their relationship, she lived with a horse dealer, a fact that emerged during her breach of promise case. Her former servant, Rebekah Spriggs, not only confessed about Elizabeth's lover, but admitted that she herself lived with a Mr Eliot, insisting, 'She was not a lady in keeping or a gay lady, as only one gentleman came to see her.' Unsurprisingly, the jury found for the defendant.[9] Though she lost her case, Irvine had profited from Vickers over their seven-year union, and she had also acquired a new protector before the trial. As long as she remained attractive, she had little reason to change her profession.

In fact, some kept women used their sexuality aggressively, demanding compensation from their partners. Mary Ann Clarke, mistress of the Duke of York, used the threat of her memoirs to negotiate a lump payment of £7,000 and a £400 annuity when the relationship was over. Wilson also extracted money from various lovers when she wrote her memoirs; many paid to be removed from its pages.[10] Few women got money on this scale, but many used their sexuality to good effect. Emmeline Hairs, an 'adventuress', was the mistress of Sir George Elliot, an MP, in 1887. He gave her large sums of money, including £3,000, supposedly an investment in her nonexistent coal business.[11]

In contrast to these predatory cases, most of these relationships involved emotional attachments. Irvine had numerous affectionate letters from Vickers, who called her 'the only woman I ever loved'. Handley claimed to have struggled greatly when he decided he had to part from Keenan.[12] For the most part, the affection was mutual. Indeed, some of these unions were extraordinarily long-lived. In contrast to Clarke, Madame de St Laurent happily cohabited with the Duke of Kent for twenty-seven years. Though he had to leave her to marry legally in 1817, they both found the parting painful. Even more remarkably, Elizabeth Armistead began her career in a high-class brothel and had numerous protectors, but she eventually settled down with Charles James Fox. The couple loved each other so devotedly that they married in 1795.[13]

Not all women relied solely on their incomes as mistresses. Some professions gave women the opportunity to supplement their earnings with protection from wealthy admirers. The main avenue to such a career was the theatre. Upper-class men often became enamoured with the glamourous figures on the stage; actresses may have preferred marriage, but they knew that it was unlikely and so accepted protection. Dora Jordan, the most prominent example, knew the Duke of Clarence would not marry her, since he would never get George III's permission. Thus, before they cohabited, Dora negotiated an annual allowance of £840. Like many of the actresses who had protectors, Jordan continued to go on stage; her lover's allowance simply added a much higher degree of financial security for her and their ten children.[14] Though rarely as exalted as royalty, most protectors of actresses were noblemen or wealthy entrepreneurs who could offer high incomes. May Gore acted in the 1890s and lived with Lord Sudley for two years. When his family induced him to leave her, he settled £500 on her. May then lived with another gentleman, a Mr Stourton, at which point Sudley tried to get her back. She eventually agreed, allegedly because he promised marriage. When he broke off with her again, he offered her an annual allowance of £100 which she indignantly refused.[15]

Clearly, women approached these unions on the understanding that they deserved compensation when the affairs ended. Those who came out best had written annuities; these gave real security. For the most part, this belief was mutual. When the Duke of Clarence decided that he should find a legal wife, he negotiated a settlement for Jordan, an allowance of £4,400, though in return she gave up custody of the children when they reached thirteen. Similarly, St Laurent received a generous allowance when she retired back to France. In the case of Gore, Sudley testified that he gave her the £500 because 'I recognised that I had an obligation towards her'.[16] Compensation was crucial because marriage was superior. When Gore told Stourton that she was returning to Sudley because he offered marriage, Stourton assured her he would not 'stand in the way of her becoming a good woman'. This did not mean the couples had no affection for each other, but they recognised that without marriage, women had no security. Ann Moody, mistress of an army officer, was afraid to tell him about her debts, though she had accrued them after her confinement with his child. As the editors of the *Sunday Times* pointed out, 'a mistress must be incessantly tormented by the knowledge that she can hold on to her lord not a moment longer than his own confidence and sympathy endure'.[17]

Marriage also gave status; in contrast, prostitutes, kept women, and cohabitees shaded into one another. The Victorian courts and press largely saw all such women as 'prostitutes', and the women themselves were often confused about the issue.[18] One crucial indication was where the male partner actually lived or how often he visited. A married man, unless formally separated, had a house with his 'real' family, and his union with a working-class woman was simply an affair. Some bachelors, too, had family homes, and would not regard their habitation with a mistress as their main residence (or might ask the mistress to leave when his 'real' family visited). On the other hand, men in billets or on ships much of the year or in cramped accommodations in colleges or inns of court might well have considered their mistresses' houses as real 'homes'; indeed, some unhappily married men may also have done so. Moreover, the situation was fluid. Within a single relationship, a couple might go from being a prostitute and a 'regular', a kept woman with a protector who visited, then a live-in mistress. Each change altered a man's perception of his responsibilities. In particular, men felt more obligation to pension off women with whom they had marriage-like unions, though women who relied on goodwill, rather than written agreements, risked disappointment.

Though the determination of these women to extract support partially mitigated their class and gender disadvantages, the financial arrangements did not always pan out. Mistresses had more difficulty as they aged, since their primary asset was their attractiveness. Their paramours might grow tired of them, and they had less chance of finding anyone else as the years went on. Both Jordan and St Laurent died alone in Paris, and Jordan was heavily in debt. Mistresses had prosperity in the short run, but little security; thus, they had to be both romantic and businesslike, an uneasy combination. Nevertheless, these unions were not purely exploitative by one side or the other.

Esther Bartons

Though they did not always have happy ends, courtesans had some say about the terms of their relationships. The second, much larger group of mistresses were those who agreed to live with higher-class men because of romantic feelings, by far the most common pattern for cross-class relationships. Such women went into the unions knowing that they would probably not marry, but they settled for what they could get. Some convinced themselves that they would wed eventually, especially if they had children. Women fell in love with well-off men easily, and these men's regard was also flattering. The secrecy and forbidden nature of the relationship added to its allure.[19]

An upper-class or middle-class man's attraction to a poor woman may have been due to her supposed earthiness, but could also have been her ability to cater to his every need. Such women were also open and friendly, as well as being 'forbidden fruit'.[20] Furthermore, men's attraction to these women was partly due to proximity. Men had wide social contacts, walked the streets freely, dealt with working-class employees, and frequented music halls and other lower-class forms of entertainment. Many upper-class and middle-class men delayed marriage for years or were in professions (such as the army or navy) that meant long periods away from home. These men were those most likely to have long-term relationships outside of marriage with women in lower classes.

The women who agreed to these liaisons came from varying backgrounds. One prominent group was domestic servants. As Chapter 4 demonstrated, some of the bigamy cases involved women who had married into better-off families only to have their new in-laws sue in order to be rid of them. Many of the nullity of marriage suits, too, involved a young, well-off man, going through a secret ceremony with a servant.[21] Other women relied on promises of marriage. Maria Bessela, a German immigrant, worked in a Liverpool hotel as a servant. The son of her employer made romantic overtures to her, she claimed under a promise of marriage. When she became pregnant, they lived together in lodgings until after the birth of their child. He then gave her £60 to return to Germany, though she stayed there only four months. Stern believed he had discharged his obligation, but Bessela did not agree. On her return to England, she sued him for breach of promise and got £100 from the jury.[22]

For the most part, though, men did not intend marriage, and women recognised it was unlikely. A wealthy man seldom wanted to marry a servant; even if he did, his family would object. Thus, the only solution was to cohabit, often with modest financial support for the woman. Agness C., a servant, appealed to the Foundling Hospital in 1842, claiming that the father of her child was a painter. The investigators, however, found that she 'has two illegitimate children by the same man – said to be a *Gentleman* – He allows her ten shillings a week'. Not surprisingly, the Hospital rejected her petition. Catherine S., similarly, was a chambermaid in a large hotel, where she met T., 'a traveling Gentln of Fortune'. After his second visit, 'he proposed that she should become his Mistress and travel with him – she consented'. T. frankly acknowledged that he wanted a mistress only, and Catherine accepted the offer.[23]

Servants were tempting because they fulfilled all of the roles of wives, usually without pay once the cohabitation started. Louisa W. became a servant to George L., a grocer, in 1845. In 1848, his wife died, and George turned to Louisa for solace. As she put it, 'We lived together as man & wife for a year & a half – When pregnant I told him & he still promised to protect me'. Again, George did not suggest marriage, but he did pledge support. Unfortunately, he died less than a year later.[24] Men might tire of relationships with servants, but a limited responsibility continued. Foundling Hospital records showed that many men saw the women through their confinements, if not much beyond. In addition, a woman was not always ruined by a relationship with an employer; she might get a dowry. A. B. Brown lived with his servant, Mary, in 1833, and they had a daughter. Brown paid her £60 a year, a bond that continued after his death. Perhaps as a result, she married a Mr Jennings in 1835.[25] In these cases, the upper-class men did not want to rear their children, but they did provide for them, though on a modest level.

Servants with only slight class differences were particularly tempted by the vision of marrying a well-off man, so risked cohabitation. Wilkie Collins lived with his housekeeper, Caroline Graves, the widow of a solicitor's clerk. Though not rich, she was respectable, yet she lived as Collins's mistress/housekeeper in the late 1850s and early 1860s. Caroline gained an improved lifestyle and a better future for her daughter, Harriet, by doing so.[26] All the same, better educated women would not stay in free unions indefinitely. They had too much to lose, and most believed they were suitable marriage material. Thus, some women sued for breach of promise, and others abandoned the unions. Graves, for instance, married another man after Collins's mother died, almost certainly because Collins refused to marry her. Though she later returned to work for him, their relationship was never the same.[27]

What all these women had in common was their poor pay; servants, even governesses, earned little. Other mistresses were also in poorly paid jobs – millinery, needlework, and sweated labour. The amount these women earned was so small and the hours so long that the life of a mistress was attractive by comparison. Mary Ann M. was a needleworker when she met Richard S., an army officer. At first, he paid for her sexual services; he later provided her with lodgings. 'He then said he would take her under his protection – and she consented.' Though in the end he did not make her his mistress, her willingness to take this role was telling. Similarly, Eleanor T., a seamstress, met Joshua G., an attorney, in London. 'He offered to keep her and for some time he supported her and visited her at her Lodgings', though his support stopped after she had a child.[28] Only those women who held out for promises of marriage had a chance to get compensation, since juries often gave larger awards to cases which fitted the melodramatic stereotype of the well-off seducer and the poor maiden. The plaintiff in *Berry v. Da Costa*, in 1866, was a lacemaker, but she claimed that Da Costa, 'a gentleman of considerable fortune', promised marriage. Da Costa denied it and called her a prostitute, but his defence failed and the jury awarded her £2,500.[29] Again, the civil courts tacitly acknowledged men's need to compensate women they had 'ruined'. Berry's story, though, was unusual; most working women settled for protection with no promises.

Men in a variety of professions kept working-class women in the nineteenth century, another demonstration of men's sexual freedom. Other cases in the Foundling Hospital records include that of a woman who worked in a straw bonnet shop, who lived with an army colonel, and Ann D., who lived with a diamond merchant in the 1840s. Barrett-Ducrocq's sample included a dressmaker who lived with a civil servant for a year and a shop-girl with a medical student.[30] In some cases, the men were not able to support wives, while others wanted to establish themselves in their professions before settling down. James Whistler, the painter, lived with two of his models, Joanna Hifferman and Maud Franklin, in succession, Jo for over six years and Maud for fifteen. Similarly, William Orpen, also a painter, lived with his model on the continent while he made a name for himself at the turn of the century.[31]

Naturally, these unions had real disadvantages for women, due to the sexual double standard. For instance, when unable to achieve marriage, women were often too ashamed to return home. They accepted 'protection' as the best they could do, starting a downward spiral. Susan Mumm's work on Anglican convents showed many women who ended up as prostitutes due to unwise unions. Elizabeth McIntosh, a servant, was married to an army officer, but he deserted her. In desperation, she lived with another army officer in London, but he, too, left her after only three months, and she had to turn to the streets. Other sources confirm this pattern. Carolyn Thompson, a protégée of Charles Dickens, lived with a businessman for nine years. When his business failed, though, she turned to prostitution to keep from starving. In her effort to enter a higher realm of life, Thompson had, paradoxically, descended to a much lower one.[32]

On the other hand, working-class women were not invariably victims; indeed, some legal sources reveal lifelong unions. John Vidler, a wealthy coach-builder, lived for years with his servant, Mary Hall, after the death of his wife. They had several children, but he did not marry her, perhaps because his daughter from his marriage objected. Instead, he left Hall a bond of £3,000. Similarly, the testator in In re Vallance lived for thirty years with his cohabitee until his death in 1881. He left her a bond for £6,000.[33] Not only did these women have permanent unions and some provision in old age, but the Victorian courts upheld the bonds, agreeing that women should have compensation for years of faithful, if unmarried, companionship.

Non-legal sources also reveal numerous cross-class relationships that lasted for years. Friedrich Engels lived with Mary Burns, 'an illiterate Irish factory girl' for almost twenty years, until her death in 1863; he then lived with her sister Lizzie for close to ten.[34] Engels was unconcerned with his reputation, but some men with respectable ambitions also preferred not to marry. Benjamin Leigh Smith, a wealthy landowner and future radical MP, lived with Ann Longden, a milliner, in the early nineteenth century. Despite the births of five children, Benjamin and Ann remained unmarried. After her death in 1834, Smith had another liaison with Jane Buss, the daughter of an agricultural labourer, and had three more children with her. Similarly, Wilkie Collins lived with a working-class woman named Martha Rudd for over twenty years (c.1868–89), a relationship that resulted in three children.[35]

The women in these unions probably would have married if they had been asked; as in many other types of cohabitation, the man was the reluctant party. The reasons for their hesitation are many. The class difference was an obvious bar, particularly for the man's family. Still, some of these families would have preferred a lower-class wife to no wife at all; many of Collins's biographers argue that this was the case for him. Thus, in many cases, some other reason(s) must have existed. Of course, some men were already married and so could not regularise the union. William Frith, the painter, had an affair with a working-class woman named Mary Alford and had two children with her, but he could not marry her until his wife died in 1880.[36] But this reason will not suffice for bachelors.

Sometimes, the men had radical beliefs that made marriage pointless or obnoxious to them. Smith came from a long line of Unitarian reformers and may well have enjoyed being as unconventional in his personal life as in his politics. Engels, unsurprisingly, disdained bourgeois marriage. Even here, though, abstract theorising was not a complete explanation; after all, in some ways Engels's cohabitation with the Burns sisters was harmful to his work in socialism. Engels had inherited factories from his father; his relationships with factory workers were, in William Henderson's words, a reminder 'that the sons of rich millowners had often been accused of using the daughters of their operatives to gratify their own pleasure.' Arguably, Engels would have been a more effective spokesperson for the working class if he had married into it rather than cohabited.[37]

Thus, there must be other reasons still, which leads to the issue of how much the class difference affected these unions. And, indeed, many men could not overcome their condescension towards working-class women. They may even have assumed that they were doing poor women a favour by consorting with them, particularly as they paid for the privilege. This attitude was tied into the assumption that working-class women were promiscuous, or, at the least, cared little about chastity. Engels is a good example in this regard. He could not see that rather than being daring by living with a worker, he was, in fact, participating in a commonplace, and usually exploitative, relationship. As Terrell Carver has argued, Engels did not look for an 'intellectual equal' from his lovers, but for 'domestic compatibility ... Engels's intellectual mates were not women but men.'[38] These attitudes may have been subconscious, but they were still decisive.

Another factor was men's sexual freedom; they could cohabit and have full social lives. Collins dined out frequently, though neither Graves nor Rudd joined him. Smith retained his friends and was elected to Parliament, despite having five known illegitimate children. The men, then, had all the advantages of bachelorhood, yet also had 'wives'. And though some men found the secrecy a strain, others were invigorated. Collins apparently thrived on it, contrasting his situation with married men, whom he considered selfish bores. According to William Baker and William Clarke, he did not want to be 'a middle-aged married man with a growing paunch and little freedom'. He did not consider, though, that his freedom meant social restrictions for Martha and his children.[39]

The advantages for men were considerable, then, in cohabiting with poorer women. In part, these relationships were part of a 'flight from domesticity' that John Tosh has noted for the late nineteenth century. The domesticated middle-class man was only one type of masculinity; men also had attractive alternatives to the bourgeois paterfamilias, like the empire-builder. Though the alternatives might not confer as much prestige as respectable marriage and legitimate fatherhood, they were satisfactory to some men; indeed, by avoiding marriage, men had independence and freedom, two important parts of masculinity, without sacrificing a home life.[40] When such men are factored in, the number of men who resisted domesticity (at least temporarily) may well be higher than historians have thought, and the resistance may have begun earlier in the century. All the same, one should not overstate the men's freedom. These men ignored the bounds of respectability, not just by cohabiting, but by crossing class lines to do so, which explains their determined secrecy about it. Unless a man was independently wealthy (like Smith), discretion was vital, since sexual probity was important to men's professional reputations. Even Engels hid Mary Burns away when he was working at his father's factory in Manchester, and Collins and Rudd used a false name when together. Aristocrats might get away with some sexual irregularities, but middle-class men risked losing their clientele, jobs, or public acclaim. Thus, men had other models for masculinity, but these could not be pushed too far.[41]

Nor was the learning process all one way. At times, well-off men gained a better understanding of the poor through these relationships. Gustav Mayer credited the Burns sisters with influencing Engels about the working class and Ireland. After Lizzie's death, Engels wrote that her 'passionate feeling for her class' greatly influenced him. Ford Madox Brown, who lived with a working-class model before marrying her, identified with workers in the 1840s and 1850s. This was in part because of his family's republican sympathies, but, 'his feelings [were] reinforced by his liaison with a bricklayer's daughter and direct experience, through her, of working-class poverty and solidarity.' When the two were married, they often gave charity to the poor even when they did not have enough money themselves.[42]

As their influence makes clear, women were not always victims in these unions, married or not. By living with Smith, Longden did not have to struggle on as a milliner, and Buss escaped one of the poorest groups in England – rural labourers. In addition, their children married into the lower middle and middle classes. Rudd, the daughter of a shepherd, had a much higher standard of life with Collins. Her three children received excellent educations and inherited half of their father's estate. In short, not all working-class cohabitees were victims. On occasion, these relationships even led to marriage. Sir Henry Percivale de Bathe lived with a woman named Charlotte Clare; she was probably working-class, since little is known about her. They had three daughters and a son before marrying in 1870 and having two more sons. Charlotte, then, made the leap to the upper classes, and her son Hugo inherited his father's title and estates.[43] As these examples indicate, even without marriage, children of these unions could be upwardly mobile. Few were as fortunate as Hugo, but they still did better than their mothers' kin, a real advantage to poor women in accepting 'protection'.

Family and kin

In cross-class unions, both partners' families were unenthusiastic about the relationships. Men's families feared a misalliance, or, at the least, an encumbrance for the family property. They also had great distaste for 'vulgar' women, and this led to tensions and sometimes open breaches. Whistler did not live openly with either Jo or Maud while his mother lived with him. Despite this, his brother-in-law, Seymour Haden, refused to let Whistler's sister, Deborah, visit the house. This meant, in practice, that Deborah could never visit her mother. Whistler, never one to suffer fools gladly, argued fiercely with Haden, and their relationship never recovered.[44] Benjamin Smith's sisters and mother were appalled at his relationship with Longden. His mother felt he was in 'thraldom' to a conniving whore, and his sister would not even use Ann's name in letters.[45] Friends, though usually loyal, were uneasy. John Millais, the Pre-Raphaelite painter, considered Collins's unions 'unhealthy' and warned his friend, William Holman Hunt, against following the example.[46] A man's friends might regard him in two negative ways, then – as a dupe of a lower-class woman's wiles, or as a cad, taking advantage of a helpless young woman. Neither role was attractive.

Working-class women's families also disapproved, since they feared that such relationships had no future. Many pressured the men to marry or end the unions. Mary Croden, a barmaid, lived for six years with Joseph Brimble, a businessman. Croden's sister and mother tried to get Brimble to marry her, to no avail. Mary's sister confronted him openly about it, and later insisted, 'She would not have recognised him if she had not thought he intended to marry her sister.'[47] Families were right to be suspicious of upper-class lovers and to try to persuade their daughters to give them up, though they had limited success. Few working-class families repudiated their daughters, though; they instead blamed the man for 'seducing' an innocent girl. Examples abound of mothers, parents and siblings who remained loyal despite their relative's 'falls'; Ellen Blum's mother, for example, took her daughter in twice after well-off protectors disappeared.[48] Ironically, then, both families were hostile to these unions, though for different reasons.

Pygmalions

Not all men were satisfied with working-class women as mistresses; some instead wanted to transform them into wives. The myth of the upper-class man moulding a poor girl into a beautiful princess was powerful. Men who tried to accomplish it did so for a variety of reasons, including a sense of responsibility, a desire to 'redeem' fallen women, and a defiance of bourgeois snobbery. These cases were a small group in comparison with temporary unions, but their experiences were instructive. Though they might see themselves as challenging social mores, these men's desire to turn their lovers into middle-class ladies had a conventional core. These instances, in fact, were good examples of the cross-class mix of defying marital restrictions while, at the same time, accepting gender norms. In addition, though a man's motives were often good, he gained a sense of power changing a woman into whatever he wished her to be. Whether he actually succeeded in this quest was a different issue. Working-class women had much to gain by becoming middle-class wives, but they sometimes stubbornly retained aspects of working-class life.

The premier example of reshaping working-class women was the Pre-Raphaelite circle. Unlike Whistler, these artists tried to reform their models, reinforcing each other in the process. Dante Gabriel Rosetti, William Holman Hunt, and Ford Madox Brown all met and fell in love with lower-class models and tried to reinvent them as ladies. Brown and Rosetti eventually married Emma Hill and Lizzie Siddall, but Hunt was never satisfied that Annie Miller would be an acceptable bride. Still, the transition for all these couples was difficult. The men and women had to renegotiate their relationships as the women gained more education and earning power; in addition, even the most willing woman retained some of her working-class habits, and some of these women were not particularly willing.

These men were good examples of professionals who faced either several years of celibacy or unmarried liaisons. A relationship with a working-class woman was one solution to this problem, and such cohabitation had other advantages as well. In contrast to ladies, poor women accepted economic difficulties and worked when necessary. In addition, the artists were encouraged in their hopes of transforming an uneducated beauty into a middle-class wife precisely because these women were models. After all, the artists had already re-made these women on a regular basis, posing them in a variety of guises. If the painter could turn a milliner into a princess on canvas, he could certainly teach her to be a lady in real life – or so he hoped.

Ford Madox Brown was a widower with a small daughter when Emma Hill, the illiterate daughter of a bricklayer, began working as his model in the late 1840s. The two were living together by 1850, since Emma was pregnant by early 1850.[49] Yet Ford hesitated to marry her. He was not financially secure, and he also had to consider his daughter, Lucy. After Emma gave birth to a daughter in November 1850, then, Ford registered the birth in the name of 'Ford and Matilda Hill', and they lived in a cottage together unmarried.[50] Despite his hesitation, Ford educated Emma, and she studied hard while also serving tirelessly as a model for the next three years. Perhaps as result of this loyalty, Brown married her on 5 April 1853. Ford had, then, made Emma into an acceptable wife, but her transformation was incomplete. Unfortunately, Emma was an alcoholic, and her drinking was a running battle between them for the rest of their marriage.[51] Emma never entirely managed to become a lady, and Ford had to accept and make the best of her shortcomings.

Gabriel Rosetti and Lizzie Siddall had an equally tangled courtship. They met after she had become a model for the Pre-Raphaelites, rescued from a milliner's shop. Eventually Rosetti monopolised her time, but the Rosettis did not approve of a union with a milliner, even one whose father owned two cutlery shops and a warehouse. Siddall had, after all, agreed to model, which made her suspect. Nevertheless, Lizzie had advantages; she was soft-spoken, literate, and creative, and she was soon painting pictures and writing poetry. Dante encouraged this self-improvement, hoping her new career would make her acceptable.[52]

Gabriel moved into his own home in 1852 so that he could have more time with Lizzie, and she eventually lived with him there, though on what terms it is impossible to say. At one time or another, she was described as his fiancée, his mistress, and his pupil. At any rate, they were emotionally intimate. She met many of his friends, including Barbara Leigh Smith, and some of them were supportive, but she was not their equal. She was an object of patronage, since she was both sickly and a struggling artist, and also because she and Rosetti did not marry for years. Gabriel had an insecure income and was unsure about Lizzie's health, so their relationship dragged on, satisfying no one.[53] When Siddall gained a patron in John Ruskin, and thus some independence, she became harder to placate with vague promises. As a result of these factors, and her discovery of Rosetti's infidelities, the relationship grew stormy.[54] They finally married in 1860, when she seemed to be dying and Rosetti felt guilty. But the marriage did not provide a happy ending. Siddall gave birth to a stillborn child in 1861, slipped into depression, and took an overdose of laudanum in 1862 at the age of thirty-two.[55]

The third pairing, that of Hunt and Annie Miller, was even less successful. Miller was from a poverty-stricken background before she became a model, but she had a strong will of her own. The two never lived together, and probably did not have a sexual relationship, but Hunt was obsessed with her for years. He paid for various types of education for her to make her 'respectable'. Annie, for her part, used his absences to have (at the least) flirtations with both Rosetti and Lord Ranelagh, a notorious rake.[56] Miller was simply too independent to tolerate Hunt's long apprenticeship. He finally gave up on her altogether, and she went back to modeling. Not long after, she made Hunt pay to get his letters back, and then began a relationship with Thomas Ranelagh Thompson, Lord Ranelagh's cousin.[57]

None of these unions turned out quite as either party expected. Hunt was so disillusioned by his failure with Miller that he never tried with a poor woman again. Ford and Emma lived together until her death in 1890, but Ford had to watch her carefully. In 1880, he discovered that her friend, Mrs Pyne, brought alcohol to her, and he admitted, ruefully, "'Emma does talk people over in an astonishing way.'"[58] Gabriel and Lizzie married too late to be successful. As a result, when he turned to a new lover, Fanny Cornforth, a former prostitute, he did not try to make her an acceptable wife; both of them had realistically low expectations for their union.[59]

Indeed, one cannot help but conclude that the women who resisted being moulded gained the most from these unions. Emma was happy in her marriage, but Lizzie's was not fulfilling, though a life as a milliner probably would not have satisfied her either. The assertive Miller, on the other hand, achieved the Cinderella dream. In 1863 she married Thompson, had several children, and eventually lived to the age of ninety. Similarly, Cornforth looked after her own interests. When Gabriel became ill, he wrote to her "'to take the best step in life that you can for your own advantage, and quite to forget about me'". Fanny took him at his word; she used her savings to buy a pub, and a Mr Schott moved in with her. They later married, and Fanny proudly told Rosetti that she employed three servants and an accountant.[60] Galateas who stayed themselves – and took advantage of their chances – were the most likely to be successful.

The Pre-Raphaelites were an unusual group or they would not have tried to marry their models at all. But their experiences were echoed by those of other men who tried to 'redeem' poor women. George Gissing married an ex-prostitute, Nell Harrison, after living with her in London. This marriage was a disaster, since Nell was an alcoholic. Gissing's tendency to self-punishment was part of the reason he married her, but also his many sacrifices for her would have been pointless unless he 'saved' her. Morley Roberts argued that his friend 'built up a kind of theory of these things as a justification for himself ... he considered an affair of that description as sacred as any marriage.'[61] Nevertheless, after four years, George gave up any hope of reforming her, and Nell died, poverty-stricken and alone, in 1888.[62]

Not all cross-class matings were this miserable, but even the happier ones had stresses. For one thing, the couples were not always able to reconcile the husbands' families to a marriage across class lines. Frith waited over a year after the death of his wife before he married Alford, his mistress. His daughter, Jane Panton, was estranged from her father from that time on.[63] For another, working-class mistresses who became wives had to be secretive about their backgrounds. Marie Corelli's father, Dr Charles Mackay, had probably been having an affair with "'an imperfectly educated young woman'", Mary Mills, since at least 1853, when his wife Rosa left him. Mackay supported her and their daughter (born c. 1855) until a year after his wife's death, in 1861, when they married. Despite this, Corelli always asserted that her parentage was unknown, and that Mackay adopted her out of kindness.[64] In both these cases, the secrecy was partially because of the adultery, but it cannot have been easy for a second wife to know that her husband and children considered her past shameful and her family unsuitable. When poor women married their wealthier cohabitees, they had security, but not without costs.

Conclusion

Cross-class cohabitees defied two conventions of Victorian life: they had sexual relations outside of their social strata and without marriage. In doing so, they followed conventions in some ways, while challenging them in others. For instance, few cross-class couples openly cohabited. They lived in secrecy or, if they eventually married, covered up the women's pasts. Also, traditional gender power remained or got even stronger. In contrast to these disadvantages, some women lived a life of higher status than they could have hoped for in their own class. The complications of this relationship, though hardly typical, should warn against making simplistic assertions about exploitation by leering millowners or gentleman *flaneurs*. Nevertheless, the cross-class tensions in these relationships show the difficulties of making an unequal relationship work. Unless the two had a financial settlement, the lower-class party could be left with little. In addition, for a working-class woman to become an acceptable spouse, she had give up parts of herself. Though some couples made their unions work, the Victorian disapproval of cross-class matings, married or otherwise, becomes understandable in this context.

As with so many types of cohabitation, cross-class unions got limited support from the state. The civil courts upheld bonds and wills in favour of mistresses and their families, and written annuities to mistresses were an accepted part of the equation. In addition, women further down the social scale could get some compensation for their sacrifices through breach of promise suits. The courts again agreed that a man who entered an unmarried union with a woman owed her support, another partial acknowledgement of cohabitation.

Cross-class couples resembled those who could not marry, since many of the men did not believe they could reconcile their families to marriages with unsuitable women. On the other hand, women preferred marriage and married gladly when men offered. A few women and men in all classes, however, chose cohabitation purposely and openly, because they dissented from its laws, rites, or gender inequality. These couples took the most risks of all, defending their unions as more moral than marriages, refuting the role of the state in adjudicating relationships, and making their rebellion public with wide consequences for themselves and their families. Their strategies had limited success, but they led far more open lives than the other cohabitees, as Chapters 8 and 9 make clear.

Notes

1 E. Gaskell, *Mary Barton* (Oxford: Oxford University Press, 1987), pp. 154–62; 187–93.

2 The case with small class difference involved a business owner with her manager, found in *Liverpool Mercury*, 26 June 1860, p. 3; 29 June 1860, p. 7; 30 June 1860, p. 4; 28 July 1860, p. 4; 30 July 1860, p. 3; 31 July 1860, p. 3; 21 August 1860, p. 3; 22 August 1860, p. 3;

23 August 1860, p. 3; 24 August 1860, p. 6. The couple who could not marry involved a wealthy woman with a man pretending to be a gentleman, found in R. Huson (ed.), *Sixty Famous Trials* (London: Daily Express Publications, 1938), pp. 259–72; *The Times*, 23 May 1903, p. 8; 30 May 1903, p. 8; 19 June 1903, p. 11; 23 June 1903, p. 11; 24 June 1903, p. 4; 13 July 1903, p. 6; 15 July 1903, p. 11. Both of these are murder cases.

3   Mayhew, *London Labour and the London Poor*, IV, 215–16, 355–6, quote from p. 215.

4   K. Hickman, *Courtesans: Money, Sex and Fame in the Nineteenth Century* (New York: William Morrow, 2003), pp. 149–213; H. Blyth, *Skittles, The Last Victorian Courtesan: The Life and Times of Catherine Walters* (London: Rupert Hart-Davis, 1970), pp. 73–102, 245–6.

5   Mayhew, *London Labour and the London Poor*, IV, 216–17, quote from p. 217; Walkowitz, *Prostitution and Victorian Society*, pp. 13–31.

6   *Hill v. Spencer* (1767), 27 *English Reports* 416–17; 524–5; *Friend v. Harrison* (1827), 172 *English Reports* 265–6; *The Times*, 14 February 1827, p. 3 (for quote).

7   University College, London, Karl Pearson Papers (hereafter KPP), 840/4, Olive Schreiner to Karl Pearson, 11 October 1886, fols. 76–9, quote from fols. 77–8; Barret-Ducrocq, *Love in the Time of Victoria*, pp. 52–4.

8   *Keenan v. Handley* (1864), 28 *Justice of the Peace* 660; *The Times*, 8 June 1864, p. 12; 11 July 1864, p. 11.

9   NA, ASSI 1/65; *Berkshire County Chronicle*, 17 July 1869, p. 5.

10 *Authentic and Interesting Memoirs of Mrs Clarke* (Boston: J. Belcher, 1809); P. Berry, *By Royal Appointment: A Biography of Mary Ann Clarke, Mistress of the Duke of York* (London: Femina, 1970), p. 181; A. Clark, *Scandal: The Sexual Politics of the British Constitution* (Princeton, NJ: Princeton University Press, 2004), pp. 148–76; Hickman, *Courtesans*, pp. 208–11; 215–75; L. Blanch (ed.), *Harriette Wilson's Memoirs* (London: Century Publishing, 1985); Blyth, *The Last Victorian Courtesan*, pp. 123–7; 202–3; 222–5; Frances Wilson, *The Courtesan's Revenge: Harriette Wilson, the Woman Who Blackmailed the King* (London: Faber and Faber, 2003), pp. 199–232.

11 *Hairs v. Elliot, Woman* 17 (1890), p. 1; *The Times*, 18 April 1890, p. 3; 19 April 1890, pp. 5–6; 22 April 1890, p. 10.

12 *Berkshire County Chronicle*, 7 July 1869, p. 5; 28 *Justice of the Peace* 660.

13 M. Gillen, *The Prince and his Lady: The Love Story of the Duke of Kent and Madame de St Laurent* (London: Sidgwick & Jackson, 1970); Hickman, *Courtesans*, pp. 105–47; I. M. Davis, *The Harlot and the Statesman: The Story of Elizabeth Armistead and Charles James Fox* (Abbotsbrook, Bucks: Kensal Press, 1986), pp. 53–7, 79–121.

14 Tomalin, *Mrs Jordan's Profession*, p. 127.

15 *Gore v. Sudley, Cardiff Times*, 13 June 1896, p. 6.

16 Tomalin, *Mrs Jordan's Profession*, pp. 253–7; 284–304; Gillen, *The Prince and his Lady*, pp. 230–8.

17 *Gore v. Sudley, Cardiff Times*, 13 June 1896, p. 6; R. Altick, *Deadly Encounters: Two Victorian Sensations* (Philadelphia, PA: University of Pennsylvania Press, 1986), p. 94 (for quote).

18 See Gillis, *For Better, For Worse*, 201.

19 Barret-Ducrocq, *Love in the Time of Victoria*, pp. 61–73.

20 *Ibid.*, 52–4.

21 For example, *Pouget v. Tomkins, falsely calling herself Pouget* (1812), in 1 *Phillimore's Reports* 499–506.

22 *Bessela v. Stern* (1877), 2 *Law Reports, Common Pleas Division*, 265–72; *The Times*, 8 February 1877, p. 10.

23 LMA, A/FH/A8/1/3/49/1, Petition # 3, 9 March 1842; A/FH/A8/1/3/42/1, Petition # 75, 5 August 1835.

24 LMA, A/FH/A8/1/3/57, Petition #85, 27 July 1850.

25 *Jennings and Wife v. Brown and Others* (1843), 9 *Meeson & Welsby's Reports of the Exchequer* 496–501.

26 W. Clarke, *The Secret Life of Wilkie Collins* (Stroud: Alan Sutton Publishing, 1989), pp. 89–106; C. Peters, *The King of Inventors: A Life of Wilkie Collins* (London: Secker and Warburg, 1991), pp. 189–202.

27 Clarke, *Secret Life of Wilkie Collins*, pp. 114–28. See also *Thomas v. Shirley* (1862), 11 *Weekly Reporter* 21; *The Times*, 6 November 1862, p. 8; 7 November 1862, p. 9.

28 LMA, A/FH/A8/1/3/42/1, Petition # 116, 9 December 1835; A/FH/A8/1/3/24/1, 8 February 1817 (no number).

29 *Berry v. Da Costa* (1865–66), 1 *Law Reports, Common Pleas Division* 331–6; *The Times*, 15 January 1866, p. 11; 26 January 1866, p. 11.

30 LMA, A/FH/A8/1/3/26, 3 January 1819 (no number); A/FH/A8/1/3/57/1, 9 February 1850, Petition #14; Barret-Ducrocq, *Love in the Time of Victoria*, p. 65.

31 R. McMullen, *Victorian Outsider: A Biography of J. A. M. Whistler* (New York: E. P. Dutton, 1973), pp. 90–152; 164–86; 242–4; S. Weintraub, *Whistler: A Biography* (New York: Weybright and Talley, 1974), pp. 68–122; 154–327; G. H. Fleming, *James Abbott McNeill Whistler: A Life* (New York: St Martin's Press, 1991), pp. 88–120; 170–255; Holyroyd, *Augustus John*, I, 101.

32 S. Mumm, '"Not worse than other girls"', 529–30; E. F. Payne, *The Charity of Charles Dickens: His Interest in the Home for Fallen Women and A History of the Strange Case of Caroline Maynard Thompson* (Boston, MA: The Bibliophile Society, 1929), pp. 52–8. See also Mayhew, *Life and Labour of the People of London*, IV, 243–4; Bartley, *Prostitution*, pp. 6–12.

33 *Hall v. Palmer* (1844), 67 *English Reports* 491–4; *The Times*, 8 May 1844, p. 8; 9 May 1844, p. 6; *In re Vallance – Vallance v. Blagden* (1884), 48 *Justice of the Peace* 598.

34 T. Carver, *Friedrich Engels: His Life and Thought* (New York: St Martin's Press, 1990), pp. 150–61; S. Marcus, *Engels, Manchester and the Working Class* (New York: Random House, 1974), pp. 98–101 (quote from p. 99); G. Mayer, *Friedrich Engels: A Biography* (London: Chapman & Hall Ltd, 1936), pp. 43, 69, 124–48, 171–4, 190–6, 226.

35 S. Herstein, *A Mid-Victorian Feminist: Barbara Leigh Smith Bodichon* (New Haven, CT: Yale University Press, 1985), pp. 1–10; P. Hirsch, *Barbara Leigh Smith Bodichon, 1827–1891: Feminist, Artist and Rebel* (London: Chatto & Windus, 1998), pp. 8–15; 96–8; Clarke, *The Secret Life of Wilkie Collins*, pp. 107–22; 169–85.

36 A. Noakes, *William Frith: Extraordinary Victorian Painter* (London: Jupiter, 1978), p. 134. For other examples, see R. L. Patten, *George Cruikshank's Life, Times and Art* 2 vols (London: Lutterworth Press, 1996), II, 286–8; 391; 491–6; 513–17; and C. Tomalin, *The Invisible Woman: The Story of Nelly Ternan and Charles Dickens* (New York: Penguin Books, 1990), pp. 96–149; 167–96.

37 Mayer, *Friedrich Engels*, p. 226; W. O. Henderson, *The Life of Friedrich Engels* 2 vols (London: Frank Cass, 1976), I, 104 (for quote), 220–1; Marcus, *Engels, Manchester, and the Working Class*, pp. 100–1; Carver, *Friedrich Engels*, pp. 150–8. Engels did marry Lizzie Burns on her deathbed.

38 Carver, *Friedrich Engels*, p. 159; Marcus, *Engels, Manchester, and the Working Class*, pp. 100–1.

39 Peters, *The King of Inventors*, pp. 196–9; 295–9; 415–16; W. Baker and W. Clarke (eds), *The Letters of Wilkie Collins* 2 vols (London: Macmillan, 1999), I, xxxiii (for quote); II, 368, 376; W. Collins, 'Bold words by a bachelor', *Household Words* 14 (1856), 505–7.

40 Tosh, *A Man's Place*, pp. 170–94; Brady, *Masculinity and Male Homosexuality*, pp. 25–49.

41 Tosh, *Manliness and Masculinities*, p. 76.

42 Mayer, *Friedrich Engels*, pp. 191–6; 226, quote from p. 226; T. Newman and R. Watkinson, *Ford Madox Brown and the Pre-Raphaelite Circle* (London: Chatto and Windus, 1991), pp. 120–3, quote from p. 121.

43 Hirsch, *Barbara Leigh Smith Bodichon*, p. 97; Clarke, *The Secret Life of Wilkie Collins*, p. 186; D. Petre, *The Secret Orchard of Roger Ackerley* (New York: George Braziller, 1975), pp. 62–3.

44 D. Du Maurier (ed.), *The Young George Du Maurier: A Selection of his Letters, 1860–67* (London: Peter Davies, 1951), p. 227; McMullen, *Victorian Outsider*, p. 120; Weintraub, *Whistler: A Biography*, pp. 89–90.

45 Hirsch, *Barbara Leigh Smith Bodichon*, pp. 10–13; 97; quote from p. 10.

46 Holman-Hunt, *My Grandfather*, p. 174.

47 *Croden v. Brimble*, ASSI 22/42; *Bristol Mercury*, 4 July 1896, p. 3.

48 *Blum v. Reeve*, *Oxfordshire, Buckinghamshire, and Northamptonshire Telegraph*, 16 July 1873, p. 3.

49 Newman and Watkinson, *Ford Madox Brown*, pp. 45–6.

50 *Ibid.*, pp. 54–64, quote from p. 64; J. Marsh, *Pre-Raphaelite Sisterhood* (London: Quartet Books, 1985), pp. 37–43.

51 V. Surtees (ed.), *The Diary of Ford Madox Brown* (New Haven, CT: Yale University Press, 1981), pp. 79–80; 139; 182; Newman and Watkinson, *Ford Madox Brown*, pp. 72–96; Marsh, *Pre-Raphaelite Sisterhood*, pp. 104–6, 240–1.

52 J. Marsh, *The Legend of Lizzie Siddal* (London: Quartet Books, 1989), pp. 149–65; *Pre-Raphaelite Sisterhood*, pp. 15–36; D. Cherry and G. Pollock, 'Woman as sign in Pre-Raphaelite literature: A study of the representation of Elizabeth Siddall', *Art History* 7 (1984), 207–11; B. Bauer, 'Rescuing Ophelia: Gendered Interpretations of the Life and Work of Elizabeth Siddall' (BA thesis, Smith College, Northampton, MA 1995), pp. 39–44.

53 D. Cherry, *Painting Women: Victorian Women Artists* (New York: Routledge, 1993), p. 189; Bauer, 'Rescuing Ophelia', p. 45; Herstein, *A Mid-Victorian Feminist*, pp. 95–7; 100–1; S. Weintraub, *Four Rossettis*, pp. 74–8; W. Rosetti (ed.), *Pre-Raphaelite Diaries and Letters* (London: Hurst and Blackett, Ltd, 1900), pp. 43–7; Marsh, *The Legend of Lizzie Siddal*, pp. 42–6; 147–8; *Pre-Raphaelite Sisterhood*, pp. 47–50, 88–90.

54 Weintraub, *Four Rossettis*, pp. 86–98; Cherry, *Painting Women*, pp. 99–100.

55 Weintraub, *Four Rossettis*, pp. 108–25; Newman and Watkinson, *Ford Madox Brown*, pp. 132; 138–9; Marsh, *Pre-Raphaelite Sisterhood*, pp. 115–17; 130–5; 177–85, 197–203; 210–23.

56 Clark Amor, *William Holman Hunt*, pp. 102–59; Marsh, *Pre-Raphaelite Sisterhood*, pp. 58–66; 107–9.

57 Clark Amor, *William Holman Hunt*, pp. 159–79; Marsh, *Pre-Raphaelite Sisterhood*, pp. 223–8.

58 Newman and Watkinson, *Ford Madox Brown*, pp. 178–89, quote from p. 179.

59 Weintraub, *Four Rossettis*, pp. 127–8; 135; 161; 201–2; Marsh, *Pre-Raphaelite Sisterhood*, pp. 141–59; 233–40.

60 Weintraub, *Four Rosettis*, pp. 219–20; Marsh, *Pre-Raphaelite Sisterhood*, pp. 227–8; 306–28; 353–4, quote from p. 325.

61 Halperin, *Gissing*, pp. 16–19; 26–37; Selig, *George Gissing*, pp. 8–9; P. Coustillas, *London and the Life of Literature*, pp. 22–3; M. Roberts, *The Private Life of Henry Maitland* (London: The Richards Press, 1958), pp. 28–33; 40–3; 49–57; 75–6; 109; quote from p. 75.

62 Halperin, *Gissing*, pp. 41–5, 102–4.

63 Noakes, *William Frith*, p. 139; J. Panton, *More Leaves from a Life* (London: Eveleigh Nash, 1911), pp. 181; 197–8.

64 T. Ransom, *The Mysterious Marie Corelli: Queen of the Victorian Bestsellers* (Stroud: Sutton Publishing, 1999), pp. 9–14, quote from p. 11; E. Bigland, *Marie Corelli: The Woman and the Legend* (London: Jarrolds Publishers Ltd, 1953), pp. 12–19.

8

Radical couples, 1790–1850

F ROM THE 1790s to the early twentieth century, some couples consciously dissented from the marriage ceremony because of its indissolubility, the influence of the state or the church on it, or the disabilities that it gave to women. Often the dissent from marriage was a part of a larger critique – for example, by anarchists, socialists, or feminists. At times, too, those who disliked marriage did so from bitter experience, radicalised by their own marital failures. Whatever the cause, these unions diverged by gender. Because of the economic weakness of women, they seldom wholeheartedly supported experimentation, and power relationships existed even in supposedly free unions. In addition, marital dissent brought a raft of complications with wider kin and society.

What differentiated many radicals was not necessarily their behaviour, since so many non-radical people cohabited. The public nature of the dissent, and the couples' broad analyses of marriage, set them apart. Radicals felt duty-bound to explain their actions in order to make their society into a better place. In the final two chapters, I first explore how and why free unions either did or did not work in particular couples and radical groups. Second, I emphasise the continuity of the critiques of marriage. Many of the complaints about the institution were long-lived, stretching back to the early modern period. Most groups, then, diagnosed the ills of marriage similarly, though they differed on the suggested cures.

Marital dissenters throughout the century insisted they were more moral and equitable than those who supported legal marriage, and few supported 'free love', i.e., promiscuity. Instead, they wanted to make unions between men and women as 'real' as possible. The majority did not want to abolish marriage, but to reform it by focusing on the relationship as the barometer of a genuine marriage. A 'true' marriage was one of hearts and minds, whatever its legal status. Thus, their suggestions were for monogamous partnerships, but with flexibility about divorce and equal rights for women. Indeed, for marriage to be an equal 'contract', the rights and duties would have to be the same for both partners, and both should have a say in the terms. Unsurprisingly, then, calls for divorce reform and equality for women recurred again and again. In addition, the view of marriage as a contract sat uneasily with a belief in marriage as a sacrament, so resistance to the church also threaded through these critiques.

Though these ideas seem mild to modern ears, they alarmed most people in the nineteenth century. Opponents of reform feared that without strict laws of marriage and divorce, society would disintegrate. In particular, they feared that men would not behave responsibly towards women or children, a concern for many women's advocates as well. In addition, religious leaders fought against secularising marriage, insisting that marriage was a sacred rite. Though Parliament had undermined this view in 1753, conservatives fought a rearguard action against any more change for the rest of the century. Those who wanted to challenge marriage, then, faced a daunting task.

Pioneers and revolutionaries

The roots of marital dissent go back at least to the seventeenth century. In particular, the period of the Civil Wars saw an outpouring of criticism for the church and traditional marriage practices. Puritans had long advocated marriage as a love relationship, but other groups went even further in the 1640s and 1650s. Quakers, for instance, promoted women's equality by eliminating the vow of obedience, and other groups pressed for divorce on equal grounds. The government of the Interregnum even passed a civil marriage statute. In some ways, these arguments prefigured later critiques, but, as John Gillis has pointed out, many were backward-looking and just as patriarchal as the system they disdained. Nor did they survive the restoration of order in 1660; Parliament repealed civil marriage, and the church and state marriage system returned in full force for the next century.[1]

Sustained public debate about marriage only returned at the end of the eighteenth century. The 1790s was a fervent decade for change in England. Reformers drew inspiration from the French Revolution and agitated for a more representative Britain. Though most of the energy of the movement went into the public sphere, the fight against despotism turned to the home as well. After all, if one believed that all humans were born with reason, then women had reason as well as men. And if they did, the restrictions of their lives within marriage were unjust. Furthermore, many of these reformers had a rational approach to religion, so did not regard marriage as a sacrament and had no horror of divorce. Tom Paine, Robert Burns, and Thomas Spence all had heterodox views about marriage, arguing for married women's equality within marriage and that divorce should be more available. As Spence put it, "'what signifies Reforms of Government or Redress of Public Grievances, if people cannot have their domestic grievances redressed?'"[2]

All the same, few of these writers practiced free unions in their own lives, and most of those who cohabited did so because they had no choice. For instance, Mary Robinson, a former actress, was a fervent supporter of Charles James Fox and an early feminist, but her cohabitation with Banastre Tarleton was unmarried because she was already married to someone else.[3] Two writers in this period were exceptions to this rule – William Godwin and Mary Wollstonecraft. Both stressed the centrality of human reason, but their approaches to marital problems differed. Godwin saw the issue as one of personal liberty, while Wollstonecraft centred on women's difficulties. Both influenced later radicals, but also had uneven personal lives. In spite of – in fact, because of – their pioneering behaviour, their reputations posed problems for future cohabitees.

Godwin expressed his opinion of marriage in his work, *Enquiry Concerning Political Justice*, in 1793. He was influenced in his views of marriage by Thomas Holcroft, his friend and collaborator. Holcroft argued that 'All individual property is an evil – Marriage makes woman individual property – Therefore marriage is evil'.[4] Godwin adopted this logic in his work, calling marriage 'the worst of monopolies' for both sexes. Anything that shackled the human mind – law, property, militarism – was wrong, and he included marriage on this list. The whole process was irrational to Godwin: 'The method is, for a thoughtless and romantic youth of each sex, to come together, to see each other, for a few times, and under circumstances full of delusion, and then to vow eternal attachment.' Marriage only worked, then, when both partners lied to themselves and pretended to have the same opinions of each other no matter how much changed. He suggested abolishing it in favour of a system in which 'each man would select for himself a partner, to whom he will adhere, as long as that adherence shall continue to be the choice of both parties.' He did not ignore women's problems but argued that a rational economic system would support them.[5]

Godwin's first point, in particular, resonated throughout the nineteenth century. How could anyone promise to feel the same way forever? And how could marriage be moral if it lacked emotional and physical unity? On the other hand, Godwin's second point, and his suggestion for replacing marriage, appealed more to men than women. He assumed the major actors in both free unions and marriages would be men, as in his statement that 'each man would select for himself a partner'. Furthermore, he did not address the dangers to women adequately; their economic weakness left them vulnerable to desertion. Godwin's suggestion that free unions would last only as long as this was the 'choice of both parties' was also problematic. What if one of the partners wished to be free but the other did not?

Wollstonecraft had a better grasp on women's problems. In fact, in her work *Vindication of the Rights of Woman*, she argued that men who seduced women 'should be *legally* obliged to maintain the woman and her children'.[6] In addition, in her unfinished novel, *Maria, or the Wrongs of Woman*, she critiqued marriage thoroughly. The plot detailed all the possible horrors for women under patriarchy, including brutality, rape, greed, and desertion, as Maria struggled to free herself from her evil husband. Wollstonecraft also defended Maria's unmarried relationship with Henry Darnford; because it was based on affection, it was a true marriage. Wollstonecraft did not disdain the institution, since 'the odium of society impedes usefulness', but she wanted reforms, since marriage demanded slavish obedience of women, even to stupid or vice-ridden husbands.[7] She shared Godwin's belief in reason, but she had a better estimate of women's difficulties, due to their economic weakness and poor education. She also understood more clearly the power of emotion over women.[8]

Godwin and Wollstonecraft's own relationships showed the risks of marital experimentation without societal changes. Wollstonecraft's decision, in 1793, to live with Gilbert Imlay in France became a watchword of sexual danger for women in the nineteenth century. Imlay was an American speculator and revolutionary, and the two fell in love in the midst of the French Revolution. Though she did not demand a wedding, Wollstonecraft believed their union was a lifelong commitment. She took Imlay's name and registered their daughter, Fanny, as legitimate. Her letters to Imlay resembled those of a wife, and she was consumed by the power of her affection, writing, 'You have, by your tenderness and worth, twisted yourself more artfully round my heart than I supposed possible.'[9] Still, the fact that Mary was not a wife made her uneasy. She wrote in 1794, 'if a wandering of the heart, or even a caprice of the imagination detains you, there is an end to all my hopes of happiness.'[10] To Mary, the union was a marriage, based on affinity and respect; unfortunately, her partner did not share her commitment.

Gilbert registered Mary as his wife, and, in revolutionary France, this constituted a marriage, though it was not legal in England. Despite this, he had lost interest in her by early 1795, and Wollstonecraft was so bewildered by the change that she did not let go completely until many months later.

She joined Imlay at Le Havre, and when he left for England, she reluctantly returned to her homeland in order to salvage the relationship. She even agreed to go on a business trip to Scandinavia for him, acting as his 'best friend and wife', in the summer of 1795, but it was all to no avail.[11] Her agony at the end of the union led her to attempt suicide twice; in fact, her emotional need for Imlay was perhaps greater for having no legal bond to coerce it. Mary only accepted defeat when Imlay had rejected her multiple times in favour of a new lover. She had seen herself as a pioneer, but she was instead, as Janet Todd put it, 'an abandoned woman whose lover had tired of her.'[12]

Wollstonecraft's plight showed the dangers of cohabitation for women. For one thing, her child had no legal father. Imlay promised to set aside money for Fanny, but he never did so, and Mary refused to resort to humiliating legal proceedings to get it. Second, Wollstonecraft's freedom in the union was highly contingent. Because of her love for Gilbert, she found it difficult to disentangle herself from him, even after months of cruelty. Wollstonecraft did not see the freedom of her union as a positive, though she had criticised the English legal system for leaving women with no redress against faithless husbands. She believed that marriage was only real as long as the emotions binding the couple remained, but she had not anticipated Imlay's love would die before hers.[13] In short, Wollstonecraft's first union showed the difficulty of ending nonmarital relationships. Neither partner could conceive of what kind of separation should follow an informal union; in addition, those who saw themselves as pioneers were particularly loath to admit failure.[14] This squalid end forced Wollstonecraft to admit that her brave experiment was, to the eyes of society, no more than a brief affair with a worthless man.

Wollstonecraft's relationship with Godwin was different, both because of her prior experience and because Godwin was more considerate. Godwin, despite his writings about marriage, was probably a virgin when he met Wollstonecraft for the second time in January 1796. Wollstonecraft, then, took the lead, visiting Godwin at his home, and the two began a sexual relationship in August. The couple apparently did not consider marrying. In the first edition of his memoirs, Godwin proclaimed it ridiculous 'to require the overflowing of the soul to wait upon a ceremony,' but in his more chastened second edition, he admitted, that his 'prejudices' made him reluctant to take part in a ceremony that 'I should undoubtedly, as a citizen, be desirous to abolish.'[15] So the couple met clandestinely and had separate social lives. Though this decision appeared mutual, Mary's past experience made her uneasy and touchy, and she hinted at times about marriage. For example, when she sent him some linen, she wrote that she enjoyed 'acting the part of a wife, though you have so little respect for the character.'[16] But Godwin refused to take the hints.

The crisis in their relationship developed when Wollstonecraft confirmed in December 1796 that she was pregnant. The relationship could no longer be discreet, and Mary's situation was dire. Rather than a pseudo-wife to Imlay, she would be a fallen woman with two illegitimate children. Thus, Mary urged William to marry her and, reluctantly, he agreed. They married quietly on 29 March 1797. Godwin faced a great deal of ridicule when the marriage became public in April. He admitted that he had been inconsistent, but defended himself on the grounds that he had to consider Mary's well-being: 'Nothing but a regard for the happiness of the individual, which I had no right to injure, could have induced me to submit to an institution which I wish to see abolished'.[17] As long as society stayed traditional, sexual experiments disadvantaged women. Rather than watch Mary suffer, William married her.

Wollstonecraft's experiences were painful enough to discourage many women from entering free unions. If she had not married, she would have had no chance at a useful social life; and, indeed, her tarnished reputation greatly limited her influence on the later women's movement. Godwin, too, had been converted. After Wollstonecraft's death, he married Mary Jane Clairemont, again after first getting her pregnant. Indeed, the two married twice, since she gave a false name in the first wedding and feared it was not legal. Neither Godwin nor Wollstonecraft repudiated their beliefs, but living out these ideals in the unreconstructed world proved impossible.

The 'romantic' generation

Godwin and Wollstonecraft influenced subsequent generations in both the working and middle classes. Godwin's most famous follower was Percy Shelley, though the latter was already a radical when he met Godwin. He had been expelled from Oxford for writing a pamphlet in support of atheism, quarrelled with his father, and then married without his father's permission. In 1812, he wrote to Godwin to begin the friendship. Like Godwin, Shelley's attitude towards marriage was complex. In *Queen Mab*, he insisted that love was the only binding power between two people; when it died, the marriage was over.[18] Yet Shelley married Harriet Westbrook twice – once in Scotland and once in England, explaining his decision by pointing out the difficulties for any dishonoured woman.[19]

Most romantics expressed sexual rebellion by marrying legally and then having affairs. Lord Byron's notorious amours, married and single, were an example of this advocacy of 'free love'.[20] Shelley's marital behaviour, though distinct from this, also had aspects of both defiance and compliance. Though he did not limit his sexual activities to his wives, he went through three weddings and stayed with his second wife until his death. The one way Shelley stood out from other men of his time was his public elopement with Mary Godwin while he was still married, particularly since both Mary and Percy insisted that they were following the precepts of her parents when they did so. Percy loved another woman; how could living with Harriet be moral? Shelley's situation fitted with Godwin's early objections to marriage. Harriet and Percy were 'thoughtless and romantic' youths (sixteen and nineteen) when they married. And Shelley had clearly deluded himself about the eternal nature of his love. Thus, he felt justified in following his heart.[21]

Shelley was so confident of Godwin's approval that he told William of their plans to elope in July 1814. Godwin, appalled, made Shelley promise to give up this scheme, but Mary and Percy ran away together on 28 July, taking Mary's stepsister, Jane, with them. Godwin refused to see Mary as long as she cohabited with Shelley, and the couple were baffled by his reaction. As William St Clair has pointed out, though, Godwin had good reason to differentiate his behaviour from his daughter's. William and Mary had been discreet, were both in their thirties, and had not broken up a marriage. In contrast, Percy and Mary had openly defied society, were very young, and had hurt Harriet Shelley deeply.[22] Thus, Godwin's reaction was understandable, if not heroic.

The Godwin/Shelley menage now had two generations of marital nonconformity, and the result was a variety of family tensions. For instance, Mary Godwin and Fanny Imlay barely knew their maternal aunts, since neither approved of their sister's private life. In addition, Mary Jane's jealousy of Godwin's first wife may have made her an unsympathetic stepmother; Mary claimed her stepmother ill-treated her. The elopement brought these tensions to a boil. On one side, Mary Jane blamed Mary for Jane's 'fall'; on the other, Mary Godwin held her stepmother responsible for her father's harshness. Ironically, the main victim of the feud was Fanny Imlay, who committed suicide in the midst of the scandal. Her reasons remain murky, but most likely she believed she did not belong in the household, since she was not related to William or Mary Jane. Though some of these problems happened in many families (like step-parenting), others (illegitimacies and elopements) were the result of unusual marital practices.[23] At the least, both Godwin's and Mary Jane's sexual careers made them ill-suited to lecture Percy and Mary about morality, though this did not much hinder them.

In the end, Harriet Shelley's suicide ended the estrangement, since

Percy and Mary married as soon as possible, especially because Mary, pregnant for the third time, insisted on it. Again, a free union ended in a conventional marriage, and Godwin, for one, could not have been happier about it.[24] As St Clair has noted, by December 1816, Godwin and Shelley, two dissenters from marriage, had gone through the ritual six times. In the end, the advantages of the marriage ceremony (which Shelley called 'magical') overrode any objections to it. Though Shelley did not receive custody of his children, he and Mary were welcomed back to Godwin's home and went out in society. The family repercussions, though, did not end, since Shelley's father never forgave him or Mary.[25]

The Godwin/Shelley elopement defied the 'monopoly' of marriage, since Percy renounced his vows to Harriet. All the same, his choice to cohabit was dictated by his limited options. Mary and Percy would probably have married had he been able to do so; at any rate, they did not hesitate when they had the opportunity. Thus, though they were more openly defiant than Wollstonecraft and Godwin in some ways, they were more conventional in others. Like her mother, Mary disliked being a 'fallen woman'; she was, for instance, deeply hurt that none of her friends visited her after her elopement. Radical women were particularly upset at these defections, since they assumed that their friends and families were progressive.[26]

Despite his marriages, Shelley's example influenced many later radicals. Barbara Taylor has demonstrated Shelley's influence on Robert Owen. In addition, Richard Carlile, the radical printer, admired Shelley throughout his life, as did W. J. Linton, who was active in reforming circles.[27] Nor were middle-class activists immune. Radical Unitarians quoted Shelley frequently in their literature, and George Henry Lewes asked Mary Shelley if he could write her husband's biography. Into the 1890s, Shelley's reputation as a marital radical attracted admirers, including anarchists, socialists, and novelists.[28]

In general, then, early nineteenth-century marital dissenters influenced many later movements. All the same, men appreciated Shelley more than women. Women feared that men free to leave unions would not hesitate to do so. After all, the majority of free unions in the Romantic period had little to do with theorising against marriage. Byron's scandalous career was a case in point. He quickly moved from lover to lover, and since he was already married after 1815, the best he could offer was protection to any paramours. Women looked at his career and assumed that his freedom was a cover for promiscuity. Shelley and Godwin were more attractive models, but both had married in the end. This gender divide continued as working-class radicalism spread; though they might dislike the Hardwicke

Act, working-class couples, especially the women, were leery of too much sexual freedom.

Working-class radicalism, 1800–50

John Gillis has pointed out that the period from 1780 to 1840 saw a change in working-class attitudes towards marriage. Illegitimacy and pre-bridal pregnancies sky-rocketed, and, in the north and west, women remained in the paternal home after having illegitimate children. Other couples, resentful at the expense of the banns, self-married through 'besom' marriages or 'tally' arrangements. Men and women seemed indifferent to the moral aspects and refused to pay fees to the church or state. All the same, these couples did not usually espouse any ideology, and the majority did not publicise their unmarried state. They had their own rituals, and most regarded themselves as married. In fact, often their parsons did not know they were living 'tally' until specifically informed.[29]

Thus, though the amount of working-class cohabitation was large in the early nineteenth century, only a few were consciously radical. These consisted of a wide variety of persuasions, including religious dissenters, socialists, and feminists. Religious concerns led to free unions for several different reasons. For instance, some Irish Catholic immigrants and Dissenters disdained the requirement that they go through an Anglican ceremony and refused to do so. However, this grievance was of limited duration, since marriage by registrar became law in 1836.[30]

Despite this change, marginal religious groups continued to rebel against legal marriage. For the most part, these associations stressed celibacy and asceticism, as in Joanna Southcott's movement in the 1790s.[31] Many of them separated legal husbands and wives and wed their leaders to several different 'spiritual wives', but these unions were, theoretically, without sexual contact. The Abode of Love, which had only sixty adherents, was one such group. The leader, known as Prince, was already married, yet he had 'spiritual unions' with women followers. His union with Miss Paterson, though, resulted in the birth of child, an unexpected result, since Prince assumed 'his carnal life had passed away'. The group faced several problems in the wake of this development, but the fact that there was only one child indicated that such breakdowns were rare.[32] Ascetic movements generally held to their principles of celibacy, though splinter groups might not. Joanna Southcott likely remained a virgin, but some of her followers, such as John Wroe, failed due to sexual scandals.[33]

On the other hand, other radical religious groups did not demand celibacy. As J. F. C. Harrison put it, 'If a man believed that he had attained perfection and was no longer capable of sin ... he was free to do all manner of things which were normally forbidden. Free love, for instance, was a sign or symbol of spiritual emancipation.'[34] Some groups argued that they should follow the example of the early church, where all things were held in common, including, allegedly, spouses. Luckie Buchan, who saw herself as the third part of the Godhead, lived with a married man. Buchan wrote that 'Where the Holy Spirit of God occupies all the person, and reigns throughout the flesh, it matters not much whether they marry or not.'[35] The Communist Church, led by the Barmbys, was another example. They had a feminist critique of marriage, and a close relationship with the White Quakers, a church led by Joshua Jacob and Abigail Beale, who were in a free union (Jacob had abandoned his wife).[36] Though such religious groups were small (the Buchanites had only sixty members), they contributed another strand to the general marital experimentation of the first half of the century.

Secular movements were larger and more vocal. Leaders of the working class spread rationalist critiques of marriage in the 1820s and 1830s. In particular, Richard Carlile, a radical publisher, argued for more marital, sexual, and gender freedom. Under the influence of Francis Place, he converted to the cause of birth control in the 1820s. In 1826, he published *Every Woman's Book*, in which he argued that celibacy hurt both men and women far more than sex outside of marriage. Thus, he suggested the use of birth control for both married and unmarried couples.[37] Carlile also argued that the state should only interfere in unions if the couples had children. Like Godwin, he believed that indissoluble marriage deformed reason, since those 'unhappily united to one whom they find it impossible to love' nevertheless tried 'to appear otherwise than they are.'[38] Carlile argued that the virtue of each union was determined by the motive of the couple for being together, and 'chastity' consisted of being together for the right reason, married or not.

Carlile's dissent went beyond the theoretical, since his own marriage was unhappy. He and Jane Carlile separated in the early 1830s, and not long afterwards, he met Eliza Sharples. Sharples, twenty-eight, had converted to 'freethought and political radicalism' from her father's Methodism. She came to London and wrote to Carlile (he was in prison); encouraged by his replies, she visited him. These visits eventually resulted in a passionate love affair. Sharples's views about women's equality and marriage were similar to Carlile's. She argued that women suffered from indissoluble marriage, and criticised their 'undue submission, which constitutes slavery'. Her publication, *The Isis*, included transcripts of trials that showed the hypocrisy of the current system – such as bigamies and wife sales. About the latter, she wrote, 'How much better would a quiet separation have been, and each left to a new and free choice.'[39]

Carlile and Sharples were discreet for some time, since a scandal would damage Carlile's career. Sharples, unhappy about the secrecy, asked 'him to acknowledge her as his "wife" rather than as a "hole and corner" mistress' especially after she gave birth to his son in April 1833. Carlile finally made things public in September when he published a lengthy defence. He characterised his first marriage as 'a degrading and soul-destroying restraint'. He had, then, 'divorced' his wife, and 'have now taken to wife a woman with whom I am happy'.[40] Thus, Carlile pointed out that his first marriage was over before he began his second. He added in October 1834 that his settlement on his wife was generous, and that 'I have not failed in any promise made to her, save that of the silly one of pledging association for life'. Carlile tried to blunt a growing chorus of criticism by highlighting the deliberate nature of his decision.[41]

Sharples publicly defended her union as well. Like Carlile, she argued that their relationship was based on reason and mutuality. She was even more insistent than Carlile that theirs was not a rejection of marriage. They were in a free union because they had no other choice: 'though we passed over a legal obstacle, it was only because it could not be removed'.[42] Sharples argued that their happiness was a sign that they had done the right thing, and she was proud to have 'set a good example'. To stress her new status, she took Richard's name. Sharples believed that women were intellectually equal to men and that only a marriage of equals would succeed. Presumably, she had entered such a marriage.[43]

Carlile and Sharples, in sum, both believed in the equality and 'morality' of their union. In some ways, they lived up to their ideals. Though Carlile was a strong influence on Sharples's intellectual development, she also influenced him, as when she 'converted' him to rational Christianity in 1832. They had three more children (their first child died young) and were still together when Carlile died in 1843. On the other hand, Richard, fourteen years older, was the dominant personality, and Eliza's career stopped with the births of four children. In addition, as a middle-class woman, Eliza found the poverty and isolation of her situation difficult, since her family repudiated her. According to Joel Wiener, Carlile was disillusioned with her by 1835, seeing her as 'a woman of limited ability who lacked the determination to pursue "serious" objectives'. When he went on a trip to Manchester in 1836, he left her in London and took his older son with him instead.[44]

In addition, Carlile's career never recovered from his conversion to rational Christianity and his union with Sharples. Criticism of their behaviour dogged him. He was also dismayed at the birth of their fourth child, writing to a friend that it was 'folly'. (Despite his work on birth control, he was strangely traditional about Eliza's fecundity.) Money problems were the root of his reaction; he did not have the income to support two families. Like many working men, his means were insufficient to support his ideals, and his second family suffered the most. After his death, Sharples was destitute and turned to needlework. Charles Bradlaugh, who boarded with her, saw her as a '"broken woman, who had her ardour and enthusiasm cooled by suffering and poverty"'. After her death in 1852, her Owenite friends supported her children.[45]

Carlile and Sharples both argued that one of the reasons that their union was 'moral' was its mutuality. They had great difficulty, though, in overcoming their physical and economic problems. Carlile resented Sharples's concentration on her children, rather than on philosophy, once the babies began to arrive. Radical couples, because of their shared work in reform movements, had special problems when the woman's concentration on the domestic clashed with the man's work. In addition, though both Carlile and Sharples argued for freeing women's sexuality, they did not take into account the consequences of such activities. More crucially, they could only imagine individual solutions to these social problems. Their relationship showed that sexual experiments, and particularly women's emancipation in them, were doubly difficult in the working class.

Carlile's writings acted as a bridge between the revolutionaries of the 1790s and the Owenite movement of the 1820s to 1840s; he and Eliza had contacts with both groups. Unlike previous radicals, though, Robert Owen concentrated on economic issues. As Barbara Taylor has shown, Owen's social critique was broad; for him, the three major evils were religion, private property, and marriage. Owen believed that all of society had to change for any single reform to work, and his vehicle was communal living. In theory, this system would solve the problem of women's fear of desertion in free unions; if society as a whole cared for all members, women did not need individual providers. Moreover, Owenites argued that women could not be free until they were released from a contract that treated them as chattels.[46]

Owen's views of marriage echoed many earlier rationalist criticisms. Like Godwin, Owen considered it 'absurd and farcical' for two people to promise 'to love each other, without any reference to the changes which may arise in the appearance, qualities, and character of the parties.' Owen insisted that marriage was 'only a legitimate and varnished prostitution.' Both sexes suffered, but women did so the most, since they belonged to their husbands and vowed to obey, thus soon becoming entirely artificial.

Owen blamed 'priestly' superstitions and the system of private family homes for this situation. Nuclear families perpetuated ignorance and inequality. Only communal living could rectify these evils.[47] He also challenged conventional arguments about virtue and chastity. He argued that 'The pure and genuine chastity of nature' existed only when unions were from love alone; otherwise, they were 'the most degrading prostitution'. Furthermore, Owen, echoing Wollstonecraft, argued that chastity was necessary for both sexes, 'for if men are not chaste, how is it possible for women to be so?'[48]

Particularly in his assertions about women's equality, Owen had support from others in the movement, mostly famously William Thompson and Ann Wheeler, in their work, *Appeal of One Half the Human Race, Women, Against the Pretensions of the other Half, Men*, published in 1825. In a much-quoted passage, Thompson scoffed at idea of marriage as a contract: 'A contract implies the voluntary assent of both the contracting parties … Have women been consulted as to the terms of this pretended contract?' Thompson pointed out that marriage gave all the power and advantages to men and all the duties to women, and compared it to the 'contract' between slaves and their masters.[49] Frances Morrison, one of Owen's most fervent supporters, echoed these themes. Born Frances Cooper, she lived with James Morrison for some years before they married, partly because she had 'an almost pathological distrust' of marriage. She would not marry him 'until she knew "if he was kind"', and she may not have done so at all except that she became pregnant.[50] Though her own marriage was happy, Frances complained about women's social limitations, and denounced the sexual double standard. Morrison agreed with Owen that the only hope for women was to organise society 'rationally'.[51] Similarly, Charles Southwell, a Socialist speaker in the 1840s, insisted that women must be educated so they would marry for the right reasons; a woman should be 'the FRIEND AND COMPANION OF MAN' rather than a 'cringing slave'.[52]

The Owenite movement, then, made a strong argument against traditional marriage. But what to put in its place? Owen proposed an inexpensive ceremony without the interference of church or state. The couple simply stated their intention publicly to be married. They then went through a year's probation after which they could divorce by mutual consent, though they had to wait six months for the community to attempt reconciliation. Owenites insisted that their system was cheaper, simpler, and more flexible than the traditional one. Joshua Hobson wrote in 1838 that it 'recognizes no authority but that of love – no tie but that of tenderness'. Because only happy couples stayed together, men and women developed rationally and virtuously.[53]

In some Owenite communities, like Queenswood, couples married by these terms, at least in the 1830s. Most couples were already married when they arrived there, so the numbers were few, but the possibility remained. Other communities were more radical. The most notorious Owenite community was Manea Fen, led by William Hodson. Hodson lived with his deceased wife's sister and so had little respect for the marriage laws, though he insisted to the national association that he followed Owenite principles. All the same, he wrote to a friend in 1839 that he wanted to abolish 'the buying and selling of each other' in his community. Whatever the actual practices, the Manea Fen community boasted to the local press that they did not follow the regular English customs.[54] In addition, the Lawrence Street chapel, a Southcottian church, offered a place where 'couples simply married themselves.' Owenites may have taken advantage of this option, though after 1840, Owen urged his followers to marry civilly.[55]

Self-divorce, as opposed to self-marriage, was a more difficult proposition. Southwell insisted that Owen supported divorce only when it was mutual, rather than the repudiation by one party of the other. Southwell admitted that the distinction could be hard to make, since when only one partner wanted to leave there would be 'some difficulty.'[56] Southwell himself left his wife because she was unfaithful, and later cohabited with his wife's aunt. He complained about the lack of provision for divorce: 'The woman with whom I lived was faithful; the woman I married was false ... which of these two women best deserved all the kindness and consideration in my power to bestow?' Nevertheless, when his wife became ill and begged him to return, he did so; he did not practice repudiation himself.[57]

Owenite self-divorces indeed were usually mutual. In a much publicised case in 1842, the Cheltenham Owenites drew up a divorce contract between Amelia and James Vaughan. The Vaughans agreed to separate, and William Stanbury contracted to take over the care of Amelia. If either man reneged on the contract, he had to pay a fine of £10, while James got custody of their son once he turned two years old. As Taylor has pointed out, despite their disdain for wife sales, the Owenites had drawn up a contract similar to those already used in plebeian circles, transferring responsibility for Amelia from one man to another. In addition, this 'divorce' led to a long, scandalised story in the newspaper, in part because Stanbury had left his wife and children, though the paper grudgingly admitted he gave them 'a weekly allowance.' The ire of the local population showed the difficulty of allowing divorces; the newspaper insisted that Socialism 'has become a mere byeword [sic] for immorality and licentiousness.'[58]

Of course, those who were married only by agreement could be divorced even more easily, and this situation was risky for women. For instance, Southwell's cohabitee wanted him to marry her bigamously (and illegally, because of the affinal tie). She hoped this would protect her from desertion, but he refused. Her concern was justified, since he later returned to his wife. In 1839, a servant named Mary Bennett accused John Joyes of marrying her in the 'socialist' manner, and then abandoning her after the birth of their child. The local Owenites disputed this story, but it pointed up the difficulties for women, particularly after several Owenite communities failed in the early 1840s.[59] After all, the only reason women could take part in free unions was the promise of communal support. Without that, they had only the dubious mercy of the Poor Law if their relationships failed.

Some Owenite leaders did take that risk. As mentioned earlier in this chapter, Frances Cooper and James Morrison cohabited for five years (1822–27), though they later married. Emma Martin, a crusader against religion, lived with Joshua Hopkins, a labourer, in a free union for six years until her early death in 1851. When young, Emma had married Isaac Martin and had three daughters with him, but she was miserable in the marriage. In 1839, she left him, and became a lecturer for Socialism, particularly debating with others on 'Marriage and Divorce'. In 1845, after a struggle to support herself and fierce criticism from religious groups, she formed a free union with Joshua and retired from lecturing, giving birth to a daughter in 1847. Her union with Hopkins succeeded, probably because Joshua believed in both workers' and women's emancipation.[60] At her funeral, G. J. Holyoake described their relationship in idealised terms: 'no affection was ever purer, no union ever more honourable to both parties'. Emma suffered from much criticism, even within Socialist groups, and she was often short on funds, but at least her home life was happy. Her union was an example both of the disadvantages and the rewards for working women in 'true', but irregular, bonds.[61]

Owenites challenged the biblical basis of marriage and highlighted the problems with England's marriage laws. Especially, they combined women's and class issues in ways that few others had done. They shared a belief in reason and perfectability with those who came before them, but went further in their solutions. Still, even at the height of the movement, Owenite couples in free unions were the minority. Most couples who joined Owenism were already married; others joined after 1840, when Owen encouraged civil marriage. And many of those who did take part in free unions eventually married; those who did not often could not do so.

Furthermore, much of the Owenite practices were in tune with the working class around them rather than a break with tradition. Unhappy poor couples practiced self-marriage and divorce; they just did not make a public stand about it. And despite many Owenites' emphasis on feminism, their communities still expected the women to do the domestic tasks. As it turned out, Owenite communities were hardly paradises for women, who were burdened with both domestic and non-domestic work and had little say in governing the societies. Taylor argues that the Owenite movement became increasingly conservative about marital issues after 1840, especially among women. Morrison, for instance, insisted that socialists must continue to marry, "'in order to insure that fidelity which the vehemence of temporary passion could never guarantee.'" In short, women socialists had less enthusiasm for sexual experimentation as time went on.[62]

The Owenite movement's collapse in the 1840s was due to economic failure more than these marital dilemmas. Owen became convinced that the success of the movement depended on upper-class sponsors and lost interest in experiments. After the movement petered out, couples who had lived in free unions may or may not have stayed in that situation. Without the community support, women cohabitees were in a difficult situation, so they may have insisted on legalising their relationships (if possible). After the 1840s, the working-class movement focused on Chartism and trade unions and supported domesticity and male suffrage, thus excluding women from leadership and limiting their opportunities for marital dissent. According to Anna Clark, this outcome was the result of 'bitter political and trade union struggles' and was contrary to much working-class history. Nevertheless, the leadership in critiquing marriage and pushing for gender equality shifted to the middle class.[63]

Radical Unitarians, 1820–50

As Kathryn Gleadle has shown, the largely middle-class members of Radical Unitarianism pushed for women's equality and marriage reform. The nucleus of this group was in W. J. Fox's South Place Chapel in London, and the vessel for their ideas was the journal *The Monthly Repository*. The Radical Unitarians' core philosophy, based on John Locke, argued for individual reason and education. Though most Unitarians were liberal rather than socialist, many supported Owenism, and Owen reprinted selections from the *Repository* in his publications. Eventually, the South Place Chapel attracted a wide range of liberals and radicals, including J. S. Mill, George Henry Lewes, W. J. Linton, and Eliza Cook.[64]

According to Gleadle, what separated 'radical' Unitarians from the mainstream was their devotion to women's rights. Like many of the previous writers, they argued that women's education stressed submission to men and thus warped women's development; further, they insisted that women should have wider political and economic opportunities. On the issue of marriage, these writers agreed with Owen's criticisms of the institution, especially its gender inequality and indissolubility. Mary Leman Grimstone, for example, related women's oppression directly to marriage, since women had no say in the terms of the contract and only men could sue for divorce: 'there can be no contract without two parties'. She was especially critical of the sexual double standard, since a woman 'binds herself a slave to one to avoid becoming the victim of many'.[65]

A particular goal for the radical Unitarians was to promote the idea of marriage as a civil contract. They argued that the religious part of the service was hypocritical and that the insistence on seeing the ceremony as a sacrament made divorce reform impossible. Like their predecessors, they also insisted that a true marriage was one of hearts and minds, whatever its legal state. In addition, they detailed many reasons to avoid the sanction of the church even when love was true. W. J. Linton, for example, disliked the 'public exhibition' of weddings. Thus, though most of these reformers married, they tried to do so in ways that rejected wifely subordination, such as eliminating the word 'obey' in the wife's vows.[66]

A minority of Radical Unitarians did not marry legally, and their stories are instructive. The main actors were W. J. Linton and Emily Wade, W. J. Fox and Eliza Flower, Thomas Southwood Smith and Margaret Gillies, Richard Hengist Horne and Mary Gillies (Margaret's sister), and, to a lesser extent, Thomas Wade and Lucy Bridgman. (A discussion of J. S. Mill and Harriet Taylor appears in Chapter 9.) In four out of five of these examples, the couples were unable to marry legally. Emily Wade was Linton's deceased wife's sister; in the three other cases, one of the partners was married. In short, these couples grappled with the difficulties of marriage laws because of their circumstances and not just from theoretical beliefs. However, their radicalism usually predated their unions; thus, their cohabitation deepened their dissent rather than causing it. Because so many of them were middle class and publicly active, their unconventional home lives had to be explained away or carried out discreetly. Ironically, reforming 'hypocritical' marriage laws required some hypocrisy.

The leader of the Radical Unitarians, W. J. Fox, had married in 1820, but the marriage was largely over by the late 1820s; he and his wife separated in 1832. Despite his own unhappiness, Fox argued for women's suffrage, for women's equality within marriage, and against the sexual double standard.[67] His ideas were confirmed when he met Eliza Flower through her father Benjamin, a Unitarian publisher. Fox was Eliza's guardian after Benjamin's death in 1829, and they fell in love. The two were intellectually and emotionally compatible, since Flower was well-educated and an excellent musician. Though Fox and Flower did not have a sexual affair, his wife was jealous, and her complaints led to Fox's resignation from his congregation in 1834. They eventually asked him to return, but he decided to leave again in 1835, because he wanted to live openly with Flower.[68]

Fox respected Flower's abilities a great deal; her contributions to his work deepened his belief in women's equality. For her part, Eliza was devoted to him and his family, gaining the confidence of his mother and sister. All the same, Flower sacrificed more than Fox in their irregular household. She lost many of her friends and had less time for her own work. His needs were always paramount; for example, in 1839, the family moved to Westminster, which was not a good place for the consumptive Flower but was better for Fox's career. In addition, Fox and Flower apparently did not unite physically, though Fox insisted such a union was not immoral. According to Crabb Robinson, Fox asserted that 'though no illicit intercourse had in fact taken place ... it was merely accidental, there being nothing in their principles against their so acting'. Somewhat contradictorily, Fox drew a distinction between divorce and remarriage, so he did not feel free to start a new union, despite denying its immorality. As he put it, '"I hold myself to be morally divorced – remarriage is quite another question."'[69]

Fox's scruples did not lessen the scandal. The Association of Unitarian Ministers expelled him in 1835 when he set up his home with Flower.[70] The assumption of immorality infuriated Fox, but he should have expected it. Opponents had branded all marriage reformers as free lovers since the 1790s; they were hardly likely to draw a different conclusion about a man who worked for divorce reform while living with a woman not his wife. Nonetheless, the help that Flower gave to Fox during their eleven years together allowed him to work more steadily. Flower, too, gained from their association, since Fox printed her songs in *The Monthly Repository*. Little indication of trouble or unhappiness between them survives; indeed, their affectionate letters indicate otherwise. Eliza's horizons were more circumscribed than William's, but she remained loyal until her death from consumption in 1846. One can also easily overstate their social isolation, too, since the couple had the support of the other Radical Unitarians.[71]

Still, one cannot help comparing the situation of Fox and Flower to the more private unions of the Gillies sisters. Margaret Gillies's union with Thomas Southwood Smith has already been discussed in Chapter 5. Southwood Smith's unhappy marriage prevented them from marrying, but they lived together for many years and worked for various causes.[72] Southwood Smith and Gillies had a mutually supportive relationship and both had fulfilling careers. They did not publicly acknowledge their relationship, however, and Southwood Smith's wife did not object to it (she even lived with them when she was unwell). They observed the proprieties, in other words. They thus did not give ammunition to their opponents, though they also lost the opportunity to speak out for marriage reform. On the other hand, considering the criticism that Fox received, perhaps they would have had little influence on the subject anyway if their union was public knowledge.

Unacknowledged relationships involved trade-offs, since the couple appeared to be hypocritical by defying marriage laws but rarely speaking about them. But Gillies and Southwood Smith both worked for other changes – those of sanitary laws and mining conditions – that might have failed had they lived openly together. The couple also protected and supported Mary Southwood Smith. Like Flower and Fox, they did not have children, a necessity for their situation to remain discreet; one is simply unable to know if this was by choice or circumstance, since they never wrote about it. Despite an occasional whisper of scandal, their devotion to each other survived through many years. The support of the radical Unitarians was also crucial; again, the alternative social group made a great difference.[73]

Mary Gillies was Margaret's older sister, a firm feminist who argued for associated housing for married couples and women's right to work. Mary's life changed when Richard Hengist Horne became part of their circle. Horne was a self-taught poet who struggled to make a living from his writings. His acceptance into the group gave him intellectual and social contacts and influenced him to direct his reforming zeal to helping the working class and supporting women's rights. Primarily, he came under the influence of Mary, the most important person in his adult life. Mary was his confidante, his assistant, his workmate, and, as he put it, 'My oldest, truest friend'.[74]

The exact relationship between Richard and Mary is a mystery. They did live together for a time (in 1846), but they never openly cohabited, and Horne later married a younger woman. The couple were emotionally, but probably not physically, intimate. Still, Mary often acted as a wife – planning meals for Richard, sewing flannel into his waistcoat, offering emotional support. When Horne became editor of the *Monthly Repository*, she was his firmest helper, doing editorial and secretarial tasks.[75] Why the two did not marry is puzzling; Ann Blainey speculates that Mary did not like the physical side of marriage and women's subordination. Perhaps Horne also did not want to; Mary was three years older and had her own career. For whatever reason, the friendship was enough for both of them.[76]

All the same, when Horne did marry, in 1847, he chose a young girl named Kate St George Foggo; she was half his age and, seemingly, malleable and innocent. Mary took the news well and remained his friend, but the intensity of their relationship lessened. Still, they never lost touch with each other, and he was shattered when she died in 1870. Their relationship may have been closer because they did not live together, giving each other independence. But the success of their union was, again, its discretion. If they were sexually involved, they have left little indication of it, and certainly neither allowed her or his personal feelings to interfere with duties or work.[77]

Fox and Flower lived openly together, and the Gillieses practiced discretion. A third option was to marry, legally or illegally, as in the unions within the Wade/Linton family. Thomas Wade was a young poet when he entered the South Place circle. Lucy Susannah Bridgman was a concert pianist who had married a confectioner and had one son by the time she met Wade, probably in 1834. When Wade and Bridgman became lovers is unclear; she still had a different address from Wade's in 1839. Nevertheless, she gave birth to Wade's son, and Wade celebrated their 'chainless union' in poems in the mid-1830s. They, then, followed their hearts rather than the law. Still, they married as soon as Bridgman was widowed in the early 1840s. Theirs was, to all appearances, a happy match; at any rate, Wade left his widow his estate at his death in 1875.[78]

In contrast to his brother-in-law, W. J. Linton was an artisan, not middle-class, and made his living from his engravings. His financial problems were more severe, then, than the others in the Craven Hill group. Linton's union with Emily Wade was not legal because she was his sister-in-law; they did not make a conscious choice to cohabit. Still, Linton chose the Wade sisters in part because of their independence and intelligence; he described them as "'such women in their purity, intelligence … as Shelley might have sung as fitted to redeem a world.'" Also, despite his choice to marry, Linton publicly disdained state and church controls, insisting that "'all legislative interference with marriage'" should be abolished. He resented the 'illegitimate' status of his children, too; forty years later he wrote a poem complaining about it.[79]

Linton had married Lara Wade in 1837; after her death in 1838, both her mother and sister Emily moved in with him. When he and Emily became intimate is impossible to know, but she had his son in 1842. Linton insisted that 'No truer marriage ever Couple made', and they had six more children over the next several years. Linton supported this brood by his engravings, all the while also working for Chartism and publishing radical journals. Unsurprisingly, Emily's intellectual development halted, yet she never wavered in her support for William. When he began the *English Republic*, she wrote "'It is a doubtful speculation … but it is no use fretting or fearing … dear W must serve his Great Cause.'" (The journal failed in 1854.) The privation and menial toil took its toll, and Emily died of consumption in 1856, having never lessened her affection for her husband.[80] Linton and Wade's marriage was happy; indeed, in later years, Linton compared his third wife, Eliza Lynn, unfavourably with his second. All the same, though the relationship was a complete success for William, it was only partially so for Emily. Wade could hardly pursue her own interests when she was caring for a family that grew every year, especially on an uncertain income. Wade stated after the birth of her fourth child that she wanted no more children, yet she had three more in 1851, 1852, and 1854. She made Linton's work possible, but at the cost of burying her own potential.[81] Because they had economic problems and several children, they contrast with the other Craven Hill couples; their affinal union was more acceptable to the wider society, yet their economic woes made their lives more difficult.

The work of the Radical Unitarians in promoting women's rights and in challenging marriage laws was crucial to future reform movements; their writings influenced the women's movement that began in the 1850s.[82] The free unions of the Radical Unitarians, however, were hedged with many caveats. Most were undertaken because they had no choice, at least some of them were platonic, and others were discreet. In addition, the gender roles of these households were traditional; the women's careers were slowed or stopped (except Gillies and Bridgman Wade), particularly when the couples had children. None of the women expressed resentment, but none suggested that men share the domestic duties, even when the women had careers. In this, they were similar to the Owenites, an interesting cross-class convergence.

The middle-class standing of most of these couples protected them from financial struggles; Fox and Southwood Smith could afford to support two families. But that same class standing also enjoined public silence. Fox and Southwood Smith succeeded in many movements for change, but they did not have much influence on divorce reform. Fox worked openly on the issue but was compromised by his personal interest, and the others avoided it entirely. Thus, whichever choice the couples made, their happy, non-marital relationships had limited influence on the marriage debate.

Conclusion

The first half of the nineteenth century was one of vigorous marital nonconformity. Many groups articulated dissents against marriage, mostly stemming from a belief in perfectability and human reason. In addition, these movements criticised two elements: marital indissolubility and women's legal disabilities. Still, even in the most radical groups, the majority of couples married, and those who cohabited usually did so because they had no choice. In this, they were similar to the cohabiting couples around them; their only differences were their philosophical (and often public) justifications for their choices.

In all of these groups, women and children had special difficulties. Because men did not do domestic work and did not give birth to children, women's needs often got buried under housekeeping. Even more crucially, the freedom in these unions was contingent; women, no matter how well-educated or independent, were more likely to sacrifice their needs for men than vice versa. Also, a system of unions that lasted only as long as both parties wished them to do so begged the question of what to do when one party wanted to leave. This was particularly acute for deserted women, who had damaged reputations and few economic prospects. And only the Owenites had a solution to the problems of children, since they eschewed single family units. With all others, children might bear the brunt of their parents' radicalism; the fate of Fanny Imlay, like that of her mother, hovered over radical couples throughout the century.

Despite these dilemmas, most of these couples did not suffer total isolation. All of them had like-minded people around them to offer support, even in the respectable classes. Poor couples, of course, had more problems because they could seldom support more than one family, but sometimes, as with Owenism, they found temporary solutions. Whatever the gender and class terms, and whatever the degree of radicalism, the number of men and women willing to support new family forms showed strong dissent from the English laws and church. Unsurprisingly, then, the dissent continued into the middle and late nineteenth century.

Notes

1 Gillis, *For Better, For Worse*, pp. 100–5.

2 Quoted from Gillis, *For Better, For Worse*, pp. 222; Taylor, *Eve and the New Jerusalem*, p. 8.

3 R. Bass, *The Green Dragoon: The Lives of Banastre Tarleton and Mary Robinson* (New York: Henry Holt and Company, 1957), pp. 197–207; 264; 316–76; P. Byrne, *Perdita: The Life of Mary Robinson* (London: Harper Perennial, 2005), pp. 211–54; 293–305; 350–1.

4 Quoted from P. Marshall, *William Godwin* (New Haven, CT: Yale University Press, 1984), p. 88.

5 W. Godwin, *Enquiry Concerning Political Justice* 3 vols (Toronto: University of Toronto Press, 1946), II, 507–12, quotes from pp. 508, 507, and 509; Marshall, *William Godwin*, pp. 88–90.

6 M. Wollstonecraft, *A Vindication of the Rights of Woman* (New York: Scribner and Welford, 1890), pp. 118–19.

7 M. Wollstonecraft, *Maria: or The Wrongs of Woman* (New York: W. W. Norton & Company, 1975), pp. 89, 128 (for quote); *Vindication*, p. 72; C. Kegan Paul (ed.), *Mary*

Wollstonecraft: Letters to Imlay (London: Kegan Paul, 1879), pp. 84–7.

8   J. Todd, *Mary Wollstonecraft: A Revolutionary Life* (New York: Colombia University Press, 2000), pp. 426–32.

9   Kegan Paul, *Mary Wollstonecraft*, pp. 40–1; Wollstonecraft to Imlay, February 1794.

10 *Ibid.*, p. 85, Wollstonecraft to Imlay, 30 December 1794, pp. 84–7; Todd, *Mary Wollstonecraft*, pp. 231–60.

11 Kegan Paul, *Mary Wollstonecraft*, p. 102, Wollstonecraft to Imlay, 10 February 1795, pp. 100–3; Todd, *Mary Wollstonecraft*, pp. 261–87; 303–64, quote from p. 303.

12 Kegan Paul, *Mary Wollstonecraft*, pp. 112–14; Todd, *Mary Wollstonecraft*, p. 354.

13 Kegan Paul, *Mary Wollstonecraft*, p. 187–9.

14 W. Godwin, *Memoirs of the Author of a Vindication of the Rights of Woman* (London: Penguin Books, 1987), p. 245 and note.

15 *Ibid.*, p. 258 and note.

16 R. Wardle (ed.), *Godwin & Mary: Letters of William Godwin and Mary Wollstonecraft* (Lincoln, NE: University of Nebraska Press, 1977), pp. 14–23, 40–1; Wollstonecraft to Godwin, 10 November 1796, p. 46 (for quote).

17 Quoted in Marshall, *William Godwin*, p. 186.

18 W. St Clair, *The Godwins and the Shelleys: A Biography of a Family* (New York: W. W. Norton, 1989), pp. 316–21; Marshall, *William Godwin*, pp. 302–5.

19 St Clair, *The Godwins and the Shelleys*, pp. 321–2.

20 A. Elfenbein, *Byron and the Victorians* (Cambridge: Cambridge University Press, 1995), pp. 47–89; P. Grosskurth, *Byron: The Flawed Angel* (New York: Houghton Mifflin, 1997).

21 M. Seymour, *Mary Shelley* (New York: Grove Press, 2000), p. 96; St Clair, *The Godwins and the Shelleys*, pp. 356–66.

22 St Clair, *The Godwins and the Shelleys*, pp. 371–3; Marshall, *William Godwin*, pp. 305–21; Seymour, *Mary Shelley*, pp. 98–130; K. C. Hill-Miller, *'My Hideous Progeny': Mary Shelley, William Godwin, and the Father–Daughter Relationship* (Newark, NJ: University of Delaware Press, 1995), pp. 32–42.

23 Hill-Miller, *'My Hideous Progeny'*, pp. 22–5; Seymour, *Mary Shelley*, pp. 48–50; 57–63; 70–2; Marshall, *William Godwin*, pp. 240–54; 295–8.

24 Marshall, *William Godwin*, p. 324.

25 St Clair, *The Godwins and the Shelleys*, pp. 414–22; Seymour, *Mary Shelley*, pp. 175–8; Marshall, *William Godwin*, pp. 323–5; P. R Feldman and D. Scott-Kilvert (eds), *The Journals of Mary Shelley, 1814–44* 2 vols (Oxford: Clarendon Press, 1987), I, 1–8; 44.

26 Seymour, *Mary Shelley*, p. 116.

27 Taylor, *Eve and the New Jerusalem*, pp. 43–4; 172–82; R. Owen, *The Marriage System of the New Moral World* (Leeds: J. Hobson, 1838), pp. 87–91; J. Wiener, *Radicalism and Freethought in Nineteenth-Century Britain: The Life of Richard Carlile* (Westport, CT: Greenwood Press, 1983), p. 123; W. J. Linton, *Three Score and Ten Years, 1820 to 1890: Recollections* (New York: Charles Scribner's Sons, 1894), p. 26.

28 K. Gleadle, *The Early Feminists: Radical Unitarians and the Emergence of the Women's Rights Movement, 1831–51* (London: St Martin's Press, 1995), p. 63; Seymour, *Mary Shelley*, pp. 556–7; 'Shelley on marriage', *Anarchist* 1, #4 (1886), 7; E. Aveling and E. Marx Aveling, *Shelley's Socialism* (Oxford: Leslie Peger, 1947), pp. 12–13; J. Rose, *The Intellectual Life of the British Working Class* (New Haven, CT: Yale University Press, 2001), pp. 35–6; 48; 120; 195; G. Allen, *The Woman Who Did* (Oxford: Oxford University Press, 1995), p. 75; T. Hardy, *Jude the Obscure* (London: Macmillan, 1968), p. 424.

29 Gillis, *For Better, For Worse*, pp. 190–219.

30 Gillis, *For Better, For Worse*, pp. 219–21; 'Marriage and protest', *The Christian Reformer, or, The Unitarian Magazine and Review* 2 (1835), 60; 'Marriages', *The New Moral World* 1 (1834–35), 24; Outhwaite, *Clandestine Marriage in England*, pp. 145–64; Anderson, 'The incidence of civil marriages', pp. 50–87.

31 Gillis, *For Better, For Worse*, pp. 219–21.

32 W. H. Dixon, *Spiritual Wives* 2 vols (London: Hurst and Blackett, 1868), I, 226–329, quote from p. 325; 'The Agapemone', *The Leader* 1 (1850), 150; and 'Spiritual wives', *Westminster Review* 89 (1868), 456–79.

33 J. F. C. Harrison, *The Second Coming: Popular Millenarianism, 1780–1850* (New Brunswick, NJ: Rutgers University Press, 1979), pp. 138–47.

34 *Ibid.*, p. 16.

35 *Ibid.*, pp. 16–17, 32–8, quote from p. 36.

36 Taylor, *Eve and the New Jerusalem*, pp. 172–5, 330–1.

37 Wiener, *Radicalism and Freethought*, pp. 80–90; 124–30; R. Carlile, 'Every Woman's Book', in M. L. Bush (ed.), *What is Love? Richard Carlile's Philosophy of Sex* (London: Verso, 1998), p. 97.

38 Bush, *What is Love?*, p. 12; Carlile, 'Every Woman's Book', pp. 78–9 (for quote).

39 H. Rogers, '"The prayer, the passion and the reason" of Eliza Sharples: Freethought, women's rights and Republicanism, 1832–52', in E. Yeo (ed.), *Radical Femininity: Women's Self-Representation in the Public Sphere* (Manchester: Manchester University Press, 1998), pp. 53–7, first quote from p. 53; Wiener, *Radicalism and Freethought*, pp. 180–1, second quote from p. 181; E. Sharples, *The Isis: A London Weekly Publication* (London: David France, 1832), pp. 25, 203–4; third quote from p. 204.

40 Wiener, *Radicalism and Freethought*, pp. 194–9, first quote from p. 196; R. Carlile, 'Moral marriage', *The Gauntlet* (1833), 521–2; second quote from 521.

41 'Moral marriage', 521; R. Carlile, 'Family affairs', *A Scourge for the Littleness of 'Great' Men* 3 (1834), 17–21, quote from 19; Rogers, '"The prayer, the passion, and the reason"', 56–7.

42 Sharples, *The Isis*, p. v (for quote); Rogers, '"The prayer, the passion and the reason"', 56.

43 Sharples, *The Isis*, p. v (for quote); Rogers, '"The prayer, the passion and the reason"', 63–5.

44 Sharples, *The Isis*, pp. 202–3; Wiener, *Radicalism and Freethought*, pp. 218–23; 257 (quote from p. 219); Rogers, '"The prayer, the passion and the reason"', 56–7.

45 Wiener, *Radicalism and Freethought*, p. 221; Rogers, '"The prayer, the passion and the reason"', 72–4, quote from 74.

46 Taylor, *Eve and the New Jerusalem*, pp. 15–24.

47 Owen, *The Marriage System*, pp. 16–35, 68–9; first quote from p. 16; 'Police', *Crisis* 3 (1833), 47 (second quote).

48 Owen, *The Marriage System*, pp. 49–58, quotes from pp. 49, 50.

49 W. Thompson, *Appeal of One Half the Human Race, Women, Against the Pretensions of the Other Half, Men* (New York: Bur Franklin, 1970), pp. 55–9; quote from pp. 55–6.

50 Taylor, *Eve and the New Jerusalem*, pp. 75–7; J. Sever, 'James Morrison and *The Pioneer*', unpublished manuscript, British Library, pp. 8–10, quotes from p. 10.

51 F. Morrison, *The Influence of the Present Marriage System upon the Character and Interests of Females* (Manchester: A. Heywood, 1838), pp. 2; 13. See also Philia, 'To the editor of the *Crisis*', *Crisis* 3 (1834), 258; Kate, 'Female improvement', *The New Moral World* 1 (1834–35), 263–4.

52 C. Southwell, *An Essay on Marriage Addressed to the Lord Bishop of Exeter* (London: E. Roe, 1840), p. 17.

53 Gillis, *For Better, For Worse*, p. 225; E. Yeo, 'Robert Owen and radical culture', in S. Pollard and J. Salt (eds.), *Robert Owen: Prophet of the Poor* (London: Macmillan, 1971), 101–2; J. Hobson, *Socialism as it Is!* (Leeds: J. Hobson, 1838), p. 138.

54 Taylor, *Eve and the New Jerusalem*, pp. 252–8; quote from p. 256.

55 Yeo, 'Robert Owen and radical culture', 101–2, quote from 102.

56 Southwell, *An Essay on Marriage*, p. 8.

57 C. Southwell, *Confessions of a Free Thinker* (London: Publisher unknown, 1848?), pp. 24–40, quote from pp. 34–5.

58 HO 45/981 (for quotes); Taylor, *Eve and the New Jerusalem*, pp. 198–9.

59 Southwell, *Confessions of a Free-Thinker*, pp. 30–4; Yeo, 'Robert Owen and radical culture', 102; Taylor, *Eve and the New Jerusalem*, pp. 199–201.

60 Taylor, *Eve and the New Jerusalem*, pp. 68–73; 130–57.

61 Taylor, *Eve and the New Jerusalem*, pp. 130–57; G. J. Holyoake, 'Emma Martin', *The Leader* 2 (1851), 985 (for quote).

62 Taylor, *Eve and the New Jerusalem*, pp. 205–16, quote from p. 212.

63 Clark, *The Struggle for the Breeches*, pp. 266–9, quote from p. 268.

64 Gleadle, *The Early Feminists*, pp. 4–21; 33–45; M. L. G[rimstone], 'Men and women', *Crisis* 3 (1834), 236. See also R. Watts, *Gender, Power and the Unitarians in England, 1760–1860* (London: Longman, 1998), pp. 92–3, 116–17.

65 M. L. Grimstone, 'Female education', *Monthly Repository* 9 (1835), 106–12, first quote from 110; 'The protective system of morals', *Monthly Repository* 9 (1835), 683–8; second quote from 685.

66 H. Glynn, 'The morality of easy divorce', *The Leader* 1 (1850), 157; Junius Redivivus, 'On the condition of women in England', *Monthly Repository* 7 (1833), 217–31; F. B. Smith, *Radical Artisan: William James Linton, 1812–97* (Manchester: Manchester University Press, 1973), p. 21; W. J. Linton, 'Effects of legislating upon love or some reasons against lawful wedlock', *The National* (1839), 327–9, quote from 327; Gleadle, *The Early Feminists*, pp. 111–20.

67 Mineka, *The Dissidence of Dissent*, pp. 178–81; Garnett, *The Life of W. J. Fox*, pp. 43–5; 107–113; G. Wallas, *William Johnson Fox, 1786–1864* (London: Watts & Co., 1924), p. 29; W. J. Fox, 'The dissenting marriage question', *Monthly Repository* 7 (1833), 142; 'The condition of women, and the marriage question', *Crisis* 2 (1833), 174.

68 Garnett, *Life of W. J. Fox*, pp. 158–68; Mineka, *Dissidence of Dissent*, p. 188.

69 Mineka, *Dissidence of Dissent*, pp. 191–9; 286–8, quotes from pp. 194, 196; Garnett, *Life of W. J. Fox*, pp. 166–76; 186–8; 202; Wallas, *William Johnson Fox*, pp. 26–7.

70 Mineka, *Dissidence of Dissent*, p. 188; see also Watts, *Gender, Power and the Unitarians in England*, 116–17.

71 Garnett, *Life of W. J. Fox*, p. 74.

72 Guy, *Compassion and the Art of the Possible*, pp. 2–3; Yeldham, *Margaret Gillies RWS*, pp. 1–4; R. K. Webb, 'Southwood Smith: The intellectual sources of public service', in D. Porter and R. Porter (eds), *Doctors, Politics and Society: Historical Essays* (Atlanta, GA: Rodopi, 1993), 46–80.

73 Yeldham, *Margaret Gillies RWS*, pp. 58–61.

74 Gleadle, *The Early Feminists*, pp. 51; 92; 98; A. Blainey, *The Farthing Poet: A Biography of Richard Hengist Horne, 1802–1884, A Lesser Literary Lion* (London: Longmans, 1968), pp.

58–65; quote from p. 63.

75 Blainey, *The Farthing Poet*, pp. 62–9.

76 *Ibid.*, pp. 25–8; 152–5.

77 *Ibid.*, pp. 168–70; 202–5; 242–3.

78 J. McLean, *The Poems and Plays of Thomas Wade* (Troy, New York: The Whitson Publishing Company, 1997), pp. 5–14, quote from p. 10.

79 Smith, *Radical Artisan*, pp. 14–17; 21; 43; first quote from pp. 14–15, second from p. 21.

80 *Ibid.*, pp. 42–51; 99–120, first quote from p. 43; second quote from p. 102.

81 *Ibid.*, pp. 114; 148.

82 Gleadle, *The Early Feminists*, pp. 177–83.

9

Radical couples, 1850–1914

THE LAST HALF OF THE nineteenth century saw two major phases in marital radicalism. The first phase, lasting roughly from 1850 to 1880, was primarily theoretical. Most couples, whatever their reservations about the institution, chose to marry legally during this period. Mid-century was the high tide of Victorian respectability, and couples could achieve reforms only if they disassociated themselves from scandals. Thus, the working-class movement turned to trade unionism and its version of domesticity, and feminists concentrated on legal equality. Those couples who could not marry lived together discreetly or formed platonic partnerships. The *fin-de-siècle* period (1880–1914) was different. Socialism and anarchism gained adherents and made numerous public statements against 'bourgeois' marriage. The feminist movement, though always leery about sexual experiments, explored alternatives to marriage. Novelists and essayists challenged the status quo on such issues as divorce and illegitimacy. The number of cohabiting couples remained small, but a growing minority publicly dissented from marriage and regarded the reticence of mid-century as hypocritical. Interestingly, many of these reformers had the same reasons for disliking marriage as those in the 1790s. As secularists, most distrusted its religious aspects; they also objected to women's position in the institution. In addition, because the Divorce Act of 1857 was so limited, the indissolubility of marriage remained a major grievance.

Despite this opening of rhetorical space, continuities remained. As before, women faced more problems when they had 'fallen'. Women's economic position remained precarious, and they continued to struggle with the issue of emotional attachment; though free to leave irregular unions, women often did not do so. Indeed, because radical couples tried to make a point with their lives, their unions were under greater pressure. Ironically, in an age when some legal marriages were dissolved, free unions became even more difficult t o end, in part because few men or women challenged monogamy. Only a minority questioned how free couples could be if they remained in unhappy unions, married or not. Unable to solve these problems, most radicals of the end of the century theorised for the future, but lived respectably in the present.

Rationalism, secularism, Hintonians

Two forms of mid-century radicalism descended from the agendas of the early nineteenth century. The circle around *The Leader*, edited by Leigh Hunt, and later *The Westminster Review*, edited by John Chapman, followed the agenda of the Radical Unitarians. Both publications pushed for liberalism and freethinking. Leigh Hunt's son, Thornton Hunt, and his friend George Henry Lewes produced the *Leader*, and, for a time, they partnered with W. J. Linton. In addition, they wrote articles promoting marriage reform and women's rights. All the same, these men kept up the appearance of 'normal' family life in the midst of wider sexual relationships.

Lewes, for example, joined Hunt's circle in 1835 and had many ties to radical politics and literature. Despite his marriage to Agnes Jervis in 1841, he embraced, in Rosemary Ashton's phrase, 'free love inside marriage.' Biographers are short on specifics, but Lewes apparently had numerous affairs. His radical principles, nevertheless, were sorely tested when his wife began a relationship with Hunt (who was also married). Lewes evinced little jealousy, but he became disillusioned and stopped registering Hunt's children as his own after the birth of Rose in 1851. Lewes's support for sexual freedom was tempered by his domestic unhappiness; he had discovered the disadvantages of free love inside a legal – and thus indissoluble – marriage. He and Agnes separated in 1855, yet Lewes did not protest when she registered more children under his name, one as late as 1857.[1] Though his enthusiasm waned, Lewes lived out his beliefs with a refreshing gender equality.

Another practitioner of 'free love within marriage' was the *Westminster Review*'s publisher, John Chapman. Chapman had 'utter contempt for monogamy', according to Gordon Haight. He was married and also had a mistress living in his house as a governess. Despite an already complicated love life, he may have seduced Marian Evans, and he tried to persuade Barbara Leigh Smith to run away with him.[2] In short, these men did not let their married ties prevent them from sexual intrigues, but they also seldom made open breaches. Indeed, with the exception of Lewes, most of them saw sexual freedom as primarily for men. Their discretion allowed them to have public acceptance while working for social change.

Outward conformity, though, had disadvantages. Lewes's separation left him rudderless and unhappy. In this state, he met Marian Evans when they were both working for the *Westminster Review*. Evans, the daughter of a clergyman, became a freethinker in her youth and translated Feuerbach's *Essence of Christianity* in 1854. She agreed with Feuerbach's definition of marriage: 'Marriage … must be the free bond of love … a marriage which is not spontaneously concluded, spontaneously willed, self-sufficing, is not a true marriage'. In addition, after reading *Jane Eyre*, she described the law that forced men to stay with insane wives as 'diabolical'. She and Lewes also both admired George Sand's work and sexual freedom.[3] Thus, once they had fallen in love, they were both willing to forego respectability. Their elopement to Germany in 1854 marked the beginning of their twenty-four year union.

Evans and Lewes had one of the most outwardly successful free unions in the nineteenth century, but they would have married had they been able to do so. Because of their prominence, they could not be discreet, and Evans disliked the idea of secrecy in any case. Unfortunately, their openness did not gain them the support of most of their friends. For instance, George Combe disapproved of them, but he did not criticise Charles Bray, who had a mistress and two illegitimate children. Combe justified this hypocrisy by insisting that all sexual adventures must be discreet; otherwise, the reform movement suffered. Similarly, Joseph Parkes disdained them, despite the fact that he also had a mistress.[4] Mid-Victorians, then, were most shocked by Evans and Lewes because they were open about their affair. Yet Evans and Lewes were actually similar to other adulterous middle-class cohabitees. They lived as if married, and Marian took George's name and referred to him as her husband. Neither opposed marriage in itself, but they dissented from marriage law. In the end, the apparent success of their union argued for reform without any public campaigning.

Other mid-Victorian reform movements followed radical ideas while avoiding open free unions. This period saw the beginnings of the National Secular Society and the Malthusian League, with the former promoting rights for atheists, and the latter for birth control. These movements shared many adherents, and all were careful to avoid 'free love'. Supporters either settled for platonic relationships, as with Charles Bradlaugh and Annie Besant, or they said they were 'married'.[5] The leaders of the Malthusian League for most of the nineteenth century, Charles Drysdale and Alice Vickery, for example, were close partners, but their marital status is unclear. Rosanna Ledbetter argues that they married in the early 1870s, but kept the marriage a secret. J. Miriam Benn, in contrast, insists that they never married, since no marriage certificate has come to light.[6] The evidence is not strong enough either way to make a definitive statement. Vickery and Drysdale later became active in the Legitimation League, which worked for the registration of acknowledged illegitimate children, so they may have had a personal stake in this issue. In addition, Alice regarded coverture as the worst aspect of English law, comparing it to slavery. She resented the loss of identity for married women, and sometimes signed her articles with her maiden name.[7] In the end, their actual status matters little, since they let people believe that they were married. They championed controversial causes, so they avoided any appearance of impropriety. The disadvantages of their discretion (if they were not married) was that they could not use the undoubted success of their partnership as an example of a happy free union.

As these examples indicate, rationalists of the early nineteenth century had a long legacy of marital and gender reforms, tempered by the strict morality of the mid-Victorian years. But what of the religious dissents from marriage? Some of these groups continued into the 1850s; the Abode of Love still existed in the 1860s. But these groups were dwindling, and few new ones emerged. The one major movement was that of James Hinton, and most of his influence was in the late nineteenth century, when people like Havelock Ellis, the sexologist, read his work. Hinton, a doctor, had become a philosopher in an effort to remove his spiritual doubts. He argued that because of constant change, moral codes had to adapt. A strict moral code was often immoral in practice; one should, then, follow the spirit, not the letter, of the law.[8] Oddly, from this, Hinton developed a theory of marriage. He identified prostitution as the main problem of his age, and his solution was polygamy. Women should be willing, as moral beings, to share their husbands, as long as all the unions were love matches. Since men were naturally polygamous, and women naturally monogamous, they must compromise in order to be happy.[9]

Not surprisingly, Hinton's ideas had a limited appeal. Edith Ellis pointed out that he assumed that women must do all the sacrificing and serving, while men reaped the rewards; his polygamy was actually polygyny. As Olive Schreiner later asked in a letter to Havelock Ellis, 'Would he have been satisfied if his wife had had six "spiritual husbands"'? In addition, he made no effort to deal with women's dependence, simply changing its legal status. Hinton's celebration of women's sexual feelings gained him some followers before his death, and he had a great influence on many later reformers.[10] But his sexual theories made others suspicious, especially because of Hinton's own reputation. Emma Brooke, a late nineteenth-century feminist, accused him of trying to seduce her when she was young. When she refused, he 'had the hypocrisy to add that he wished to teach me the duty and loveliness of yielding myself to "others [sic] needs" & wishes, and of over-coming all "self-regarding" impulses'. Other women also complained of his advances, and rumours circulated that he kept mistresses, went mad, or had syphilis.[11] Whatever the truth of these accusations, they indicate how wary men and women were of any promotion of free love. Hinton's female followers were a small group, and few lived out his precepts. And his reputation suffered further when his son Howard deserted his wife and then committed bigamy in 1886 with Maud Weldon, the mother of his twins.[12] Religious radicalism, never a large movement, shrank even smaller in mid-century.

Some of the ideas of the early nineteenth century, then, persisted into the 1870s. Rationalists remained committed to women's rights and to reforming marriage laws. Indeed, they could celebrate some victories, including the founding of women's colleges and the Matrimonial Causes Act of 1857. In particular, the debates over the latter gave critiques of marriage law a very public forum. Legislators argued over the definition of marriage – a relationship, a contract, a sacrament, or all three? – and delineated the power relations between husband and wife, frankly accepting the sexual double standard. Such a compromised bill offered more fodder for reformers and critics in mid-century and beyond, as well as secularising marriage and divorce, a major goal of groups like the Radical Unitarians.[13] In fact, freethinking, though still a minority, grew in both numbers and influence. Obviously, institutionalisation was a step forward, but it also meant that reformers became a part of the system. As a result, their members conformed to conventional norms in their own lives.

Feminism and marriage

The 1850s saw the beginning of a formal feminist movement and the establishment of the *Englishwoman's Review*, led by Barbara Leigh Smith and Bessie Raynor Parkes. The Langham Place group attracted a number of women who concentrated on legal and economic changes to help women. Smith, for example, stressed the disabilities of married women, and many women shared her reservations. For example, Florence Fenwick-Miller did not take her husband's name when she married in 1877; others omitted the word 'obey' from their ceremonies.[14] In short, like the Radical Unitarians, most mid-Victorian feminists chose to marry, if on liberated terms. In Barbara Caine's words, most concluded that 'unless they proceeded in a decorous and cautious way, they would have no chance of succeeding'. And they were correct; only middle-of-the-road feminists gained much support. Smith, illegitimate and unconventional, stayed in the background, agreeing that '[r]espectability was the key to acceptance'.[15]

The partnership of Harriet Taylor and John Stuart Mill shows this new dynamic. Although chronologically they belonged in Chapter 8, their actions were more typical of mid-century. Harriet Hardy was a member of Fox's South Place Chapel. She married John Taylor in 1826 and had three children, but she soon grew bored with her husband and resented his sexual demands. She went to her minister, Fox, for advice, and he introduced her to Mill, the great liberal philosopher. They became close friends, sharing a belief in feminism and divorce reform. Though emotionally intimate, they did not elope. Mill feared the scandal, and Taylor was uncertain that Mill would be any less demanding than her husband. Eventually, the couple formed a platonic union, and Harriet never broke with her husband. Thus, they avoided an open breach and scandal. This concern for public probity continued after Taylor's death in 1849; Harriet insisted on a long mourning period before she married Mill.[16]

Taylor and Mill worked for women's rights and for divorce reform after their marriage. Both agreed with previous reformers that first marriages were often made by people too young and thoughtless to know what they wanted. As a result, Mill argued that the law should allow childless couples to change partners until they found one that suited them. Taylor, for her part, critiqued marriage because it was more binding on the wife than the husband. Nevertheless, their main rebellion was not to cohabit, but to register a protest against coverture when they married. In this way, they acted as a bridge between the two halves of the century.[17]

Thus, the majority of Victorian feminists who disapproved of marriage chose celibacy rather than free unions. Moreover, the few feminists who did try unconventional arrangements had great difficulties. Smith, independently wealthy, was one of the few mid-century feminists to consider doing so. In 1855, John Chapman urged her to live with him. Barbara was attracted to the idea, probably because of her disgust with women's position in marriage. However, Benjamin Smith was horrified and insisted that she abandon the idea (though he had two cohabiting relationships and eight illegitimate children himself). Barbara, after a considerable struggle, did so.[18] Eventually, she resolved her dilemma by marrying Eugene Bodichon, who gave her enough personal freedom to pursue her interests. She made concessions to society, then, but retained much of her independence.

Elizabeth Wolstenholme was another feminist who dissented from marriage. Wolstenholme cohabited with Ben Elmy, most likely beginning in 1874. Elmy was a freethinker, while Wolstenholme had worked for the women's movement since the early 1870s. Both came from, in Sandra

Stanley Holton's phrase, 'the Manchester school of liberalism'. Thus, they wanted no part of a religious ceremony and were committed to women's rights. They probably went through an informal ceremony early in 1874, but did not marry legally for months, and then only under pressure from women's rights' workers. Wolstenholme was pregnant, and her colleagues feared that a scandal would damage the movement. Reluctantly, Elmy and Wolstenholme married in the autumn of 1874, but even then Wolstenholme did not regain her position in the movement.[19] The sexual limits for feminists at mid-century could not have been clearer.

Feminism became more radical and assertive in the 1880s and 1890s. Women's rights workers celebrated controversial figures such as Wollstonecraft and argued for women's independence. As Lucy Bland has shown, feminists fiercely criticised marriage as immoral and campaigned to change both its laws and social conventions. Still, most of them, in Bland's phrase, 'did not reject marriage *per se*. On the contrary, they wished it to be radically reformed.' Rather than arguing for free sexuality for women, they instead demanded chastity from men and regarded divorce with horror. Most also saw cohabitation as just another opportunity for male sexual aggression. A more common strike against marriage was lifelong spinsterhood, and even this choice was less popular than marriage.[20]

As a result, Edwardian feminists who emphasised women's sexual freedom were outside the mainstream. One such group was the Freewoman circle. The *Freewoman*, edited by Dora Marsdon from 1911 to 1913, published frank articles about sexuality. The major editorial stance of the journal was that women should be self-supporting and marriage must change radically. A typical article insisted that 'Indissoluble-Monogamy ... is an unjustifiable tyranny, and psychologically monstrous and morally dangerous ... marriage is not marriage when love is dead.' The editors also insisted that the expression 'free love' was redundant: 'All love is free. When love is bound it shows the modifications of its nature which will soon turn it into something else.' In other articles, writers bluntly asserted that legal marriage was little better than prostitution, while others argued for legal recognition for mistresses and illegitimate children.[21]

That some readers of the journal took part in free unions is probable, though the evidence is thin. One couple, Mary and Stanley Randolph, identified themselves as partners in a free union in June 1912. They asserted that they did not want to 'suffer so subtle and pure a thing as love to have attached to it even that amount of mistrust that the legal union postulates.' The couple had lost their jobs through their decision, and wrote to find like-minded people. The difficulties of such couples came out in the next few weeks, since another correspondent, B. L., criticised their sharing of the same last name. Mary and Stanley claimed they left out the second name only because of limited space, but B. L. insisted 'it will be futile for people to carry out "free unions" and then conceal the fact from the world'.[22] The Randolphs were ostracised for being too radical on the one side, and not progressive enough on the other. Little wonder, then, that few couples followed their example. But B. L's argument for openness was typical of the period, repudiating the 'hypocrisy' of mid-Victorians.

Though the circulation of the periodical was small, it sponsored Freewoman discussion groups who heard papers from such people as anarcho-communist Guy Aldred and sexologist Havelock Ellis. These circles collected together men and women who became increasingly thoughtful about marriage and free unions. Ruth Slate and Eva Slawson were lower middle-class women (from working-class families) who were radicalised by their association with the Freewoman circle. Both wanted independence, but both also wanted unions with men, and these were often contradictory desires. Eva was not against marriage, since she did not think free unions would work: 'I see grave difficulty in women continuing to support themselves by employment, at any rate during maternity.' Ruth, similarly, was a feminist who married because of the lack of good alternatives. She and Hugh Jones became lovers in 1918. According to Tierl Thompson, 'they would have preferred not to marry', but were unwilling to upset their families, so married in December of 1918.[23]

Ruth's decision to marry legally may also have been influenced by the experiences of her friend, Françoise Lafitte. Lafitte came from a middle-class French family, but her father lost all his money, so she came to England to teach French. While there, she got involved with the Freewoman Circle and socialism. Eventually, she met John Collier, 'a representative of American Syndicalism'. She fell in love with him and agreed to live with him (he was married to a woman in the United States). Françoise did not want a legal marriage anyway, 'for I acknowledged no need for ceremony, civil or religious.'[24] Unfortunately, Françoise was disillusioned with John almost at once. According to her, John saw women only as sexual outlets. When she became pregnant, she knew she could not rear a child with him, so she walked out on her union after only a few months. The experience made her more feminist than before; she asserted that men had to be friends with women or their relationships would fail. Lafitte lived with friends and worked as long as she could until she gave birth to her son, François, in 1913.[25]

Lafitte's ideas about this union were interesting. For one thing, she always called her relationship with Collier a marriage and used her married name at Freewoman meetings. For another, she revolted against

John's sexual demands more than any other aspect of their relationship, something to which many married women could relate. Nevertheless, she did not refuse him access to her body until she left him. Third, Françoise left John because she was going to have a child, rather than staying with him because she needed support. Her decision showed the change in feminism in this period, as she rapidly moved to a belief in free love and a woman's right to her own body. Lafitte had found both the advantages and disadvantages of free unions for women, and in her opinion, the advantages lay with freedom.[26]

Françoise's experience proved, at least to her, that legal forms guaranteed nothing about love and marriage. She legally married Serge Cyon, a Russian radical, before the First World War, for security and comradeship. This relationship was no more successful than her first union. Cyon married her to get a stepmother for his son and a housekeeper, and acted like a patriarch. When she found his behaviour unbearable, Françoise walked away again, even though she had a second child. She paid a price for this decision; she was desperately poor, and her husband harassed her for years. In fact, her legal marriage was a bigger problem than the cohabitation had been. Because of her marriage, British law classified Françoise as Russian, her husband's nationality. Her status caused her endless difficulties during both world wars and the Cold War. She eventually entered a second free union with Havelock Ellis, a relationship of twenty years. But officially she remained a Russian 'alien'. These experiences made her even less impressed with women's 'advantages' in marriage.[27]

Few feminists were as bold as Françoise, but many recognised the legal and emotional difficulties for women in marriage and out, as well as some 'radical' men's reluctance to embrace true equality. What made Lafitte unusual was her willingness to brave ostracism and poverty and leave both men. Few women made that choice. Thus, most feminists urged that women concentrate on marriage reforms rather than trying experiments, and those who discussed sexuality emphasised male aggression rather than women's freedom. As the Owenites had discovered, sexual freedom without economic equality was dangerous.

Socialism and 'free love'

Ambivalence also plagued another major movement that spanned the century, socialism. After the collapse of Owenism, the working-class movement turned away from gender equality and instead championed domesticity. As Anna Clark put it, 'Domesticity provided a way of both defending working-class families and appealing to women without threatening men.' In addition, economic conditions, particularly the decline of cottage industry, made women unable to support illegitimate children. With no hope for communal childcare or economic aid, most women did not risk desertion and poverty.[28] Thus, legal marriage was the norm.

One working-class movement that continued critiquing marriage was the nascent Communist movement. Both Marx and Engels disdained the 'bourgeois' institution, and Engels 'accepted without reservation Owen's views on marriage'. Like Owen, Engels and Marx blamed religious and indissoluble marriage for prostitution and male libertinism. Marx insisted that communism, in destroying private property, would also destroy the need to use wives as instruments of production and thus end this hypocrisy.[29] Nevertheless, the influence of Marxism on the English working class was limited until the end of the nineteenth century. Most workers preferred to join unions, and if they read the *Manifesto*, they focused on its economic and political programme rather than its argument about marriage. Thus, communist ideas about marriage had almost no impact before the *fin-de-siècle*.

Still, Engels lived in two free unions during the mid-Victorian years, both with Irish mill workers. As discussed in Chapter 7, Engels's relationships caused uneasiness. Interestingly, the reactions to Engels's cohabitation with working women echoed the concerns of other reformers in this period. As Terrell Carver points out, the Marxes may have feared that Engels's 'free love' would damage socialism. Furthermore, Engels had to follow many hypocritical practices, especially when he was with Mary Burns. He was a Manchester businessman during those years, so he hid her in a suburb – the typical middle-class man's dodge. They took the name Mr and Mrs Frederick Boardman, and Mary's sister kept house for them to add another layer of respectability. Engels had to be able to carry out his social obligations, but the hypocrisy was unfortunate.[30]

Engels's relationships with the Burns sisters also foreshadowed one of the central problems for socialism in dealing with women. Engels's ties to Mary and Lizzie further sensitised him to workers' struggles, but did not give him much insight into gender. Engels, throughout his life, remained a typical Victorian man, regarding women as primarily domestic.[31] Though Communists believed that women should enter the public sphere, they did not expect men to take a greater part of the domestic labour. Instead, like the Owenites, Engels trusted communal arrangements and technology to lift the domestic load from women. Moreover, because Socialists regarded capitalism as the problem, they underestimated patriarchy. For a number of reasons, then, Socialism had limited influence between 1850 and 1880.[32] In short, the working class muted its challenge to marriage in mid-century, much like the middle classes.

Socialism took on a renewed life in the *fin-de-siècle*, buttressed by a number of middle-class converts and new associations. The leader of the Marxists in the 1880s and early 1890s was Engels, since Marx died in 1883. Engels set out the basic Marxist position to marriage and the family in *The Origins of the Family, Private Property, and the State* in 1884; this book and August Bebel's *Woman and Socialism* were the key documents of socialist thought on women's issues, since socialist publications disseminated their basic tenets widely.[33] According to Engels, marriage arrangements followed the economic system; in other words, the capitalist system required monogamy. The key moment was the establishment of property, since men wanted their property to pass down to their own blood and so insisted on female monogamy. Under communism, such property in women would no longer exist. The community would support women during pregnancy and child-rearing, freeing them from maintenance by individual men. Couples, then, would form unions as they saw fit with no interference from the state.[34]

Interestingly, Engels's critique of marriage was similar to those from earlier in the century. His main objections were married women's disabilities and its indissolubility. Also like previous writers, Engels did not have solutions to all problems; his vision of the communist family was vague, saying simply that the new generation 'will make their own practice and their corresponding public opinion about the practice of each individual – and that will be the end of it.'[35] Engels's position had other weaknesses, as scholars have pointed out. Men's domination of women was more than economic; it was physical, mental, and emotional, a fact he never acknowledged. He also ignored the question of what to do if the relationship failed, even though he believed men to be less faithful than women.[36] Unsurprisingly, then, most socialist organisations, following Engels and Bebel, did not deal successfully with these questions.

The difficulties and omissions of the Socialist theory of marriage came to the fore in the most prominent socialist free union in the late nineteenth century, that of Eleanor Marx and Edward Aveling. Eleanor was Karl's youngest daughter, a translator and typist who served the Socialist movement in a variety of capacities. Aveling was a scientist, secularist, and socialist. He had married Isabel Frank in 1872, but the marriage soon failed. Marx and Aveling met in 1883 and decided to live together in 1884.[37] They cohabited for fourteen years, openly eschewing marriage. Indeed, in a publication in 1886, they critiqued marriage as 'worse than prostitution.' All the same, they did not favour easy divorce, since this disadvantaged women. Their ideal, which could only happen under socialism, was 'true' monogamy: 'the complete harmonious, lasting blending of two human lives.'[38]

The Marx/Aveling relationship unfortunately never approached this ideal. Aveling had few scruples about money or women. Olive Schreiner, Eleanor's friend, believed that Marx was unhappy almost from the beginning, and some of Marx's letters bear this out.[39] Despite her quick disillusionment with her partner, Eleanor always insisted that she was married. She took Edward's name, put up with his infidelities and neglect, nursed him in his illnesses, and left him all her money. The freedom of this union, then, was only for Aveling, just the situation most feminists feared. Though historians have been baffled at Marx's loyalty, Aveling was sexually attractive to her, and he also worked by her side in the socialist cause. Still, one cannot help thinking that the gender differences were key. Marx regarded herself as married, no matter what the state of their union; indeed, she felt bound by their union precisely because it was based on love alone. Aveling, on the other hand, always considered himself free whatever the circumstances. He married Isabel but lived with Eleanor for fourteen years. After his wife's death in 1892, he continued to live with Eleanor, but secretly married Eva Freye, an actress, in 1897. He was simply indifferent to the legal status of his relationships; like the bourgeois men he criticised in 1886, he did as he pleased, married or not.[40]

Eleanor was financially independent, particularly after 1895, when she received part of Engels's estate, and she had no children. Thus, she could have walked away from Aveling, yet she did not do so. Ruth Brandon argues that Eleanor had to believe in both Aveling and the Socialist movement to prove 'that her life was not a failure.' After Edward's betrayal, she could no longer remain deluded. When she learned about his second marriage is unclear; it may have been in late 1897 or immediately before her death in March 1898. At any rate, when she could no longer cope, Eleanor committed suicide, leaving Edward all of her money. Since he died only four months later, Eleanor's money went to Eva, her rival, within six months of her death.[41]

The tragedy of Eleanor Marx showed the limitations of the socialist position on marriage and free unions. Marx, after all, had not stayed with Aveling due to economic weakness or children. She did so because she was too emotionally tied to do otherwise. Free unions did not undo the power relations between a couple, and most socialists and feminists underestimated the difficulties of untangling emotional commitments as opposed to legal ones. Not all men were like Aveling, but Engels had admitted in his work on the family that 'sex feeling' often changed, particularly in men. When it did so, the spurned partner had to find a way to accept desertion, never an easy proposition. And because she regarded their relationship as a 'truer' marriage than most legal unions, Eleanor, like Wollstonecraft, was doubly reluctant to admit to failure.[42]

Socialist unions were also complicated by the fact that not all Socialist groups accepted them. Eleanor and Edward belonged to the Social Democratic Federation (SDF) and the Socialist League, neither of which condemned them, though the SDF was unenthusiastic.[43] Other organisations were openly hostile. This was quite a reverse of the position of Owen in the 1840s, and showed how much socialism had institutionalised by the end of the century. Socialist leaders feared the 'sex question' would leave them open to the kinds of accusations Owen had faced, siphoning off support. In addition, many regarded such questions as distractions, taking energy from the fight against capitalism. This was related to the socialist assumption that feminism was a luxury of bored bourgeois women. Socialists assumed that promoting female equality – in marriage or anywhere else – would alienate working-class men, while promotion of free love would do so with working-class women (who feared desertion). The issue simply was not a winner, electorally or otherwise, and as more poor men got the vote, these considerations mattered. As Karen Hunt put it, even the more flexible SDF regarded the issue as 'politically embarrassing.'[44]

Couples who cohabited, then, faced grave problems, especially in groups that had electoral ambitions. Tom Mann was secretary of the Independent Labour Party (ILP) in the 1890s. He had married Ellen Edwards in 1879 and they had four daughters, but he fell in love with Elsie Harker, an opera singer and Labour activist, in the late 1890s. Mann and Harker began their union in Brighton in 1898, and this decision coincided with Mann's ousting from the ILP, due to rumours about his drinking and womanising. Though these scandals were untrue, Mann could not refute them because of his union with Harker. Thus, he and Elsie lived in Australia from 1902 to 1910. When they returned to England in 1910, Mann briefly joined the SDF, and later became a Communist, but he never rejoined the ILP.[45]

Interestingly, Mann did not use arguments against marriage to justify his desertion of his first wife; he and Harker seemingly shared socialist unease with 'free love'. Instead, the couple, like most working-class cohabitees, pretended to be married, an understandable decision in light of their difficulties. The discretion helped socially, but economic difficulties remained. Ellen never divorced Mann, and she received his widow's pension when he died in 1941. Mann had to write his will carefully to leave the rest to Harker. Despite these strains, this second union, lasting forty years, was happy, so he probably never regretted his choice. But they lived together because they could not marry, not by choice.[46] And the ILP's reaction to their 'marriage' showed its deep hostility to any marital nonconformity.

The ILP's moralism was also clear in the case of George Belt and Dora Montefiore. Belt, a married man with four children, was a bricklayer and organiser for the ILP. Montefiore was a widow from a well-off family. She became a feminist after her husband's death and also joined the Social Democratic Federation. The couple apparently met working in the labour movement. Belt was unhappy with his wife, who did not share his interest in socialism. He had a breakdown in 1899, and when he was released from the hospital, he left with Montefiore. Mrs Belt complained to the ILP, and the leaders promptly fired George. Montefiore continued her roles with the SDF, since it considered the marriage question one of personal conscience, but the women's movement was a different story. At an International Women's Conference in 1899, Margaret McDonald, warned by her husband Ramsay, blocked Dora from giving a paper.[47]

One cannot build too many arguments on these two incidents; after all, both involved men deserting their families. Nevertheless, the less established parts of the socialist movement clearly supported unconventional unions more readily. The traditional branches of working-class activism, as well as feminism, kept the mid-Victorian insistence on sexual purity – or at least the appearance of it. This situation baffled Montefiore. She wrote to Keir Hardie, 'They [socialists] are for the most part free thinkers as to dogmas … Why should they not be free to think out their thoughts on the sex question also?'[48] But labour workers feared such experiments would doom their wider goals.

Like the ILP, the Fabian Society had its bouts of hypocrisy. The Fabians were a number of largely middle-class writers and reformers who wanted to bring about socialism by permeating the regular parties with socialist ideas. The society attracted an interesting set of adherents, including H. G. Wells, G. B. Shaw, and Hubert Bland and Edith Nesbit. Wells was by far the most radical on the issues of women and marriage. He argued in 1902 that the state had no right to interfere in sexual relationships unless the couple had children. In the place of legal monogamy, Wells suggested people enter free sexual unions. As Jane Lewis has pointed out, Wells believed that sexual freedom would be far more liberating for women than suffrage.[49] However, he soon discovered that he was out of step with both socialism and feminism on this issue.

As discussed before, Wells left his first wife to live with his second, and he had numerous affairs during his second marriage. His affair with Amber Pember Reeves led to an elopement to France and a public scandal. Wells's openness about his beliefs, and his willingness to live by them, horrified his colleagues, but Wells found their hypocrisy maddening. For instance, Hubert Bland had sex with Edith Nesbit before they married and was persistently unfaithful thereafter, including affairs with his daughter's schoolfriends. Yet, since he made no open scandal, he was a member in good standing and one of Wells's chief critics.[50] One can understand Wells's exasperation with this situation, but he was not entirely consistent himself. In J. R. Hammond's phrase, 'equality of the sexes on the lines he was advocating would lead to greater freedom for men unaccompanied by any corresponding enlargement of freedom for women.' After all, if the state supported all offspring, men had even less responsibility than before, while women were still confined to domesticity. Nor did Wells envision women having affairs as men did. Wells admitted later that he argued for his sexual ideas with 'no thought of how I would react if presently my wife were to carry them into effect'.[51]

As pointed out in Chapter 5, Wells's relationship with Rebecca West showed the difficulties of free unions in this hostile atmosphere. Indeed, his sexual career gave some credence to socialists and feminists who doubted 'free love'. As Jane Lewis argues, 'the practical effect of Wells's "equal sexual treatment" was inevitably to make women more sexually available to men'.[52] Furthermore, because of the censorious reaction of many Socialist and Feminist groups, such couples forfeited their main support group. They thus faced increasing difficulties in balancing the demands for equality and freedom with conventional sexual expectations of groups like the ILP or the Fabians. In other words, the historian must be careful not to overstate the radicalism of the last half of the nineteenth century.

Another example of the paradoxical influence of socialism and feminism was the case of Edith Lanchester and James Sullivan. Edith, the daughter of an architect, became a socialist and worked as Eleanor Marx's secretary and as an SDF/ILP speaker. James Sullivan was an Irish labourer who worked for the SDF, where the two met in the early 1890s. Sullivan and Lanchester (known to each other as Shamus and Biddy) fell in love; it was an unusual match, considering their class differences. Even more unusually, Edith refused to marry James. Marriage, she insisted, 'is really a private concern of the individual, binding only by mutual love and esteem, and terminable by mutual consent.' Lanchester and Sullivan also refused to hide the decision; Edith told both the landlady and her family about their plans.[53]

Not surprisingly, the couple met strong resistance. Some in the socialist movement tried to talk Edith into marrying, and her parents and siblings were appalled. According to their daughter, Elsa, James preferred to marry, but Edith flatly refused. As a result, her father and brothers committed her to a lunatic asylum in October 1895. The SDF and the leaders of the

Legitimation League rallied to her support, and Sullivan eventually got her freed. The two then lived together for the rest of their lives, having a son and a daughter. Both Edith and James worked in the socialist movement and reared their children to follow freethinking and to support workers' and women's rights. They stayed together until James's death in 1945 (Edith died in 1966).[54]

The longevity of the Lanchester/Sullivan union testifies to its success. Though they had their differences (Biddy was a vegetarian and Shamus was not), the couple managed to overcome them. Still, their daughter Elsa, the future film star, insisted that their relationship had its peculiarities. For one thing, the children knew their maternal aunts and grandmother, but not the uncles who helped kidnap their mother, or their grandfather. In addition, Elsa always believed James wanted to be married. He wore a guard ring for years, because, she surmised, 'it made him feel a little bit properly married'. Edith had purposely never worn one.[55]

Moreover, the Lanchester/Sullivan union, at least according to Elsa, was not necessarily happy. Elsa records several ways that Edith belittled her partner, and Edith may have found it difficult to adapt to life with a working-class man. Elsa speculated that the fact that the two had made a public stand forced them to stay together: 'their *Cause* united them – and time does not reward political enthusiasm. From it all I learned that the cloak of respectability was, paradoxically, one of the keys to freedom. But this cloak involves a degree of hypocrisy … [and] Biddy and Shamus were never hypocrites.' Elsa speculated that if her parents had found alternative partners, they might have wanted to divorce, but they could not since they had never married: 'In defying convention they were chained by it.'[56] Elsa may not have been right; she had several differences with her mother. But she was correct that couples in free unions could not end them without admitting the failure of their ideals.

Free unions within socialist groups illustrate some important points. First, ironically, the women in these unions often had more social support than the men. Marx remained popular with her colleagues, though none of them liked Aveling, and Lanchester became a heroine in the Socialist movement, hailed for her bravery and honesty, while Sullivan, in Elsa's words, 'didn't seem to get much credit.'[57] Second, power relationships in the family remained. Strong women could hold their own, but radical beliefs did not always overcome emotional ties. Third, cohabiting partnerships were sometimes as binding as marriages. Because these relationships were exemplary, they could not fail. Ironically, their 'freedom' led to less liberty, while hypocrisy allowed room to manoeuvre. Fourth, these couples' unions, like those of the Godwin household, led to tensions in their wider families.

Lanchester's family was the most extreme example of this, but problems emerged for many cohabitees.

Finally, the class make-up of these couples is instructive. Two of them were cross-class unions, both with a middle-class woman and a working-class man; the majority of the rest were lower-middle and middle-class couples. The working class was largely uninvolved in cohabiting from radical motives. As Anna Martin's work showed, working-class women resented the gender and class biases in the divorce law, but they were not opposed to marriage. And, as Jonathan Rose has pointed out, most working-class people remained profoundly ignorant of sexual experiments; the *fin-de-siècle* age of 'liberation' passed them by.[58] In socialism, ironically, middle-class women were more adventurous than those in the working class.

The Legitimation League

As radicalism grew and splintered, new groups emerged. One example was the Legitimation League, founded in 1893 in Leeds. The League was dedicated to achieving legal recognition for all acknowledged illegitimate children (those from stable free unions). The members expanded the goals in 1897 '[t]o educate public opinion in the direction of freedom in sexual relationships'. The founder was Oswald Dawson, a man from a wealthy Quaker family, who lived in a free union with Gladys Heywood. The first president was J. H. Levy, followed quickly by Wordsworth Donisthorpe, a doctor. The League moved to London in 1897 and increased its membership and public profile, though Donisthorpe resigned at this point, since he disapproved of the change in emphasis. His replacement was Lillian Harman, an American supporter of free love. The secretary of the League and the editor of their journal, *Adult*, was George Bedborough. The League was a small group and had little visibility until the Lanchester case. Because of the publicity of that incident, the League ran into trouble in 1898. Bedborough was arrested in March for selling Havelock Ellis's *Sexual Inversion* to a policeman. The League never recovered from the financial and social blows and petered out in 1899.[59]

The members of the Legitimation League dissented from legal marriage vocally. They published numerous explanations for their stance. Bedborough argued that neither sex could be 'truly free, until men and women alike agree to forego all *rights* in each other's person'. He further argued that the female members of the League who cohabited did so because they 'wanted their freedom, and therefore they acted as paramours instead of wives'. William Dunton, who lived with Emma Briggs, agreed with this last point about the sexual double standard in marriage: 'to any woman worth considering, there could be nothing more intolerable.' Some women members also openly disdained marriage. Emma Wardlaw Best, who lived with Arthur Wastall, asserted that they did not want 'any bond save that of love' in their partnership.[60]

Though these reasons sound feminist, at times, the leaders of the League put individual liberty ahead of women's concerns. Donisthorpe, for example, dismissed women's concern about desertion and possible poverty.[61] Unsurprisingly, then, some women members expressed concerns about free unions. Mary Reed wrote that free love hurt women more than men, and she doubted the existence of many 'really happy "free" marriage[s]'.[62] In addition to these differences, the League had to refute accusations of promiscuity. Members often had to explain that they supported monogamy, if not marriage. Gladys Dawson, for example, said she believed in free love in the same way that she believed in a free press or free trade – people should make their own arrangements without state intervention – but not in polygamy. In addition, most members expected some sort of registration, since they wanted their children acknowledged.[63] In other words, most members wanted more freedom and flexibility, but not promiscuity.

One of the most interesting aspects of the League was that many of the members combined theory and practice. Because its original purpose centred on acknowledged illegitimate children, it attracted those with a direct interest in that issue. The League provided an officer who registered such children, and *Adult* printed public announcements about free unions. Oswald and Gladys Dawson gave notice that they were in a permanent union, as did William Dunton and Emma Briggs in 1895 and Emma Best and Arthur Wastall in 1898. *Adult* also ran personal ads for a time to help those interested in free unions, and both men and women advertised for partners, often 'with a view to permanent union.'[64]

The problems of finding a like-minded people was the least of the difficulties for these couples, however. Dawson was ousted from the Personal Rights Association when his free union became public. In addition, one neighbour, a man named Naylor, began a spate of petty harassments. Nevertheless, Dawson insisted that Gladys had to deal with far more 'insults and innuendos' than he, a statement Gladys affirmed.[65] As usual, landladies were a particular concern. Eliza Millard, who lived in a free union with Dr Percy MacLoghlin in Southport in the 1890s, had many troubles in this regard. The couple saw each other for ten years without cohabiting, but Millard had to move frequently, because her landladies 'objected to a gentleman friend visiting the house and staying the night.' As a result, they moved in together, but remained targets for social scorn;

a boy pelted Eliza with mud in 1898, and Percy's defence of her landed him in an assault trial.[66]

Because of the demise of the League after only six years, the historian is left to wonder how the Dunton, Dawson, and Best/Wastall unions endured. Donisthorpe continued to publish critiques of marriage into the Edwardian period, and Vickery and Drysdale, who were also affiliated with the League, stayed together for life, but the others fade from view.[67] The purpose of the League was a strange mix of radicalism and conservatism. In an effort to remove the influence of the state from their personal lives, the members formed a group that registered their irregular marriages and acknowledged their children, giving a different kind of public sanction.[68] In addition, the League had a limited audience, since they only wanted to register 'acknowledged' illegitimates. Donisthorpe flatly rejected children who emerged from 'ephemeral, coarse and brutal passion,' calling them 'the bastards of the people.'[69] The slight appeal of their ideas is, thus, understandable. Working-class couples who were dissatisfied with the law were more likely to petition for divorce reform than join the League. And if they wanted revolution, they had other alternatives at the end of the century.

Anarchism

The anarchist movement in Britain began in the mid–1880s and was renewed by waves of emigrés from Europe throughout the period before the First World War. Many famous anarchists ended up in London for at least some time, including Peter Kropotkin and Louise Michel. Thus, anarchism, like Marxism, tended to have a number of immigrant members and to be concentrated in the poorer areas of cities. It was a minority group in England; most workers preferred socialism. All the same, several small anarchist groups operated in England, often working in conjunction with other radical organisations.[70]

Anarchism critiqued the power of the state as well as capitalism. Anarchists wanted authority to rise from below, either in the form of federated communes or in direct democracy. They also championed individual liberty more than socialists. Thus, anarchists regarded marriage as another example of state oppression.[71] At base, they disapproved of marriage for two reasons. First, they insisted that love could not be coerced. A typical article asserted that 'Love needs no legal chains', and some anarchists even eschewed monogamy. Second, Anarchists supported women's rights and argued that the 'emancipation of woman from her domestic slavery is to be found in the abolition of the marriage laws.'[72]

Anarchists also revived the Owenite interest in communal living, and several small communities formed in the Edwardian period. The most prominent was at Whiteway, in Gloucester, founded in 1898. Some couples married legally there, but others decided to form non-marital partnerships. According to Nellie Shaw, who lived with Francis Sedlak for thirty-three years, their objections to marriage were similar to those of all anarchists: love should be free, marriage made women chattels, and divorce was 'tedious and expensive'. Whiteway couples also disliked patriarchal control of children within marriage. Because of these objections, Whiteway saw seven free unions in the first group of settlers and four more in the second. The couples united in a variety of ways, some with religious rites, wedding rings, and a change of names, but others with none of these. In short, individuals were free to do what suited them best.[73]

Some of the unions failed, with unfortunate results. One couple broke up due to the desertion of the man, yet he came back and caused a scene when his partner formed a second union. The ensuing publicity caused a great deal of trouble.[74] Yet others lasted for decades, including Shaw's. From this fact, she concluded that free unions 'compare quite favourably with legal marriage … But at the same time I cannot claim they are much better.' Some marriages were free and supportive, and some free unions were full of 'property sense'. Thus, the success or failure was 'more a matter of temperament than anything else'.[75] As this conclusion shows, one strength of the anarchist movement was its firm individualism, so that each couple made its own decision, even in communal settings.

Outside of these small communities, some anarchist leaders also participated in free unions. Guy Aldred, anarchist-communist, lived in a free union with Rose Witkop between 1908 and 1921. Aldred was born in London in 1886, the son of a naval officer and a parasol maker. His parents never lived together, and both of them married bigamously later in their lives, a circumstance that made Guy sceptical about marriage. In 1907, he met Rose after he had converted to atheism and anarchism. Witkop was a Polish Jew who had immigrated to Britain, following her older sister, Millie. She was a feminist and supporter of workers' rights. The couple fell in love, and though their courtship was chaste for some time, both had unconventional ideas about marriage.[76]

Aldred's disdain for legal marriage was one of his firmest articles of faith. His objections were in line with most anarchist positions. He insisted that a promise to love forever was 'void from the very start for neither party knew if it would hold for life.' Aldred also believed in women's rights, calling marriage 'serfdom' and 'rape by contract'. He railed against the requirement that women change their names at marriage; this proved married women's 'function was to be a chattel.'[77] As a communist, he also argued that an overhaul of the economic system was necessary for women to be free. All the same, he was against promiscuity. He believed that people were becoming more monogamous, not less, and that celibacy would eventually predominate among the most 'evolved' part of humanity.[78]

Witkop left little writing of her own, though she agreed with Aldred on many of these points. Only seventeen when she met Aldred, she was already a poised and accomplished radical. She was a socialist-anarchist first, and a feminist second. For example, she wrote a piece for the *Voice of Labour* that argued that economic changes were more important than women's suffrage. Still, she added that each woman 'is a slave in every sense of the word both in the factory and in her household.' Like Aldred, Witkop made a 'distinction between the terms lust, licence, prostitution, and free love'. She wanted relationships of 'staunch friendship, unsullied by obligations and duties, ties and certificates.' She was also more assertive than Guy, according to him. Aldred wanted a chaste union, but Rose disagreed. She gave birth to their son in 1909, getting her way on this as well as other matters.[79]

Aldred and Witkop had a difficult relationship. In his memoirs, Guy reported that Rose had several affairs. Guy insisted that he was not jealous, but the relationship did not survive her infidelities, though they did not separate formally until after the First World War. They also disagreed on politics; for example, Guy objected to Rose's preoccupation with birth control reform. Beyond these differences, Aldred was conscious of the difficulties of uniting two disparate people. Before he lived with Rose, he wondered, 'Would each partner to the union remain the person the other mated?' Later, Aldred argued that love was not enough to make a relationship work; the couple must suit each other as well.[80]

Witkop and Aldred also endured much family opposition to their union. Guy's mother was anti-Semitic and feared losing her son's economic support. Despite her own bigamous marriage, she also disapproved on moral grounds, which exasperated Guy. Rose's family was equally hostile; her mother was particularly distressed, since Rose was the third of the four daughters in the family to reject wedlock. Mrs Witkop also disliked that Aldred was not Jewish (a neat reversal of Guy's mother's reaction). Nor did Polly and Milly, her two sisters, much like Guy, though they eventually came around. Only Aldred's grandfather was supportive: 'he did not think ceremony or state registration mattered if we each had the courage to stand firm.'[81] The couple also experienced social difficulties. One night when they were out, a policeman called Rose a prostitute. Aldred threatened to lodge a complaint so the constable apologised, but Rose was 'much upset.'

Moreover, when Rose went into the hospital to give birth to their son, the hospital authorities would not let Guy see Rose 'and treated her as "a fallen woman"'.[82]

In addition to these practical problems, Aldred suffered from the union's failure; his memoir is extremely touchy about it. He repeats over and over again that it was purer and braver than any others. A typical passage called their union 'one of principle and challenge', which 'placed our union far above most of the eccentric matings that occurred in the Socialist and Anarchist movement.' Aldred even assumed that theirs was the first union that was both open and voluntary. This showed not only Aldred's ignorance of other couples, but also his need to feel superior. Since the freedom of their union had left him alone, he continued to defend the purity of their principles as compensation for his loss. A final irony was that Rose and Guy did marry in 1926, since the government threatened to deport her due to her radical activities, and Guy wanted to protect the mother of his son. They married, then, after their personal relationship was long over. Despite Guy's protestations, marriage did have its compensations.[83]

Aldred's doubts about other free unions could be wrong-headed, but he was not completely off-base. Polly Witkop, Rose's sister, lived with a German refugee named Simmerling, because he had a wife in Germany. Aldred criticised her for going by the name of 'Mrs Simmerling' and for not standing up to her lazy partner. Although overly harsh, he did at least see that a free union did not preclude traditional gender roles; in fact, Polly later had to marry for convenience because Simmerling deserted her. Radical men, then, were not necessarily feminists and might be totally unscrupulous. A Russian anarchist named Tchishikoff lived with a young woman named Zlatke in the East End, but left her pregnant and alone when his legal wife arrived from Russia.[84] In other words, male libertinism was present in anarchist circles, especially since for some of them, 'free love' was an article of faith.

In addition, the middle-class members of the anarchist movement usually married legally, as did much of the leadership. The middle classes had more to lose, and middle-class women, in particular, hesitated to risk their reputations. One exception was Olivia Rosetti, daughter of William (Gabriel's brother) and Lucy Rosetti. Olivia and her younger siblings, Arthur and Helen, edited an anarchist journal, the *Torch*, from 1891 to 1895. Olivia fell in love with Antonio Agresti, an Italian engraver and anarchist, who had fled Florence in 1885. Early in 1896, the two 'united' their lives when Agresti returned to Italy. All the same, the two married in Florence in 1897, so their rebellion was short-lived; it also coincided with the withdrawal of all the Rosettis from the movement.[85]

On the other hand, at least one free union in the anarchist movement was both happy and long-lived. Rudolf Rocker and Milly Witkop's relationship spanned almost sixty years. Milly had been the first of her family to come to London from Polish Russia in 1894, when she was only fifteen. She worked hard to bring over her entire family in 1897, and she had, by that time, begun working with the East End Jewish radicals. Rocker was a German who emigrated to France and then England. His family was Social Democratic, and he became involved with Jewish anarchists in Paris. He lived with a woman in Germany and then France, and they had a son in 1893, but they did not remain together, since they had no 'spiritual bond between' them. Rocker came to England in 1895, and he devoted himself to the Jewish East End, where he met Witkop. The two quickly became a couple.[86]

Rocker and Witkop's views of marriage came out most clearly when they tried to emigrate to the United States in 1898. When they arrived in New York, the officials asked for their marriage certificate, and Rudolf admitted that they had none, explaining, 'Our bond is one of free agreement between my wife and myself.' The woman official then asked Millie how she could agree with such a notion, since it promoted 'free love'. Millie replied that she would not 'consider it dignified as a woman and a human being to want to keep a husband who doesn't want me'. She added, 'Love is always free … When love ceases to be free, it is prostitution.' Unsurprisingly, this ended the conversation. Eventually, the authorities told the couple that they must marry or leave. Rocker and Witkop returned to England rather than submit, a stand that gave them brief notoriety in England and the United States.[87]

Rocker and Witkop had a firm partnership during the next several years. Millie committed her savings to helping launch his newspaper, the *Arbeter Fraint*, and also set the type for his publications. They had one son, Fermin, and also took in Rudolf's son from his previous union. When Rocker was interned in the First World War, Millie stuck by him until she herself was arrested in 1916. When the government offered to send her to Russia with Fermin, but without Rudolf, in 1918, she refused. Rocker finally got out in March 1918, and ended up in Amsterdam. He requested Millie's release, and she and Fermin joined him in the autumn of 1918. The Rockers lived in Europe until 1933, when the Nazis ran them out of Germany, and, for the second time, they emigrated to the United States. In order to get into the country, they finally married – thirty-five years after refusing to do so the first time.[88]

Both before and after the legal ceremony, Witkop and Rocker were a devoted pair, sharing a passion for anarchism and socialism. Their happiness resulted in part from Rocker's practice of equality. According to William Fishman, 'Rocker lived out his conviction that, in every sense, relations between the sexes should be free, and without artifice.' After Millie's death in 1955, Rocker wrote a touching tribute to her: 'She opened a door in my heart which had been unknown to me before ... She was a part, and surely the best part of my life.' In this case, the ritual did not seem to matter one way or the other. Thirty-five years of unmarried bliss were followed by twenty-two years of the married variety, but the couple considered themselves married whatever their status. They referred to each other as husband and wife, and Milly sometimes used Rudolf's last name. Aldred criticised them for this, but free choice surely means being able to live in a union on one's own terms.[89]

As the Rocker/Witkop union showed, Anarchists' insistence on freedom from state interference meant that they faced the dilemma of what it meant squarely. If one should be free to do as one wished, did this preclude legal marriage? And did sexual freedom mean promiscuity? Despite their reputations, most anarchists replied to the latter question in the negative. Rocker, for instance, wanted Tchishikoff removed from leadership due to his behaviour. In addition, though the Anarchists were far more consistent about women's sexual freedom than most groups, they had their limits. As Hermia Oliver put it, though Peter Kropotkin gave women leadership positions in the movement, 'Sophie [his wife] cooked the dinner.' Indeed, at Whiteway, the women did all the domestic labour, despite also doing 'men's' work.[90] And, as long as the state gave advantages to the legally wed, the choice not to do so entailed penalties; thus, there were times, as Godwin had argued, that marriage was convenient or even necessary.

Conclusion

The story of marriage dissent had come full circle – from the anarchism of Godwin to that of Aldred. Some interesting continuities emerge from this chronological survey. First, the two main problems with legal marriage for radicals from the 1790s to 1914 remained its legal bias towards women and its indissolubility. Since these two disadvantages could be solved through legislation, the choice for radicals was whether to take part in the institution while working for reform or to take a stand and refuse to marry. Only a few chose the second option. A second continuity was the insistence that the problem with the institution was with its legal form, not with monogamy. All but a handful of radicals argued that the natural tendency of men and women was to have one partner. Indeed, when partners did practice sexual freedom, their relationships rarely survived. Free unions, then, kept many of the emotional attachments and jealousies of marriage. Furthermore, the emphasis on the relationship as key made it difficult to end the unions easily. Relationships founded on ideals were rare, so every success or failure was magnified exponentially. The ironic result was that these unions were more binding, in some ways, than marriages. Women, especially, often found freedom illusory.

Gender and class concerns changed over the course of the century. Though working-class couples were more likely to live in irregular unions, few of them were ideological after the demise of Owenism. Indeed, socialism reversed itself on the issue from the 1840s; most groups were, at best, unenthusiastic about free unions. Only anarchism had a large contingent of workers, and this was a small movement; furthermore, most of its leaders were also monogamous. Gender concerns also had continuities and discontinuities. Throughout the century, women in free unions faced more discrimination than men, but some women embraced sexual freedom by the end of the century. In addition, precisely because of their difficulties, 'women who did' were heroines of their movements far more than their male partners.

Finally, another change in the movement was the tendency of radicals to define the 'best' type of free union, something that eventually became epidemic. Because so many radicals were already sectarians on political and economic issues, they applied this same spirit to their domestic affairs. Those radicals who were discreet, rather than open, about their relationships could be criticised for betraying the principles of the movement. In addition, those who could not marry legally were somehow less 'pure' than those who chose cohabitation freely. Though most groups offered an alternative social support system, they could also be sites of dissension.

Radicals critiqued the marriage laws, but the majority wanted committed unions, so were similar to those who cohabited for non-radical reasons. These couples considered themselves married, took each other's names, and called each other husband and wife. Most reformers wanted to expand the definition of marriage rather than to dissolve it. A major difference, though, with non-radical cohabitees was that family and friends were more supportive of those who could not marry than those who would not. Still, some families reconciled with cohabitees. By the end of the century, middle-class families, at least on a limited scale, joined those working-class parents who refused to desert their children or grandchildren entirely. This problem was solved more easily, of course, in those families in which the parents and children shared radical beliefs, but it was not unknown elsewhere. All in all, the freedom of free unions was contingent on a number of factors – class, gender, generation, and, most importantly, the success of the relationship. This was also true of many non-radical free unions, and shows the difficulty of generalising about the 'best' type of union, in the nineteenth or any other century.

Notes

1 Ashton, G. H. Lewes, pp. 5–56; 89–99; 120–32, quote from p. 5; D. Williams, Mr George Eliot: A Biography of George Henry Lewes (New York: Franklin Watts, 1983), pp. 14–20; 28–32; 66–70; Hughes, George Eliot, pp. 131–44.

2 G. Haight, George Eliot and John Chapman (New Haven, CT: Yale University Press, 1940), pp. 16–19, quote from p. 16.

3 Haight, George Eliot and John Chapman, pp. 80–1; Haight, George Eliot Letters, I, 277; Ashton, G. H. Lewes, pp. 52–3; Hughes, George Eliot, pp. 144–50.

4 Ashton, G. H. Lewes, pp. 157–9; Hughes, George Eliot, pp. 60–1; 114; 126–7; 150–5; Haight, George Eliot and John Chapman, pp. 88–9; Hirsch, Barbara Leigh Smith Bodichon, p. 111.

5 R. Ledbetter, A History of the Malthusian League, 1877–1927 (Columbus, OH: Ohio State University Press, 1976), pp. 16–19; A. Besant, 1875 to 1891: A Fragment of Autobiography (London: Theosophical Publishing Society, 1891), pp. 4–5; N. F. Anderson, '"Not a fit or proper person": Annie Besant's struggle for child custody, 1878–79', in Nelson and Holmes (eds), Maternal Instincts, 13–36.

6 Ledbetter, History of the Malthusian League, pp. 81–2; J. M. Benn, Predicaments of Love (London: Pluto Press, 1992), pp. 114–15.

7 Benn, Predicaments of Love, pp. 182–3; Ledbetter, History of the Malthusian League, p. 60; A. Vickery, 'Is the wife still a chattel?' Journal of the Divorce Law Reform Union 1 (1900), 8–9; and A Woman's Malthusian League (London: G. Standring, [1927?]).

8 R. First and A. Scott, Olive Schreiner (New Brunswick, NJ: Rutgers University Press, 1980), pp. 125–9; E. Ellis, James Hinton: A Sketch (London: Stanley Paul & Co., 1918), pp. 50–76; 92–104. For a positive assessment of Hinton, see S. Koven, Slumming: Sexual and Social Politics in Victorian London (Princeton, NJ: Princeton University Press, 2004), pp. 14–18.

9 Ellis, James Hinton, pp. 121–84.

10 Ellis, James Hinton, pp. 153; 178; 232; 252; Schreiner's letter quoted from P. Grosskurth, Havelock Ellis: A Biography (New York: New York University Press, 1985), p. 98.

11 British Library, Havelock Ellis Papers (hereafter HEP) ADD 70528, fols. 38–40. Emma Brooke to Havelock Ellis, 5 August 1885; fol. 41, Notes on Hinton, c. August 1885. See also KPP 10/61/1, Emma Brooke to Karl Pearson, 4 December 1885; Grosskurth, Havelock Ellis, pp. 51–4.

12 KPP 10/61/7, Ralph Thicknesse's notes on Howard Hinton's trial for bigamy, 27 October 1886; Grosskurth, Havelock Ellis, pp. 100–2. Trial in The Times, 15 October 1886, p. 3; 16 October 1886, p. 4.

13 Shanley, Feminism, Marriage and the Law, 22–48; Poovey, Uneven Developments, 51–88.

14 Herstein, A Mid-Victorian Feminist, pp. 72–5; 113; B. Caine, English Feminism, 1780–1980 (Oxford: Oxford University Press, 1997), pp. 98–101; P. Levine, '"So few prizes and so many blanks": Marriage and feminism in later nineteenth-century England', Journal of British Studies 28 (1989), 150–74; Feminist Lives in Victorian England: Private Roles and

Public Commitment (Oxford: Basil Blackwell, 1990), pp. 42–4, 69–71.

15 Caine, *English Feminism*, p. 97; Herstein, *A Mid-Victorian Feminist*, p. 85.

16 P. Rose, *Parallel Lives: Five Victorian Marriages* (New York: Vintage Books, 1984), pp. 99–119.

17 *Ibid.*, pp. 119–26.

18 H. Burton, *Barbara Bodichon, 1827–1891* (London: Murray, 1949), p. 188; Haight, *George Eliot and John Chapman*, pp. 88–92; Herstein, *A Mid-Victorian Feminist*, pp. 106–10; Hirsch, *Barbara Leigh Smith Bodichon*, pp. 105–17.

19 S. S. Holton, 'Free love and Victorian feminism: The divers matrimonials of Elizabeth Wolstenholme and Ben Elmy', *Victorian Studies* 37 (1993–94), 199–222, quote from 203; *Suffrage Days: Stories from the Women's Suffrage Movement* (London: Routledge, 1996), pp. 36–47.

20 Caine, *English Feminism*, pp. 131–72; D. Rubenstein, *Before the Suffragettes: Women's Emancipation in the 1890s* (New York: St Martin's Press, 1986); L. Bland, *Banishing the Beast: Sexuality and the Early Feminists* (New York: The Free Press, 1995), pp. 124–85, quote from p. 133; M. Jackson, *The Real Facts of Life: Feminism and the Politics of Sexuality, c. 1850–1940* (London: Taylor & Francis, 1994), pp. 1–33; Levine, *Feminist Lives*, pp. 79–102; C. Dyhouse, *Feminism and the Family in England, 1880–1939* (Oxford: Basil Blackwell, 1989), pp. 145–84.

21 'The new morality – III', *Freewoman* 1 (1912), 122 (first quote); 'The editor's reply', *Freewoman* 1 (1911), 93 (second quote); 'The immorality of the marriage contract', *Freewoman* 2 (1912), 81–3; A. B., 'The failure of marriage', *Freewoman* 2 (1912), 386–7; E. S. P. H., 'The sanctions of modern monogamy', *Freewoman* 1 (1911), 74; W. Foss, 'The problem of illegitimacy', *Freewoman* 1 (1912), 485–6.

22 M. Randolph and S. Randolph, 'Free unions', *Freewoman* 2 (1912), 79 (for first quote); B. L., 'Free unions', *Freewoman* 2 (1912), 99; M. Randolph and S. Randolph, 'Interpretations of sex', *Freewoman* 2 (1912), 118; B. L., 'Free unions', *Freewoman* 2 (1912), 138–9, second quote from 138.

23 T. Thompson (ed.), *Dear Girl: The Diaries and Letters of Two Working Women, 1897–1917* (London: The Woman's Press, 1987), pp. 151; 181; 219; 308–9, quotes from 181 and 308.

24 F. Delisle, *Françoise: In Love with Love* (London: Delisle, 1962), pp. 210–17, quotes from 210 and 217.

25 *Ibid.*, pp. 218–35.

26 'The discussion circle', *New Freewoman* I (1913), 166; Delisle, *Françoise*, pp. 222–30; 236; Thompson, *Dear Girl*, pp. 178; 186.

27 F. Delisle, *Friendship's Odyssey: In Love with Life* (London: Delisle, 1964), pp. 4–9; 36–50; *The Pacifist Pilgrimage of Françoise and Havelock* (London: The Mitre Press, 1974), pp. 80–3; 121–7.

28 Clark, *The Struggle for the Breeches*, pp. 197–232, quote from p. 221; J. Gillis, *For Better, For Worse*, pp. 231–59.

29 E. Frow and R. Frow, *The New Moral World: Robert Owen & Owenism in Manchester and Salford* (Preston: Lancashire Community Press, 1986), p. 21 (for quote); Marcus, *Engels, Manchester, and the Working Class*, pp. 88–116; K. Marx and F. Engels, *The Communist Manifesto* (London: Penguin, 1967), pp. 100–1; J. D. Hunley, *The Life and Thought of Friedrich Engels* (New Haven, CT: Yale University Press, 1991), pp. 71–3.

30 Carver, *Friedrich Engels*, pp. 145–61.

31 *Ibid.*, pp. 145–8.

32 Gillis, *For Better, For Worse*, p. 229.

33 F. Engels, *The Origin of the Family, Private Property, and the State* (New York: International Publishers, 1973); K. Hunt, *Equivocal Feminists: The Social Democratic Federation and the Woman Question, 1884–1911* (Cambridge: Cambridge University Press, 1996), pp. 23–36.

34 Engels, *Origin of the Family*, pp. 96–145.

35 *Ibid.*, pp. 143–5, quote from p. 145; Hunley, *Life and Thought of Friedrich Engels*, pp. 71–2.

36 Engels, *Origin of the Family*, pp. 135; 145; Hunt, *Equivocal Feminists*, pp. 24–9.

37 Y. Kapp, *Eleanor Marx* 2 vols (New York: Pantheon Books, 1972, 1976), I, 253–72; II, 15–18; R. Brandon, *The New Women and the Old Men: Love, Sex and the Woman Question* (London: Secker & Warburg, 1990), pp. 14–22.

38 E. Aveling and E. Marx Aveling, *The Woman Question* (London: Swan Sonnenschein, Le Bas, & Lowery, 1886), pp. 9–10; 15–16, first quote from 10, second from 15.

39 HEP, Diary, ADD 70525, fol. 161; Kapp, *Eleanor Marx*, II, 27–8.

40 Kapp, *Eleanor Marx*, II, 16–18, 677–80.

41 Brandon, *The New Women and the Old Men*, pp. 139–53, quote from p. 140.

42 Hunt, *Equivocal Feminists*, pp. 93–4.

43 *Ibid.*, pp. 93–117.

44 *Ibid.*, p. 115.

45 Tsuzuki, *Tom Mann*, pp. 102–8; 124; 140; J. White, *Tom Mann* (Manchester: Manchester University Press, 1991), pp. 11; 105–10.

46 Tsuzuki, *Tom Mann*, pp. 212–13; 266; White, *Tom Mann*, p. 142.

47 D. Montefiore, *From a Victorian to a Modern* (London: E. Archer, 1927), pp. 30–58; 154–6; 206; C. Collette, 'Socialism and scandal: The sexual politics of the early labour movement', *History Workshop Journal* 23 (1987), 102–3; 106–8.

48 Collete, 'Socialism and scandal', 109–10, quote from 109.

49 H. G. Wells, *Socialism and the Family* (London: A. C. Fifield, 1906), pp. 29–40; 44–60; Hunt, *Equivocal Feminists*, pp. 111–15; J. Lewis, 'Intimate relations between men and women: The Case of H. G. Wells and Amber Pember Reeves', *History Workshop Journal* 37 (1994), 76–83; Wells, *Experiment in Autobiography*, pp. 394–409.

50 Lewis, 'Intimate relations between men and women', 84–6; J. Briggs, *A Woman of Passion: The Life of E. Nesbit, 1858–1924* (London: Penguin Books, 1989), p. 306.

51 Hammond, *H. G. Wells and Rebecca West*, both quotes from p. 75; E. M. Watson, 'Wellsian prototypes of freewomen', *Freewoman* 1 (1912), 397–8.

52 Lewis, 'Intimate relations between men and women', 94.

53 E. Lanchester, *Elsa Lanchester Herself* (London: Michael Joseph, 1983), pp. 1–3; Rubenstein, *Before the Suffragettes*, pp. 58–9; O. Dawson, *The Bar Sinister and Licit Love: the First Biennial Proceedings of the Legitimation League* (London: W. Reeves and George Cornwell, 1895), pp. 282–3; O. Dawson, 'Lanchester and liberty', *The Labour Annual for 1896* (London: Clarion Company, 1896), 59–60, quote from 60.

54 Rubenstein, *Before the Suffragettes*, pp. 59–63; Lanchester, *Elsa Lanchester Herself*, pp. 3–5; 10; Hunt, *Equivocal Feminists*, pp. 94–104.

55 Lanchester, *Elsa Lanchester Herself*, pp. 32–40; 59–60, quote from p. 59.

56 *Ibid.*, p. 316.

57 *Ibid.*, p. 14.

58 Martin, *Working Women and Divorce*, p. 3; Rose, *Intellectual Life of the British Working Class*, pp. 206–20.

59 Rubenstein, *Before the Suffragettes*, pp. 45–7 (quote from p. 45); Benn, *Predicaments of*

Love, pp. 154–9; Brady, *Masculinity and Male Homosexuality*, pp. 141–52; Hunt, *Equivocal Feminists*, pp. 106–9; F. Richards (ed.), *At Scotland Yard: Being the Experiences during Twenty-Seven Years' Service of John Sweeney* (London: Grant Richards, 1904), pp. 176–91; J. Quail, *The Slow Burning Fuse: The Lost History of British Anarchists* (London: Paladin, 1978), pp. 214–16; A. Goldwyn, 'The Legitimation League', *Free Review* 8 (1897), 295–8.

60   G. Bedborough, 'The Legitimation League', *Shafts* (1897), 125; W. Donisthorpe, *The Outcome of Legitimation* (London: Legitimation League, 1897), p. 14; Dawson, *The Bar Sinister and Licit Love*, p. 284; *Adult* 1 (1897–98), 138, 147 (for quote).

61   W. Donisthorpe, 'The future of marriage', *Fortnightly Review* 59 (1892), 258–71; *The Outcome of Legitimation*, pp. 8–9.

62   M. Reed, 'A question of children: A symposium', *Adult* 2 (1898), 204.

63   Labadie Collection, University of Michigan, Legitimation League, *The Rights of Natural Children: Verbatim Report of the Inaugural Proceedings of the Legitimation League* (London: W. Reeves, 1893), pp. 54–5; 69; Dawson, *The Bar Sinister and Licit Love*, p. 50.

64   O. Dawson, *Personal Rights and Sexual Wrongs* (London: William Reeves, 1897), pp. 9–28; Legitimation League, *The Rights of Natural Children*, p. 10; Dawson, *The Bar Sinister and Licit Love*, p. 9; *Adult* 1 (1898), 147–8; 1 (1897), back covers of issues 4 and 5 (for quote).

65   Donisthorpe, *The Outcome of Legitimation*, p. 6; Dawson, *The Bar Sinister and Licit Love*, pp. 190–9; 225, quote from p. 199.

66   'The Millard and Thompson cases', *Adult* 2 (1898), 84–7, quote from 85.

67   *Adult* 1 (January 1898), 139; Legitimation League, *The Rights of Natural Children*, pp. 17–18; W. Donisthrope, 'To the editors of *The Freewoman*', *Freewoman* 1 (1912), 171; 'Problem plays and novels', *Freewoman* 2 (1912), 66–7.

68   O. Dawson, 'Labour and legitimation', *The Labour Annual for 1895* (Manchester: The Labour Press Society, 1896), 91.

69   W. Donisthorpe, 'Bastardy', *Free Review* 1 (1893–94), 330–42, quote from 342.

70   H. Oliver, *The International Anarchist Movement in Late Victorian London* (London: Croom Helm, 1983); Quail, *The Slow Burning Fuse*, pp. 19–21, 47–61; G. Cores, *Personal Recollections of the Anarchist Past* (London: Kate Sharpley Library, 1992).

71   P. Shipley, *Revolutionaries in Modern Britain* (London: The Bodley Head, 1976), pp. 172–6; W. C. H., *Confessions of an Anarchist* (London: Grant Richards, 1911), pp. 89–98; 127; 133; G. Aldred, *No Traitor's Gait! The Autobiography of Guy A. Aldred* 2 vols (Glasgow: Strickland Press, 1957), II, 318.

72   Verax, 'The logic of free-love', *Anarchist* 1, #7 (1886), 4–5, first quote from 5; W. C. H., *Confessions*, p. 133 (for second quote); H. Seymour, 'The anarchy of love', *Anarchist* 2, #5 (1888), 3, 6; 'The anarchy of love', *Anarchist* 2, #6 (1888), 3, 6–7.

73   N. Shaw, *Whiteway: A Colony in the Cotswolds* (London: C. W. Daniel Company, 1935), 128–30, quote from 128; J. Thacker, *Whiteway Colony: The Social History of a Tolstoyan Community* (Stroud: Alan Sutton, 1993), pp. 9–14.

74   Thacker, *Whiteway*, pp. 17–19.

75   Shaw, *Whiteway*, p. 131.

76   Aldred, *No Traitor's Gait!*, II, 309–20; J. T. Caldwell, *Come Dungeons Dark: The Life and Times of Guy Aldred, Glasgow Anarchist* (Barr, Ayrshire: Luath Press, Ltd, 1988), pp. 9–24; 55–7; G. Aldred, *From Anglican Boy Preacher*, p. 46; Quail, *A Slow Burning Fuse*, pp. 241–2; 248–9; 280–3.

77   G. Aldred, *No Traitor's Gait!*, II, 322–8; 353; 372, first quote from 372, fourth from 353; 'Labour and Malthusian heresy', *Voice of Labour* 1 (1907), 138; 'Socialism, women, and

the suffrage', *Voice of Labour* 1 (1907), 146 (for second quote), 150 (for third), 154; *The Religion and Economics of Sex Oppression* (London: Bakunin Press, 1907), pp. 26–32; *From Anglican Boy Preacher*, pp. 46–52.

78 Aldred, *No Traitor's Gait!*, II, 322–4; 'Questions of sex-oppression', *Freewoman* 2 (1912), 179; *From Anglican Boy Preacher*, p. 52; *Religion and Economics of Sex Oppression*, pp. 36–40.

79 Aldred, *No Traitor's Gait!*, II, 313–16; 399; 403; R. Witkop, 'Votes for women', *Voice of Labour* 1 (1907), 51 (first quote); R. Witkop, 'A retort', *The Freewoman* 1 (1912), 273 (rest of quotes).

80 Aldred, *No Traitor's Gait!*, II, 403–6; 423–31; 327 (for quote); I:443; Caldwell, *Come Dungeons Dark*, pp. 201–7.

81 Aldred, *No Traitor's Gait!*, II, 320–3; 327; 372–4; 399; 424, quote from p. 327.

82 *Ibid.*, II, 328, 399; 403, quotes from pp. 328; 399; Caldwell, *Come Dungeons Dark*, pp. 84–5; 102–3.

83 Aldred, *No Traitor's Gait!*, I, 444; II, 385; 400, quote from p. 385; Caldwell, *Come Dungeons Dark*, pp. 221–34.

84 Aldred, *No Traitor's Gait!*, II, 320; R. Rocker, *The London Years* (London: Robert Anscombe & Co., 1956), pp. 190–1; W. J. Fishman, *East End Jewish Radicals, 1875–1914* (London: Duckworth & Company, 1975), p. 270.

85 Oliver, *The International Anarchist Movement*, pp. 33–8; 120–5; 159–60; W. Rosetti, *Some Recollections of William Michael Rosetti* 2 vols (New York: Charles Scribner's Sons, 1906), II, 446–57.

86 Rocker, *London Years*, pp. 98–101, quote from p. 98; Fishman, *East End Jewish Radicals*, pp. 229–37; M. Grauer, *An Anarchist 'Rabbi': The Life and Teachings of Rudolf Rocker* (New York: St Martin's Press, 1997), pp. 42–3; 74–7.

87 Rocker, *London Years*, pp. 101–5, quotes on pp. 102–3; Grauer, *An Anarchist 'Rabbi'*, pp. 77–8.

88 Rocker, *London Years*, pp. 249–359; Grauer, *An Anarchist 'Rabbi'*, pp. 92–3; 127–39; 175–6; 208–12; Oliver, *International Anarchist Movement*, pp. 141–3.

89 Fishman, *East End Jewish Radicals*, p. 268; R. Rocker, *Milly Witkop Rocker* (Orkney: Ciefuegos Press, 1956), pp. 9, 19 (for quote); Aldred, *No Traitor's Gait!*, p. 399.

90 Oliver, *International Anarchist Movement*, p. 153; Shaw, *Whiteway*.

Conclusion

OHABITEES WERE the exceptions, not the rule, in nineteenth-century England. As such, one could dismiss them as unimportant in the broader scheme of family history. Yet these couples confronted the question of what makes a marriage in ways that made state and religious authorities distinctly uncomfortable. Cohabitees could do this because cohabitation was both similar and different from marriage, depending on circumstances. For those who wanted to be married, it was a second choice, but one which pointed up the inequities of English law. For those who chose not to marry, cohabitation was a positive state in itself, particularly for marital radicals. In either case, it interrogated marriage as a sacrament, legal state, and relationship.

In many ways, cohabitees resembled married couples and emulated aspects of marriage as much as possible. First, the intense desire for a public ritual was clear. Women wanted a ceremony, in part to satisfy their consciences and in part to please their 'friends', but many men also saw it as important. Thus, working-class couples 'jumped the broom', exchanged rings at others' weddings, or went out of the parish to marry illegally. Middle-class couples married abroad or announced their decision to cohabit through formal letters. Though not legal or sanctified by religion, these events nevertheless bound the couple together publicly and often included symbols like marriage lines, wife-sale 'papers', and rings. Second, most cohabitees expected a lifetime commitment and monogamy (at least for women); this was true even in the 'criminal' classes. Except for a few rare middle-class couples and radicals, cohabitees reared families and lived among their neighbours as before. The emotional investment of the partners was often intense and binding; many remained committed to unions that were clearly dysfunctional without any legal obligation to do so. Indeed, ending these unions was fraught with difficulties in all classes, as violence cases make clear. Third, many neighbours tolerated cohabitees (except those seen as 'homewreckers') especially because of the class and gender inequalities of the marriage laws. And even in censorious neighbourhoods, unless something went badly wrong, these couples 'passed' as married precisely because they resembled the married so closely.

All of these similarities were important, but the biggest ones related to gender. Both male and female cohabitees, even those in radical circles, expected men and women's 'spousal' roles to stay the same. Women did the domestic labour and kept the house, and men were breadwinners and the ultimate authorities. Occasionally, professional women also worked, but they still had responsibility for the home and any children or stepchildren. In general, as well, women regarded these commitments as more binding than men did, since the sexual double standard was, if anything, heightened by the economic and social vulnerabilities of 'fallen' women. Women tended to see irregular unions as 'marriages' whatever their legal status, while some men could see themselves as 'free' even in legal marriages.

These similarities to marriage, though, differed by class. The middle classes could escape some of the legal and social consequences of nonconformity, since they could marry and live abroad, and the men could support more than one family more easily. Better-off couples also had more resources to help change the laws in their favour, through pressure groups and petitioning. Working-class couples had no such options and so tended to get into trouble with the law more often. Yet the working class had more advantages socially, due to the more flexible sexual norms of the lower classes. No ostracism was total, but middle-class women suffered the most from societal and familial disapproval. A woman with a bad sexual reputation had a lesser status in all classes, but this was a much more serious loss the higher one moved up the scale. A woman lost her social standing, her job (if any), or even her children if her personal life became known. Middle-class men had fewer restraints, but they did not escape all censure; a middle-class man's sexual reputation mattered to his professional prospects, and the courts were especially hard on educated men who 'fell' or who did not keep their promises.

Thus, stable cohabitation and marriage shared many traits and sometimes reinforced class and gender norms. All the same, cohabitees could not emulate all aspects of marriage; even those most firmly emotionally 'married' could not change the legal and social circumstances. Most important, cohabitation had little legal standing, and any children of such unions were illegitimate even if the parents later married. As a result, all legal documents required extremely careful handling. Otherwise, unmarried 'widows' risked losing legacies from their cohabitees and any hope of charitable support, and their children might lose inheritances to legitimate rivals. Even more seriously, working-class women cohabitees faced difficult problems in the event of desertion or death of their partners. The downward spiral of female cohabitees showed the difference in status between a wife and a 'mistress' most clearly; a woman could go from a pseudo-wife to a prostitute in an alarmingly short time. Though less marked, men also faced some disadvantages in cohabitation. The criminal law at times punished cohabiting men more harshly than husbands, assuming that male cohabitees 'chose' to live unrespectably. And cohabitees' conflicts, unlike those of spouses, sometimes related to women's independence as much as men's; women cohabitees, unlike wives, controlled their own property, had custody over any children, and (in theory) could leave men who would not commit to them. In short, men gained freedom from cohabitation, but in doing so they forfeited some of their legal authority.

Couples could also not emulate the social acceptance of marriage. Neighbours and family might tolerate the relationships, but rarely as the best possibility. Some working-class parents and siblings never stopped trying to get the couple to the altar or to break them up, and middle-class couples who did not remain discreet faced snubs and isolation. Vicars and church missionaries also applied pressure to enforce marriage, whatever the attitudes of the couples themselves. In general, those who could not marry got more ready sympathy than those who did or would not marry, because their situation was not of their own making. But this kind of sympathy assumes 'fault' existed, even if it did not rest with the couples, and that the situation was not ideal. Because of these legal and social issues, cohabitation was never quite the same as marriage, despite a number of similarities, and this fact had many consequences.

Consequences

Despite legal and social disabilities, not all the results of cohabitation were negative. Couples who cohabited voluntarily enumerated several advantages to explain their choices. For one thing, they had more privacy and less interference from church and state, and they also paid no fees. For another, both men and women believe they could leave bad relationships more easily than marriages. Though this freedom did not always materialise in practice, the ability to escape a failed union in Victorian England was rare, due to the strict divorce laws, and, consequently, prized. In addition, as radicals pointed out, women also evaded the legal effects of coverture. In fact, by the end of the century, radical groups lionised pioneering women more than their male partners, and such groups acted as alternative social support in case of exile from family and society.

Still, many of the consequences were problematic, especially for women. Social ostracism was immediate with any open breach of the moral code, though this was usually not total for women and less serious for men. All the same, a 'fallen' woman became entirely dependent on her 'protector' and subject to great anxieties for her own and her children's futures. The lack of social support was related to the economic risks of cohabitation for women. Women had few job prospects and bore children, leaving them far more vulnerable to poverty. A poor woman with a well-off lover might climb out of the working class and see her children do much better than she could otherwise have hoped, but she also might receive no financial help at all. In short, the risks were considerable, and the success stories were exceptional. The relative powerlessness of women was especially evident in men's greater reluctance to marry in all groups of cohabitees and in cross-class unions, where the disadvantages of class and gender combined. Only a few unusual women, late in the century, broke free from convention without great financial and social cost. Feminist wariness of sexual experimentation must be understood in the context of these grave disabilities.

Of course, these consequences differed by class. Working-class couples had more social leeway, but came up against financial constraints in all types of cohabitation, especially adulterous unions, since the men could seldom provide for two families. In these situations, one of the families, usually the illegitimate one, suffered from want, often ending in the workhouse. The constant interaction between cohabiting poor couples and the Poor Law authorities, in fact, showed how difficult these constraints could be; the magistrates dealt with illegitimate families in a bewildering array of situations. These laws, in combination with the harsh Poor Laws, left JPs with limited options for deserted women and children.

The legal and economic consequences intertwined and made the situation more complex. Women who were not wives lost legal standing and could not enforce a husband's duty to provide, though a limited responsibility for illegitimate children existed despite the New Poor Law. Nevertheless, the legal difficulties at the assize level and even some police courts tended to fall on men and did not exclude those in the middle and upper classes. Judges, in particular, blamed men for cohabitation and believed men should support female cohabitees and any children they had fathered. The courts tried to uphold male promise-keeping and domesticated masculinity and, at times, ignored female unchastity. Such a stand at times put them in conflict with local Justices of the Peace, who differed with high court judges on how to deal with some types of cohabitation, especially bigamies. And the conflict did not end there. When judges did react with strictness, as in violence cases or in illegal marriages, juries often defied them. Some men (and women) were able to use these disagreements to evade punishment for flouting marriage laws. Interestingly, those who got more sympathy were the poor, since they could plead ignorance and necessity more plausibly.

The religious consequences of cohabitation were also mixed. On the one hand, the Anglican church enjoyed a virtual monopoly on valid marriages from 1753 to 1836 and thus fought any reforms to loosen the marital regime. Indeed, the expression 'living in sin' reflects the established church's view of any couple dissenting from the strict marriage laws. Church leaders led the charge against divorce reform, changes to affinity and consanguinity laws, and any further secularisation of marriage. As a result, some poor couples resented the power of the church and its fees and avoided marriage altogether, and middle-class couples married elsewhere. Similarly, reformers often saw the church as a major obstacle to 'sensible' marriage and divorce laws, since the church insisted on defining marriage as a sacrament, and, thus, indissoluble. In this way, the church drove otherwise conventional people out of the fold. On the other hand, some churches, like dissenting congregations and the Catholic church, chipped away at the Anglican monopoly of defining marriage, helping to change it. In addition, even within the church, vicars often waived their fees to help the poor, and energetic clergymen could be the best friends of women with reluctant partners; more than once, church pressure brought a man to the altar. Some women may well have been grateful for the help. Overall, however, the power of the church in influencing people's views of marriage declined; even when couples remained firm believers, they challenged the clergy's interpretation of scripture, as with affinal marriages.

Cohabitation also had a strong effect on family, friends, and wider communities. Marriages, except in rare instances, were joyful occasions, but responses to irregular unions were highly ambivalent. Of course, some people rejected all those who lived 'outside the law', but these were the exceptions. Most families and friends agreed that marriage was 'better', but they were willing to widen the definition of marriage to include bigamous, affinal, and some consanguineous and adulterous unions, as they had done (at times legally) before 1753. Though unenthusiastic, working-class families accepted irregular spouses, and took in daughters and illegitimate offspring if necessary. Even middle-class society made exceptions, as with marriage with a deceased wife's sister; many otherwise strict moralists disputed the laws of affinity. In these situations, parents and siblings (especially sisters) were vitally important; female kin rarely entirely deserted 'erring' daughters and sisters. Cohabiting unions often illustrated the continuing importance of nuclear and even extended families, especially in times of trouble. Family members could not prevent an irregular union, but they could influence its duration, success, and the fate of women and children if the union failed.

The relationship between parents and children could also be complex. Of course, children whose parents 'passed' as married might never know the difference, blending in with other poor children seamlessly. Only if the family faced legal problems or had to rely on the Poor Law authorities would the lack of marriage lines intrude. Still, illegitimate children had no legal standing. They were far more likely to be born in the workhouse, a serious stigma, and they also had no automatic right to paternal support. They, then, faced desertion by their fathers (and sometimes mothers). In the poor, this might mean that the child would be shuttled between state care, charities, and foster homes, as well as living with various relatives, a thoroughly unsettled home life.[1] In better-off families, legitimate relatives could fight the children for any legacies, unless their parents had worded their wills carefully. On some occasions, siblings sued each other over inheritances; this was particularly likely when some siblings were legitimate and others illegitimate. Though some families blended together well, illegitimacy complicated the family dynamic.

Two situations showed particular difficulties. First, in adulterous unions, children might well resent the intrusion of a 'homewrecker' as a step-parent; the Frederic children, for instance, sharply disliked their father's second family, the children of Kate Lyon.[2] Though some adulterous stepmothers and fathers were popular, like Margaret Gillies, others were not. In addition, the state's disapproval of adulterous unions meant that a woman might lose custody of her children, not being a 'proper person' to raise them; this even happened to a rare father, like Percy Shelley, who did not see his children with Harriet after his elopement. Second, mixed-class unions had potential to help children, yet, for the most part, these offspring did not have the same opportunities as their legitimate peers. Many, like the children of Benjamin Smith, were considerably richer than they would have been if they had grown up among their poor mothers' kin, but few fathers were as generous as Smith. Most did not give their illegitimate children the same status as themselves, just better than their mothers'. In some ways, these children fitted neither class of their parents, not as low as their mothers and not as high as their fathers, a confusing situation.[3] Cohabitation had legal, economic, and emotional consequences for all family members; because they were the most vulnerable, children saw these consequences most starkly, for good or ill.

Implications

Cohabitation was not widespread, but it was also not shockingly exceptional, and the majority of people accommodated themselves to at least some of its forms. This conclusion complicates common assumptions about the divide between the respectable and unrespectable poor. Poor families needed each other too much to be too nice about the matter and, in any case, 'passing' as married was fairly easy, especially in urban areas, so many cohabitees would have blended into their neighbourhoods with little ado. Also, people moved in and out of respectability, depending on circumstances and sometimes luck. A former mistress might inherit a bond, use it as a dowry, and attract a respectable husband; an adulterous couple might be enabled to marry by the death of a spouse. These couples regained some social standing, even in the middle classes. On the other hand, couples could slide down the social scale if the courts invalidated their marriages, and poorer women might slip from cohabitee to prostitute in short order. A simple dichotomy is not adequate to embrace this complicated social terrain, even within the poorest groups.

In addition, the experience of these couples in the nineteenth century showed that changes over time in cohabitation were only partly to do with changes in behaviour. In the early part of the century, marital nonconformity peaked and a sizeable minority of families had illegitimacies or cohabiting relationships. After mid-century, the number of such couples declined, and families admitted to irregular unions far less often. But not all of this change was numerical; some couples continued to live together but simply stopped talking about it openly. Similarly, in the better-off classes, the end of the century was a time of more open challenge to marriage, rather than the beginning, but more in words rather than actions. Thus, as many historians have shown, marital choices did not necessarily follow the rhetoric about marriage; indeed, discretion and hypocrisy often masked freedom in practice, and vice versa. In short, the prescriptive language defined what was 'normal' one way, while people's behaviour defined it another. One of the arguments of this book, then, is that historians need to look at what people actually did as well as what they said, to understand social change.

Cohabitation also comments on the relationship of the English state to family formation. The English marriage laws were a mix of religious and secular traditions, cemented by precedent and common law. Consequently, the enforcement of laws of marriage fell on a wide array of local and national courts whose interpretations overlapped and sometimes conflicted. One result of this idiosyncratic regime was that both civil and criminal courts were flexible about cohabiting unions. Judges upheld many cohabitation contracts and legacies in wills to partners or children. Like the couples themselves, many judges and jurors regarded cohabitees as 'practically married', and juries were notoriously unwilling to convict poor people who had married illegally, no matter how blatant their behaviour. Yet these mixtures also meant that the courts' reaction to cohabitation could be surprisingly harsh (as in violence cases) and inconsistent. Moreover, the adjudication of family life did not all come from the top. The actions of thousands of couples (as in bigamy cases) pressured judges to use their discretion in favor of cohabitation and eventually led to changes in the law itself. By looking at hundreds of cases, rather than simply appeals, this study shifts the perspective on domestic legal reform in the nineteenth century to the role of ordinary people. A person's sense of 'being married' often conflicted with the state's definition, so many people took action well in advance of legal changes.

A final contribution of this book concerns definitions and the marriage debate. Victorians struggled to define both cohabitation and marriage; the differences were crucial in legal forms, but often elusive in practice. At one end of the spectrum were those who included only those unions with both state approval and religious sacraments as 'real' marriages. At the other end were those who insisted that 'true' marriages were relationships and ideas, with no need of legal or spiritual sanction. Most Victorians fell somewhere between these two extremes, but a surprising number supported some kinds of reforms (as in affinal marriages or divorce reform) by the end of the century. Thus, the definition differed between groups of people – religions, classes, and neighbourhoods.

This variability helps explain the slowness of change and the anxiety of many people in reforming marriage. Of course, many reasons existed for this delay, including fears of 'hurting' marriage and the implacable opposition of the church party in Parliament. However, another reason for the great anxiety was the recognition that the definition of marriage was variable. In making the laws of marriage, Parliament was, in many cases, determining who was married and who was not. In other words, though theoretically eternal and sacred, marriage was, on the contrary, permeable and unstable. One might be living in sin one day and respectably married the next, or, alternatively, married on one side of the Scots–English border and unmarried on the other. The relativity of marriage was summed up by one respondent to the 1912 Royal Commission, who stated, 'I do not look upon compliance with man-made marriage laws as being synonymous with morality, seeing that those man-made laws differ in every country in the world.'[4] Each time Parliament reformed marriage, MPs faced this uncertainty anew. Secularisation and relativity in marriage were two long-term outcomes of the Hardwicke Marriage Act of 1753, and many people found this unsettling. In short, the century brought not so much a new definition of marriage as a destabilising of it. The Hardwicke Act restricted the definition of marriage, and in the resulting century, the English slowly widened it again, first by practice and later by law.

The conservative attack on any reform of marriage is understandable in light of the instability. Though many Victorians believed that marriage would be strengthened by a few judicious reforms, for conservatives, the reforms themselves were the problem. Ignoring much of the history of marriage laws, conservatives insisted that people should not make the decision on who was married and who was not; marriage was sacred, eternal, and immutable. If not, marriage became an idea or an act of will. This was why, in many ways, those cohabitees who insisted that they were 'married' were a bigger threat to marriage than those who openly defied it. If marriage was a relationship and an idea, rather than a sacrament and an institution, it was possible to marry without any sanction at all. Conservatives had reason to fear that every time the marriage law changed, the relativistic approach took another step forward, and the sanctity of legal marriage took another step backward.

As many examples in this work showed, though, refusing to change anything, no matter how crying the need, was also risky. People who could not make legal marriages went outside the law and made their own, further destabilising its meaning. As many reformers pointed out, a law that was completely outside of public opinion would not be followed – and, indeed, many people held the law in contempt, which hardly raised respect for marriage. The fact that some of those who could marry turned into marital radicals was a clear example of the danger of refusing to address serious domestic grievances. These arguments were strong, but not persuasive enough in the nineteenth century, which only illustrates how much was at stake for the participants.

Marriage rejection?

Despite the controversy, the evidence of this book points to English people's attachment to marriage, however defined. The number of people who wanted to marry far outnumbered those who disdained it, and even those who chose not to marry usually preferred monogamy and envisaged lifelong partnerships. Moreover, though some people preferred privacy, the majority craved public acknowledgement, to the point of breaking the law to get it. And the vast majority of couples, including radicals, believed the state did have a role in relationships whenever the partners became parents.

Thus, marriage, though much modified, has survived the onslaughts of mass cohabitation and no-fault divorce.

Of course, the contemporary English marital regime is much looser. Divorce is easier, cheaper, and quicker, and the rate has soared; illegitimacy is no longer a serious stain on a child; and living together is a normal part of a long-term relationship and does not inevitably lead to marriage. Still, many couples do marry when they have children or if they want a public acknowledgment of their relationship.[5] The number of couples who never marry is the highest in British history, but it has not yet replaced marriage. In the 2001 census, cohabiting couples made up 10 per cent of households (the figure for 1991 was 5 per cent). This is a large increase, but still a minority. And though fewer people are getting married, those weddings have become more costly and elaborate; the average cost of a wedding in 2008 was £20,000, and in 1996 the wedding market in the UK accounted for £3.33 billion. In other words, the white wedding has become culturally more significant as the legal and social roles of marriage have diminished. In addition, most cohabitees do not support promiscuity. Marriage is less popular, but committed relationships remain the goal.[6]

Nor have women's disabilities entirely disappeared. Numerous social and legal changes granted women more equality, including suffrage, equal pay statutes, and protection from domestic abuse. The birth-control pill gave women control of their fertility, and the lessening of restrictions on abortion in 1967 also limited unwanted births. The welfare state has eased the financial burdens of motherhood, and has chipped away at the advantages that men had from the sexual double standard. Yet women remain more likely to stay home with children, married or not, and do more of the housework than men, even when both couples work full-time.[7] Women in cohabiting relationships value their independence, but these unions have not brought equality.

The legal changes of the twentieth century have ended the heavy-handed adjudication of divorce and marriage. Most English people agree that consenting adults should be allowed to marry and divorce as they wish. All the same, legal differences between cohabiting unions and marriages remain. Men have fewer rights to their children born out of wedlock than to those born inside the institution. Cohabitees are not entitled to each other's pensions in the case of death, and court decisions over property disputes also disadvantage those without legal ties. Many cohabitees are annoyed at having to consider these factors, particularly as they do not want state intervention in their lives and strongly value their privacy.[8] Again, cohabitees show a mix of disliking the legal and public aspects, but wanting the state to acknowledge their commitment.

Obviously, the differences between the Victorians and the English population today outweigh the similarities. Still, the survival of marriage, if in an attenuated form, into the twenty-first century shows that the institution has weathered the changes in its definition and roles. The emphasis on the relationship, and on individual happiness as a goal, has not eliminated couples' desire for a public commitment. Indeed, gay couples received the right to civil unions in 2005, thereby opening up a whole new group of people to participate in the institution – but also to argue over its definition. For some cohabitees, their union is a partnership, not a marriage. But for others, it is still a relationship where the two live 'as husband and wife', and often ends with those titles becoming literally true. Does this, then, include same-sex couples? A religious aspect? Gender equality? Does it lessen the social and familial pressures in cross-class or mixed-race families? And, most especially, can any legal system adjudicate fairly in a relationship when one partner wants to continue while the other does not? No marital regime has all the answers. And though the English have more alternatives to marriage than ever before, the reformed original is still the most popular choice, as it was for the majority of those 'living in sin' in the nineteenth century.

Notes

1 Frost, "'The black lamb of the black sheep'", 299–303.
2 Myers, *Reluctant Expatriate*, pp. 93; 152–61.
3 See, for instance, Whistler's treatment of his illegitimate children in Fleming, *James Abbott McNeill Whistler*, pp. 278–80; 299–300; Weintraub, *Whistler: A Biography*, pp. 153; 258; 376–7; 423; McMullen, *Victorian Outsider*, pp. 140; 186; 271.
4 *Report of the Royal Commission*, II, 386.
5 Cretney, *Family Law*, p. 518; J. Lewis, *The End of Marriage? Individualism and Intimate Relations* (Cheltenham: Edward Elgar, 2001), p. 134; Gillis, *For Better, For Worse*, pp. 308–16; H. Cooke, *The Long Sexual Revolution: English Women, Sex, and Contraception, 1800–1975* (Oxford: Oxford University Press, 2004), pp. 332–5.
6 Cretney, *Family Law*, p. 33.
7 Gillis, *For Better, For Worse*, pp. 316–21; Lewis, *The End of Marriage?*, pp. 147–57.
8 Cretney, *Family Law*, pp. 520–4; 563–5; Lewis, *The End of Marriage?*, pp. 138–40.

Bibliography

Primary sources

Manuscript collections

National Archives, Kew Gardens, London

ASSI 1/65 Oxford Circuit Minute Books
ASSI 22/42 Western Circuit Minute Books, Civil
ASSI 54/5 Northern Circuit Minute Books
ASSI 75/2 South Wales Circuit Minute Book (Civil Court)
CRIM 10/23–86 Central Criminal Court Reports
DPP 1/6 Director of Public Prosecution Case Files
MEPO, 3/121 Metropolitan Police Records
PCOM 1/43–155 Old Bailey Sessions Papers
HO 45 and 144 Home Office Files
TS 18/1 and 25/1100 Treasury Solicitor's Files

Other manuscript collections

British Library, London, Francis Place Papers
British Library, London, Havelock Ellis Papers
British Library, Newspaper Annexe, Colindale, General Collection
British Library of Political and Economic Science, University of London, Mill-Taylor Collection
Institute of Advanced Legal Studies, London, Law Reports
Lambeth Palace Archives, London, Court of Arches Records
Lancaster University, Centre for Northwest Regional Studies, Elizabeth Roberts Oral History Collection, 1890–1940
London Metropolitan Archives, Foundling Hospital Records, Rejected Petitions, 1810–56
Special Collections Library, University of Michigan, Labadie Collection
University College, London, Karl Pearson Papers

Government documents

Parliamentary Papers: Judicial Statistics of England and Wales. London: Her Majesty's Stationery Office, 1857–1906
Reports From Commissioners on the Laws of Marriage and Divorce with Minutes of Evidence Appendices and Indices. 3 vols. Shannon, Ireland: Irish University Press, 1969–71

Irish University Press Series of British Parliamentary Papers: Reports, Returns, and Other Papers Relating to Marriage and Divorce with Proceedings and Minutes of Evidence, 1830–96. Shannon, Ireland: Irish University Press, 1971

Royal Commission on Divorce and Matrimonial Causes. 3 vols [Volumes 18–20 of *Parliamentary Papers* of 1912]. London: His Majesty's Stationery Office, 1912

Newspapers

Annals of Our Time
Berkshire County Chronicle
Birmingham Daily Mail
Bristol Mercury
Cardiff Times
Chester Guardian and Record
Cornish Times
Croydon Journal
Devizes and Wiltshire Guardian
Devonport Independent and Plymouth Gazette
Devonport Independent and Plymouth and Stonehouse Gazette
Dorset County Chronicle and Somersetshire Gazette
Durham Chronicle
Durham County Advertiser
East Sussex News
Gloucester Chronicle
Hampshire Advertiser and County Newspaper
Illustrated Police News
Lancaster Guardian
Lancaster Standard
Leeds Daily News
Leeds Intelligencer
Leeds Mercury
Leicester Chronicle
Lewes Times
Liverpool Mercury
Manchester Weekly Times
Newcastle Chronicle
Northampton Daily Chronicle
Norwich Mercury
Nottingham and Midland Counties Daily Express
Nottingham Evening Post
Oxford Chronicle and Berks and Bucks Gazette
Oxfordshire, Buckinghamshire, and Northamptonshire Telegraph
Portsmouth Times and Naval Gazette County Journal
Shrewsbury Free Press
Shrewsbury Free Press and Shropshire Telegraph

South Wales Daily News
Staffordshire Advertiser
Surrey Adverstiser and County Times
Swansea and Glamorgan Herald and the Herald of Wales
The Times
Tonbridge Telegraph
Warwick and Warwickshire Advertiser
Western Daily Mercury
Western Times
Yorkshire Gazette

Law Reports

Addams's Reports
Annual Register
Barnewall and Alderson's Reports
Cox's Criminal Cases
English Reports
Gibson's Law Notes
House of Lords Appeals Cases
Justice of the Peace
Kay and Johnson's Reports
Law Reports, Chancery Division
Law Reports, Common Pleas Division
Law Reports, Crown Cases Reserved
Law Reports, House of Lords
Law Reports, Magistrates Cases
Law Reports, Queen's Bench Division
Law Times
Meeson and Welsby's Reports of the Exchequer
Mylne and Keen's Reports
Phillimore's Reports
Vesey and Brames Reports
Weekly Reporter

Books and articles

A. B. 'The failure of marriage'. *Freewoman* 2 (1912): 386–7
Ackerley, J. R. *My Father and Myself*. London: The Bodley Head, 1968
Adult 1 (1897–98): 138–9, 147–8
'The Agapemone'. *The Leader* 1 (1850): 150
Aldred, G. *From Anglican Boy-Preacher to Anarchist Socialist Impossiblist*. London: Bakunin Press, 1908
——'Labour and Malthusian heresy'. *Voice of Labour* 1 (1907): 138
——*No Traitors Gate! The Autobiography of Guy A. Aldred*. 2 vols. Glasgow:

Strickland Press, 1957

——'Questions of sex-oppression'. *Freewoman* 2 (1912): 179

——*The Religion and Economics of Sex Oppression*. London: Bakunin Press, 1907

——'Socialism, women, and the suffrage'. *Voice of Labour* 1 (1907): 146, 150, 154

Allen, G. *The Woman Who Did*. Oxford: Oxford University Press, 1995

Atlay, J. B. *The Victorian Chancellors*. 2 vols. London: Smith, Elder, & Co., 1906–08

Authentic and Interesting Memoirs of Mrs Clarke. Boston, MA: J. Belcher, 1809

Aveling, E. and E. Marx Aveling. *Shelley's Socialism*. Oxford: Leslie Peger, 1947

——*The Woman Question*. London: Swan Sonnenschein, Le Bas, & Lowery, 1886

Bedborough, G. 'The Legitimation League'. *Shafts* (1897): 125

Besant, A. *1875 to 1891: A Fragment of Autobiography*. London: Theosophical Publishing Society, 1891

B. L. 'Free unions'. *Freewoman* 2 (1912): 99

——'Free unions'. *Freewoman* 2 (1912): 138–9

Blanch, L. (ed.) *Harriette Wilson's Memoirs*. London: Century Publishing, 1985

Booth, C. *Life and Labour of the People in London*. 17 vols. London: William & Norgate, 1891–1904. Reprint edition: New York: AMS Press, 1970

Bowen-Rolands, E. *Seventy-Two Years at the Bar: A Memoir*. London: Macmillan, 1924

Bramwell, Lord. 'Marriage with a deceased wife's sister'. *Nineteenth Century* 20 (1886): 403–15

Carlile, R. 'Every Woman's Book'. In *What is Love? Richard Carlile's Philosophy of Sex*, 81–104. M. L. Bush (ed.) London: Verso, 1998

——'Family affairs'. *A Scourge for the Littleness of 'Great' Men* 3 (1834): 17–21

——'Moral marriage'. *The Gauntlet* (1833): 521–2

Chaplin, C. *My Autobiography*. New York: Simon and Schuster, 1964

Clarke, E. *The Story of My Life*. London: John Murray, 1923

Clarke, R. 'Marriage within the prohibited degrees'. *Justice of the Peace* 26 (1862): 334

Cleveland, A. R. *Woman Under the English Law*. London: Hurst and Blackett, 1896

Coleman, J. *Charles Reade as I Knew Him*. London: Treherne & Co., 1903

Coleridge, Lord. Tract #13 in 'What the Liberals say'. In *Tracts Issued by the Marriage Law Defence Union*, 10–13. London: Marriage Law Defence Union, 1884

Collins, W. 'Bold words by a bachelor'. *Household Words* 14 (1856): 505–7

Cookson, J. *Thoughts on Polygamy*. Winchester: J. Wilkes, 1782

Davies, M. *Life in an English Village: An Economic and Historical Survey of the Parish of Corsely in Wiltshire*. London: T. Fisher Unwin, 1909

Dawson, O. *The Bar Sinister and Licit Love: the First Biennial Proceedings of the Legitimation League*. London: W. Reeves and George Cornwell, 1895

——'Labour and legitimation'. In *The Labour Annual for 1895*, 91. Manchester: The Labour Press Society, 1896

——'Lanchester and liberty'. In *The Labour Annual for 1896*, 59–60. London: Clarion Company, 1896

——*Personal Rights and Sexual Wrongs*. London: William Reeves, 1897

Delisle, F. *Françoise: In Love with Love*. London: Delisle, 1962

——*Friendship's Odyssey: In Love with Life*. London: Delisle, 1964

——*The Pacifist Pilgrimage of Françoise and Havelock*. London: The Mitre Press, 1974

'The discussion circle'. *New Freewoman* 1 (1913): 166

Dixon, W. H. *Spiritual Wives*. 2 vols. London: Hurst and Blackett, 1868

Donisthorpe, W. 'Bastardy'. *Free Review* 1 (1893–94): 330–42

——'The future of marriage'. *Fortnightly Review* 59 (1892): 258–71

——*The Outcome of Legitimation*. London: Legitimation League, 1897

——'Problem plays and novels'. *Freewoman* 2 (1912): 66–7

——'To the editors of *The Freewoman*'. *Freewoman* 1 (1912): 171

'The editor's reply'. *Freewoman* 1 (1911): 93

Ellis, E. *James Hinton: A Sketch*. London: Stanley Paul & Co., 1918

Engels, F. *The Origin of the Family, Private Property, and the State*. New York: International Publishers, 1973

E. S. P. H. 'The sanctions of modern monogamy'. *Freewoman* 1 (1911): 74

Eversley, W. *The Law of Domestic Relations*. 6th edn London: Sweet and Maxwell, 1951

Fairfield, C. *Some Account of George William Wilshere, Baron Bramwell of Hever*. London: Macmillan and Co., 1898

'False declaration of marriage'. *Justice of the Peace* 65 (1901): 428

Foss, W. 'The problem of illegitimacy'. *Freewoman* 1 (1912): 485–6

Foulkes, W. *A Generation of Judges*. London: Sampson Law, Marston, Searle & Rivington, 1886

Fox, R. M. *Drifting Men*. London: The Hogarth Press, 1930

Fox, W. J. 'The condition of women, and the marriage question'. *Crisis* 2 (1833): 174

——'The dissenting marriage question'. *Monthly Repository* 7 (1833): 136–42

Fulford, F. *The Rector and His Flock: A View of the Cambridgeshire Village of Croydon in Early Victorian Days*. David Ellison (ed.) Bassingbourn, Cambridge: Bassingbourn Booklets, 1980

Garnett, R. *The Life of W. J. Fox: Public Teacher and Social Reformer, 1786–1864*. London: John Lane, 1909

Gaskell, E. *Mary Barton*. Oxford: Oxford University Press, 1987

Glynn, H. 'The morality of easy divorce'. *The Leader* 1 (1850): 157

Godwin, W. *Enquiry Concerning Political Justice*. 3 vols. Toronto: University of Toronto Press, 1946

——*Memoirs of the Author of a Vindication of the Rights of Woman*. London: Penguin Books, 1987

Goldring, D. *South Lodge: Reminiscences of Violet Hunt, Ford Madox Ford and the English Review Circle*. London: Constable & Co., 1943

Goldwyn, A. 'The Legitimation League'. *Free Review* 8 (1897): 295–8

Greenwood, J. *The Seven Curses of London*. London: Stanley Rivers & Co., 1869

Grimstone, M. L. 'Female education'. *Monthly Repository* 9 (1835): 106–12

——'Men and women'. *Crisis* 3 (1834): 236

——'The protective system of morals'. *Monthly Repository* 9 (1835): 683–8

Hardy, T. *Jude the Obscure*. London: Macmillan, 1968

Higgs, M. *Glimpses into the Abyss*. London: P. S. King & Sons, 1906

Hobson, J. *Socialism as it Is!* Leeds: J. Hobson, 1838

Holyoake, G. J. 'Emma Martin'. *The Leader* 2 (1851): 985–6

Hooper, W. *The Law of Illegitimacy*. London: Sweet and Maxwell, 1911

Howitt, M. *An Autobiography*. 2 vols. London: William Isbister, Ltd, 1889

Hunt, V. *I Have This to Say: The Story of My Flurried Years*. New York: Boni and Liveright, 1926

Hunt, W. H., Sir Frederick Pollock, et al. *Deceased Wife's Sister Bill: Letters from William Holman Hunt, Sir Frederick Pollock, and Others*. London: Marriage Law Reform Association, 1901

'The immorality of the marriage contract'. *Freewoman* 2 (1912): 81–3

Jerrold, C. *The Story of Dorothy Jordan*. New York: Benjamin Blom, 1914

Kate. 'Female improvement'. *The New Moral World* 1 (1834–35): 263–4

Kegan Paul, C. (ed.) *Mary Wollstonecraft: Letters to Imlay*. London: Kegan Paul, 1879

Kirk, Sir John. 'The creche and the ragged school union'. *Progress, Civic, Social, Industrial: The Organ of the British Institute of Social Services* 2 (1907): 183–5

Lanchester, E. *Elsa Lanchester Herself*. London: Michael Joseph, 1983

'The law relating to marriages as it affects the law of settlement'. *Justice of the Peace* 2 (1838): 65–7

Legitimation League. *The Rights of Natural Children: Verbatim Report of the Inaugural Proceedings of the Legitimation League*. London: W. Reeves, 1893

Lindsay, Lady. 'Some recollections of Miss Margaret Gillies'. *Temple Bar* 81 (1887): 265–73

Linton, W. J. 'Effects of legislating upon love or some reasons against lawful wedlock'. *The National* (1839): 327–9

—— *Three Score and Ten Years, 1820 to 1890: Recollections*. New York: Charles Scribner's Sons, 1894

'Marriage and protest'. *The Christian Reformer, or, The Unitarian Magazine and Review* 2 (1835): 60

'A marriage of affinity'. *Justice of the Peace* 68 (1904): 521

'Marriages'. *The New Moral World* 1 (1834–35): 24

Martin, A. *Working Women and Divorce*. London: David Nutt, 1911

Marx, K. and F. Engels. *The Communist Manifesto*. London: Penguin, 1967

Mayhew, H. *London Labour and the London Poor*. 4 vols. New York: Dover, 1968.

Mearns, A. *The Bitter Cry of Outcast London*. Anthony Wohl (ed.) Leicester: Leicester University Press, 1970

'The Millard and Thompson cases'. *Adult* 2 (1898): 84–7

Minto, W. (ed.) *Autobiographical Notes of the Life of William Bell Scott*. 2 vols. New York: Harper and Brothers, 1892

Montefiore, D. *From a Victorian to a Modern*. London: E. Archer, 1927

Morrison, F. *The Influence of the Present Marriage System upon the Character and Interests of Females*. Manchester: A. Heywood, 1838

'The new morality – III'. *Freewoman* 1 (1912): 121–2

Owen, R. *The Marriage System of the New Moral World*. Leeds: J. Hobson, 1838

——'Police'. *Crisis* 3 (1833): 47

Panton, J. *More Leaves from a Life*. London: Eveleigh Nash, 1911

Payne, E. F. *The Charity of Charles Dickens: His Interest in the Home for Fallen Women and A History of the Strange Case of Caroline Maynard Thompson*. Boston, MA: The Bibliophile Society, 1929

Petre, D. *The Secret Orchard of Roger Ackerley*. New York: George Braziller, 1975

Philia. 'To the editor of the *Crisis'*. *Crisis* 3 (1834): 258

'Presumption in favour of marriage'. *Justice of the Peace* 45 (1881): 711–12

The Queen against Thomas Smethurst. London: Butterworths, 1859

Quilter, H. *Is Marriage a Failure?* New York: Garland, 1984

Randolph, M. and S. Randolph. 'Interpretations of sex'. *Freewoman* 2 (1912): 118

——'Free unions'. *Freewoman* 2 (1912): 79

Redivivus, Junius. 'On the condition of women in England'. *Monthly Repository* 7 (1833): 217–31

Reed, M. 'A question of children: A symposium'. *Adult* 2 (1898): 204

Richards, F. (ed.) *At Scotland Yard: Being the Experiences during Twenty-Seven Years' Service of John Sweeney*. London: Grant Richards, 1904

Ridley, J. 'Increase in bigamy'. *Justice of the Peace* 74 (1910): 125

Roberts, M. *The Private Life of Henry Maitland*. London: The Richards Press, 1958

Roberts, R. *The Classic Slum: Salford Life in the First Quarter of the Century*. London: Penguin Books, 1973

——*A Ragged Schooling: Growing Up in the Classic Slum*. London: Fontana Paperbacks, 1984

Rocker, R. *The London Years*. London: Robert Anscombe & Co., 1956

——*Milly Witkop Rocker*. Orkney: Ciefuegos Press, 1956

Rose, C. *European Slavery; or Scenes from Married Life*. Edinburgh: Andrew Elliot, 1881

Rosetti, W. (ed.) *Pre-Raphaelite Diaries and Letters*. London: Hurst and Blackett, Ltd, 1900

——*Some Recollections of William Michael Rosetti*. 2 vols. New York: Charles Scribner's Sons, 1906

Rounsfell, J. W. *On the Road: Journeys of a Tramping Printer*. A. Whitehead (ed.) Horsham: Caliban Books, 1982

Rowntree, B. S. *Poverty: A Study of Town Life*. London: Macmillan, 1901

Seymour, H. 'The anarchy of love'. *Anarchist* 2, #5 (1888): 3, 6

——'The anarchy of love'. *Anarchist* 2, #6 (1888), 3, 6–7

Sharples, E. *The Isis: A London Weekly Publication*. London: David France, 1832.

Shaw, N. *Whiteway: A Colony in the Cotswolds*. London: C. W. Daniel Company, 1935

'Shelley on marriage'. *Anarchist* 1, #4 (1886): 7

Sims, G. *How the Poor Live and Horrible London*. London: Chatto & Windus, 1883

Skinner, J. *Journal of a Somerset Rector, 1800–1834*. H. Coombs and P. Coombs (eds) Oxford: Oxford University Press, 1984

Southwell, C. *Confessions of a Free Thinker*. London: Publisher unknown [1848?]

——*An Essay on Marriage Addressed to the Lord Bishop of Exeter*. London: E. Roe,

1840

'Spiritual wives'. *Westminster Review* 89 (1868): 456–79

Surtees, V. (ed.) *The Diary of Ford Madox Brown*. New Haven, CT: Yale University Press, 1981

Thompson, W. *Appeal of One Half the Human Race, Women, Against the Pretensions of the Other Half, Men*. New York: Bur Franklin, 1970

Tracts Issued by the Marriage Law Defence Union. London: Marriage Law Defence Union, 1884

Verax. 'The logic of free-love'. *Anarchist* 1, #7 (1886): 4–5

Vickery, A. 'Is the wife still a chattel?' *Journal of the Divorce Law Reform Union* 1 (1900): 8–9

——*A Woman's Malthusian League*. London: G. Standring [1927?]

Watson, E. M. 'Wellsian prototypes of freewomen'. *Freewoman* 1 (1912): 397–8

W. C. H. *Confessions of an Anarchist*. London: Grant Richard, 1911

Wells, H. G. *Experiment in Autobiography: Discoveries and Conclusions of a Very Ordinary Brain (Since 1866)*. New York: Macmillan, 1934

——*H. G. Wells in Love: Postscript to an Experiment in Autobiography*. G. P. Wells (ed.) London: Faber and Faber, 1984

——*Socialism and the Family*. London: A. C. Fifield, 1906

Witkop, R. 'A retort'. *Freewoman* 1 (1912): 273

——'Votes for women'. *Voice of Labour* 1 (1907): 51

Wollstonecraft, M. *Maria: or The Wrongs of Woman*. New York: W. W. Norton & Company, 1975

——*A Vindication of the Rights of Woman*. New York: Scribner and Welford, 1890

Women's Suffrage Journal 13 (1882), 119

Women's Suffrage Journal 16 (1885), 93

Yeames, J. *Life in London Alleys, with Reminiscences of Mary McCarthy and Her Work*. London: F. E. Longley, n.d.

Secondary sources

Articles and books

Abrams, L. 'Concubinage, cohabitation and the law: Class and gender relations in nineteenth-century Germany'. *Gender and History* 5 (1993): 81–100

Altick, R. *Deadly Encounters: Two Victorian Sensations*. Philadelphia, PA: University of Pennsylvania Press, 1986

——*Victorian Studies in Scarlet*. New York: W. W. Norton, 1970

Anderson, N. F. 'The "marriage with a deceased wife's sister bill" controversy: Incest anxiety and the defense of family purity in Victorian England'. *Journal of British Studies* 21 (1982): 67–86

——'"Not a fit or proper person": Annie Besant's struggle for child custody, 1878–79'. In *Maternal Instincts: Visions of Motherhood and Sexuality in Britain, 1875–1925*, C. Nelson and A. S. Holmes (eds), 13–36. New York: St Martin's Press, 1997

Ander son, O. 'Emigration and marriage break-up in mid-Victorian England'. *E conomic History Review* 50 (1997): 104–9

——'The incidence of civil marriage in Victorian England and Wales'. *Past and Present* 69 (1975): 50–87

Ashton, R. G. H. *Lewes: An Unconventional Victorian*. London: Pimlico, 2000

Asker, M. *Lawrence: The Uncrowned King of Arabia*. London: Viking, 1998

Auerbach, N. *Ellen Terry: Player in Her Time*. New York: W. W. Norton, 1987

August, A. *Poor Women's Lives: Gender, Work, and Poverty in Late-Victorian London*. London: Associated University Presses, 1999

Ayres, J. (ed.) *Paupers and Pig Killers: The Diary of William Holland, A Somerset Parson, 1799–1818*. Stroud: Sutton Publishing, 1984

Ayers, P. and J. Lambertz. 'Marriage relations, money, and domestic violence in working-class Liverpool, 1919–39'. In *Labour and Love: Women's Experience of Home and Family, 1850–1940*, J. Lewis (ed.), 195–219. Oxford: Basil Blackwell, 1986

Bailey, V. *This Rash Act: Suicide Across the Life Cycle in the Victorian City*. Stanford, CA: Stanford University Press, 1998

Baker, W. and W. Clarke (eds). *The Letters of Wilkie Collins*. 2 vols. London: Macmillan, 1999

Baker, W. (ed.) *Letters of George Henry Lewes*. 3 vols. Victoria, BC: English Literary Studies, 1995

Ballinger, A. *Dead Woman Walking: Executed Women in England and Wales, 1900–1955*. Aldershot: Ashgate, 2000

Barret-Ducrocq, F. *Love in the Time of Victoria: Sexuality, Class, and Gender in Nineteenth-Century London*. London: Verso, 1991

Bartholomew, G. W. 'The origin and development of the law of bigamy'. *Law Quarterly Review* 74 (1958): 259–71

——'Polygamous marriages and English criminal law'. *Modern Law Review* 17 (1954): 344–59

Bartley, P. *Prostitution: Prevention and Reform in England, 1860–1914*. London: Routledge, 2000

Barton, C. *Cohabitation Contracts: Extra-Martial Partnerships and Law Reform*. Aldershot: Gower Publishing Company, 1984

Bass, R. *The Green Dragoon: The Lives of Banastre Tarleton and Mary Robinson*. New York: Henry Holt and Company, 1957

Behlmer, G. *Friends of the Family: The English Home and Its Guardians, 1850–1940*. Stanford, CA: Stanford University Press, 1998

Belford, B. *Violet: The Story of the Irrepressible Violet Hunt*. New York: Simon and Schuster, 1990

Benn, J. M. *Predicaments of Love*. London: Pluto Press, 1992

Bennett, B. *The Damnation of Harold Frederic: His Lives and Works*. Syracuse, NY: Syracuse University Press, 1997

Bentley, D. *English Criminal Justice in the Nineteenth Century*. London: The Hambledon Press, 1998

Berry, P. *By Royal Appointment: A Biography of Mary Ann Clarke, Mistress of the*

Duke of York. London: Femina, 1970

Bigland, E. *Marie Corelli: The Woman and the Legend*. London: Jarrolds Publishers Ltd, 1953

Blainey, A. *The Farthing Poet: A Biography of Richard Hengist Horne, 1802–1884, A Lesser Literary Lion*. London: Longmans, 1968

Bland, L. *Banishing the Beast: Sexuality and the Early Feminists*. New York: The Free Press, 1995

Blyth, H. *Skittles, The Last Victorian Courtesan: The Life and Times of Catherine Walters*. London: Rupert Hart-Davis, 1970

Brady, S. *Masculinity and Male Homosexuality in Britain, 1861–1913*. New York: Palgrave Macmillan, 2005

Brandon, R. *The New Women and the Old Men: Love, Sex and the Woman Question*. London: Secker & Warburg, 1990

Briggs, J. *A Woman of Passion: The Life of E. Nesbit, 1858–1924*. London: Penguin Books, 1989

Brooks, P. *The Melodramatic Imagination: Balzac, Henry James, Melodrama, and the Mode of Excess*. New Haven, CT: Yale University Press, 1976

Burton, H. *Barbara Bodichon, 1827–1891*. London: Murray, 1949

Bush, M. L. (ed.) *What is Love? Richard Carlile's Philosophy of Sex*. London: Verso, 1998

Byrne, P. *Perdita: The Life of Mary Robinson*. London: Harper Perennial, 2005

Caine, B. *English Feminism, 1780–1980*. Oxford: Oxford University Press, 1997

Caldwell, J. T. *Come Dungeons Dark: The Life and Times of Guy Aldred, Glasgow Anarchist*. Barr, Ayrshire: Luath Press Ltd, 1988

Carver, T. *Friedrich Engels: His Life and Thought*. New York: St Martin's Press, 1990

Chadwick, R. *Bureaucratic Mercy: The Home Office and the Treatment of Capital Cases in Victorian Britain*. New York: Garland Publishing, 1992

Cherry, D. *Painting Women: Victorian Women Artists*. New York: Routledge, 1993

Cherry, D. and G. Pollock. 'Woman as sign in Pre-Raphaelite literature: A study of the representation of Elizabeth Siddall'. *Art History* 7 (1984): 206–27

Chinn, C. *They Worked all Their Lives: Women of the Urban Poor in England, 1880–1939*. Manchester: Manchester University Press, 1988

Clark, A. 'Domesticity and the problem of wife beating in nineteenth-century Britain: Working-class culture, law and politics'. In *Everyday Violence in Britain, 1850–1950*, S. D'Cruze (ed.), 27–40. New York: Longman, 2000

——*Scandal: The Sexual Politics of the British Constitution*. Princeton, NJ: Princeton University Press, 2004

——*The Struggle for the Breeches: Gender and the Making of the British Working Class*. Berkeley, CA: University of California Press, 1995

Clark Amor, A. *William Holman Hunt: The True Pre-Raphaelite*. London: Constable, 1989

Clarke, W. *The Secret Life of Wilkie Collins*. Stroud: Alan Sutton Publishing, 1989

Cobb, B. *Trials and Errors*. London: W. H. Allen, 1962

Cocks, H. G. *Nameless Offenses: Speaking of Male Homosexual Desire in Nineteenth-Century England*. London: I. B. Tauris, 2003

Collette, C. 'Socialism and scandal: the sexual politics of the early labour movement'. *History Workshop Journal* 23 (1987): 102–11

Collie, M. *George Gissing: A Biography.* Folkestone: William Dawson and Sons, Ltd, 1977

Colwell, S. 'The incidence of bigamy in 18ᵗʰ and 19ᵗʰ century England'. *Family History* 11 (1980): 91–102

Conley, C. *The Unwritten Law: Criminal Justice in Victorian Kent.* Oxford: Oxford University Press, 1991

Cooke, H. *The Long Sexual Revolution: English Women, Sex, and Contraception, 1800–1975.* Oxford: Oxford University Press, 2004

Cores, G. *Personal Recollections of the Anarchist Past.* London: Kate Sharpley Library, 1992

Coustillas, P. (ed.) *The Letters of George Gissing to Gabrielle Fleury.* New York: The New York Public Library, 1964

——*London and the Life of Literature in Late Victorian England: The Diary of George Gissing, Novelist.* Hassocks, Sussex: The Harvester Press, 1978

Craig, E. *Gordon Craig: The Story of His Life.* New York: Alfred A. Knopf, 1968

Cretney, S. *Family Law in the Twentieth Century: A History.* Oxford: Oxford University Press, 2003

Curtis, L. P. *Jack the Ripper and the London Press.* New Haven, CT: Yale University Press, 2001

Davidoff, L. 'The separation of home and work? Landladies and lodgers in nineteenth- and twentieth-century England'. In *Fit Work for Women*, S. Burman (ed.), 68–92. New York: St Martin's Press, 1979

——*Worlds Between: Historical Perspectives on Gender and Class.* London: Polity Press, 1995

Davidoff, L. and C. Hall. *Family Fortunes: Men and Women of the English Middle Class, 1780–1850.* Chicago: University of Chicago Press, 1987

Davin, A. *Growing Up Poor: Home, School and Street in London, 1870–1914.* London: Rivers Oram Press, 1996

Davis, A. 'Youth gangs, masculinity and violence in late Victorian Manchester and Salford'. *Journal of Social History* 32 (1998): 349–69

Davis, I. M. *The Harlot and the Statesman: The Story of Elizabeth Armistead and Charles James Fox.* Abbotsbrook, Bucks: Kensal Press, 1986

Davis, J. 'A poor man's system of justice: The London police courts in the second half of the nineteenth century'. *Historical Journal* 27 (1984): 309–35

Davis, T. *Actresses as Working Women: Their Social Identity in Victorian Culture.* London: Routledge, 1991

D'Cruze, S. *Crimes of Outrage: Sex, Violence, and Victorian Working-Class Women.* DeKalb, IL: Northern Illinois University Press, 1998

Du Maurier, D. (ed.) *The Young George Du Maurier: A Selection of his Letters, 1860–67.* London: Peter Davies, 1951

Dyhouse, C. *Feminism and the Family in England, 1880–1939.* Oxford: Basil Blackwell, 1989

Elfenbein, A. *Byron and the Victorians.* Cambridge: Cambridge University Press,

1995.

Elwin, M. *Charles Reade: A Biography*. London: J. Cape, 1931

Feldman, P. R. and D. Scott-Kilvert (eds). *The Journals of Mary Shelley, 1814–44*. 2 vols. Oxford: Clarendon Press, 1987

Finnegan, F. *Poverty and Prostitution: A Study of Victorian Prostitutes in York*. Cambridge: Cambridge University Press, 1979

First, R. and A. Scott. *Olive Schreiner*. New Brunswick, NJ: Rutgers University Press, 1980

Fishman, W. J. *East End Jewish Radicals, 1875–1914*. London: Duckworth & Company, 1975

Fleming, G. H. *James Abbott McNeill Whistler: A Life*. New York: St Martin's Press, 1991

Forster, E. M. *Marianne Thornton: A Domestic Biography, 1797–1887*. New York: Harcourt, Brace and Company, 1956

Foyster, E. *Marital Violence: An English Family History, 1660–1857*. Cambridge: Cambridge University Press, 2005

Fredeman, W. (ed.) *The Letters of Pictor Ignotis: William Bell Scott's Correspondence with Alice Boyd, 1859–1884*. Manchester: John Rylands University Library, 1976

——*A Pre-Raphaelite Gazette: The Penkill Letters of Arthur Hughes to William Bell Scott and Alice Boyd, 1886–97*. Manchester: John Rylands University Library, 1967

Frost, G. "'The black lamb of the black sheep': Illegitimacy in the English working class, 1850–1939". *Journal of Social History* 37 (2003): 293–322

——*Promises Broken: Courtship, Class, and Gender in Victorian England*. Charlottesville, VA: University Press of Virginia, 1995

——"'She is but a woman': Kitty Byron and the English Edwardian criminal justice system". *Gender and History* 16 (2004): 538–60

Frow, E. and R. Frow. *The New Moral World: Robert Owen & Owenism in Manchester and Salford*. Preston: Lancashire Community Press, 1986

Gettman, R. *George Gissing and H. G. Wells: Their Friendship and Correspondence*. Urbana, IL: University of Illinois Press, 1961

Gilfoyle, T. J. 'The hearts of nineteenth-century men: Bigamy and working-class marriage in New York City, 1800–1890'. *Prospects* 19 (1994): 135–60

Gillen, M. *The Prince and his Lady: The Love Story of the Duke of Kent and Madame de St Laurent*. London: Sidgwick & Jackson, 1970

Gillis, J. *For Better, For Worse: British Marriages, 1600 to the Present*. New York: Oxford University Press, 1985

Gleadle, K. *The Early Feminists: Radial Unitarians and the Emergence of the Women's Rights Movement, 1831–51*. London: St Martin's Press, 1995

Grauer, M. *An Anarchist 'Rabbi': The Life and Teachings of Rudolf Rocker*. New York: St Martin's Press, 1997

Grosskurth, P. *Byron: The Flawed Angel*. New York: Houghton Mifflin, 1997

——*Havelock Ellis: A Biography*. New York: New York University Press, 1985

Gruner, E. R. 'Born and made: Sisters, brothers, and the deceased wife's sister bill'.

Signs: Journal of Women in Culture and Society 24 (1999): 423–47

Guy, J. R. *Compassion and the Art of the Possible: Dr Southwood Smith as Social Reformer and Public Health Pioneer.* Cambridgeshire: Octavia Hill Society & Birthplace Museum Trust, 1994

Haight, G. *George Eliot and John Chapman.* New Haven, CT: Yale University Press, 1940

——(ed.) *George Eliot Letters.* 7 vols. New Haven, CT: Yale University Press, 1954–55

Halperin, J. *Gissing: A Life in Books.* Oxford: Oxford University Press, 1982

Hammerton, A. J. *Cruelty and Companionship: Conflict in Nineteenth-Century Married Life.* London: Routledge, 1992

Hammond, J. R. *H. G. Wells and Rebecca West.* New York: Harvester/Wheatsheaf, 1991

Harbron, D. *The Conscious Stone: The Life of Edward William Godwin.* New York: Benjamin Blom, 1971

Hardwick, J. *An Immodest Violet: The Life of Violet Hunt.* London: Andre Deutsch, 1990

Harrison, J. F. C. *The Second Coming: Popular Millenarianism, 1780–1850.* New Brunswick, NJ: Rutgers University Press, 1979

Henderson, W. O. *The Life of Friedrich Engels.* 2 vols. London: Frank Cass, 1976

Henriques, U. 'Bastardy and the new poor law'. *Past and Present* 37 (1967): 103–29

Herstein, S. *A Mid-Victorian Feminist: Barbara Leigh Smith Bodichon.* New Haven, CT: Yale University Press, 1985

Hickman, K. *Courtesans: Money, Sex and Fame in the Nineteenth Century.* New York: William Morrow, 2003

Higginbotham, A. 'Respectable sinners: Salvation Army rescue work with unmarried mothers, 1884–1914'. In *Religion in the Lives of English Women, 1760–1930*, G. Malmgreen (ed.), 216–33. Bloomington, IN: Indiana University Press, 1986

Hill-Miller, K. C. *'My Hideous Progeny': Mary Shelley, William Godwin, and the Father–Daughter Relationship.* Newark, NJ: University of Delaware Press, 1995

Hirsch, P. *Barbara Leigh Smith Bodichon, 1827–1891: Feminist, Artist and Rebel.* London: Chatto & Windus, 1998

Holman-Hunt, D. *My Grandfather, His Wives and Loves.* London: Hamish Hamilton, 1969

——*My Grandmothers and I.* New York: W. W. Norton & Company, 1960

Holmes, A. S. '"Fallen mothers": Maternal adultery and child custody in England, 1886–1925'. In *Maternal Instincts: Visions of Motherhood and Sexuality in Britain, 1875–1925*, C. Nelson and A. S. Holmes (eds), 37–57. New York: St Martin's Press, 1997

Holton, S. S. 'Free love and Victorian feminism: The divers matrimonials of Elizabeth Wolstenholme and Ben Elmy'. *Victorian Studies* 37 (1993–94): 199–222

——*Suffrage Days: Stories from the Women's Suffrage Movement.* London: Routledge, 1996

Holroyd, M. *Augustus John: A Biography.* Vol. I: *The Years of Innocence.* London:

Heinemann, 1974

——*Augustus John: A Biography.* Vol. II: *The Years of Experience.* London: Heinemann, 1975

Hughes, K. *George Eliot: The Last Victorian.* London: Fourth Estate, 1998

Hunley, J. D. *The Life and Thought of Friedrich Engels.* New Haven, CT: Yale University Press, 1991

Hunt, K. *Equivocal Feminists: The Social Democratic Federation and the Woman Question, 1884–1911.* Cambridge: Cambridge University Press, 1996

Huson, R. (ed.) *Sixty Famous Trials.* London: Daily Express Publications, 1938

Jackson, L. *Child Sexual Abuse in Victorian England.* London: Routledge, 2000

Jackson, M. *The Real Facts of Life: Feminism and the Politics of Sexuality, c. 1850–1940.* London: Taylor & Francis, 1994

Judd, A. *Ford Madox Ford.* Cambridge, MA: Harvard University Press, 1991

Kapp, Y. *Eleanor Marx.* 2 vols. New York: Pantheon Books, 1972, 1976

Karl, F. *George Eliot: Voice of a Century.* New York: W. W. Norton, 1995

Knelman, J. *Twisting in the Wind: The Murderess and the English Press.* Toronto: University of Toronto Press, 1998

Koven, S. *Slumming: Sexual and Social Politics in Victorian London.* Princeton, NJ: Princeton University Press, 2004

Kuper, A. 'Incest, cousin marriage, and the origin of the human sciences in nineteenth-century England'. *Past and Present* 174 (2002): 158–83

Ledbetter, R. *A History of the Malthusian League, 1877–1927.* Columbus, OH: Ohio State University Press, 1976

Lemmings, D. 'Marriage and the law in the eighteenth century: Hardwicke's Marriage Act of 1753'. *Historical Journal* 39 (1996): 339–60

Leneman, L. *Alienated Affections: The Scottish Experience of Divorce and Separation, 1684–1830.* Edinburgh: Edinburgh University Press, 1998

Levine, P. *Feminist Lives in Victorian England: Private Roles and Public Commitment.* Oxford: Basil Blackwell, 1990

——'"So few prizes and so many blanks": Marriage and feminism in later nineteenth-century England'. *Journal of British Studies* 28 (1989): 150–74

Lewis, J. *The End of Marriage? Individualism and Intimate Relations.* Cheltenham: Edward Elgar, 2001

——'Intimate relations between men and women: The case of H. G. Wells and Amber Pember Reeves'. *History Workshop Journal* 37 (1994): 76–98

McClelland, K. 'Masculinity and the "representative artisan" in Britain, 1850–1880'. In *Manful Assertions: Masculinities in Britain since 1800*, M. Roper and J. Tosh (eds), 74–91. London: Routledge, 1991

Mack, J. E. *A Prince of Our Disorder: The Life of T. E. Lawrence.* Boston, MA: Little, Brown, and Co., 1976

McLean, J. *The Poems and Plays of Thomas Wade.* Troy, New York: The Whitson Publishing Company, 1997

McMullen, R. *Victorian Outsider: A Biography of J. A. M. Whistler.* New York: E. P. Dutton, 1973

Mahood, L. *The Magdalenes: Prostitution in the Nineteenth Century.* London:

Routledge, 1990

Marcus, S. *Engels, Manchester and the Working Class.* New York: Random House, 1974

Marsh, J. *The Legend of Lizzie Siddal.* London: Quartet Books, 1989

——*Pre-Raphaelite Sisterhood.* London: Quartet Books, 1985

Marshall, P. *William Godwin.* New Haven, CT: Yale University Press, 1984

Mayer, G. *Friedrich Engels: A Biography.* London: Chapman & Hall Ltd, 1936

Melville, J. *Ellen and Edy: A Biography of Ellen Terry and her Daughter, Edith Craig, 1847–1947.* London: Pandora, 1987

Menefee, S. P. *Wives for Sale: An Ethnographic Study of British Popular Divorce.* Oxford: Basil Blackwell, 1981

Mineka, F. E. *The Dissidence of Dissent: The Monthly Repository, 1806–1838.* Chapel Hill, NC: University of North Carolina Press, 1944

Mitchison, R. and L. Leneman. *Girls in Trouble: Sexuality and Social Control in Rural Scotland, 1660–1780.* Edinburgh: Scottish Cultural Press, 1998

Mizener, A. *The Saddest Story: A Biography of Ford Madox Ford.* New York: Carroll and Graf Publishers, 1971

Morris, P. 'Incest or survival strategy? Plebeian marriage within the prohibited degrees in Somerset, 1730–1835'. In *Forbidden History: The State, Society, and the Regulation of Sexuality in Modern Europe,* J. Fout (ed.), 139–69. Chicago: University of Chicago Press, 1992

Mumm, S. '"Not worse than other girls": The convent-based rehabilitation of fallen women in Victorian Britain'. *Journal of Social History* 29 (1996): 527–46

Myers, R. M. *Reluctant Expatriate: The Life of Harold Frederic.* Westport, CT: Greenwood Press, 1995

Newman, T. and R. Watkinson. *Ford Madox Brown and the Pre-Raphaelite Circle.* London: Chatto and Windus, 1991

Noakes, A. *William Frith: Extraordinary Victorian Painter.* London: Jupiter, 1978

Norman, S. (ed.) *After Shelley: The Letters of Thomas Jefferson Hogg to Jane Williams.* London: Oxford University Press, 1934

Oliver, H. *The International Anarchist Movement in Late Victorian London.* London: Croom Helm, 1983

Outhwaite, R. *Clandestine Marriage in England, 1500–1850.* London: The Hambledon Press, 1995

Parker, P. *Ackerley: A Life of J. R. Ackerley.* New York: Farrar Straus Giroux, 1989

Parker, S. *Informal Marriage, Cohabitation and the Law, 1750–1989.* New York: St Martin's Press, 1990

Parry, L. (ed.) *Trial of Dr. Smethurst.* London: William Hodge & Company, 1931

Patten, R. L. *George Cruikshank's Life, Times, and Art.* 2 vols. London: Lutterworth Press, 1996

Pearson, H. *Labby: The Life and Character of Henry Labouchere.* New York: Harper and Brothers, 1937

Peters, C. *The King of Inventors: A Life of Wilkie Collins.* London: Secker and Warburg, 1991

Plomer, W. (ed.) *Kilvert's Diary, 1870–79: Selections from the Diary of the Rev. Francis*

Kilvert. London: Penguin Books, 1977

Poovey, M. *Uneven Developments: The Ideological Work of Gender in Mid-Victorian England.* Chicago: University of Chicago Press, 1988

Poynter, F. N. L. 'Thomas Southwood Smith – the man (1788–1861)'. *Proceedings of the Royal Society of Medicine* 55 (1962): 381–92

Quail, J. *The Slow Burning Fuse: The Lost History of British Anarchists.* London: Paladin, 1978

Radzinowicz, L. and R. Hood. 'Judicial discretion and sentencing standards: Victorian attempts to solve a perennial problem'. *University of Pennsylvania Law Review* 127 (1979): 1288–1349

Ransom, T. *The Mysterious Marie Corelli: Queen of the Victorian Bestsellers.* Stroud: Sutton Publishing, 1999

Ratcliffe, B. M. 'Popular classes and cohabitation in mid-nineteenth-century Paris'. *Journal of Family History* 21 (1996): 316–50

Ray, G. *H. G. Wells and Rebecca West.* New Haven, CT: Yale University Press, 1974

Reay, B. *Microhistories: Demography, Society, and Culture in Rural England, 1800–1930.* Cambridge: Cambridge University Press, 1996

Robb, G. 'Circe in crinoline: Domestic poisonings in Victorian England'. *Journal of Family History* 22 (1997): 176–90

Roberts, E. *A Woman's Place: An Oral History of Working-Class Women, 1890–1940.* Oxford: Basil Blackwell, 1984

Robinson, D. *Chaplin: His Life and Art.* London: Collins, 1985

Rogers, H. '"The prayer, the passion and the reason" of Eliza Sharples: Freethought, women's rights and Republicanism, 1832–52'. In *Radical Femininity: Women's Self-Representation in the Public Sphere*, E. Yeo (ed.), 52–78. Manchester: Manchester University Press, 1998

Rollyson, C. *Rebecca West: A Life.* New York: Scribner, 1996

Rose, J. *The Intellectual Life of the British Working Class.* New Haven, CT: Yale University Press, 2001

Rose, M. (ed.) *The Poor and the City: The English Poor Law in its Urban Context, 1834–1914.* Leicester: Leicester University Press, 1985

Rose, P. *Parallel Lives: Five Victorian Marriages.* New York: Vintage Books, 1984

Rose, S. *Limited Livelihoods: Gender and Class in Nineteenth-Century England.* Berkeley, CA: University of California Press, 1992

Ross, E. '"Fierce questions and taunts": Married life in working-class London, 1870–1914'. *Feminist Studies* 8 (1982): 575–602

——*Love and Toil: Motherhood in Outcast London, 1870–1918.* Oxford: Oxford University Press, 1993

——'"Not the sort that would sit on the doorstep": Respectability in pre-World War I London neighborhoods'. *International Labor and Working-Class History* 27 (1985): 39–59

Rubenstein, D. *Before the Suffragettes: Women's Emancipation in the 1890s.* New York: St Martin's Press, 1986

Russell, E. L. *Though the Heavens Fall.* London: Cassell and Company, 1956

St Clair, W. *The Godwins and the Shelleys: A Biography of a Family.* New York: W.

W. Norton, 1989

Samuel, R. *East End Underworld: Chapters in the Life of Arthur Harding*. London: Routledge and Kegan Paul, 1981

Scott, W. *Jefferson Hogg*. London: Jonathan Cape, 1951

Selig, R. *George Gissing*. New York: Twayne Publishers, 1995

Seymour, M. *Mary Shelley*. New York: Grove Press, 2000

Shanley, M. L. *Feminism, Marriage, and the Law in Victorian England*. Princeton, NJ: Princeton University Press, 1989

Shipley, P. *Revolutionaries in Modern Britain*. London: The Bodley Head, 1976

Smith, E. *Charles Reade*. Boston, MA: Twayne Publishers, 1976

Smith, F. B. *Radical Artisan: William James Linton, 1812–97*. Manchester: Manchester University Press, 1973

Smith, R. *Trial by Medicine: Insanity and Responsibility in Victorian Trials*. Edinburgh: Edinburgh University Press, 1981

Stone, L. *Uncertain Unions: Marriage in England, 1660–1753*. Oxford: Oxford University Press, 1992

Strachey, B. and J. Samuels (eds). *Mary Berenson: A Self-Portrait from Her Letters and Diaries*. London: Hamish Hamilton, 1983

Tabili, L. *'We Ask for British Justice': Workers and Racial Difference in Late Imperial Britain*. Ithaca, NY: Cornell University Press, 1994

Taylor, B. *Eve and the New Jerusalem: Socialism and Feminism in the Nineteenth Century*. London: Virago, 1983

Tebbutt, M. *Women's Talk? A Social History of 'Gossip' in Working-Class Neighbourhoods, 1880–1960*. Aldershot: Scolar Press, 1995

Thacker, J. *Whiteway Colony: The Social History of a Tolstoyan Community*. Stroud: Alan Sutton, 1993

Thane, P. 'Women and the poor law in Victorian and Edwardian England'. *History Workshop Journal* 6 (1978): 29–51

Thomas, D. *The Victorian Underworld*. New York: New York University Press, 1998

Thompson, E. P. *Customs in Common: Studies in Traditional Popular Culture*. New York: New Press, 1993

Thompson, F. M. L. *The Rise of Respectable Society: A Social History of Victorian Britain, 1830–1900*. London: Fontana, 1988

Thompson, T. (ed.) *Dear Girl: The Diaries and Letters of Two Working Women, 1897–1917*. London: The Woman's Press, 1987

Todd, J. *Mary Wollstonecraft: A Revolutionary Life*. New York: Columbia University Press, 2000

Tomalin, C. *The Invisible Woman: The Story of Nelly Ternan and Charles Dickens*. New York: Penguin Books, 1990

——*Mrs Jordan's Profession: The Actress and the Prince*. New York: Alfred A. Knopf, 1995

Torr, D. *Tom Mann and His Times*. London: Lawrence & Wishart, 1956

Tosh, J. *Manliness and Masculinities in Nineteenth-Century Britain: Essays on Gender, Family and Empire*. London: Pearson/Longman, 2005

——*A Man's Place: Masculinity and the Middle-Class Home in Victorian England*.

New Haven, CT: Yale University Press, 1999

Tsuzuki, C. *Tom Mann, 1856–1941: The Challenges of Labour.* Oxford: Clarendon Press, 1991

Vicinus, M. *Intimate Friends: Women Who Loved Women, 1778–1928.* Chicago: Chicago University Press, 2004

Walkowitz, J. *City of Dreadful Delight: Narratives of Sexual Danger in Late-Victorian London.* Chicago: University of Chicago Press, 1992

——*Prostitution and Victorian Society: Women, Class, and the State.* Cambridge: Cambridge University Press, 1980.

Wallas, G. *William Johnson Fox, 1786–1864.* London: Watts & Co., 1924

Walton, J. K. and A. Wilcox (eds). *Low Life and Moral Improvement in Mid-Victorian England: Liverpool Through the Journalism of Hugh Shinmin.* Leicester: Leicester University Press, 1991

Wardle, R. (ed.) *Godwin & Mary: Letters of William Godwin and Mary Wollstonecraft.* Lincoln, NE: University of Nebraska Press, 1977

Watts, R. *Gender, Power and the Unitarians in England, 1760–1860.* London: Longman, 1998

Webb, R. K. 'Southwood Smith: The intellectual sources of public service'. In *Doctors, Politics and Society: Historical Essays,* D. Porter and R. Porter (eds), 46–80. Atlanta, GA: Rodopi, 1993

Weeks, J. *Sex, Politics, and Society: The Regulation of Sexuality Since 1800,* 2nd edn London: Longman, 1989

Weintraub, S. *Four Rosettis: A Victorian Biography.* New York: Weybright and Talley, 1977

——*Whistler: A Biography.* New York: Weybright and Talley, 1974

Weisbrod, B. 'How to become a good foundling in early Victorian England'. *Social History* 10 (1985): 193–209

Wertheim, S. and P. Sorrentino (eds.) *The Correspondence of Stephen Crane.* 2 vols. New York: Columbia University Press, 1988

White, J. *Tom Mann.* Manchester: Manchester University Press, 1991

Wiener, J. *Radicalism and Freethought in Nineteenth-Century Britain: The Life of Richard Carlile.* Westport, CT: Greenwood Press, 1983

Wiener, M. 'Judges v. jurors: Courtroom tensions in murder trials and the law of criminal responsibility in nineteenth-century England'. *Law and History Review* 17 (1999): 467–506

——*Men of Blood: Violence, Manliness and Criminal Justice in Victorian England.* Cambridge: Cambridge University Press, 2004

——'The sad story of George Hall: Adultery, murder and the politics of mercy in mid-Victorian England'. *Social History* (1999): 174–95

Williams, D. *Mr George Eliot: A Biography of George Henry Lewes.* New York: Franklin Watts, 1983

Wilson, F. *The Courtesan's Revenge: Harriette Wilson, the Woman Who Blackmailed the King.* London: Faber and Faber, 2003

Wilson, J. *Lawrence of Arabia: The Authorised Biography of T. E. Lawrence.* London: Heinemann, 1989

Wohl, A. 'Sex and the single room'. In *The Victorian Family: Structure and Stresses*, A. Wohl (ed.), 197–216. New York: St Martin's Press, 1978

Wolff, R. *Sensational Victorian: The Life and Fiction of Mary Elizabeth Braddon*. New York: Garland, 1979

Wood, J. C. *Violence and Crime in Nineteenth-Century England: The Shadow of Our Refinement*. London: Routledge, 2004

Yeldham, C. *Margaret Gillies RWS: Unitarian Painter of Mind and Emotion, 1803–1887.* Lewiston, NY: Edwin Mellen Press, 1997

Yeo, E. 'Robert Owen and radical culture'. In *Robert Owen: Prophet of the Poor*, S. Pollard and J. Salt (eds), 84–114. London: Macmillan, 1971

Theses, dissertations, papers

Bauer, B. 'Rescuing Ophelia: Gendered Interpretations of the Life and Work of Elizabeth Siddall'. BA thesis, Smith College, Northampton, MA, 1995

Gandy, G. N. 'Illegitimacy in a Handloom Weaving Community: Fertility Patterns in Culcheth, Lancashire, 1781–1860'. D. Phil. dissertation, Oxford University, 1978

Savage, G. 'Defining the boundaries of marital sexuality: Bigamy, incest, and sodomy in the divorce court, 1857–1907'. Mid-Atlantic Conference on British Studies Annual Meeting, New Brunswick, NJ, 22 March 2003

Sever, J. 'James Morrison and *The Pioneer*'. Unpublished manuscript, British Library

Index

Note: Literary works can be found under authors' names